BIBLE, GENDER, SEXUALITY

BIBLE, GENDER, SEXUALITY

Reframing the Church's Debate
on Same-Sex Relationships

James V. Brownson

WILLIAM B. EERDMANS PUBLISHING COMPANY
GRAND RAPIDS, MICHIGAN / CAMBRIDGE, U.K.

Published 2013 by
Wm. B. Eerdmans Publishing Co.
2140 Oak Industrial Drive N.E., Grand Rapids, Michigan 49505 /
P.O. Box 163, Cambridge CB3 9PU U.K.
www.eerdmans.com

Printed in the United States of America

18 17 16 15 14 13   7 6 5 4 3 2 1

Library of Congress Cataloging-in-Publication Data

Brownson, James V.
Bible, gender, sexuality: reframing the church's debate on same-sex relationships /
James V. Brownson.
        p.   cm.
Includes bibliographical references (p.   ) and index.
ISBN 978-0-8028-6863-3 (pbk.: alk. paper)
1. Bible and homosexuality.
2. Homosexuality — Religious aspects — Christianity.
3. Sex — Biblical teaching.
4. Sex — Religious aspects — Christianity.
5. Marriage — Biblical teaching.
6. Marriage — Religious aspects — Christianity.
I. Title.

BS680.H67B76 2013
241'.664 — dc23

2012035589

Unless otherwise indicated, the Scripture quotations in this publication are from the New Revised Standard Version of the Bible, copyright © 1989 by the Division of Christian Education of the National Council of Churches of Christ in the U.S.A., and used by permission.

Contents

IV. Conclusions

Foreword

The church needs this book.

Presently the church is locked in a polarized debate about same-sex relationships that is creating painful divisions, subverting the church's missional intent, and damaging the credibility of its witness. We've all heard the sound-bite arguments. For some, condoning or blessing same-sex relationships betrays the clear teaching of the Bible and represents a capitulation to the self-gratifying, permissive sexual ethic of a secularized culture. For others, affirming same-sex relationships flows from the command to love our neighbor, embodies the love of Jesus, and honors the spiritual integrity and experience of gay and lesbian brothers and sisters.

The way the debate presently is framed makes productive dialogue difficult. People talk past one another. Biblical texts collide with the testimony of human experience. The stakes of the debate become elevated from a difference concerning ethical discernment to the preservation of the gospel's integrity — for both sides. Lines get drawn in the ecclesiastical sand. Some decide that, in order to be "pure," they must separate themselves spiritually from others and break the fellowship of Christ's body. Then the debate devolves into public wrangling over judicial proceedings, constitutional interpretations, and property ownership.

Mirroring the dynamics of contemporary secular politics, the debate is driven by small but vocal minorities with uncompromising positions at one end or another of the spectrum. For the majority in the "middle," who may be unclear about their own understandings, exploring their questions becomes all the more difficult because of the polarized toxicity of the debate. Furthermore, those in positions of leadership in congregations or denominations come to regard the controversy over same-sex relationships as the "third rail" of church politics: they don't want to touch it. I know this because I've been there myself.

The controversy over same-sex relationships in the church thus seems as though it's a theological and political cul-de-sac. Within the present framework, finding a way forward without significant injury, damage, and division appears difficult — if not nearly impossible. We need to push the "reset" button and figure out how to reframe this debate.

That is the intent and the promising contribution of James Brownson's book. Moreover, he resets the debate by calling us all into a deeper engagement with the Bible itself, exploring in the most thoughtful and thorough ways not just what it says but, more importantly, what these inspired words of revelation truly mean.

On the one hand, Brownson argues that many of those upholding a traditional Christian view of same-sex relationships have made unwarranted generalizations and interpretations of biblical texts that require far more careful and contextual scrutiny. On the other hand, those advocating a revised understanding often emphasize so strongly the contextual and historical limitations of various texts that they often seem to confine biblical wisdom to the broadest affirmations of love and justice.

For all, Brownson invites us into a far more authentic, creative, and probing encounter with the Bible as we consider the ethical questions and pastoral challenges presented by contemporary same-sex relationships in society — and in our congregations. In so doing, Brownson does not begin by focusing on the oft-cited seven biblical passages seen as relating to homosexuality. Rather, he starts by examining the underlying biblical assumptions made by those holding to a traditional view, and by dissecting the undergirding perspectives held by those advocating a revised view.

Then he goes on to explore foundational biblical perspectives in four crucial areas: the pattern of male-female relationships, and Scripture's understanding of the bond of marriage, procreation, and celibacy. Against this backdrop Brownson then offers one of the most thorough and biblically insightful interpretations of Romans 1:24-27 that has been written in reference to same-sex relationships. His mastery of biblical scholarship illumines the meaning of phrases and words that readers often fail to carefully examine or understand. To conclude, he looks at other specific passages often referred to in the debate over same-sex relationships and sheds important light on their contextual meaning and applicability.

One of Brownson's central insights is that the traditional argument against same-sex relationships rests on an assumption of male and female "complementarity." He does not find convincing biblical support for such a complementarian view. Moving the dialogue to this level, in my view, will prove to be enormously helpful. Instead of being trapped in shallow debates over the meaning of a few isolated biblical passages, Brownson grounds his approach in foundational biblical understandings of gender and sexuality. He takes the Bible seriously, engaging it faithfully and deeply, and he encourages the reader to do the same.

James Brownson is uniquely qualified for this task. He serves as the James and Jean Cook Professor of New Testament at Western Theological Seminary in Holland, Michigan, a seminary of the Reformed Church in America. For eight years he also served as dean of that institution. Students are consistently drawn to his love of the Bible, his passion for understanding the meaning of the gospel in our world today, and his commitment to the church's mission.

Beyond being a gifted teacher and administrator, Brownson has faithfully served the Reformed Church in America in numerous capacities, including as moderator of its Commission on Theology. Never content with simply exploring truth in a classroom, Jim Brownson is a faithful teacher of the church. His desire is to see biblical theology enrich the life and witness of congregations, and this book is his latest contribution in that consistent task.

When Christians confront difficult ethical issues, we bring to our discernment the tradition of what the church has said, our understanding of the Bible, and the testimony of our experience, all illuminated by the Holy Spirit. Even when we are not consciously aware of these three dimensions, they each still play some part. The challenge is to keep them in balance — and in dialogue with each other. Problems come when we try to isolate just one of these as the only source of truth and fail to recognize how they depend on one another. The church's debate over same-sex relationships has often reflected the weaknesses of a one-dimensional approach to discerning truth.

We also can fail to recognize how our trust in the Spirit, working through tradition, the Bible, and our own experience, continuously guides us into all truth, including the deepest truths within Scripture itself (John 16:13). Especially those of us from the Reformed tradition understand that this is an ongoing process, continually being enlivened by the Spirit's work, as experience and Scripture interact in the life of the Christian community.

Recently I listened to a sermon by Rev. Adam Hamilton, who is the lead pastor at the Church of the Resurrection near Kansas City. With over 16,000 members, this is the largest congregation of the United Methodist Church in the United States, and Hamilton is known for his evangelical convictions as well as his congregation's social outreach. Rev. Hamilton was preaching a series entitled "Wrestling with the Bible," in which he was helping the congregation understand difficult or puzzling passages and get to the deeper truths of Scripture.

In the sermon that I heard, Rev. Hamilton dealt with scriptural passages dealing with the role of women, slavery, and homosexuality. I was particularly intrigued by what he said about slavery. The Bible contains no fewer than 326 references to slavery. All but two of them, Hamilton explained, either condone slavery or assume that it was a given part of the social structure. Yet today, no one needs to be convinced that slavery is utterly opposed to God's intention, and that opposition to slavery was and is a compelling biblical mandate.

But in the middle of the nineteenth century, Christians could argue that the tradition of the church, the clear witness of Scripture, and even their human experience (if they were not slaves) all convinced them that slavery was ordained by God. Many made exactly those arguments. It took the persistent work of the Holy Spirit, and a deeper engagement with Scripture that went beyond what had been assumed for centuries was the meaning of many texts — along with careful attentiveness to the human experience of those who suffered — to lead some Christians to support the cause of abolition.

Of course, many will argue that the issues of slavery and of same-sex relationships should not be comparable. But the church's struggle with slavery does illustrate forcefully how assumed understandings of Scripture, based on simple readings of the texts, have been overturned through a deeper engagement with the truth of God's Word, enlivened by the witness of human experience.

Today, the church must find a new way forward from its present crippling and incriminating battle over same-sex relationships. Doing so will involve a fresh and sincere commitment by all to engage the deep truths of God's Word and to listen intently to the witness of gay and lesbian brothers and sisters, all within the trusting fellowship of the church, where we expect the Spirit to lead us into the fullness of God's truth and life. This book by James Brownson can serve as a valuable means to keep us all faithfully and fearlessly engaged in asking what the words of the Bible mean.

This study opens a door, through rigorous biblical interpretation, that could welcome those in same-sex relationships into the full life, ministry, and witness of the church. Personally, I find his biblical arguments persuasive. Other readers may not. But in the end, the goal of this book is not persuasion, but invitation. We are simply asked to look honestly, prayerfully, and openly at how we understand the full meaning of the Bible as it applies to same-sex relationships.

Perhaps most importantly, *Bible, Gender, Sexuality* can play a critical role in doing what its subtitle proposes: *Reframing the Church's Debate over Same-Sex Relationships*. And, in so doing, it can demonstrate that the commitment to take the Bible with all the seriousness and fidelity that our Reformed tradition requires may still leave some questions yet to be answered and some honest differences still requiring further discernment. But then we will know that such differences are ones that need not divide Christ's body, poison our life, or impair our mission. That is the first essential step if we truly believe that God's Spirit is leading us into all truth.

Therefore, the church needs this book.

WESLEY GRANBERG-MICHAELSON

PART I

Why Another Book on Same-Sex Relationships?

1

Introduction and Overview

The church is stuck on the question of homosexuality. In many North American denominations, despite vote after vote and debate after debate, questions remain, tempers flare, and peace and clarity seem continually elusive. In the last two decades, no issue has been more polarizing or contentious, particularly for mainline churches. Even though a major focus of this debate within the church in North America has come down to whether openly gay or lesbian Christians in committed relationships may be ordained to positions of church leadership, the fundamental question is not one of church polity. At bottom — at least for most churches of the Reformation — the question has to do with Scripture and ethics. What is the moral vision regarding gender and sexuality that Scripture commends? How flexible and adaptable is that vision in different cultures and contexts? And where do gay and lesbian people, gender identities, and marriage fit within that vision in the context of post-Christian North American society, where divorce rates are high, sexual promiscuity is common, AIDS and other sexually transmitted infections are a powerful threat, and where too many pregnancies end in abortion, and too many babies will never have two parents?

These larger questions and problems regarding gender and sexuality in North American culture illuminate why the question of homosexuality has become so polarizing. Traditionalists on the homosexuality question believe that the church must read the "plain sense" of Scripture clearly on this issue.[1] And they generally believe that Scripture plainly and clearly re-

---

1. It is not easy to know how to designate various parties in the homosexuality debate. To speak of the debate as taking place between "conservatives" and "liberals" doesn't quite

3

gards all same-sex erotic behavior to be immoral.[2] How, they ask, will the church find the strength to bear witness in word and deed to all of Scripture's other teachings regarding sexuality in a context where the larger culture increasingly ignores the biblical vision for sexuality and marriage and experiences deep brokenness as a result? In this context, then, the question of the ethics of homosexuality becomes for many traditionalists a "line in the sand" that will determine whether the church as a whole will lose its capacity to speak a clear word from God to its surrounding culture.

For revisionist Christians, however, this attempt to draw a "line in the sand" is fundamentally misguided. They see deliberations over the ethics of homosexuality as an opportunity for the church to consecrate same-sex unions, drawing gay and lesbian persons into a biblical and traditional vision of faithful, committed unions that can stand as a witness against the prevailing patterns of promiscuity, divorce, and brokenness that characterize so much sexual experience in the wider North American culture.[3] Moreover, from the perspective of revisionists who want the church to have a greater openness to gays and lesbians, the broader concern expressed by traditionalists regarding sexual confusion and brokenness in

---

do justice to the fact that some who identify themselves as theological conservatives also argue for a greater openness in the church's position toward gay and lesbian people (and I would include myself in this camp). In this book I use the words "traditionalists" and "revisionists" to describe contrasting approaches to the church's "traditional" teaching on homosexuality, which has generally been negative and restrictive. For some contrasting moments in the tradition, see, for example, John Boswell, *Same-Sex Unions in Premodern Europe* (New York: Villard Books, 1994).

2. See, for example, John R. W. Stott, *Same-Sex Partnerships? A Christian Perspective* (Grand Rapids: F. H. Revell, 1998); Stanley J. Grenz, *Welcoming But Not Affirming: An Evangelical Response to Homosexuality* (Louisville: Westminster John Knox, 1998); Robert A. J. Gagnon, *The Bible and Homosexual Practice: Texts and Hermeneutics* (Nashville: Abingdon, 2001); William J. Webb, *Slaves, Women and Homosexuals: Exploring the Hermeneutics of Cultural Analysis* (Downers Grove, IL: InterVarsity, 2001); Thomas E. Schmidt, *Straight and Narrow? Compassion and Clarity in the Homosexuality Debate* (Downers Grove, IL: InterVarsity, 1995); Marion L. Soards, *Scripture and Homosexuality: Biblical Authority and the Church Today* (Louisville: Westminster John Knox, 1995).

3. See, for example, David G. Myers and Letha Scanzoni, *What God Has Joined Together: A Christian Case for Gay Marriage* (San Francisco: HarperSanFrancisco, 2005); William Stacy Johnson, *A Time to Embrace: Same-Gender Relationships in Religion, Law, and Politics* (Grand Rapids: Eerdmans, 2006); Eugene F. Rogers, *Sexuality and the Christian Body: Their Way into the Triune God*, Challenges in Contemporary Theology (Oxford: Blackwell, 1999); Jack Bartlett Rogers, *Jesus, the Bible, and Homosexuality: Explode the Myths, Heal the Church*, rev. ed. (Louisville: Westminster John Knox, 2009).

North American culture often has the character of scapegoating. They note that drawing a line in the sand on the question of homosexuality will do nothing, in itself, to lower the divorce rate, reduce abortions, and heal the brokenness of heterosexuals who have difficulty living moral lives.[4] They observe how easy it is for many churches to take such a strong position on this issue, when the only gay or lesbian people who may have any contact with those churches are deeply closeted. In light of some recent research indicating that the overall divorce rate among Christians differs little from the prevailing divorce rate in North America, revisionists wonder whether gay and lesbian people are being forced to pay the price for a church that has lost its way and its voice in addressing our current context effectively.[5]

Such polarization is easy to document; finding a way forward is more difficult. Even if we bracket out the larger problems facing the church's teaching on sexuality in our culture, even if traditionalists and revisionists work extremely hard at listening to each other and understanding each other, deep differences remain. These deeper divisions are hermeneutical in character: they arise from different ways of interpreting biblical texts and applying them to contemporary life.[6]

The Necessity of Interpretation

These deeper differences are the focus of this book: they are not so much disagreements about what the biblical text *says* (though such disagreements do occur at a few points, and I will explore them when they occur), but primarily disagreements about what the biblical text *means* for Christians today. They are disagreements over how Scripture is to be interpreted.

It may be helpful to further explore this distinction between what a text

---

4. See esp. Myers and Scanzoni, *What God Has Joined Together*, pp. 23-36.

5. See the statistics gathered by George Barna at: http://www.barna.org/barna-update/article/15-familykids/42-new-marriage-and-divorce-statistics-released. Yet these issues are complex, and other studies indicate that those who attend church more frequently — or who are married in a religious ceremony — tend to have lower divorce rates overall. See Margaret L. Vaaler, Christopher G. Ellison, and Daniel A. Powers, "Religious Influences on the Risk of Marital Dissolution," *Journal of Marriage and Family* 71 (Nov. 2009).

6. Note, for example, the work done by two Mennonites who disagree on this issue, but are together committed to peacemaking: Ted Grimsrud and Mark Nation, *Reasoning Together: A Conversation on Homosexuality* (Scottdale, PA: Herald Press, 2008).

says and what it means. Most Christians agree that Gentile Christians today are not required by Scripture to observe the kosher laws regarding clean and unclean foods that are found in the Old Testament. The reason is that such laws are explicitly eliminated for Gentiles in the New Testament because of the epoch-changing work of Christ and the leading of the Spirit in the early church (see Acts 10, 15; Rom. 14:14; Galatians). So in this case, what a specific passage such as Leviticus 11 or Deuteronomy 14 *means* for Christians today depends on its place in the larger witness of Scripture as a whole — a larger witness that clearly relativizes the applicability of these passages for Gentile Christians.

Other examples can be adduced that, though slightly more controversial, still generate wide assent among Christians. Many Christians, for example, do not believe that Scripture requires them to kiss each other as a Christian form of greeting, despite the fact that in five separate New Testament passages Christians are commanded to "Greet one another with a holy kiss"(see Rom. 16:16; 1 Cor. 16:20; 2 Cor. 13:12; 1 Thess. 5:26; 1 Pet. 5:14). In the ancient Mediterranean world, this cultural practice was the norm both inside and outside the church (and continues today). But other cultures find other ways of expressing the warmth, intimacy, and affection embodied in the scriptural commendation of a "holy kiss."[7] In these cultures, a literal obedience to what these texts *say*, coming as it does from an alien culture, would probably create more disharmony and discomfort than it would express warmth, intimacy, and affection. Rather, many Christians intuitively grasp what they believe the text *means*. They sense that a deeper principle is at stake here in this exhortation to a holy kiss: not simply the external behavior of pressing one's lips against another's cheek or lips, but a call to those forms of greeting that convey warmth and close relationships. In this case, it is cultural diversity — a diversity brought on by the mission of the church set forth in the New Testament — that provides a framework for interpreting specific biblical passages and discerning the particular ways they are to be applied in differing contexts.

This brings us to the heart of the deeper controversy. Most thoughtful

---

7. Yet one should be cautious about oversimplifying the meaning of gestures such as the "holy kiss." For an extensive discussion of the wide range of meanings acquired by the "holy kiss" in the early church, see Michael Philip Penn, *Kissing Christians: Ritual and Community in the Late Ancient Church*, Divinations (Philadelphia: University of Pennsylvania Press, 2005). The gesture cannot simply be reduced to its transcultural significance without some loss of meaning and nuance.

Christians on both sides of the homosexuality debate are not biblical literalists who take every single statement or command of Scripture at face value. Rather, most acknowledge that there are central texts, which articulate major themes of Scripture as a whole, and there are peripheral texts, which articulate subsidiary — and sometimes culturally particular — themes that are less relevant to every time or place. There are Scripture passages that lay out broad, general principles, and there are biblical texts that make specific exceptions to those broad principles.

Let's look at some rather obvious examples. In Genesis 34, the sons of Jacob murder all the males of the city of Shechem in retaliation for the rape of their sister Dinah. Most Christians would argue that this behavior cannot serve as a precedent for Christians today, since Scripture elsewhere clearly rejects such retaliatory and escalating use of violence.[8] In Genesis 38, Tamar, the daughter-in-law of Judah, plays a prostitute and incestuously sleeps with her father-in-law (cf. Lev. 18:10) because Judah failed to provide a husband for her according to the law of levirate marriage after her husband (Judah's son) had died (cf. Deut. 25:5-10). Despite the fact that Judah declares that Tamar was "more righteous" than he (Gen. 38:26), and despite the fact that Tamar is explicitly listed in the genealogy of Jesus himself (Matt. 1:3), Christians recognize that her behavior recounted in Genesis 38 arose under extreme circumstances and is not an example for others to imitate. All these judgments are *hermeneutical* (i.e., interpretive) judgments that arise from the attempt to situate specific passages within the larger movement of Scripture as a whole.

These hermeneutical principles apply not only in the "difficult" or marginal passages we have just explored in Genesis 34 and 38; the same principles apply even in passages that are central and foundational to the biblical witness. Consider, for example, the way the Heidelberg Catechism, an important confessional and teaching document from the Reformation period, explains the meaning of the sixth commandment, "Thou shalt not kill" (Exod. 20:13 [KJV]):

> I am not to belittle, insult, hate, or kill my neighbor — not by my thoughts, my words, my look or gesture, and certainly not by actual deeds — and I am not to be party to this in others; rather, I am to put away all desire for revenge. I am not to harm or recklessly endanger

---

8. See Gen. 49:5-7 for an explicit renunciation of this behavior within the Genesis narrative itself.

myself, either. Prevention of murder is also why government is armed with the sword.[9]

The Catechism's exposition moves well beyond a strictly literal application to one that includes the literal meaning, but also extends much further as well (and also creates some room for exceptions in the government's use of the "sword"). John Calvin, in his commentary on the sixth commandment, takes this line of discussion even further:

> God not only forbids us to be murderers, but also prescribes that everyone should study faithfully to defend the life of his neighbor, and practically to declare that it is dear to him. . . . There are, consequently, two parts in the Commandment, — first, that we should not vex, or oppress, or be at enmity with any; and secondly, that we should not only live at peace with men, without exciting quarrels, but also should aid, as far as we can, the miserable who are unjustly oppressed, and should endeavour to resist the wicked, lest they should injure men as they list.[10]

Here we see the Catechism, along with the wider Reformation tradition, making explicit a number of forms of moral logic that it regards as implicit in the command not to kill: what the text means as well as what it says. The exposition recognizes, for example, that the commandment presupposes a deep and profound value placed on all human life. This implies that, not only must I not kill my neighbor, but I also must not "belittle, insult, or hate" my neighbor. Calvin extends the same notion even further: he calls for constructive resistance to oppression and injustice. This fuller exposition clearly goes far beyond the literal meaning of the words "thou shalt not kill"; it is grounded in the teaching of Jesus in Matthew 5:21-24, which itself is grounded in the deep value of human life found in texts such as Genesis 9:6: "Whoever sheds the blood of a human, by a human shall that person's blood be shed; for in his own image God made humankind." Here we see, early in Genesis, that the prohibition of murder is grounded in the fact that humans are created in God's image: they bear an intrinsic value

---

9. Christian Reformed Church, *Ecumenical Creeds and Reformed Confessions* (Grand Rapids: CRC Publications, 1987), 52, Lord's Day 40, Q&A #105.

10. John Calvin, *Commentaries on the Four Last Books of Moses: Arranged in the Form of a Harmony,* trans. Charles William Bingham, vol. 3, Calvin's Commentaries (Grand Rapids: Eerdmans, 1950), p. 21.

that must be respected in all circumstances and that grants them an inherent dignity, which must not be taken away.

This example from the Heidelberg Catechism and John Calvin shows clearly that the *meaning* of Scripture for Christians today must be not be drawn from just one passage but from the way any particular passage of Scripture is located within the larger themes and movements of Scripture as a whole. We must discern the deeper and more comprehensive moral logic that undergirds the specific commands, prohibitions, and examples of the biblical text. We do not interpret rightly any single passage of Scripture until we locate the text within this larger fabric of meaning in Scripture as a whole. This is necessary for two reasons: first, this kind of exposition, building on underlying values, allows the extension of core principles of biblical commands or prohibitions into new terrain not directly addressed by the literal commandment. Second, this exploration of underlying values can assist us in addressing exceptions and unusual circumstances that are not easily addressed by the literal commandment (such as why, and under what circumstances, if at all, lethal force might be justified in attempting to preserve the lives of persons).

Imagination and Biblical Interpretation

It is relatively easy for most people to understand the broad principles outlined above. They make sense to us because we have been taught over the centuries to read the Bible in these ways. But it is not always easy to clearly discern the various forms of underlying moral logic that give shape to the biblical witness when we are in a new cross-cultural context and are forced to come up with answers to questions that no one has ever asked before. We can see, already in the New Testament, how the early church struggled with these issues when Gentiles began receiving the Spirit and coming to faith in Jesus. Should the Jewish disciples of Jesus require these Gentiles to become circumcised and to eat kosher food, as other converts to Judaism were expected to do in that day? This was not an easy question, and it disrupted the life of the church for some time, requiring the "apostolic council" of Acts 15 to come to some resolution. Paul's letter to the Galatians shows the contentiousness of the same issue in another context, and Paul's continued treatment of the question in texts such as Romans 14:14 reveals that the issue continued to be contentious quite a while after the apostolic council had offered its ruling to the larger church. It was not easy for early Jewish Christians to let go of their ways of reading their Hebrew Bible texts that required circumcision and kosher observance of all of God's people.

In order for those early Christians to discern this deeper pattern in Scripture, they had to rekindle their imaginations to read and put together a range of biblical texts in a different way, discerning a different and deeper set of interconnections, analogies, and resonances in the Bible as a whole. In this context, "imagination" does not connote the conjuring up of images or beliefs that have no grounding in reality; rather, it refers here to the ability to see the deeper meanings and patterns that emerge in the context of cross-cultural engagements. Early Christians spoke of this as the leading of the Holy Spirit (Acts 15:28). Yet the dynamics of the discussion leading up to Acts 15 make it clear that this leading was not simply a supernatural "voice from the blue," but that it involved history, experience, wisdom, debate, and judicious assessment of a variety of forms of evidence, stories, and experiences. When the apostle James declared, "It seemed good to the Holy Spirit and to us," he was not elevating human wisdom to an equivalent status with the guidance of the Holy Spirit, but instead underscoring the way the Spirit works through these complex human processes of constructing patterns of discernment, meaning, and vision.[11]

The same discipline was required when Galileo called into question the earth-centered structure of the cosmos that people had always imagined — a structure of the cosmos that they saw reflected in Scripture itself. Suddenly, a whole range of texts needed to be reread, and some passages assumed to be literal in their description of the sun moving around the earth had to be read in different ways. The same dynamics can be seen in the nineteenth-century debate over slavery and the twentieth-century debate concerning women in leadership in the church. In each of these cases, the Bible was not simply discarded when it didn't cohere with changes happening in society. Instead, the changes happening in society and across cultures caused people to go back to the biblical texts and read them with fresh eyes — looking more deeply and searching for different underlying values and forms of moral logic that they had not seen so clearly before.

I believe that something akin to this pattern is happening in the present debate concerning homosexuality. The church's experience with gay and

---

11. For a discussion of the relevance of these issues to the question of homosexuality, see D. Heim, M. L. Stackhouse, L. T. Johnson, and D. M. McCarthy, "Homosexuality, Marriage and the Church: A Conversation," *Christian Century,* July 1-8, 1998.

lesbian people is raising questions that have never been asked before and confronting people with dilemmas they have never faced before. Many of these questions are arising in fresh ways simply because our culture is becoming more direct and frank in its discussion of sexual issues. What was previously relegated to the silence of "the closet" and to euphemistic speech is now being discussed more directly and openly. And with this greater directness and openness of speech comes the need to face questions that the church has not faced so directly and explicitly before. In particular, in this new context the church is faced with gay and lesbian Christians who exhibit many gifts and fruits of the Spirit and who seek to live in deep obedience to Christ. Many of these gay and lesbian Christians seek, not to suppress their sexual orientation, but rather to sanctify it, thus drawing intimate gay and lesbian relationships into the sanctifying work of the Spirit. In this new context, what had seemed like adequate solutions in general, when specific cases were barely discussed, has become more problematic as the church deals with cases that don't seem to fit within the old paradigms.

Something like this has happened in my own life. Five years before I began writing this book, I had already been engaged in studying the issues related to homosexuality, and I had done some teaching and writing on the subject. At that time I took a moderate, traditionalist position on the issues. But then something happened that altered my life in major ways: my eighteen-year-old son told my wife and me that he believed he was gay. I wish I could say that, since I had always been such a thoughtful and empathic scholar, when I was faced with this case in my own family, I would simply find the conclusions I had already arrived at in my prior study on this subject to be adequate. But I must confess — to my regret and embarrassment — that this was not the case. I realized, in fact, that my former work had stayed at a level of abstraction that wasn't helpful when it came to the concrete and specific questions I faced with my son. Indeed, the answers that I thought I had found seemed neither helpful nor relevant in the case of my son.

For example, I had made a sharp distinction in my earlier thinking between homosexual *orientation* (which my denomination had declared was not necessarily sinful) and homosexual *behavior* (which, I had believed, was forbidden by Scripture).[12] But in my son's case, the issue was not sex-

---

12. "The homosexual must be accepted in his homosexuality. If this is not the case he is left with the choice of leaving the fellowship, wearing the mask of heterosexuality, or being contemptuously condemned. Most choose the mask" ("Christian Pastoral Care for the Ho-

ual activity; he was simply trying to understand his own emotional makeup and disposition. The traditionalist treatment of sexual orientation seemed shallow and unhelpful to my wife and me when we looked at our son. We found the neo-Freudian explanations for the familial origins of male homosexuality (absent father, dominant mother) to make little sense in the dynamics of our household. Moreover — and this was perhaps the most important thing — our own son's resolute good humor and good will, his natural leadership abilities and good grades in school, his physical strength and quickness (a black belt in Tae Kwon Do), and his easygoing nature all seemed clearly and self-evidently to say, "There is nothing wrong here!" Or to put it a bit more precisely, we considered him a normal and healthy high school senior, someone in need of the grace of God, as we all are, but not deeply troubled (apart from his anxiety about talking to us about his sexual orientation).

I did not change my mind right away. I told my son that there were many things I didn't understand, and that I was going to have to do a lot more thinking and praying and studying. I told him I loved him, and I urged him, regardless of his sexual orientation, to be faithful, wise, and loving in the use of his body. I spent some subsequent time in depression, grieving the loss of the heterosexual future for my son that I had dreamed of. Then slowly, over several years, along with many conversations with my son, my wife, and many others, I returned to the literature to try to sort out the issues more deeply, to determine how we could best support and encourage our son — and to discover how I might better serve the church as a biblical theologian. I decided, from the beginning, that I wanted to discern, as deeply as I could, what the most central and truest message of Scripture was for my son. If my study brought me to the conclusion that my son should remain celibate, I was prepared to make that my prayer. But if my study led me to different conclusions, I was also prepared to follow those lines of inquiry as clearly and as consistently as I could. The goal was not to justify a certain conclusion; rather, it was to discern, as best I could, the truth. This book is one of the results of that effort.

But here is the point I want to make from this personal story: that dramatic shock to my life forced me to reimagine how Scripture speaks about

---

mosexual," reprinted in James I. Cook and Reformed Church in America, Commission on Theology, *The Church Speaks: Papers of the Commission on Theology, Reformed Church in America, 1959-1984*, Historical Series of the Reformed Church in America, 15 [Grand Rapids: Eerdmans, 1985], p. 262).

homosexuality. The texts had not changed, but my assumptions about what they were self-evidently saying was put to the test. My core Reformed commitment to the centrality of Scripture had not changed; but I needed to confront the equally Reformed conviction that the church must always be reforming itself according to the Word of God. This principle assumes that what Scripture *seems* to say is not always identical to how it truly should inform Christian faith and practice. I have been forced to dig more deeply, to reread texts that seemed clear, and those that have always seemed puzzling, in an effort to find new patterns and configurations in which both the texts themselves, and a range of human experience, might cohere more fully. I have found some of the exegesis in traditionalist positions to be lacking (as well as some of the exegesis in revisionist positions). I have made many new discoveries as well. I believe that this is the essential exercise that the church must always engage in when it encounters new questions and new problems. We go back and read the old texts again, and we discover more there than we thought we knew.

Ultimately, however, this rereading of the biblical text is not something done by individuals in isolation. Rather, it is an exercise of the whole church. This book is thus not an attempt to give a "final word" on homosexuality and gay or lesbian relationships for the whole church, arising from my own limited experience. Nor is it merely a personal manifesto, expressing a private attempt to seek coherence between the personal experience of a few people and the biblical text. Rather, it is an invitation to the whole church to enter into a deeper conversation about sexual ethics in the hope that the collective imagination of the church may be deepened and widened to see the Bible in new ways, and to embrace its message more deeply in a new context. Ultimately, the church must engage these issues corporately, for two reasons. On the one hand, corporate discernment protects the church from erroneous readings of the text that may be well-intentioned but misleading. This means that this book cannot be held above such careful examination either. On the other hand, corporate readings are necessary to avoid the fracturing of the church that comes from the loss of commonly embraced and shared readings of the Scripture.

The Methodology of This Book

In order to cultivate a wider capacity to read biblical texts in fresh ways, I do not begin this book with a direct study of the passages that seem to speak explicitly to same-gender erotic relationships. Instead, I begin with the points where the conversation about homosexuality seems most stuck and problematic — both on the traditionalist and on the revisionist sides of the debate. Unless we confront more directly what is not working in present assumptions, the debate cannot move forward. Consequently, in the second and third chapters I will explore in more detail some central problems, first with the traditionalist case, and then with the revisionist case. The overall goal of the discussion is to explain why further work is needed — and to show where the focus of this further work should lie.

After this review of the present state of the conversation, I turn in the central section of the book to four very broad forms of moral logic that are critical for understanding what Scripture has to say about sexuality in general: patriarchy, the "one-flesh" bond of marriage, procreation, and celibacy. My aim is to gain a broad understanding of the recurring key themes, motifs, and arguments that shape the Bible's discussion of sexuality and marriage — broadly considered. After covering this wide canvas, I conclude each chapter with a brief exploration of the implications of that chapter's discussion for one or more aspects of the current debate within the church concerning gay and lesbian relationships.

With this broad picture in place, I turn in the next four chapters to other forms of moral logic that are critical in the debate over homosexuality and same-sex unions. In these four chapters, the focus is not on those *positive* elements that comprise a comprehensive biblical vision, but instead on the *negative* texts that mark the boundaries of acceptable sexual practice in Scripture. The four topics addressed in these chapters all come from the central New Testament text in the debate on homosexuality, Romans 1:24-27: lust, purity, honor/shame, and natural law. Again, in each case, I begin each chapter with a broad biblical survey of relevant material and conclude by drawing out the implications of the study for the interpretation of Romans 1:24-27 in particular, and for the debate about gay and lesbian unions in general.

In the last chapter of this book I summarize some of the main points of the study, and then return to the texts that speak more specifically to same-sex relations in Scripture: the Sodom and Gomorrah story in Genesis 19 and its parallel in Judges 19; the prohibitions of same-sex relations in Leviticus 18:22 and 20:13; and the New Testament texts that are central to the debate: Romans 1:26-27, 1 Corinthians 6:9, and 1 Timothy 1:10. This book will have covered many issues that pertain to these texts in the preceding chapters, but a more consolidated and integrated perspective will emerge in this last chapter.

In all of this, my hope is to reinvigorate the imagination of the church in the midst of this controversy, not to leave the witness of Scripture behind, but to see and embrace it more deeply and freshly, so that we may discover its wisdom in the presence of new questions and information that the church has not considered before. I want to invite readers to take a closer look at a wider range of texts than have ordinarily been reviewed as part of this debate. Issues of sexuality in Scripture are complicated — not only issues related to homosexuality and gay unions, but a wide range of issues on the meaning of marriage and celibacy, the significance of procreation, the acceptable place of divorce in the church, the roles of men and women, and so on. In the face of such complexity, the temptation is either to revert to simple answers from the past or to avoid the particularity of the biblical texts and simply focus on broad principles such as justice and love. Neither approach will help us move beyond the current impasse in the church. But with a wider capacity to imagine the coherence of biblical teaching on sexuality in fresh ways, the church just may find a way forward in this controversy that is both more faithful to Scripture and also more effective in guiding men and women today (gay, lesbian, and straight) into the fullness of life in Christ. That is my hope and goal in this book.

Summing Up

- In the midst of polarized and polarizing debates, it is important to ask, not only what a text *says*, but what it *means*. This entails determining the moral logic that shapes biblical prohibitions or commands — discerning why a text says what it does and clarifying its underlying values and assumptions.
- Determining this underlying moral logic is particularly important when interpreting Scripture in cross-cultural contexts.
- At numerous points in the history of Christian interpretation of Scripture, the church has needed to exercise its imagination to discern a wider and more encompassing form of moral logic underlying biblical commands and prohibitions.
- This book seeks to accomplish such an exercise with a renewed and widened imagination regarding the moral logic underlying Scripture's discussion of same-sex intimate relationships.

2

The Traditionalist Case and Its Problems

The preceding chapter introduced the concept of a variety of forms of moral logic that undergird the commands and prohibitions of Scripture. In that chapter I argued that an effective cross-cultural reading of Scripture requires attentiveness to these underlying forms of moral logic. But it is at this point — when we begin to explore these underlying forms of moral logic that give shape and meaning to any specific passage — that we encounter the deeper divisions within the church on the question of the ethics of same-sex relationships. In this chapter I will explore the ways in which traditionalist interpreters identify one critical form of moral logic in the debate, and I will identify some key problems with that analysis. In particular, I want to expose difficulties with the category of "gender complementarity," which plays a central and pivotal role in the traditionalist case.

It is not difficult to get to the crux of the matter in the traditionalist case against homosexual behavior. For almost all traditionalists, the core issue is found in the central biblical text in the church's debate over the ethics of homosexuality:

> [26]For this reason God gave them up to degrading passions. Their women exchanged natural intercourse for unnatural, [27]and in the same way also the men, giving up natural intercourse with women, were consumed with passion for one another. Men committed shameless acts with men and received in their own persons the due penalty for their error. (Rom. 1:26-27)

Most interpreters on both sides of the debate accept that, in this passage, Paul is portraying very negatively men who have sexual relations with

16

other men.[1] Or, to put it even more precisely, Paul is using male same-sex erotic behavior as a particularly egregious example of Gentile corruption: it is the consequence of the Gentiles' idolatry and a symptom of their alienation from God. However, differences arise when we press further and ask *why* Paul condemns what he does, what kind of same-sex behavior he has in mind, and how such condemnation should inform the church's attitude toward committed same-sex unions today.[2]

Some traditionalist interpreters point to the vehemence and intensity of Paul's language here — the use of words and phrases such as "degrading," "unnatural," "consumed with passion," "shameless," and "error" — as evidence that Paul is articulating a deeply held conviction and not an occasional judgment. But noting the vehemence or intensity of the text does not yet identify its underlying moral logic. Paul may be speaking intensely here, but in observing that we have not yet discerned *why* the same-sex relations he depicts are to be understood as wrong.

Most traditionalist interpreters, however, do not simply observe Paul's vehemence here. Beyond this, the most common form of moral logic that traditionalists discern in this passage has to do with the claim that same-sex erotic behavior defies the purpose of God found in the creation narrative in Genesis. The reason same-sex erotic behavior is portrayed negatively — and the reason heterosexual sex outside of marriage is also wrong — is that God created man and woman (Genesis 2) to complement each other in the bond of marriage. According to this interpretation, male and female are both similar and different, and this combination of similarity and difference — or gender complementarity — is foundational to human identity, and to the institution of marriage. Therefore, the only appropriate place for sexual activity is within the "one-flesh" union of marriage between a man and a woman. This is what is meant by Paul's claim (in Rom. 1:26-27) that same-sex erotic relations are "unnatural." This behavior violates divine intentions regarding gender complementarity, which are embodied in the creation itself.[3] It is this vision of gender complementarity, so the case goes,

1. Whether Rom. 1:26 ("their women exchanged natural intercourse for unnatural") refers to same-sex erotic behavior among women is more disputed (see chapter 11, especially pp. 223-26, below, for further discussion).

2. As we shall see, the form of moral logic Paul is using here also directly impacts whether one regards Rom. 1:26 as referring to same-sex behavior among women (see esp. chapter 11 for further discussion).

3. All these issues will be explored in much more detail in coming chapters. But for some basic references to this line of interpretation, see Gagnon, *The Bible and Homosexual*

that provides the basic moral logic underlying the various biblical texts that speak against same-sex erotic unions.

When framed in this way, the case appears — at least to many — to be decisively closed. Because both male-male and female-female erotic unions cannot embody the gender complementarity intended by God in creation, they are to be avoided in all circumstances. They can never be understood as fulfilling the will of God for human life, regardless of the extent to which they are marked by love, commitment, mutuality, justice, or any other value. Indeed, it is precisely this kind of analysis that leads many traditionalists to wonder why revisionists even attempt to argue for an alternative view.

Analyzing "Gender Complementarity"

However, on further analysis, the case is not as airtight as it might seem. The reason is simple: gender complementarity is not really a form of moral

---

Practice: Texts and Hermeneutics, p. 254: "Paul in effect argues that even pagans who have no access to the book of Leviticus should know that same-sex eroticism is 'contrary to nature' because the primary sex organs fit male to female, not female to female or male to male. Again, by fittedness I mean not only the glove-like physical fit of the penis and vagina, but also clues to complementarity provided by procreative capacity and the capacity for mutual and pleasurable stimulation." See John R. W. Stott, *Same-Sex Partnerships? A Christian Perspective* (Grand Rapids: Revell, 1998), p. 32: "[Genesis 2] is particular and affirms the complementarity of the sexes, which constitutes the basis for heterosexual marriage." See also Thomas E. Schmidt, *Straight and Narrow? Compassion and Clarity in the Homosexuality Debate* (Downers Grove, IL: InterVarsity, 1995), p. 85: "[Homosexual behavior] is 'revolting,' not because heterosexuals find it so — they have their own dirt to deal with (Rom. 2:22) — but because it epitomizes in sexual terms the *revolt* against God. It is sinful because it violates the plan of God, present from creation, for the union of male and female in marriage." See also William J. Webb, *Slaves, Women and Homosexuals: Exploring the Hermeneutics of Cultural Analysis* (Downers Grove, IL: InterVarsity, 2001), p. 253: "A biblical perspective on gender calls for 'men to be men' and 'women to be women.' Gender distinction needs to be celebrated as a transcultural value within the Christian community." Marion L. Soards, *Scripture and Homosexuality: Biblical Authority and the Church Today* (Louisville: Westminster John Knox, 1995), p. 23: "God's purpose for humanity, as Paul and the others knew it from created order, scripture, and perhaps the words of Jesus, was for man and woman, male and female, to find fulfillment in the complementary sexual union that God intended in the creation." In reference to Gen. 2:24, Richard Hays says: "Thus the complementarity of male and female is given a theological grounding in God's creative activity: God has made them to become 'one flesh'" (Hays, "Relations Natural and Unnatural: A Response to J. Boswell's Exegesis of Rom. 1," *Journal of Religious Ethics* 14, no. 1 [1986]: 191).

logic in its own right. Instead, it is really simply a *category* that represents a variety of different values or forms of moral logic, which may be related to each other in complex ways. To speak of gender complementarity is to speak of a complex interaction of similarities and differences between the genders. But simply to use the term "complementarity" does not yet specify exactly what these differences are, and in what sense the differences are divinely intended as part of the structure of creation itself. When we move across time, and across different cultural settings, the specific ways in which the genders may be understood as similar and different often shift dramatically. A key difference in one culture (e.g., length of hair) may be quite irrelevant to the differentiation of genders in another. Indeed, when we probe further, we discover that different interpreters — all of whom use the term "gender complementarity" — have quite different understandings of exactly what this phrase actually means when they interpret the biblical texts.

Consider, for example, the question of the *hierarchy of genders*. There are some evangelical Christians who believe that this lies at the heart of what Scripture intends by "gender complementarity." They point to passages such as Genesis 3:16b: ". . . yet your desire shall be for your husband, and he shall rule over you." This "rulership" of husbands over wives represents the essence of gender complementarity for these interpreters.[4] And they cite numerous other biblical texts in support of this position, regarding this as the essential difference that distinguishes male from female. God wills that males should lead and females should follow. Same-sex erotic unions are wrong because they lack this dynamic interaction between initiative and receptivity. In fact, some of these interpreters argue that the abandonment of gender hierarchy will eventually and almost inevitably lead the church (wrongly) to approve same-sex unions, precisely because of the loss of this crucial aspect of gender complementarity, understood in terms of hierarchy.[5]

Other Christians, even those who may agree that the notion of gender complementarity excludes all same-sex erotic unions, do not agree that hi-

---

4. The standard text for this view of gender complementarity is John Piper and Wayne A. Grudem, *Recovering Biblical Manhood and Womanhood: A Response to Evangelical Feminism* (Wheaton, IL: Crossway Books, 1991), which includes extensive discussions of the following texts: Gen. 1–3; 1 Cor. 11:2-16; 1 Cor. 14:33-36; Eph. 5:21ff.; 1 Tim. 2:11-15; 1 Pet. 3:1-7.

5. See Wayne A. Grudem, *Evangelical Feminism: A New Path to Liberalism?* (Wheaton, IL: Crossway Books, 2006); Kevin DeYoung, *Freedom and Boundaries: A Pastoral Primer on the Role of Women in the Church* (Enumclaw, WA: Pleasant Word, 2006).

erarchy is the divinely intended meaning of gender complementarity. William Webb, for example, affirms gender complementarity and rejects same-sex erotic unions, while also explicitly rejecting the notion that this complementarity expresses itself in a hierarchy between the genders.[6] Instead, he argues for a "role distinction based upon biological differences between men and women," and suggests that some such role differences might include greater involvement of women in the early stages of child rearing, due to the need for the presence of a nursing mother.[7]

Robert Gagnon, whose massive study *The Bible and Homosexual Practice* is cited by many as the definitive exposition of the traditionalist's case, presses still further the focus on biological differences as the root meaning of gender complementarity. Like Webb, Gagnon also rejects a hierarchical understanding of gender complementarity, arguing explicitly that the Bible "does not condemn same-sex intercourse (at least primarily) because of the threat that such intercourse poses to male dominance over females." Rather, he argues:

> Scripture rejects homosexual behavior because it is a violation of the gendered existence of male and female ordained by God at creation. . . . Same-sex intercourse represents a suppression of the visible evidence in nature regarding male-female anatomical and procreative complementarity.[8]

This "anatomical and procreative complementarity" comprises the heart of Gagnon's argument about why same-sex erotic unions are morally wrong.[9] More importantly, he believes that this is *Scripture's* reason for rejecting same-sex unions in those passages that speak to the subject. When Paul speaks of same-sex erotic acts as "contrary to nature" in Romans 1, anatomical and procreative complementarity is what he is thinking about

---

6. Webb, *Slaves, Women and Homosexuals;* see also Webb, "Gender Equality and Homosexuality," in Ronald W. Pierce, Rebecca Merrill Groothuis, and Gordon D. Fee, *Discovering Biblical Equality: Complementarity without Hierarchy,* 2nd ed. (Downers Grove, IL: InterVarsity, 2005), pp. 401-13.

7. Webb, *Slaves, Women and Homosexuals,* p. 241.

8. Gagnon, *The Bible and Homosexual Practice,* pp. 485, 487-88.

9. Language focusing on anatomical and/or procreative complementarity appears seventeen times in his briefer essay of 52 pages, summarizing his argument, in Dan Otto Via and Robert A. J. Gagnon, *Homosexuality and the Bible: Two Views* (Minneapolis: Fortress Press, 2003); see pp. 44, 46, 48, 61, 62, 65 (his central argument), 72, 78, 79, 80, 84, 85, 88, 89, 90, 91.

or assuming. The same holds true, says Gagnon, for the prohibitions of male-male erotic acts in Leviticus 18:22 and 20:13. The reason these behaviors are rejected by the biblical writers is that they violate the divinely intended "anatomical and procreative complementarity" of the genders, which Gagnon interprets as the fittedness of male and female sexual organs and their capacity to produce children.[10]

Gagnon goes on to offer a somewhat expanded understanding of gender complementarity: "Complementarity extends also to a range of personality traits and predispositions that contribute to making heterosexual unions enormously more successful in terms of fidelity, endurance, and health than same-sex ones."[11] But Gagnon does not specify more precisely what these "personality traits and predispositions" are, nor does he claim, as far as I can tell, that this form of moral logic shapes the language of the biblical writers, or that it explains why they say what they do. Rather, this is a more modern way of engaging the argument about modern same-sex unions, appealing to a certain kind of generalized experience rather than to the interpretation of biblical texts. This is not to say whether Gagnon is correct or not, but merely to observe that this sort of argument is no longer directly addressing the interpretation of biblical texts.[12]

So we come to the crux of an interpretive problem. Traditionalists all point to gender complementarity as the central form of moral logic that undergirds what they believe to be the Bible's universal rejection of same-sex erotic relationships. These relationships are "against nature," and "nature" is further explained as the complementarity of the genders. But as we have seen, when we press further to identify exactly in what ways males and females are taught or assumed in Scripture to be complementary, disagreements emerge.

---

10. Interestingly, however, Gagnon at one point at least, devalues to some extent the centrality of procreation as part of the biblical logic underlying its rejection of same-sex eroticism. In commenting on 1 Cor. 7, he says, "Paul's opposition to same-sex intercourse was not based primarily on its nonprocreative character" (Via and Gagnon, *Homosexuality and the Bible,* p. 86). It is unclear whether Gagnon's comments should be applied equally to all the biblical proscriptions against same-sex erotic activity, or only to Paul's.

11. Gagnon, *The Bible and Homosexual Practice,* p. 488.

12. Gagnon fails to distinguish between those aspects of gay culture in North America that are dominated by promiscuous relationships and those gay and lesbian persons who are in committed relationships. He provides no data on comparing gay/lesbian and heterosexual relationships that have persisted over equivalent periods of time. Hence these types of generalizations are unhelpful in assessing ethical questions surrounding committed same-sex relationships.

These disagreements involve important issues. The tendency to read gender complementarity as hierarchy has led increasingly, in the more conservative parts of the church, toward a greater tendency to restrict women in leadership at home and in the life of the church. In my own denomination (Reformed Church in America), which has ordained women to all leadership positions for more than thirty years, I hear stories of congregations that once allowed women into leadership but now question that approach, placing greater restrictions on women in leadership. Indeed, if the leadership of women violates the same underlying biblical norm of gender complementarity that same-sex intimate unions violate, then both share fundamentally in the same departure from the will of God revealed in creation, and both are, at least in that sense, equally culpable. I do not hold such a position, but some do, and it is an important question in its own right (which we shall explore further in chapter 4 below).

Biological Understandings of Gender Complementarity

But moving from hierarchy to biology as the focus of gender complementarity is not without its own problems. Such an approach raises a variety of difficult questions, particularly for contemporary application, quite apart from the question of homosexuality. For example, does this focus on the fittedness of sexual organs mean that all noncoital sexual contact among heterosexual married couples (e.g., mutual masturbation) is subject to the same condemnation? It would be difficult to find anything in Scripture to support such a view.[13] Yet another concern focuses on the apparent genitalizing of sex that results from this focus on biological differences. Sexuality in general, and lovemaking in particular, is about much more than how certain body parts fit together. The biological differences between the sexes seem a rather slender basis on which to build an entire marriage ethic. Moreover, such an approach leads us directly into the difficult contemporary debate about essentialism (gender differences are primarily biologi-

13. Even the use of the Onan story in Gen. 38 to condemn solitary masturbation occurs only in rabbinical sources much later than the writing of the New Testament. See M. L. Satlow, "'Wasted Seed,' the History of a Rabbinic Idea," *Hebrew Union College Annual* 65 (1994). Another kind of argument condemning mutual masturbation might be based on a different stream in the Christian tradition, focusing not on the fittedness of sexual organs, but on the nonprocreational nature of such activity. See chapter 6 below, where I argue that procreation cannot function as the defining essence of sexual intercourse or marriage.

cally based) versus constructivism (gender differences are primarily socially constructed) in gender identity. Sorting out what is "biological" and
what is "cultural" in the meaning of maleness and femaleness is an enormously complicated task.[14]

  These are difficult questions, and they raise some doubt about whether
emphasizing the biological dimension to gender complementarity can be
used consistently in a contemporary context. But for our purposes in this
study, none of these problems is central. The more basic question is this: Is
"anatomical and procreative complementarity" really the basic form of
moral logic that the *biblical writers* have in mind or assume when they condemn same-sex erotic relations? If so, we should certainly expect to find biblical passages that treat this subject of the biological complementarity of the
genders directly and explicitly. The issue is not, first of all, whether this way
of understanding "gender complementarity" makes sense to us. The first
question is whether this is what the biblical writers have in mind and what
Scripture as a whole teaches. This is in keeping with the overall goal, outlined
above, to discern the "moral logic" that undergirds Scripture's commands
and prohibitions. If biological gender differences really are what the Bible
has in mind when it rejects same-sex erotic relations, we ought to expect to
find other passages of Scripture that make this connection between gender
and biology clear.[15] But if we do not find other texts that draw a clear connection between gender and biological differences, then we may be guilty of
imposing an alien set of assumptions onto the texts that forbid same-sex
erotic relations. We may be misreading the basic forms of moral logic that
shape the biblical writers' minds when they speak as they do against same-
sex erotic relations. In other words, we still may not have determined *why* the
biblical writers speak negatively about these relationships.

  There are not many passages in Scripture that speak of a connection
between biology and gender; in fact, some would argue that there are none
that speak to this issue. But one text that has played a very large role in this
debate is the story of the creation of woman in Genesis 2. Here is where
Robert Gagnon, the foremost traditionalist interpreter, makes his case for

---

14. For an exploration of some of these complexities, see Lisa Sowle Cahill, *Sex, Gender,
and Christian Ethics,* New Studies in Christian Ethics (Cambridge, UK: Cambridge University Press, 1996).

15. I take this to be a rather straightforward application of the principle articulated by
Martin Luther in the Reformation: "Sacred Scripture is its own interpreter." For further discussion, see Paul Althaus, *The Theology of Martin Luther* (Philadelphia: Fortress Press, 1966),
pp. 76ff.

the link between gender complementarity and the biological differences between the sexes. Gagnon's reading has exercised enormous influence, so it will be necessary to explore it in some detail.

Gagnon begins his discussion of this text by commenting on the creation of human beings in Genesis 1:26-28:

> [26]Then God said, "Let us make humankind in our image, according to our likeness; and let them have dominion over the fish of the sea, and over the birds of the air, and over the cattle, and over all the wild animals of the earth, and over every creeping thing that creeps upon the earth." [27]So God created humankind in his image, in the image of God he created them; male and female he created them. [28]God blessed them, and God said to them, "Be fruitful and multiply, and fill the earth and subdue it; and have dominion over the fish of the sea and over the birds of the air and over every living thing that moves upon the earth."

Gagnon comments: "Filling or populating the earth with humans is a precondition for ruling it, and procreation is a precondition for filling the earth. The complementarity of male and female is thereby secured in the divinely sanctioned work of governing creation."[16] Yet Gagnon acknowledges that procreation, while important, is not the whole meaning of gender complementarity.[17] He goes on to say: "'Male and female he created them' probably intimates that the fullness of God's 'image' comes together in the union of male and female in marriage [not, one could infer, from same-sex unions]" (p. 58).

This connection between gender differentiation and the image of God acquires greater significance in Gagnon's exposition of Genesis 2, the story of the creation of woman. Referring to the comment earlier in the narrative, "It is not good that the man should be alone" (Gen. 2:18), Gagnon writes the following about the creation of woman in Genesis 2: "The solution that God arrived at was not the independent creation of another

16. Gagnon, *The Bible and Homosexual Practice*, p. 57. Hereafter, page references to this work appear in parentheses in the text.

17. Gagnon argues that, even in a context of overpopulation as the world experiences it today, a procreative understanding of marriage and gender differentiation is still important because it "avoids a detachment of sexuality from stable family structures," and because "God's people in particular play a special role in discerning God's will for the created order and for communicating that will to the next generation" (*The Bible and Homosexual Practice*, p. 58).

'*adam,* a replica of the first, but rather to 'build' a complementary being from a portion of '*adam's* own self, a 'rib' (2:21-22)" (p. 60). He continues, "Only a being made from '*adam* can and ought to become someone with whom '*adam* longs to reunite in sexual intercourse and marriage, a reunion that not only provides companionship but restores '*adam* to his original wholeness" (p. 61).

The last phrase of Gagnon's sentence is particularly important: the sexual union depicted in Genesis 2 assumes the reconstituting of the original "wholeness" that was split into male and female. Gagnon states this even more directly in his comments on Genesis 2:24: "Therefore a man leaves his father and his mother and clings to his wife, and they become one flesh." Gagnon says:

> The sexual union of man and woman in marriage, of two complementary beings, in effect makes possible a single, composite human being. So great is the complementarity of male and female, so seriously is the notion of "attachment" and "joining" taken, that the marital bond between man and woman takes precedence even over the bond with the parents that physically produced them. A descriptive statement about the creation of woman thus provides etiological justification for prescriptive norms regarding marriage. (p. 61)

Gagnon is even more explicit in a later writing:

> In Genesis 2:18-24, a binary or sexually undifferentiated human (the *adam*) is split into two sexually differentiated beings. Marriage is treated by the Yahwist as a reunion of two complementary sexual others, a reconstitution of the sexual unity of the original *adam.*[18]

Gagnon is not alone in this reading. John Stott has a similar view: "Out of the undifferentiated humanity of Adam, male and female emerged. And Adam awoke from his deep sleep to behold before him a reflection of himself, a complement to himself, indeed a very part of himself."[19] Thomas Schmidt writes in a similar vein: "*Because union is the remedy of incompleteness* ('for this reason,' Gen 2:24), humans possess a drive to 'leave and cleave' in marriage."[20]

18. Via and Gagnon, *Homosexuality and the Bible,* p. 61.
19. Stott, *Same-Sex Partnerships?* p. 33.
20. Schmidt, *Straight and Narrow? Compassion and Clarity in the Homosexuality Debate,* p. 44 (italics added).

We may summarize this exposition of a "biological" interpretation of gender complementarity by noting some recurring themes. This argument clearly assumes that the complementarity of male and female bodies together is needed to fully represent the image of God, and that the sexual union of male and female in marriage constitutes a recovery of the original androgynous unity of the first created being (ʿadam — Gen. 1:27), and thus the fullness of the image of God, in which the original ʿadam was created. The one-flesh union of marriage thus necessarily and exclusively requires the union of the "flesh" of one male and one female. Therefore, it is the bodily differences of male and female that are centrally in view in Genesis 2.

Critiquing Biological Understandings of Gender Complementarity

I want to address four basic assumptions made by these various expositions of the Genesis stories, each of which represents, I believe, a misreading of the text. When we have cleared away these mistaken assumptions, it becomes considerably less clear that the creation narratives teach a biological complementarity of the genders. I will argue the following countertheses: (1) The original ʿadam of Genesis 1:26–2:18 is not a binary, or sexually undifferentiated, being that is divided into male and female in Genesis 2:21. (2) The focus in Genesis 2 is not on the *complementarity* of male and female, but rather on the *similarity* of male and female. (3) The fact that male and female are both created in the divine image (Gen. 1:27) is intended to convey the value, dominion, and relationality *shared* by both men and women, but not the idea that the complementarity of the genders is somehow necessary to fully express or embody the divine image. (4) The "one-flesh" union spoken of in Genesis 2:24 connotes not physical complementarity but a kinship bond.

(1) The original ʿadam of Genesis 1:26–2:18 is not a binary, or sexually undifferentiated, being that is divided into male and female in Genesis 2:21.

As we consider this issue, it may be helpful to have the text from Genesis 2:18-24 before us:

> [18]Then the LORD God said, "It is not good that the man should be alone; I will make him a helper as his partner." [19]So out of the ground the LORD God formed every animal of the field and every bird of the

air, and brought them to the man to see what he would call them; and whatever the man called every living creature, that was its name. [20]The man gave names to all cattle, and to the birds of the air, and to every animal of the field; but for the man there was not found a helper as his partner. [21]So the LORD God caused a deep sleep to fall upon the man, and he slept; then he took one of his ribs and closed up its place with flesh. [22]And the rib that the LORD God had taken from the man he made into a woman and brought her to the man. [23]Then the man said, "This at last is bone of my bones and flesh of my flesh; this one shall be called Woman, for out of Man this one was taken." [24]Therefore a man leaves his father and his mother and clings to his wife, and they become one flesh.

In support of the notion that the original 'adam was a binary, or sexually undifferentiated, being, Gagnon points to the ambiguity of translating the Hebrew word commonly rendered "rib" *(sela')* in Genesis 2:21, noting that its normal use refers to the side of an object, and that nowhere else in Scripture is it used as a part of the human body. He goes on to cite a third-century CE rabbi, Samuel bar Nahman, who thought of Adam as an androgynous being who was sliced in half — down the side.[21] It might be observed, in passing, that the rabbinical reading may be more influenced by Plato's *Symposium,* which portrays a similar creation of gendered beings by the splitting of originally androgynous or binary creatures.[22] Yet this interpretation of the Genesis text is deeply problematic. There are no other places in Scripture that interpret the creation account in this way. Moreover, the details of the language in the text contradict this reading.

We begin with an analysis of some of those details. Gagnon clearly needs to come clean on his blurry "binary or sexually undifferentiated" characterization of his postulated original 'adam. The two terms are not equivalent; furthermore, each has its problems. If the original 'adam is a single sexually undifferentiated or androgynous being, then Gagnon can-

---

21. Gagnon, *The Bible and Homosexual Practice,* p. 60, n. 44.

22. In Plato's *Symposium,* Aristophanes describes the creatures this way: ". . . each of these beings was globular in shape, with rounded back and sides, four arms and four legs, and two faces, both the same, on a cylindrical neck, and one head, with one face one side and one the other, and four ears, and two lots of privates, and all the other parts to match" *(Symposium,* §189e-190a, cited in Edith Hamilton and Huntington Cairns, eds., *The Collected Dialogues of Plato, Including the Letters,* Bollingen Series, 71 [New York: Pantheon Books, 1961], p. 542).

not account for the plural "male and female he created *them*" in Genesis 1:27. But if one gives weight to Genesis 1:27 and postulates that the original *'adam* is binary, with two centers of consciousness (but not two distinct bodies), then one cannot account for the statement in 2:18, "It is not good for the *'adam* to be alone," since two distinct centers of consciousness can scarcely be said to be "alone." Gagnon's evasive use of both terms obscures the difficulties with either as a consistent way to read the text.

But there are even more substantial problems with Gagnon's postulation of an original binary or sexually undifferentiated *'adam*. Genesis 2:23 says: "[T]his one shall be called Woman *[ishah]*, for out of Man *[ish]* this one was taken." The words *ish* and *ishah* are not generic terms; they are specifically *gendered* terms for man and woman. But this is not what one would expect, if Gagnon's reading were correct. If Gagnon were correct, the woman would not be taken from the male *(ish)* but from the binary or sexually undifferentiated human *('adam)*. But this is not what the text says. In other words, Genesis 2:23 assumes that the first human *('adam)* is *already* male *(ish)* *before* the woman is taken from his side.[23] The same perspective on this verse is reflected in 1 Corinthians 11:8, which also speaks of woman being made "from man" in explicitly gendered terms. All this is incompatible with Gagnon's reading of the text.[24]

This means that the Genesis 2 account cannot be used to argue that heterosexual union in marriage reconstitutes the original, binary, or androgynous *'adam*. The creation of woman does not arise from the splitting of an original binary or sexually undifferentiated being. Sexual union is never portrayed in Scripture as the recovery of a primordial unity of the two genders.[25] Gagnon is simply wrong when he claims, "Marriage is

23. The Greek words for "from the man" in Gen. 2:23 used in the Septuagint, the first Greek translation of the Old Testament, are also gendered *(ek tou andros)* rather than androgynous. Hence there is no reason why the New Testament writers who relied on the Septuagint would have viewed the creation of woman as the division of a sexually androgynous *'adam*.

24. If anything, one might connect the notion in Gen. 2:23b that the female comes "from" the male to the ancient idea that the female is an incomplete and derivative version of the male, though the canonical witness does not seem to move in this direction, despite some similar echoes in texts such as 1 Cor. 11:8-9. In the latter text, note how any potential reading of the text in terms of male superiority (woman was made from man, 1 Cor. 11:8) is immediately countered by 1 Cor. 11:11-12: "Nevertheless, in the Lord woman is not independent of man or man independent of woman. For just as woman came from man, so man comes through woman; but all things come from God."

25. Interestingly, this vision of an original androgyny does appear in early Gnostic texts, even though it does not appear in the canonical texts. For a more extended discussion and

treated by the Yahwist as a reunion of the sexual unity of the original *adam*."[26] Others who follow the same line of interpretation are equally mistaken. The Genesis text portrays marriage as a solution, not for "incompleteness," but for *aloneness* (Gen. 2:18).

It is also worth observing that this understanding of gender differences via a "myth of incompleteness" (arising from Plato rather than from the Hebrew Bible) raises some serious practical and relational problems as a theory of gender complementarity. First, it leaves single people in a permanent state of deficiency with no hope of remedy apart from marriage. This contrasts markedly with the positive portrayals of celibacy in the New Testament (e.g., Matt. 19:11-12; 1 Cor. 7:7-9). But there are even problems for married couples. This myth may incline people to a greater focus on themselves, seeing their partners as a means to complete themselves and their own self-construction, rather than as genuine *others* who may have differing agendas, concerns, desires, or interests — extending well beyond stereotypical gender differences. Such differences may not only complement dispositions of the partner; they may also contrast, or even conflict with, those of the partner, requiring the difficult and sacrificial work of Christian love — including, in some cases, death to the self — in order to forge and sustain a bond of unity. This "myth of incompleteness" may thus obscure the ways in which marriage involves the hard work of creatively *constructing* a form of shared life built on the unique interests and gifts of each partner, rather than merely *recovering* a preexisting and divinely established, "hard-wired" form of complementarity. Viewed more holistically, marriage does not look backward to the recovery of a primordial unity; rather, it looks forward, like all forms of human community, to what may creatively emerge in the common space between two persons who share kinship and a common destiny.

(2) The focus in Genesis 2 is not on the complementarity of male and female, but on the similarity of male and female.

This observation arises from a simple reading of the narrative of Genesis 2:18-24. The story begins with God's declaration, "It is not good that the

---

citations from a range of such texts, see Andrew T. Lincoln, *Ephesians*, Word Biblical Commentary (Dallas: Word Books, 1990), pp. 382-83.

26. Via and Gagnon, *Homosexuality and the Bible*, p. 61.

man should be alone. I will make him a helper as his partner." As many commentators have pointed out, there is no sense of inferiority in the word "helper" (Hebrew *ezer*); in fact, in numerous passages, God is spoken of using the same word (e.g., Exod. 18:4; Deut. 33:7, 26, 29; 1 Sam. 7:12; Ps. 33:20; 70:6; 115:9-11; 121:2; 124:8; 146:5; Dan. 11:34). The narrative continues as God brings all the animals before the man as potential solutions to the problem of the man's aloneness. But a solution is not found. The narrator declares in 2:20, "But for the man there was not found a helper as his partner." In other words, the animals are not similar to the man — in the way that the woman will be. The animals are certainly different from the man, but that is not what the story is interested in. It is pursuing not differences but someone *similar* to the man, someone similar enough to be "his partner" (in contrast to the animals, who are not sufficiently similar), and someone strong enough to be his "helper."[27]

This line of interpretation is confirmed by the response of the man when he meets the woman (2:23): "This at last is bone of my bones and flesh of my flesh." On the surface of it, this appears to be a discovery of sameness, not difference. Furthermore, if one looks elsewhere in Scripture for similar language, one discovers that this language is always used to express kinship (Gen. 29:14; Judg. 9:2; 2 Sam. 5:1; 19:12-13; 1 Chron. 11:1). In the other texts where this language occurs, there is not a hint of any notion of complementarity; the entire focus is that those who share flesh and bone share something important in common with each other. In this case, the man discovers a far deeper commonality with the woman than he shares with the animals. That seems to be the meaning that is reflected in the structure of the narrative itself. The focus is not so much on complementarity but on *shared* identity, nature, and experience between the man and the woman, over against the rest of the creation. In a way that is similar to the language of the "image of God" used in Genesis 1:26-27, this narrative distinguishes both man and woman from the rest of creation, and it celebrates a unique commonality that is shared by men and women, over against all the rest of creation (symbolized by the animals). The primary movement in the text is not from unity to differentiation, but from the isolation of an individual to the deep blessing of shared kinship and community. Of course, the story envi-

---

27. The Hebrew phrase translated by the NRSV as "as his partner" *(kenegdo)* is usually understood as "corresponding to him" or "in front of, or beside him." The phrase certainly allows for the notion of difference as well. Yet this aspect of difference remains undeveloped in the remainder of the passage.

sions marriage as the most basic form of this community, and it assumes that marriage is constituted by a husband and wife. But the text doesn't really explore gender differences at all; instead, it places the emphasis on the value of shared human experience between the man and the woman.[28]

(3) The fact that male and female are both created in the divine image (Gen. 1:27) is intended to convey the value, dominion, and relationality shared by both men and women, but not the idea that the complementarity of the genders is somehow necessary to fully express or embody the divine image.

Genesis 1:27 links the "image of God" with the creation of humanity as male and female: "So God created humankind in his own image, in the image of God created he them; male and female created he them." This raises an obvious exegetical question: What is the relationship between the image of God and maleness and femaleness? For at least some of the traditionalist interpreters I have been referring to, the image of God is only fully seen in the sexual union of male and female. Gagnon writes, "'Male and female he created them' probably intimates that the fullness of God's 'image' comes together in the union of male and female in marriage [not, one could infer, from same-sex unions]."[29] Other traditionalist commentators do not attempt to link the image of God with gender complementarity. For example, Thomas Schmidt says: "I am *not* confident that we can derive [from Gen. 1:27] a definition of creation 'in God's image' as either sexual differentiation or human fellowship."[30]

We should heed Schmidt's caution. Throughout much of Christian history, the notion that gender differentiation is part of the image of God ("male and female as the image of God in stereo") has occasionally surfaced as a marginal voice, but it has never occupied a significant place in the Christian understanding of the *imago Dei*.[31] The reason is a simple one. If both

---

28. Paul K. Jewett writes, "We can only conclude, then, that when the narrative in Genesis 2 speaks of the woman as made from the man, the intent is to distinguish her from the animals, as essentially like the one from whom she is taken." Jewett and Marguerite Shuster, *Who We Are: Our Dignity as Human; A Neo-Evangelical Theology* (Grand Rapids: Eerdmans, 1996), pp. 161-62.

29. Gagnon, *The Bible and Homosexual Practice*, p. 58.

30. Schmidt, *Straight and Narrow?* p. 44.

31. This despite the most ambitious attempt by Karl Barth to argue that a complemen-

male and female must be present together in order to fully constitute the image of God, then those who are single do not fully reflect the image of God. This runs deeply against the grain of many passages in the Bible. But even more importantly, the New Testament clearly proclaims that Jesus is, par excellence, the image of God (e.g., 2 Cor. 4:4; Col. 3:10; 1 Cor. 15:45). Unless we are to postulate an androgynous savior, something the New Testament never even contemplates, we cannot say that the image of God requires the presence of both male and female. It is far better to interpret Genesis 1:27, which insists that both male and female are created in the divine image, to mean that all the dignity, honor, and significance of bearing the divine image belong equally to men and to women. We need not delve into the entire debate about what exactly the image of God signifies. For our purposes it is enough to say what is *not* signified by the divine image: gender complementarity.

(4) The "one-flesh" union spoken of in Genesis 2:24 connotes, not physical complementarity, but a kinship bond.

Traditionalist interpreters might grant each of the previous countertheses, yet still not be persuaded that Genesis 2 is unconcerned with gender complementarity. Perhaps, they might say, the Genesis text does not portray an originally androgynous ʿadam, subsequently divided into male and female. Perhaps the narrative of Genesis 2 does contain significant elements emphasizing the similarity between the man and the woman, over against the rest of the creation. Perhaps the creation of male and female in the "image of God" does not connote gender complementarity, but rather gender equality before God. Still, some will argue, we must reckon with Genesis 2:24 and the language it uses: "Therefore a man leaves his father and his mother and clings to his wife, and they become one flesh." Given the fact that the woman is created from the "flesh and bone" of the man (2:23), doesn't the language of "one flesh" in the following verse connote a reunification of what was divided in the creation of the woman? If so, doesn't this suggest that the marital union fulfills some sort of incompleteness in the flesh of either gender — on its own? And if this is indeed the case, doesn't Scripture locate gender complementarity precisely in the physical "flesh" of the male and female?

---

tary understanding of gender is essential to the image of God (see Karl Barth et al., *Church Dogmatics*, Study Edition (London/New York: T & T Clark, 2009), 3.1 §41.

This objection cannot be sustained: it is contradicted both by the lexical meaning of "flesh" in the Hebrew Bible and by the extended use of the term "one flesh" in the New Testament. The standard lexicon of the Hebrew Bible includes Genesis 2:24 under the general heading that defines the Hebrew word for "flesh" *(basar)* as "relatives."[32] In other words, "one flesh" means "one kinship group." This is in keeping with the parallels to "flesh and bone"; the reference implicit in "one flesh" here is not to the recovery of a mystic or primordial unity, but rather to the establishment of a kinship bond.

This is evident, first of all, in the way Genesis 2:24 unfolds: "Therefore a man leaves his father and his mother and clings to his wife, and they become one flesh." One of the elements of this verse that catches the attention of commentators is that the man "leaves his father and mother." What makes this puzzling is that, in most ancient Mediterranean cultures, sons do not usually "leave" their parents when they get married. Indeed, in any society in which agriculture plays a significant role, such leaving can be economic suicide. Sons stay on the land and work the land with their fathers. In many of these cultures, the marriage of a son simply means the addition of another room onto the house of the extended family. While some commentators speculate that this language about leaving father and mother comes from an early period when society was organized matrilineally, this solution bears no confirmation elsewhere in any of the antecedents of ancient Israelite culture, and it leaves the text oddly disconnected from its larger cultural and canonical context. It makes more sense to recognize that what is already in view here at the beginning of 2:24 is the realignment of primary kinship ties. Despite the fact that sons are still to honor their parents, when they marry, the location of primary kinship moves from the family of origin to the new family constituted by marriage. Only such an interpretation can make sense of the reference to "leaving."

If the "leaving" of the first half of the verse connotes the dissolution of one primary kinship tie, the "one-flesh" language at the end of the verse connotes the establishment of a new one, between husband and wife. This is in keeping with the lexical meaning of "flesh" that I noted above. So the focus in Genesis 2:24 is not on explaining the origin of "the extremely powerful drive of the sexes to each other," as von Rad and many others argue (nowhere else in Scripture is this verse interpreted in this

---

32. *A Hebrew and English Lexicon of the Old Testament,* ed. F. Brown, S. R. Driver, and C. A. Briggs (Oxford: Clarendon Press, 1979).

way).[33] Rather, the focus is on the formation of the essential and foundational building blocks of human community — the ties of kinship.[34]

This approach to the text is confirmed by the way Jesus himself interprets Genesis 2:24 in the New Testament. Both Mark 10:8 and Matthew 19:5-6 portray Jesus as citing Genesis 2:24 in the context of a question about divorce. According to Jesus, as recounted in Mark, the fact that "the two shall become one flesh" means that divorce — the negation of the essential mutual obligations of kinship — is unacceptable and contrary to the will of God. Although Matthew's account adds an "exception clause" in the case of sexual immorality, the essential reading of Genesis 2:24 is the same: the one-flesh union is centrally concerned about kinship obligations, which are established by God in marriage and thus cannot be set aside by human beings (Mark 10:9, Matt. 19:5-6).

The same essential line of interpretation is found in Paul's reference to Genesis 2:24 in 1 Corinthians 6:16-17: "Do you not know that whoever is united to a prostitute becomes one body with her? For it is said, 'The two shall be one flesh.' But anyone united to the Lord becomes one spirit with him." For Paul, the central problem concerning sex with a prostitute is that sexual union enacts a deeper union ("one body") with a prostitute that is completely inappropriate. Or to put it in different terms, Paul urges the Corinthians not to say with their bodies (by enacting sexual unions with prostitutes) what they are not saying with the rest of their lives (by recognizing the kinship ties and obligations of marriage). The same connection between "one-flesh" language and the call to mutual obligations is evident in Ephesians 5:31-33, where the Pauline tradition identifies the union between Christ and the church as reflecting the same one-flesh bond, characterized by mutual care (Eph. 5:28-29). Only this focus on mutual care and kinship obligation can make sense of the language in a few New Testament texts that speak of men as well as women as brides to Christ (e.g., 1 Cor. 11:2; Rev. 19:7ff.). Clearly, the physical complementarity of the genders cannot be in view in these texts that speak of the church as the bride of Christ.

33. Gerhard von Rad, *Genesis: A Commentary,* rev. ed., The Old Testament Library (Philadelphia: Westminster, 1972), p. 85.

34. Gordon Wenham writes: "'They become one flesh.' This does not denote merely the sexual union that follows marriage, or the children conceived in marriage, or even the spiritual and emotional relationship that it involves, though all are involved in becoming one flesh. Rather, it affirms that just as blood relations are one's flesh and bone, so marriage creates a similar kinship relation between man and wife" (Wenham, *Genesis,* 2 vols., Word Biblical Commentary [Waco, TX: Dallas Word Books, 1987], I:71).

Conclusions

The results of this exploration of "one-flesh" language in Genesis 2:24 and gender complementarity are thus evident. Both in its immediate context, and in the wider canonical context, the language of "one flesh" in Genesis 2:24 does not refer to physical gender complementarity, but to the common bond of shared kinship. Therefore, to say that the same-sex erotic acts depicted in Romans 1:26-27 are "against nature" because they violate the physical complementarity of the genders depicted in the one-flesh union of Genesis 2:24 is simply mistaken. This line of interpretation cannot be sustained, either by a close reading of the Genesis accounts themselves, or by a larger consideration of other wider canonical references to "one flesh" in the creation story, or by other references to the language of "one flesh" in the Pauline corpus. Of course, to say that a doctrine of physical or biological gender complementarity is not the key to understanding Romans 1:26-27 and other biblical texts regarding same-sex erotic relationships is hardly the end of the matter. At this point, the argument is simple: appeals to a doctrine of physical or biological gender complementarity grounded in the creation narratives do not illuminate the moral logic by which Pauline and other biblical texts condemn same-sex erotic relations. Despite the fact that such gender complementarity, allegedly taught in the creation narratives, is the most commonly cited reason why commentators believe Scripture teaches that same-sex erotic relations are wrong, the texts themselves do not support this claim, as we have seen.

This conclusion does not alter the simple observation that Paul views "unnatural" same-sex erotic relations very negatively in Romans 1, as do other biblical writers in other passages. It is simply to recognize that the most common attempts to explain the underlying moral logic that shapes this outlook are inadequate and unhelpful. But even such a conclusion is a sort of progress. The old ground must be cleared before a new framework of understanding can be built in its place. However, this "clearing of old ground" also clears away a great deal of theological speculation based on the notion of gender complementarity. Consider, for example, some of Robert Gagnon's comments at the conclusion of his summary essay:

> There is a world of difference between erotic attraction to the sex that one belongs to and erotic attraction to the sex that one does not. *So far as the erotic dimension is concerned,* the former is sexual self-deception: a desire either for oneself or for what one wishes to be but

in fact already is. It is a misguided attempt at completing the sexual self with a sexual same when true integration, as the story of Gen. 2:21-24 illustrates, requires a complementary sexual other.[35]

Clearly, Gagnon has built an entire psychological/psychotherapeutic theory of gender and eroticism on his interpretation of Genesis 2:24, an interpretation that cannot be exegetically sustained.

As far as the creation accounts are concerned, then, gender complementarity, viewed through the lens of the physical or biological difference between the genders, cannot be construed as the basis for the Bible's rejection of same-sex erotic relations. Later (in chapter 4 below) I will explore the extent to which a hierarchical understanding of gender complementarity may underlie Paul's concerns in Romans 1 — and scriptural perspectives more generally. Chapter 6 will engage yet another way that "gender complementarity" is commonly understood in Roman Catholic teaching, focusing on procreation. But our exploration up to this point suggests that "gender complementarity," either construed in abstract terms or identified more specifically as biological or physical complementarity, is not a helpful way to discern the moral logic underlying scriptural teachings on sexual ethics. If an argument appealing to gender complementarity is to be used at all, it must spell out more specifically what other kind of complementarity is in view, and it must test that more detailed understanding against the canonical evidence.

Of course, some will argue that there must be *some* differences between male and female that Paul has in mind when he rejects same-sex erotic relations in Romans 1, since he refers explicitly to gender in verses 26-27; and there must be some reason why Leviticus 18 and 20 also refer explicitly to gender when they say that it is an abomination for a man to "lie with a male as with a woman." But to make this observation is not yet to discern *why* exactly same-sex erotic relations are seen as wrong in these texts. What is it about "appropriate" gender roles, functions, natures, or identities that is being violated in these cases referred to in Romans 1 and Leviticus 18 and 20? In this chapter I have argued that biological or physical gender complementarity is not an appropriate exposition of the moral logic underpinning these texts, because the larger canonical witness does not support this reading. The coming chapters will attempt to set forth a more compelling and scripturally coherent account of the moral logic that underpins these pro-

---

35. Via and Gagnon, *Homosexuality and the Bible,* p. 91 (italics in original).

hibitions, as well as the wider biblical vision for marriage, gender, and sexuality. In so doing, I hope to illuminate how the relevance of these texts to contemporary sexual ethics may be more clearly discerned.

But before I build that new structure of understanding, I must also deal with some obstacles and problems that have arisen on the revisionist side of the homosexuality debate.

Summing Up

- An analysis of the form of moral logic underlying most traditionalist positions shows that what traditionalists find most fundamentally wrong with same-sex intimate relationships is that they violate divinely intended gender complementarity.
- But "gender complementarity" is really more like a category under which a variety of forms of moral logic may appear. Some of these more specific forms, such as hierarchy, are not universally embraced among traditionalists as the deep meaning of gender complementarity.
- The most widely embraced form of gender complementarity among traditionalists focuses on the anatomical or biological complementarity of male and female. The physical union of male and female in this view represents the overcoming of the incompleteness of the male on his own or the female on her own.
- But this hypothesis raises a deeper question: Is anatomical or biological gender complementarity what Scripture assumes and teaches? The central issue here is the interpretation of the creation of woman in Genesis 2.
- In response to a variety of traditionalist readings of Genesis 2, this chapter has argued the following countertheses:
  - The original 'adam of Genesis 1:26–2:18 is not a binary or sexually undifferentiated being that is divided into male and female in Genesis 2:21.
  - The focus in Genesis 2 is not on the complementarity of male and female but on the similarity of male and female.
  - The fact that male and female are both created in the divine image (Gen. 1:27) is intended to convey the value, dominion, and relationality that is *shared* by both men and women, but not the idea that the complementarity of the genders is somehow necessary to fully express or embody the divine image.

- The one-flesh union spoken of in Genesis 2:24 connotes not physical complementarity but a kinship bond.
- These countertheses demonstrate that Genesis 2 does not teach a normative form of gender complementarity, based on the biological differences between male and female. Therefore, this form of moral logic cannot be assumed as the basis for the negative treatment of same-sex relationships in biblical texts. Hence we need to look further to discern why Scripture says what it does about same-sex intimate relationships.

3

Revisionist Readings

In the previous chapter I explored some fairly deeply embedded problems with the traditionalist position on same-sex erotic relationships. I noted the extent to which a theory of gender complementarity is assumed as the underlying form of moral logic that shapes most traditionalist positions. Yet such a reading of the biblical text encounters several significant difficulties. First, it is inadequate simply to talk in abstract terms about "gender complementarity" because these words, by themselves, do not tell us anything about the specific patterns of similarity and difference that actually express themselves in the complementarity of the genders. When traditionalist arguments are pressed further, in the attempt to discern more specifically what is meant by "gender complementarity," two approaches emerge. One approach emphasizes hierarchy as the essential way in which the complementarity of the genders expresses itself normatively in Scripture. This has led, in many conservative churches in North America, to a significant retrenchment in some churches' commitment to the full equality of women in church and society — and thus a diminution of the full use of women's gifts in church and society. I believe that this represents a misreading of the biblical text, but I will address this problem in more detail in chapter 4.

Another approach emphasizes the physical or biological complementarity of the genders, basing itself on the creation narrative in Genesis 1 and 2. As I have argued in the preceding chapter, however, such a reading of the physical complementarity of the genders is nowhere else directly affirmed (or even addressed) in Scripture, and thus cannot be sustained as a comprehensive reading of the creation narratives themselves. A third approach to gender complementarity focuses on procreation. I will explore this question in more detail in chapter 6, where I will argue that procreation is not a sufficient basis on which to ground the essence of marriage.

The failure of these approaches raises in a pressing way the need to discern more clearly the underlying forms of moral logic that do shape the negative portrayal of same-sex erotic relationships in texts such as Leviticus 18:22, 20:13, and Romans 1:26-27, and in the related texts of Genesis 19, Judges 19, 1 Corinthians 6:9, 1 Timothy 1:10, and Jude 7. If we are to discern how and to what extent these texts speak to gay and lesbian Christians in committed relationships today, we must discern the underlying forms of moral logic that shape these passages, as well as the links between these passages and the wider biblical witness regarding gender and sexuality. It is not sufficiently precise to speak vaguely about "gender complementarity" without further specifying the content and dynamics of such complementarity. And, as we have seen, it is also inappropriate to appeal to physical or biological differences between the genders as the meaning of gender complementarity, since Scripture itself doesn't speak of gender differences and interaction in this way.

These observations do not yet provide a constructive reading of the texts in question, nor do they provide a clearer glimpse of the forms of moral logic that actually shape the passages that take a negative view of same-sex erotic relationships. But they do identify some significant problems with the hermeneutical foundations of the traditionalist position. One of the goals of this book is to provide a more satisfactory foundation for reading and interpreting these passages.

Understanding Revisionist Positions

But it is not only the traditionalist position that has run into problems in the debate over the church's response to gay and lesbian Christians in its midst. If traditionalist readings have been too dependent on a theory of gender complementarity that is either undefined or unsupported by a close reading of the relevant texts, revisionist readings have struggled with their own difficulties in interpretation. The overall thrust of most revisionist positions has been to emphasize the historical *distance* between the world of the biblical text (and thus the forms of sexual behavior and desire addressed by the text) and our own contemporary world. Whatever the Bible is talking about in the "seven passages" (often used by the traditionalists when they talk about same-sex behavior), so the revisionist argument proceeds, these passages are not talking about the sexual or relational experience of contemporary gay and lesbian Christians in committed relationships. Therefore, they say, the Bible is essentially silent in addressing the contemporary experience of committed, long-term same-sex relationships.

However, beneath this kind of argument lurks a problem that is sensed, in a variety of ways, by Christians who are concerned about biblical authority. Because revisionist arguments emphasize so strongly the historical distance between the Bible and contemporary experience, this interpretative strategy may implicitly call into question whether the Bible can speak directly, with sufficient specificity and power, to any issues of sexual ethics more broadly considered in contemporary life. If the Bible's approach to sexual ethics in this particular case is so removed from our world, what would prevent us from constructing the same kind of argument to apply to other areas of contemporary sexual ethics? Might we not, following the same kind of analysis, claim that the Bible cannot speak at all to the modern experience of divorce, cohabitation, abortion, incest, or polygamy? If the Bible does not speak to our contemporary experience of homosexuality, even when it does seem to speak explicitly about same-sex erotic relationships, how can the Bible speak to our contemporary sexual experience at all?

It will be helpful for us — before we probe this basic question further — to explore more precisely the nature of the revisionist interpretation of the "seven passages" that are often cited as prohibiting same-sex erotic relations. If we are to assess this larger anxiety about the use of Scripture in sexual ethics, we need a more concrete sense of the historical gap envisioned by revisionist interpreters between the world of these texts and the contemporary world. For example, in reading the story of Sodom and Gomorrah, revisionist interpreters correctly note, first of all, that other biblical texts focus on the sin of inhospitality in this story, rather than on the alleged sin of same-sex relations.[1] Moreover, they note that even if one concedes that the "wickedness" of Sodom might have included the sinfulness of the attempted rape of Lot's male guests by the men of the city, the text says nothing about consensual same-sex intimate relations in committed relation-

---

1. See John Boswell, *Christianity, Social Tolerance, and Homosexuality: Gay People in Western Europe from the Beginning of the Christian Era to the Fourteenth Century* (Chicago: University of Chicago Press, 1980), p. 94. Boswell cites the following texts: Deut. 29:23; 32:32; Isa. 3:9; 13:19; Jer. 23:14; 49:18; 50:40; Lam. 4:6; Ezek. 16:46-48; Amos 4:11; Zeph. 2:9; Matt. 10:15; Luke 17:29; Rom. 9:29; 2 Pet. 2:6; Jude 7.

ships, but instead speaks to the abhorrence of the violence and violation of rape.[2] The same analysis holds true for the parallel story in Judges 19.

Turning to the Levitical texts (Lev. 18:22; 20:13), both of which declare that it is an "abomination" for a man to "lie with a male as with a woman," Jack Rogers argues that these are concerned with "ritual purity" and are preoccupied with distinguishing Israel from its pagan neighbors. Rogers then sets this concern over against the teaching of Jesus, who is concerned not with ritual purity but with purity of heart.[3] Therefore, these texts do not address sexual ethics in the church today, which is no longer defined in terms of ritual purity.[4]

In considering the "vice lists" of 1 Corinthians 6:9 and 1 Timothy 1:10, revisionist interpreters focus on the difficulties of translating and understanding the key words involved, which refer to those who will not "inherit the kingdom of God" (1 Cor. 6:10). In 1 Corinthians 6:9, the words translated in the NRSV as "male prostitute" (arsenokoitēs) and "sodomite" (malakos) carry with them a number of interpretative problems. The word arsenokoitēs, for example, does not occur in any extrabiblical Greek texts that are prior to or contemporaneous with the biblical writings, so it is difficult to ascertain its precise meaning via comparison with other contemporary or earlier texts. Thus Boswell is attempting to argue that the word refers to male prostitutes — without any particular homosexual connotation.[5] Robin Scroggs, by contrast, emphasizes the link between both of these terms (arsenokoitēs and malakos) and the Greek practice of peder-

---

2. One other New Testament passage that is often cited when considering the Sodom and Gomorrah story is Jude 7, where Sodom and Gomorrah are condemned because they pursued "unnatural lust" (NRSV). But the Greek text here (apelthousai opisō sarkos heteras) cannot refer to same-sex desire. The phrase sarkos heteras literally means "other flesh," and the word "other" means "another of a different kind." It is the same word from which we get the English word heterosexual! The sin envisioned in the text is not lusting after someone of the same sex, but the sin of lusting after the angelic visitors — who are not human — hence the NRSV's rendering of the phrase "unnatural lust."

3. Rogers, Jesus, the Bible, and Homosexuality: Explode the Myths, Heal the Church (Louisville: Westminster John Knox, 2006), pp. 68-69.

4. For a more comprehensive and helpful discussion of the place of purity in biblical discussions of sexuality, see Louis William Countryman, Dirt, Greed, and Sex: Sexual Ethics in the New Testament and Their Implications for Today, rev. ed. (Minneapolis: Fortress, 2007).

5. Boswell, Christianity, Social Tolerance, and Homosexuality, p. 107. This interpretation has not generally been sustained by later scholarship. See the critique in Martti Nissinen, Homoeroticism in the Biblical World: A Historical Perspective (Minneapolis: Fortress Press, 1998), pp. 114ff.

asty, the sexual use of younger boys *(malakoi)* by older men *(arseno-koitai)*.[6] Dale Martin argues that we cannot know much more about the word *arsenokoitēs* than that it refers to some kind of sexual abuse or exploitation.[7] Many interpreters also note a third term, which appears next to *arsenokoitēs* in 1 Timothy 1:10: *andropodistēs*. Literally, the word means "slave-dealer" or "kidnapper." A number of revisionist interpreters have connected this word to the ancient sex trade, where young boys were captured, castrated, and sold to be used as sexual slaves.[8] These and many other revisionist interpreters argue that the negative portrayal of these abusive ancient practices cannot be used to justify the condemnation of consensual, committed, and loving same-sex unions today.

We find a similar pattern of argument, emphasizing historical distance, in revisionist treatments of Romans 1:26-27, though the complexities of the debate warrant caution against an overly facile summary here. But much of the debate has focused on what Paul means in his reference to "nature" *(phusis)* when he says that women gave up "natural intercourse for unnatural," and men gave up "natural intercourse with women" and were consumed with passion for one another. Some revisionist interpreters have followed Boswell, who argues that Paul here assumes that heterosexual persons are engaging in homosexual relationships that violate their own sexual nature, and thus these verses do not apply to those who are "naturally" attracted to others of the same sex.[9] Other interpreters argue that the word "nature" in Paul's usage means "customary" or "normal," and they understand Paul as portraying behaviors that violate ancient standards of decency, rather than universal norms established in the creation itself.[10] All these lines of interpretation suggest that Paul is speaking

---

6. Robin Scroggs, *The New Testament and Homosexuality: Contextual Background for Contemporary Debate* (Philadelphia: Fortress Press, 1983), pp. 106ff.

7. Dale B. Martin, *Sex and the Single Savior: Gender and Sexuality in Biblical Interpretation* (Louisville: Westminster John Knox, 2006), p. 43.

8. See, for example, the discussion in William Stacy Johnson, *A Time to Embrace: Same-Gender Relationships in Religion, Law, and Politics* (Grand Rapids: Eerdmans, 2006), pp. 50, 133. He notes how Roman emperors attempted, on three separate occasions, to ban the practice, which was deemed exceedingly offensive even by ancient Roman standards.

9. Boswell, *Christianity, Social Tolerance, and Homosexuality*, pp. 107ff. Boswell says: "Paul did not discuss gay *persons* but only homosexual *acts* committed by heterosexual persons" (p. 109).

10. See, for example, Martti Nissinen, *Homoeroticism in the Biblical World: A Historical Perspective* (Minneapolis: Fortress, 1998), pp. 103ff. Cf. Paul's use of the same word *(phusis)* in 1 Cor. 11:14-15: "Does not nature itself teach you that if a man wears long hair, it is degrad-

to an ancient context, with ancient assumptions — assumptions that cannot be simply transferred directly to contemporary life without significant critical assessment.

It is not my purpose, at this point, to evaluate the merits and strengths of these various arguments and interpretations of the relevant texts. I will revisit all these arguments, and many others, in the coming chapters and will explore them in greater detail. At this point, I simply want to observe a common thread that weaves its way through all these arguments (just as I observed the common thread of "gender complementarity" that pervades traditionalist arguments). The common thread in the revisionist argument is this: Whatever specific behaviors and relationships the Bible is condemning in the "seven passages" cannot be used to condemn committed same-sex unions today. These ancient texts are speaking against pagan practices, against pederasty and abuse, and against violations of commonly embraced standards of decency and "normality" that were part of the ancient world. As such, they cannot speak directly to committed, mutual, and loving same-sex unions in the contemporary church. The Bible is thus essentially silent when it comes to addressing the ethics of such unions, at least when we consider the seven passages that might be construed as having anything specific to say on same-sex sexual behavior at all.[11] Robin Scroggs summarizes this entire line of argument when he says, "Biblical judgments against homosexuality are not relevant to today's debate . . . not because the Bible is not authoritative, but simply because it does not address the issues involved."[12]

Difficulties in Revisionist Positions

It is important to note that this problem of historical distance emerges not only when dealing with biblical texts that address same-sex erotic relations. The problem comes up repeatedly in biblical texts that deal with other sexual issues as well. Over and over, we confront the historical distance between the world of the text and our own, and the difficulty of directly applying biblical teaching on sexual issues to contemporary life.

---

ing to him, but if a woman has long hair, it is her glory?" This sounds much more like "nature" as "custom" or "normality."

11. Boswell writes: "The New Testament takes no demonstrable position on homosexuality" (*Christianity, Social Tolerance, and Homosexuality*, pp. 117ff.).

12. Scroggs, *The New Testament and Homosexuality*, p. 127.

Consider an obvious example: Deuteronomy 22:28-29 says that, if a man rapes a virgin who is not betrothed, "the man who lay with her shall give fifty shekels of silver to the young woman's father, and she shall become his wife. Because he violated her he shall not be permitted to divorce her as long as he lives." To our minds and in our context, such a command seems monstrous and unthinkable, regardless of what it might have meant in the ancient world concerning the rights of fathers and the provision of economic care for women deprived of socially sanctioned marriage. This passage simply cannot be directly appropriated today: it comes from a strange world and does not fit in our context. Other examples could easily be cited: the levirate marriage law that requires the brother of a deceased husband to marry his brother's widow (Deut. 25:5-10), the practice of polygamy by the patriarchs, the abhorrence of contact with menstrual blood (Lev. 18:19), and so forth. A lot of the discussion of sexuality in the Bible is very strange to us, and it simply cannot be directly applied to contemporary life.[13] This same perception of historical distance between the world of the text and our world lies at the heart of many revisionist positions regarding same-sex relationships.

This immediately raises a further question: If the Bible does not speak directly and explicitly to contemporary committed and loving same-sex unions, how are we to construct a distinctively Christian approach to such unions? Here is where we detect the second common thread winding its way through a range of revisionist positions. If the first step is to emphasize the historical distance between the world of the text and our contemporary experience and culture, the second step is to appeal to very broad ethical principles that can be established in a wide range of biblical passages. A good example can be found in Dan O. Via's discussion in *Homosexuality and the Bible*. The brief and distilled character of his essay helps to make the underlying form of the argument more transparent. Via appeals to Jesus' words that one cannot get bad fruit from a good tree (Matt. 7:17-18; 12:33-35; 23:26); he concludes: "So if the heart is loving, the acts that flow from it cannot be evil . . . . The inner nature of a homosexual relationship does qualify the acts." He goes on to argue that "for Paul sin is harmful

---

13. Much of this strangeness arises from the fact that most understandings of marriage in the West (focusing on intimacy and love) diverge rather sharply from the dominant understanding of marriage that has characterized most of human history (focusing on extended kinship relationships and economic considerations). See Stephanie Coontz, *Marriage, a History: From Obedience to Intimacy, or How Love Conquered Marriage* (New York: Viking, 2005).

by its very nature." He goes on to conclude from this premise: "If it cannot be demonstrated that homosexual practice is harmful in itself — in mutual, consensual, committed relationships — then it cannot be shown, in Pauline terms, to be sinful."[14] In other words, any acts that proceed from a loving heart and do not harm the other person cannot be considered sinful. Or, to use words that Via does not use (but which seem to express similar perspectives), the biblical basis for assessing the ethics of committed same-sex unions consists of a focus on justice (do not harm the other and respect the other's rights) and love (act out of good will and concern for the other).[15]

Justice, Love, and Sexual Ethics

Here is where the debate becomes more focused. No one disputes that the biblical call to justice and love is a necessary component of any Christian sexual ethic. The question is not whether justice and love are necessary conditions of a Christian sexual ethic, but whether they are a *sufficient* basis on which to build an entire sexual ethic.[16] Justice and love must necessarily be part of any Christian ethical framework, since they represent some of the broadest themes of the entire biblical witness. But to speak *only* of justice and love when constructing a sexual ethic seems to imply that the Bible has nothing more to say about sex than that sexual behavior should be just and loving. Yet many Christians wonder whether the Bible has something more than this to say about the meaning of our sexuality and God's purposes for human sexuality. The question arises about whether the specificity and particularity of the biblical witness has been lost, reduced to generic principles that, though valuable, can be twisted and distorted without the larger and more specific witness of Scripture.

Some traditionalists offer examples to illustrate the problems with this more generic approach that uses justice and love as exclusive ethical criteria. Robert Gagnon, for example, makes repeated appeals to incest as a

14. Via and Gagnon, *Homosexuality and the Bible*, pp. 20-25.

15. Cf. Margaret A. Farley, *Just Love: A Framework for Christian Sexual Ethics* (New York: Continuum, 2006), which builds an entire sexual ethic on these twin themes.

16. Dale Martin, arguing for a more open posture in the church toward gays and lesbians, makes a similar distinction and notes further scholarly discussion of the inherent problems in an ethic based solely on love (Martin, *Sex and the Single Savior*, pp. 165ff.).

counterexample.[17] He argues that incestuous relationships might conceivably be expressed in long-term monogamous, consensual terms, but they would nevertheless be immoral.[18] Richard Hays presses the argument further, claiming that Paul in Romans 1 is not only arguing out of a concern for justice and love. In addition to these, Hays argues, Paul is also saying that "homosexual activities" are "symptomatic of [a] tragically confused rebellion" against God.[19] He observes: "Whatever one may decide about the weight of the love-principle, however, the fact remains that no biblical text directly contradicts the authority of Paul's teaching on this matter."[20] For Hays, justice and love are not sufficient because they do not by themselves address the purpose of God established in creation and revealed in Scripture for human sexuality.

It does not take too much imagination to extend Hays's critique to other areas of sexual ethics. Can a mere emphasis on justice and love adequately explain the nearly absolute prohibition of divorce we find in the teachings of Jesus and in the later tradition (e.g., Matt. 5:31-32; 19:3-9; Mark 10:2-12; 1 Cor. 7:10-16)? Can justice and love, by themselves, adequately address the finely nuanced discussions of marriage and celibacy we find in texts such as Matthew 19:11-12 and 1 Corinthians 7? Scripture seems to bring a wider array of concerns to its discussion of sexuality than merely the questions of justice and love. One must also come to grips with the biblical understandings of embodiment, desire, marriage, family, procreation, and many other questions. Questions of justice and love certainly factor into all these issues, but questions of justice and love do not exhaust the content of these broader issues.

But this truncation of the biblical witness concerning sexuality is not the only problem. The terms "justice" and "love" are subject to multiple interpretations in different contexts. This raises the question of whether such broad terms are adequate, not only in interpreting the biblical texts, but also in applying biblical norms to everyday life situations. For example,

17. See, for example, Via and Gagnon, *Homosexuality and the Bible*, pp. 48ff.

18. Yet Gagnon's own subsequent argument that incestuous relationships are "wrong partly because of the disproportionately high incidence of scientifically measurable, ancillary problems" (Via and Gagnon, *Homosexuality and the Bible*, pp. 48ff.) represents an implicit acknowledgment that Via's "do no harm" criterion would exclude these relationships, rendering Via's criterion sufficient in the case of this particular counterexample.

19. Hays, "Relations Natural and Unnatural: A Response to J. Boswell's Exegesis of Romans 1," *Journal of Religious Ethics* 14, no. 1 (1986): 207.

20. Hays, "Relations Natural and Unnatural," p. 208.

in modern parlance "consensual" relationships are often deemed to fulfill the requirements of justice, since they are freely chosen by participants who, acting out of legitimate self-interest, would not be expected to embrace relationships that violate their rights. But what it means that relationships are "consensual" is not always easy to determine. Power differentials, psychological problems, and other factors may indicate that even relationships that appear to be consensual may be morally wrong. Obvious examples would include incest or sexual relations with minors, but other, more complex examples are not hard to imagine. Is it not the case that "the heart is devious above all else" (Jer. 17:9), and thus that humans may well deceive themselves about whether their motives in sexual relationships are truly loving or not? If there are no principles, values, or norms beyond the very broad criteria of justice and love, with which we may construct a sexual ethic, we may find it difficult indeed to build a sexual ethic that protects us from our own tendencies to self-deception. In the minds of many, the absence of more specific and focused norms regarding sexuality posited by some revisionist readings of the Bible renders Christian ethics vulnerable to such forms of manipulation and self-deception.

It may be helpful at this point to step back for a moment and review the larger argument that this chapter has been constructing. I have attempted to identify some common threads of the revisionist case, and some characteristic problems with that case. Many revisionist arguments emphasize the historical distance between the text and contemporary life so strongly that the dominant note tends to be the irrelevance to contemporary discussions of committed same-sex unions of the "seven passages" that touch on same-sex eroticism in the Bible. What the Bible is talking about, revisionists argue, is not what contemporary gay and lesbian Christians in committed relationships are experiencing and doing. As a result, revisionists draw an ethical framework for treating loving and committed same-sex relationships, not from the texts that *seem* to speak more directly to this issue, but rather from broader biblical themes, such as justice and love. Critics, however, wonder whether this move to broader principles represents an abandonment of the specificity of the biblical witness on sexual issues and identity in particular, and whether it renders Christian sexual ethics too vulnerable to vagary, self-deception, and manipulation.

It is important to observe that such broad characterizations of "common threads" may not apply equally to all revisionist positions. Indeed, a number of more recent studies have moved well beyond a concern only with the broad ethical categories of justice and love and have attempted to synthesize a nuanced and more comprehensive Christian understanding of sexuality into a revisionist position. Among the more interesting and comprehensive are the studies by William Stacy Johnson, *A Time to Embrace*, and Eugene F. Rogers, *Sexuality and the Christian Body*.[21] In deep conversation with the broad Christian tradition, Rogers has developed a carefully crafted theology of Christian embodiment, sexuality, and marriage in which he offers interesting and provocative insights regarding how committed gay and lesbian unions might find their place in this wider vision. Johnson has argued that revisionist positions must move beyond merely a focus on liberation and justice, toward *consecration*, which entails the offering up of ourselves, including our sexual selves, in obedience to and worship of God. Other studies have offered interesting probes and suggestions for a wider ethical vision — without developing those suggestions in more systematic fashion.[22]

A New Chapter in the Debate over Same-Sex Relationships

These studies are promising beginnings to a new chapter in the church's debate over same-sex relationships. This book is an attempt to make a further contribution to this new phase of the dialogue. This "new chapter" presupposes that most of the historical work on same-sex relations in the ancient world has been completed. While we must always be open to new discoveries, it seems that scholars now have a fairly accurate picture of the relevant data on same-sex erotic relations in the ancient world.[23] Of course, there remain vigorous disputes over the *interpretation* of these data, and the question of interpretation is precisely where the focus of this

21. Johnson, *A Time to Embrace: Same-Sex Relationships in Religion, Law, and Politics*, 2nd ed. (Grand Rapids: Eerdmans, 2012); Rogers, *Sexuality and the Christian Body: Their Way into the Triune God*, Challenges in Contemporary Theology (Oxford: Blackwell, 1999).

22. Writing before he became Archbishop of Canterbury, Rowan Williams offered a range of interesting theological observations on embodiment, desire, and sexuality, creating space for gay and lesbian unions, in a brief article entitled "The Body's Grace," reprinted in Charles C. Hefling, ed., *Our Selves, Our Souls, and Bodies: Sexuality and the Household of God* (Cambridge, MA: Cowley Publications, 1996), pp. 58-68. The writings of James Alison also provide suggestive beginning points for a more comprehensively Christian understanding of sexuality that embraces heterosexuals and gays and lesbians. See, for example, Alison, *Faith Beyond Resentment: Fragments Catholic and Gay* (New York: Crossroad, 2001).

23. The most comprehensive and accessible summary is found in Nissinen, *Homoeroticism in the Biblical World: A Historical Perspective*.

"new chapter" lies. We can now see much more clearly the nature and character of sexuality and sexual behavior in the ancient world. That increased clarity of vision has shown us how the meaning and social function of sexuality has changed over time, and how we experience our sexual selves differently from women and men in the ancient world. Consequently, not everything that the Bible says about gender and sexuality is directly applicable to life today.

What is needed, however, is not simply a reversion to very broad biblical principles like justice and love. These principles are, of course, entirely necessary; but they are not sufficient in themselves to construct a biblically based, contemporary sexual ethic that can address, among many other things, the contemporary debate over homosexuality and gay and lesbian unions. Theologians such as Eugene Rogers, James Alison, and William Stacy Johnson have begun this new conversation by engaging the broad Christian tradition in a wide-ranging conversation about the meaning of sexuality and marriage in the Christian tradition. This book attempts to contribute to this new conversation in a specific and focused way, by exploring the forms of moral logic that undergird a wide range of biblical texts dealing with sexual issues. I will not focus primarily on engaging the wider Christian tradition on these issues, nor on investigating the discussions taking place in psychology or other social sciences that are part of the larger debate. Rather, my focus is on the biblical texts that deal with sexuality in general — and with same-sex erotic relationships in particular. The goal is to discern in a fresh way the underlying forms of moral logic that shape and focus biblical teaching on sexuality.

The problems of historical distance between our world and the world of the text are present not only in passages that deal with same-sex relations; they are ubiquitous. Because the world of the biblical text is different from our world in countless ways, both great and small, every reading of the biblical text is a cross-cultural encounter, the engagement of a complex interaction between similarity and difference. Discerning the wider underlying forms of moral logic that shape particular biblical texts is of enormous importance in assisting and clarifying this cross-cultural encounter. A canonical approach that seeks to identify shared themes, values, images, and concerns across the biblical witness assists the cross-cultural reading of the Bible in three specific ways.

First, the Bible itself is a multicultural document whose writing spans many centuries and cultures. Understanding the dynamics of intertextuality is enormously helpful in differentiating between those elements that are historically contingent and those that transcend time and place. For example, it is only from a wide-angle, canonical view that we can see that there are multiple ways in which marriage itself is understood in various texts: some texts accept polygamy as a given (e.g., the multiple marriages of the patriarchs), while other texts assume and presuppose monogamy (e.g., Jesus' words on divorce in Matt. 19:1-9); or, at a more mundane level, we see a variety of cultural processes by which a marriage is celebrated in the Bible, sometimes through a formal wedding ceremony, at other points without such ritual accompaniments (e.g., the marriage of Isaac to Rebekah in Gen. 24:50-67). Each instance of such diversity in the biblical witness is a flag calling attention to factors of cultural variability that need to be considered — a cultural variability sanctioned by Scripture itself.

But it is not only the *diversity* of the canonical witness that is important in discerning underlying forms of moral logic that Scripture as a whole presents to us; one must also consider the progressive and unfolding nature of the canon when sorting through questions of cultural rootedness and transcendence. The canon, in this sense, is not flat; it comes to its divinely intended end and goal in the life, death, and resurrection of Jesus, to which the New Testament bears witness. In his Sermon on the Mount, Jesus repeatedly declares, "You have heard it said . . . but I say to you." Jesus' teaching, his death, his resurrection, and the coming of the Spirit at Pentecost all provide critical vantage points from which the entire canonical witness is reread and reframed. Some elements of the scriptural witness that were assumed before as universally binding (e.g., the requirements of circumcision and kosher eating for the people of God) were suddenly reenvisioned as culturally particular. So it is not only the *diversity* of the canonical witness that alerts us to the presence of cultural particularity; it is also, more specifically, the *movement* of scriptural revelation that discloses the most important and powerful underlying forms of moral logic that transcend culture and place, but are instead rooted in the gospel, the deepest embodiment of the heart of God's self-revelation.

Third, a canonical approach can help distinguish those patterns in Scripture that are *normal,* or descriptive, from those patterns that are *normative,* or prescriptive. For example, it is clearly normal in the Old Testament for men to be in positions of leadership. But as we shall explore in the next chapter, there are some striking exceptions to that normal pattern — exceptions that call into question whether the normal (or typical) pattern in these passages should also be construed as normative (or prescriptive). Similarly, chapter 6 will note the ways in which the birth of children is understood to be a normal part of marriage. Yet Scripture never regards the absence of children as a sufficient basis for divorce, in contrast with common patterns in marriages of that day. Hence procreation is normal within marriage, but it does not constitute the normative essence of marriage. Similarly, chapter 7 will explore the complex discussions of marriage and celibacy in Scripture. Here marriage is also understood as normal, but not normative, and Jesus commends those who have "made themselves eunuchs for the sake of the kingdom of God" (Matt. 19:12). In all these cases, a canonical approach provides a clearer vantage point from which the fundamental patterns of moral logic that unite the biblical witness — amid striking cultural and situational diversity — can be more clearly discerned.

But here is the paradox that drives the methodology of this book: we cannot discern a comprehensive and culture-transcending biblical vision for sexuality unless we look broadly across the entire canonical witness for the underlying forms of moral logic that shape and unfold in the canon as a whole. And we will not be able to establish a wider, transcultural vision for human sexuality into which committed gay and lesbian unions might fit unless we establish that wider biblical framework. Hence I seek in this book to pursue a somewhat complicated juggling exercise that tries to do four things at the same time: (1) look across the canon of Scripture for those underlying forms of moral logic that shape Scripture's discussion of issues involving sexuality and marriage, broadly considered; (2) explore how each of those forms of moral logic may have elements that are particular and unique to specific cultural settings, and how other elements of that particular form of moral logic may transcend cultural boundaries and speak more broadly to God's purposes for, and gracious redemption of, human life; (3) reflect on how these broader themes impact our understanding of the "seven passages" that seem to speak more directly about same-sex erotic relationships in the ancient world; and finally, (4) explore the implications of this analysis for the contemporary debates regarding the church, homosexuality, and committed gay or lesbian unions. The goal is to move beyond abstract and ill-defined conceptions such as gender complementarity, or overly general notions such as justice and love, to a more specific and nuanced cross-cultural biblical vision for gender and sexuality, with particular attention to the implications of that vision for gay and lesbian people in the church.

Summing Up

- Most revisionist positions argue that whatever the Bible says about same-sex eroticism in the ancient world does not directly apply to contemporary committed gay or lesbian relationships.
- Therefore, many revisionist positions resort to broad biblical categories like justice and love for evaluating same-sex relationships.
- However, though justice and love are *necessary* elements of any sexual ethic, they are not *sufficient* in themselves to develop a full sexual ethic from Scripture.
- What is required is a wider canonical exploration of biblical discussions of sexuality in order to develop a cross-cultural sexual ethic that may have relevance for gay and lesbian relationships today. That kind of exploration is the goal of this book.

PART II

Recovering a Broad, Cross-Cultural Vision for the Center of Christian Sexual Ethics

4

Patriarchy

If we are to discern the underlying forms of moral logic that shape sexual ethics in Scripture, we cannot avoid the question of patriarchy, the cultural pattern in which males are assumed to be dominant and females are expected to be submissive. Although examples of this cultural pattern appear throughout Scripture, there are also countervailing movements toward a more egalitarian vision. One central challenge for understanding Scripture's approach to gender lies in discerning the relationship between these different streams within the biblical witness — and their interrelationship. Is patriarchy not only normal, but normative? And do the egalitarian examples in Scripture function as unusual exceptions, or is there a movement in the canon away from patriarchy and toward a more egalitarian vision? In this chapter I will explore these contrasting themes regarding patriarchy, and I will identify some criteria that can illumine their interrelationship. I will then address the broader question of the use of seemingly patriarchal texts in giving specific content and focus to the overarching category of "gender complementarity" in Scripture. After discerning the essential canonical themes and movements in this area, I will conclude this chapter by considering the implications of this analysis for the church's debate on same-sex unions.

Patriarchy and Egalitarianism: Contrasting Streams in the Creation Narratives

Contrasting streams regarding patriarchy appear already in the creation accounts of Genesis 1 and 2, especially when we view these texts in their wider canonical context. On the one hand, 1 Timothy 2:13 seems to assume, based on the creation accounts, that the submission of women arises from the fact that "Adam was formed first, then Eve." Priority in creation is assumed in that text to be equivalent to dominance. Furthermore, 1 Corinthians 11:8 seems to link Paul's demand that women cover their heads (a sign, for Paul, of the subordination of female to male, according to some interpreters) with the fact that Genesis 2 shows that "man was not made from woman, but woman from man." Here again, the priority of the male in the creation account and the seeming portrayal of female as derivative from male can be used to bolster patriarchal assumptions about the relationship between the genders and the role of head coverings in symbolizing that relationship.

But despite these attempts of New Testament writers to find a basis for certain forms of patriarchy in the creation narratives, we must also note the remarkable egalitarian motifs that appear in the creation stories themselves. The Genesis narrative tells us twice that both male and female are created in the image of God (Gen. 1:27; 5:1-2). As I have noted in chapter 2, this portrayal underscores the *equality* of men and women before God and in their relationship to the rest of creation. Moreover, as I also noted above, the account of the creation of woman in Genesis 2 places the emphasis on the *similarity* of men and women — that is, over against the rest of the animal world. It is not until after the Fall, in Genesis 3:16, that we find explicit discussion about patriarchy: "To the woman [God] said, 'I will greatly increase your pangs in childbearing; in pain you shall bring forth children, yet your desire shall be for your husband, and he shall rule over you.'" The parallel use of the same Hebrew words for "desire" *(teshoqah)* and "rule" *(mashal)* in Genesis 4:7 suggests that the "desire" in Genesis 3:16 is the desire for mastery, and the husband's "rule" derives not from gracious concern but from greater strength.[1] Therefore, Genesis 3:16 portrays patriarchy not as grounded in *creation*, but in the conflicted relationship between men and women resulting from the *Fall.*

Contrasting Streams in the Old Testament

This tension between patriarchal and egalitarian streams continues throughout the canon. Patriarchal assumptions appear throughout the

---

1. Genesis 4:7 declares: "If you do well, will you not be accepted? And if you do not do well, sin is lurking at the door; its desire [*teshoqah*] is for you, but you must master [*mashal*] it."

rest of the Old Testament, sometimes in obvious — sometimes in subtle — ways. The Hebrew word for "become a husband" *(ba'al)* also means "to be master" or "to rule." Women in the Old Testament do not decide to marry; they are "given in marriage" by their fathers, who receive a bride price in return. Women do not normally inherit property. They may not divorce their husbands, though their husbands may divorce them (Deut. 24:1-4). Wives are thus clearly subject to their husbands in almost every instance. Moreover, the higher valuation of men over women is evident in more subtle ways. According to Leviticus 12, a woman's time of ritual impurity after bearing a baby girl is twice as long as her time of impurity after bearing a baby boy. Throughout the Old Testament, women have fewer rights than men; they often are regarded as having less value in Israelite society; they are frequently regarded as a dangerous source of potential contamination or ritual impurity; and they rarely exercise any form of public leadership.

Nevertheless, though ancient Israel was indeed deeply patriarchal, the stories of Israel's history show remarkable moments when, despite those dominant patterns, women exercised significant public leadership. A number of examples offer striking evidence of a movement in significant contrast to the dominant patriarchal assumptions in the Old Testament. Miriam, sister of Moses, is described as a prophet (Exod. 15:20): she is portrayed in Micah 6:4 as one of Israel's judges and deliverers, and she was clearly understood as a leader. Deborah is another female prophet who appears in the narrative as "judging Israel" (Judg. 4:4-5). Huldah is yet another prophet consulted in matters of importance to the entire state by King Josiah (2 Kings 22:12-20; 2 Chron. 34:22-28). Her role is even more striking when we note that there were other male prophets also functioning during this time period, including the prophet Zephaniah, whose work is recorded in one of the books of the Hebrew canon. The fact that these stories are remembered and included at all within the canonical witness suggests that, already in ancient Israel, patriarchy is not conceived in absolute terms, and more importantly, that there is an implicit recognition in Scripture that God raises up both men and women as leaders for the covenant people, often in contrast to traditional societal expectations.

How should these countervailing currents in the Old Testament be understood in relationship to each other? Is patriarchy in the Old Testament not only normal but also normative, and are the isolated instances of women in leadership merely illustrations of a breakdown in male leadership, pointing to the failure of God's people to fulfill their divinely appointed roles?[2] Or should we take these exceptions as glimpses, already at this early point in Israel's history, of the first movements toward an egalitarian vision hinted at in the creation story?[3] In order to answer these questions, at least from a canonical perspective, we must turn to the ways patriarchy is treated in the New Testament in order to discern whether we see the kind of canonical movement that illustrates an emerging trajectory toward a more egalitarian position, or whether patriarchy is simply a norm despite a number of minor exceptions to the rule.

Contrasting Streams in the New Testament

At first glance, we see the same juxtaposition of patriarchal and egalitarian motifs in the New Testament. There are numerous examples of exhortation that look solidly patriarchal in character. The apostle Paul urges that women should cover their heads in public (1 Cor. 11:2-16), and insists, "Neither was man created for the sake of woman, but woman for the sake of man" (1 Cor. 11:9). Several chapters later, he argues that women should be silent in the congregations, and that they should ask their husbands at home if they want to learn anything, insisting that "it is shameful for a woman to speak in church" (1 Cor. 14:34-35). Ephesians 5:33 directs that "a wife should respect [literally "fear"] her husband," and the same text directs wives to be subject to their husbands as they are to the Lord (Eph. 5:22; cf. Col. 3:18). Similarly, Titus 2:5 focuses women on their roles within the household, and urges them to be submissive to their husbands — "so that the word of God may not be discredited." In the same way, 1 Peter 3:1 directs wives: "Accept the authority of your husbands." Finally — and perhaps most emphatically — 1 Timothy 2:11-15 instructs a woman to "learn in silence, with full submission." The writer declares: "I permit no woman to teach or to have authority over a man," making an appeal to the creation narrative to provide a warrant for that instruction. I will explore all these texts in more detail in the coming pages, but for now it is sufficient to note the common patriarchal theme that runs through all of them.

2. For a summary of these kinds of arguments, see Piper and Grudem, *Recovering Biblical Manhood and Womanhood: A Response to Evangelical Feminism* (Wheaton, IL: Crossway Books, 1991).

3. For counterarguments to the text cited above, see Ronald W. Pierce, Rebecca Merrill Groothuis, and Gordon D. Fee, *Discovering Biblical Equality: Complementarity without Hierarchy,* 2nd ed. (Downers Grove, IL: InterVarsity, 2005).

For many — on both the theological right and the left — these texts are straightforward: the Bible simply assumes the same patriarchal social structure throughout: men exercise authority in a variety of ways, and women submit themselves to that authority. For some on the right, this represents an ongoing norm to which members of the church should continue to devote themselves. For some on the left, this represents yet another aspect of the ancient world that we have grown past and must leave behind — similar to the Bible's acceptance of slavery or its prohibitions against usury. They feel that we must recognize that the church has grown past such ancient assumptions and that we must focus instead on broader biblical principles such as justice and love.

But both of these approaches can too easily miss the countervailing currents that operate within the New Testament, which call into question whether a simple patriarchy represents the totality of the witness of the New Testament. We see this, first of all, in the tendency I have noted already in the Old Testament: the striking portrayal of stories and statements that seem to move against the patriarchal ideal. This same tendency appears even more prominently in the New Testament, right along with the seemingly patriarchal statements we have already seen.

Consider the many cases throughout the New Testament in which women appear in significant positions of leadership and wield notable authority in the life of the early church. The book of Acts says that women are among those included with the eleven meeting in Jerusalem at the very beginning of the church, even before Pentecost (Acts 1:13-14). This means that women were among those speaking in tongues at the first Pentecost, as attested by Acts 2:17-21. This public manifestation of the presence of the Spirit is not limited to men. Indeed, Peter's sermon on Pentecost cites Joel 2:28-32, which speaks explicitly of women as prophets and recipients of the Spirit: "Your sons and your daughters shall prophesy" (Acts 2:17). Old divisions between rich and poor, and between men and women, are overcome: "Even upon my slaves, both men and women, in those days I will pour out my Spirit; and they shall prophesy" (Acts 2:18). From the very beginning, Luke's story narrates a powerful new movement that includes women in significant ways, publicly addressing the community and speaking for God.

The same pattern continues throughout the book of Acts. Women often hosted churches in their homes: Mary, the mother of John Mark, is so described in Acts 12:12; Lydia is another, the first convert in Europe and a successful businesswoman (Acts 16:14-15, 40). In a culture where few had homes of adequate size to host a meeting, such hosts/hostesses were recognized leaders and benefactors for the entire community. The two women Euodia and Syntyche in Philippi appear to have played a prominent role within that community in Philippians 4:2-3. Otherwise, why does Paul include the very public request that they agree? Paul says that they "have struggled beside me in the work of the gospel, together with Clement and the rest of my co-workers." This sounds very much like the two of them occupy prominent and leading positions in the life of the church.[4]

We also see other striking and important roles for women, particularly in light of the patriarchal background so prominent elsewhere in the Bible. The four daughters of Philip are introduced as prophets (Acts 21:9). Priscilla (and her husband, Aquila) were apparently widely known (Rom. 16:3-4) and hosted a local church (1 Cor. 16:19; Rom. 16:5). The two of them together give gentle correction to Apollos in his teaching (Acts 18:26). Luke and Paul almost always mention Priscilla first, then Aquila. She is referred to as a "co-worker" in Romans 16:3-4, a technical term, as I have noted, that Paul uses for others in positions of leadership. In a similar vein, a number of women are referred to in Romans 16 as "workers in the Lord": Mary (v. 6), Tryphaena and Tryphosa (v. 12), and Persis (v. 12). In Romans 16:7, Junia is clearly referred to as an "apostle," indicating that she is involved in the proclamation of the gospel and the planting of new churches.[5] Phoebe, in Romans 16:1-2, is a *diakonos* (translated as "deacon," or perhaps "minister") and is also spoken of as a *prostates* (translated as "benefactor," "patron," or "protector").[6] Such persons carried enormous public respect in

---

4. The following persons are called "co-workers": Priscilla and Aquila (Rom. 16:3-4); Urbanus (Rom. 16:9); Timothy (Rom. 16:21); Apollos (1 Cor. 3:6-9); Titus (2 Cor. 8:23); Epaphroditus (Phil. 2:25); Euodia and Syntyche (Phil. 4:3); Jesus called Justus (Col. 4:11); Timothy (1 Thess. 3:2); Philemon (Philem. 1:1); Mark, Aristarchus, Demas, and Luke (Philem. 1:24). Clearly, the term refers to those in leadership positions.

5. A number of later copyists were apparently scandalized by this and changed the accent on the feminine name *Junia* to reflect the masculine name *Junias,* supposedly an abbreviated form of the more common Junianus. But this abbreviated masculine form has no other attestation, and the feminine form occurs more than 250 times in Greek and Latin inscriptions found in Rome alone. (See the discussion in Bruce Manning Metzger, *A Textual Commentary on the Greek New Testament: A Companion Volume to the United Bible Societies' Greek New Testament,* 4th rev. ed., [London/New York: United Bible Societies, 1994], p. 475). There can be little doubt that the feminine form is the original reading.

6. Even the New International Version, fairly traditional in general on gender issues, translates the Greek word *diakonos* as "minister" in four passages: 1 Cor. 3:6; Col. 1:7, 4:7; 1 Tim. 4:6.

the ancient world. Note the implicit authority that Phoebe wields, so that Paul asks the Romans to help her in whatever she may "require" from them.

Those who want to insist that the Bible requires women never to exercise authority publicly over men are forced into some striking exegetical gymnastics to account for this direct evidence of women in leadership in the New Testament texts. Some of them attempt to distinguish public from private exercise of authority, claiming that women only exercised authority privately. But the New Testament documents are all public documents, and the discussion of women in leadership positions in these documents is necessarily a discussion of public leadership. Others have attempted to build on the dissertation of Wayne Grudem, who has argued that prophecy in the New Testament is not a public and authoritative office, and thus that at least the presence of women prophets does not violate patriarchal assumptions.[7] Yet such arguments seem strained at best. Ephesians 2:20 pairs apostles and prophets together as the "foundation" of the entire New Testament church; Ephesians 3:6 speaks again of this foundational revelation being disclosed to "apostles and prophets" by the Spirit. Prophets are here clearly considered to occupy a public and authoritative office, directly alongside that of apostles. But even if one were to grant some consideration to Grudem's thesis, that prophecy is (at least in some cases) subject to the discernment of elders, we still must account for why women are standing up in public and proclaiming the word of the Lord at all! Prophecy is, by its very nature, a public activity, and insofar as it is the word of God that is being proclaimed, it is authoritative. If, in some cases, others were called on to discern the authenticity of the prophetic word, this does not diminish the public and authoritative role of the prophet herself. Surely, the proclamation of the gospel on the day of Pentecost, by both men and women, was a public and authoritative exercise of Spirit-endowed prophetic speech.

So far, we have seen a number of New Testament texts that seem to give prescriptive advice or direction to women — based on patriarchal assumptions. But we have also seen a wide range of texts that bear witness to women in prominent positions of leadership, a practice that violates patriarchal assumptions that a woman's place is never in public leadership. How are we to resolve such tensions?

---

7. See the more recently updated version of his dissertation: Wayne A. Grudem, *The Gift of Prophecy in the New Testament and Today,* rev. ed. (Wheaton, IL: Crossway Books, 2000).

Resolving the Tensions

We begin to find our way through this maze by looking more broadly at the portrayal of women in the New Testament. Consider the ministry of Jesus: in a variety of ways, Jesus stood apart from the patriarchal assumptions of his day. He allowed menstruating women to touch him (Mark 5:25-34), and didn't seem worried about any kind of defilement, despite the warnings about such contact in Leviticus 15:19. He allowed a woman to let her hair down in public and to kiss his feet (Luke 7:36-50), a shocking act in that culture but an act that Jesus wholeheartedly defended. He counted women among his followers, and they were present with him at many key junctures in his ministry, including listening to his teaching in the house of Mary and Martha (Luke 10:38-42), a place for women that was unthinkable in the synagogue of Jesus' day. Women are portrayed as the last to remain with him at the cross and the first to witnesses his resurrection — against the prevailing Jewish assumption that only males were reliable witnesses.

We also see in the teaching of Jesus a number of motifs that militate against the traditional patriarchal assumptions of his day. Perhaps most importantly, Jesus clearly placed loyalty to family below loyalty to himself and to God, thereby calling into question the basic structures of society that were built around the order of patriarchal households. He declared that anyone who loved father or mother more than him was not worthy of him (Matt. 10:37). He pronounced a blessing on those who left behind all family ties for the sake of discipleship (Matt. 19:29; Mark 10:29; Luke 14:26). Matthew records Jesus' forbidding his disciples to call anyone "father" (Matt. 23:9), thereby calling into question the entire social structure of patriarchy that singles out paternal males for particular honor. Finally, Jesus taught that "in the resurrection, they neither marry nor are given in marriage" (Matt. 22:30; Luke 20:35). This saying effectively takes one's location in traditional family structures and removes it from one's core identity. In the resurrection, the ongoing task of raising up the next generation (and thus all the social structures required for this procreative enterprise) is no longer needed, and therefore no longer present. If there is no marriage in the resurrection, then there is no differentiation of the roles that constitute marriage, including the subjection of women. One's eternal identity is thus decisively severed from patriarchal structures and relationships.

The Place of Galatians 3:27-28

It is in this light that we must read the most sweeping text in the New Testament on the question of patriarchy, Galatians 3:27-28: "As many of you as were baptized into Christ have clothed yourselves with Christ. There is no longer Jew or Greek, there is no longer slave or free, there is no longer male and female; for all of you are one in Christ Jesus." Most Christians are quite familiar with the first of these pairings: "in Christ, there is no longer Jew or Greek." The book of Acts and the letters of Paul devote a great deal of attention to the way the early church was led to set aside various parts of the Old Testament law as applicable to Gentiles (i.e., "Greeks"), particularly the requirements of circumcision, Sabbath observance, and kosher eating. What is not as commonly recognized is the function of the last two pairings: "[T]here is neither slave nor free; there is no longer male and female." Yet Jesus' words declaring that there is no marriage in the resurrection gives us an important clue about why these pairings are included here. Early Christians understood that they had already begun to partake in the life of the coming eschatological age (though they also recognized that the coming age had not yet fully arrived). It is this eschatological existence — an existence that already begins to embrace the life of the world to come — that Paul speaks about here. In this new life, old distinctions of Jew and Gentile no longer have any ultimate meaning. The same is true for slave and free, and for male and female.

But why these last two in particular? Why does the life to come exclude the differentiations of slave and free and the coupling of male and female?[8] We begin to grasp the significance of these last two when we look at Aristotle's *Politics*, a window into the way people in the ancient world understood society in its most basic terms.[9] Aristotle begins that work by talking about the essential elements of any form of human community or part-

---

8. It is important to note the slight difference in Paul's conjunctions in Gal. 3:27-28: "There is no longer slave *or* free, there is no longer male *and* female." In the age to come, the difference between slave and free ceases to exist entirely. With respect to male and female, the emphasis shifts to the *coupling* of male and female that passes away (in keeping with Jesus' words about the absence of marriage in the resurrection). Gender *identity* does not necessarily disappear, but gender *roles*, at least insofar as they are defined by marriage, no longer exist in the age to come.

9. Aristotle was an early tutor of Alexander the Great, whose military machine created the first empire that encompassed the entire known world in the fourth century BCE, an empire later taken over and administered by Rome prior to the emergence of Christianity.

nership. The two most basic and essential elements of any form of human community are evident already in the family: "the union of male and female for the continuance of the species" (i.e., the procreative relationship) and "the union of natural ruler and natural subject for the sake of security" (i.e., the relationships of master and slave).[10] In other words, in the ancient world the divisions of humanity into slave and free and the coupling of male and female were considered the essential and primal building blocks of every form of human society. For Jews, these two primal divisions in human society were supplemented by a third — and equally basic — division in the ordering of the world: the distinction between Jew and Gentile that was established by God to single out the covenant people as recipients of his blessing on behalf of the world. It is also important to note that each of these relationships was also marked by the difference between superior and inferior, between insider and outsider, between greater power and lesser power.

It is against this backdrop that we can sense the radical nature of the text of Galatians 3:27-28. Here Paul is probably citing an early baptismal formula (note the reference to baptism in 3:27). We see a similar statement — linked to baptism and proclaiming the end of the fundamental divisions that make up society as the ancient world understood it — in Colossians 3:10: "In that renewal there is no longer Greek and Jew, circumcised and uncircumcised, barbarian, Scythian, slave and free; but Christ is all and in all!"[11] In both statements, life in Christ is presented as a foretaste of the new age, when old structures have disappeared and society is centered only on Christ as the source of the whole creation's life and being. It is not surprising, then, that in that same letter to the Galatians, Paul speaks about the cross, "by which the world has been crucified to me, and I to the world" (Gal. 6:14). The whole world as Paul knew it had come to an end. The gospel of Christ entails nothing less than a radical eschatological reordering of society as a whole. Paul goes on to conclude: "For neither circumcision nor uncircumcision is anything; but a new creation is every-

---

10. Aristotle, *The Politics,* trans. Harris Rackham, Loeb Classical Library (London/New York: W. Heinemann/Putnam, 1932), §1252a.

11. "Scythians" were understood in the ancient world as the most barbaric and uncivilized people of all. See Petr Pokorný, *Colossians: A Commentary* (Peabody, MA: Hendrickson Publishers, 1991), p. 170. Interestingly, in the same section cited in the preceding note, Aristotle also notes "barbarians" as a corporate embodiment of servitude, destined by nature to be ruled by the Greeks. In other words, in this Colossians text the two basic pairings are Jew-Gentile and master-slave.

thing!" (Gal. 6:15) In that "new creation" there is not merely forgiveness and reconciliation to God; there is also a new social order in which there is no longer Jew or Greek; there is no longer slave or free; there is no longer male and female.

Here we discover substantial emphases within the New Testament witness that sweep away, in categorical terms, those basic distinctions between insider and outsider, between powerful and powerless, as well as the distinctive pairing (male and female) devoted to procreation — all the distinctions that form the basis for the structures of society as it was known in the ancient world. One can readily see this theme as part of the same fabric as the many texts we noted above, in which women were exercising significant leadership, in a variety of ways, in the life of the church. These texts should be placed alongside some others in which Jews and Gentiles are eating together in table fellowship, and also perhaps alongside Paul's letter to Philemon, where he urges Philemon to receive back his slave Onesimus — "no longer [as] a slave, but more than a slave, a beloved brother" in Christ (Philem. 1:16). We see glimpses, throughout the New Testament, where the reality envisioned by Galatians 3:27-28 has begun to break into the experience of the Christian community.

Revisiting the New Testament Patriarchal Texts

Yet this same New Testament also seems, as we have noted, to assume patriarchal relationships in many places. Wives are instructed to respect and submit to their husbands; women are told to cover their heads (1 Cor. 11:3-16); to be silent (1 Cor. 14:34; 1 Tim. 2:11); and not to attempt to boss men around (1 Tim. 2:12). This sounds as if the patriarchal structures of this world are very much in place in the life of the New Testament church. How are we to justify these two strikingly different elements of the New Testament witness?

Those who wish to argue that patriarchal relationships should continue today, at least in some modified form, often move quickly to emphasize the *spiritual* equality that all believers have by virtue of faith in Christ, whether they are Jew or Gentile, slave or free, male or female. Yet they argue that this spiritual equality does not eliminate the specific role distinctions that God intends for life in this world. For example, S. Lewis Johnson says: "In the context of Galatians, the apostle simply affirms that every believer in Christ inherits fully the Abrahamic promises by grace apart from legal works."[12] But it is difficult to see what connection exists between Johnson's "legal works" and the pairings of slave-free and male-female. This fails as an exegesis of the entire verse, addressing only the Jew-Greek distinction. Nor does this entire line of emphasis give us any clear understanding of the nature and character of social relationships in the "new creation" of which Paul speaks in Galatians 6:15.

I believe that a more helpful approach is to emphasize the eschatological nature of the affirmation in Galatians 3:27-28 and similar passages — that is, their grounding in the life of the world to come. These texts are describing the same reality of which Jesus speaks when he declares that "in the resurrection, they neither marry nor are given in marriage" (Matt. 22:30; Luke 20:35). Galatians 3:27-28 describes the destiny of all Christians, a destiny initiated in baptism but experienced in this life only in glimpses and foretastes of a kind of life that is yet to come in all its fullness.

This brings us to a vitally important and broad New Testament motif: the dynamic interaction between the "already" and the "not yet" of Christian existence. (The theological term for this discussion is eschatology, the study of last things in relation to our present existence.) In many New Testament texts there is a sense that we have already "been raised with Christ" (Col. 3:1) and are "seated . . . with him in the heavenly places in Christ Jesus" (Eph. 2:6). *Already* now, resurrection life starts to break into present experience; *already* Christians are discovering a deeper family than simply the connections of blood and kinship, and they begin to address each other as "brother" and "sister"; *already* the first apostles declare to earthly authorities that they "must obey God rather than any human authority" (Acts 5:29); *already* the Spirit is poured out on all flesh, without making distinctions between male and female, between young and old, or between slave and free (Acts 2:17-18); *already* some Christians are invited to remain single rather than becoming married, preparing for a "coming distress"; and we are *already* entering into the life to come (1 Cor. 7). Paul summarizes this "already" side of the picture in 1 Corinthians 7:29-31:

> [29]I mean, brothers and sisters, the appointed time has grown short; from now on, let even those who have wives be as though they had none, [30]and those who mourn as though they were not mourning, and those who rejoice as though they were not rejoicing, and those

---

12. In Piper and Grudem, *Recovering Biblical Manhood and Womanhood: A Response to Evangelical Feminism*, p. 163.

who buy as though they had no possessions, [31] and those who deal with the world as though they had no dealings with it. For the present form of this world is passing away.

However, this emphasis on the "already" of Christian existence, with its awareness that the new creation is already breaking into life in this world, is only half of the picture. The other half is the "not yet" of New Testament eschatology. Although Christians begin to taste this new life of the age to come, they still experience the reality of this present world as well. They still experience suffering and death. Slaves still have earthly masters who expect them to obey orders. Jews and Gentiles still struggle to understand each other and to learn how to live together. Husbands and wives must still find ways to relate to each other and forge their common life, and to care for the children whom God has given them. Despite the fact that the apostles "must obey God rather than human authority," they still find themselves forced to deal with human authorities who do not always like what the apostles are doing, and who may persecute them for their beliefs and actions. Christians live in hope, awaiting the fullness of God's redemption, which is "not yet" — still lying in the future. Paul writes in Romans 8:24-25: "For in hope we were saved. Now hope that is seen is not hope. For who hopes for what is seen? But if we hope for what we do not see, we wait for it with patience." We still await aspects of our redemption that we do not yet see.

But this "already/not yet" tension was no easier for Christians in the ancient world to grasp than it is for us to understand. One of the characteristic problems that many New Testament writers grappled with arose from misunderstandings of this eschatological tension. It seems particularly evident that many early Christians grabbed onto the happy and hopeful "already" side of the picture and ran with it, ignoring the less appealing "not yet" side. We see this, for example, in Paul's first letter to the Corinthians, where he addresses a host of pastoral problems. The Corinthians were enthusiastic about their Christianity: there was an abundance of what we would call "charismatic" activity — speaking in tongues, prophesying, miracles, and so forth. Anything that would be a tremendous display of spiritual power caught their attention. But this enthusiasm was also accompanied by a number of serious problems. The community was dividing itself into groups that were pitted against each other, claiming "I am of Paul," or "I am of Apollos," or "I am of Christ" (1 Cor. 1:10-13). This was accompanied by a kind of pride in their own spiritual accomplishments (1 Cor. 12–14). At the same time, there was a disturbing indifference to the needs of others. They refused to deal with one member who was in an apparently incestuous relationship (1 Cor. 5:1-5), and they showed a disturbing greed and lack of concern for the poor at their meal celebrations (1 Cor. 11:21-22). We also see a fascination with ascetic practices in some: those who were seemingly concerned to detach themselves from bodily existence, especially avoiding marriage, probably because they claimed to be participating in the life of the coming kingdom already. Meanwhile, others in the community saw no problems with having sex with prostitutes, perhaps also claiming that they had already transcended earthly existence and thus what they did with their bodies was irrelevant to their spiritual lives (1 Cor. 6:13-20).

Many scholars suggest that a common thread weaving its way through all these pastoral problems was a lack of eschatological balance.[13] The Corinthians were enamored of Paul's gospel of a new reality breaking into this world; however, the problem was that they dissolved the "already/not yet" tension and converted this temporal tension into a dichotomy between the physical and the spiritual. They thought that, because they had already entered the spiritual realm, their bodies were essentially matters of indifference, and that bodily structures of this world were irrelevant to true spirituality. Spirituality had become for them exclusively a matter of the "already," as it was understood *spiritually*. Paul's ironic rejoinder seems to illuminate the problem:

> [8]Already you have all you want! Already you have become rich! Quite apart from us you have become kings! Indeed, I wish that you had become kings, so that we might be kings with you! [9]For I think that God has exhibited us apostles as last of all, as though sentenced to death, because we have become a spectacle to the world, to angels and to mortals. [10]We are fools for the sake of Christ, but you are wise in Christ. We are weak, but you are strong. You are held in honor, but we in disrepute. [11]To the present hour we are hungry and thirsty, we are poorly clothed and beaten and homeless, [12]and we grow weary from the work of our own hands. When reviled, we bless; when persecuted, we endure; [13]when slandered, we speak kindly. We have become like the rubbish of the world, the dregs of all things, to this very day. [14]I am not writing this to make you ashamed, but to admonish you as my beloved children. (1 Cor. 4:8-14)

13. See, e.g., the discussion in Johan Christiaan Beker, *Paul the Apostle: The Triumph of God in Life and Thought* (Philadelphia: Fortress, 1980), pp. 163ff.

Paul here contrasts the triumphalism of the Corinthians with the suffering example of the apostles. Christian faith is not about transcending and escaping the troubles of this world, but about the sacrificial offering of lives to one another in hope and love. It is the "not yet" side of the "already/not yet" tension — the embrace of suffering and sacrificial love — that the Corinthians are missing. They need to remember that the resurrection still lies before them (see 1 Cor. 15:12-23).[14]

So how does all this inform our understanding of Galatians 3:27-28 and the curious tension between texts such as this one, in which all gender distinctions seem to be obliterated, and those other texts that urge the submission of women and slaves, the wearing of head coverings, and the like? As I have already observed, we see the "already" of Galatians 3:27-28 lived out in all kinds of surprising ways in the life of the early church. Women hosted churches; they were deacons/ministers, co-workers, workers in the Lord, apostles, and prophets. But a closer look at the Corinthian correspondence begins to show the tensions we have been exploring. It appears that much of the New Testament's patriarchal language arose in instances where women were claiming a radical new sort of freedom based on their understanding of their participation in the new creation in Christ. But those claims to freedom were sometimes disrupting the life of the Christian community in noteworthy ways — and damaging the church's witness to the wider community. In other words, the New Testament's seemingly patriarchal injunctions can be understood as various attempts to rein in imbalances in the "already/not yet" tension of New Testament eschatology.

1 Corinthians 11:2-16

For example, 1 Corinthians 11:2-16 assumes that women are praying and prophesying in the public assembly, but the same text requires them to wear head coverings (or perhaps to wear their hair pinned above their head rather than hanging loosely). In a culture with at least some Jewish connections, where a woman's exposing or letting down her hair was

14. Many commentators believe that Paul's discussion of the resurrection in 1 Cor. 15 must be viewed against this backdrop. The Corinthians do not deny the resurrection because they doubt the power of God; they deny that there is a *future* resurrection, believing that whatever resurrection God intends has already happened to them.

laced with sexual overtones, it does not take much imagination to envision the problems Paul addresses in 1 Corinthians 11. Women were claiming a new kind of freedom that they believed belonged to them in their new Christian identity: they were standing up to pray and prophesy with hair down and flowing, providing plenty of titillation for some males, while their husbands may well have felt shamed because their wives were seeming to send signals of sexual availability to others rather than to them alone.[15] In the midst of all of this, the worship of the community was in disarray, and the focus had shifted from God to much more human issues.[16]

Paul responds by reminding them that they have not yet fully transcended the structures of the old creation. He reasserts signs and markers of traditional gender roles, and he urges women not to expose or let their hair down in public worship. Yet it is also worth noting what Paul does *not* say. He does not forbid women from praying and prophesying; nor does he require them to be silent here. Moreover, even though he requires women to cover their hair by his appeal to the creation story and the priority of man in creation (1 Cor. 11:9), he follows this by a qualifying comment: "Nevertheless, in the Lord woman is not independent of man or man independent of woman. For just as woman came from man, so man comes through woman; but all things come from God" (1 Cor. 11:11-12). One gets the sense that the gender distinctions Paul is speaking of here have a pragmatic basis, not a deep or ontological basis, since Paul himself cites evidence that balances an overly patriarchal reading of his words.

In other words, for Paul, the family structures that are part of this world are indeed patriarchal; other forms of social organization within families were inconceivable in his day. To the extent that people participated in these structures, they needed to recognize the limits and roles that

15. Other commentators focus attention less on the sexual overtones of exposed long hair and more on the hypothesis that the Corinthians were engaging in the ancient equivalent of cross-dressing, with women dressing like men and vice versa. See Linda Belleville, "Κεφαλή and the Thorny Issue of Headcovering in 1 Corinthians 11:2-16," in Margaret E. Thrall, Trevor J. Burke, and J. K. Elliott, eds., *Paul and the Corinthians: Studies on a Community in Conflict; Essays in Honour of Margaret Thrall*, Supplements to Novum Testamentum (Leiden: Brill, 2003), pp. 215-32. In either case, the "bottom line" was a pragmatic one: what was perceived as inappropriate behavior for men and women had become a distraction from the worship of God.

16. Paul apparently feels that he can appeal to ordinary standards of decency and shame, which he expresses repeatedly (1 Cor. 11:5, 6, 13, and 14-15). Whatever Paul wants, it is probably consistent with conventional standards of propriety for men and women.

were required of them, particularly when failure to do so would disrupt communities and shame individuals. For Paul, the tension seems clear, though manageable: insofar as Christians still participate in family life, they are not yet, in this aspect of their lives, part of the new creation (in which families are left behind). Therefore, they need to recognize, within those contexts where families are in play, the responsibilities and roles that are appropriate to family life, which are grounded in the original creation. Yet even here, the new creation seeps in around the edges: women are praying and prophesying in public, and even Paul's citation of warrants for his instructions in the creation narrative (1 Cor. 11:7-9) is qualified by a recognition of the ultimate basis of mutuality and equality that marks the relationship between the sexes (1 Cor. 11:11-12).[17]

1 Corinthians 7:3-5

That mutuality between husband and wife is even more deeply expressed in a surprising text in 1 Corinthians 7 — which is about sex within marriage. Apparently, some Corinthian Christians were advocating that married couples should cease having sex, and that they should "already" participate in the gender-free life of the coming age. Paul strongly discourages such behavior, and then he makes the following comment in 1 Corinthians 7:3-4: "The husband should give to his wife her conjugal rights, and likewise the wife to her husband. For the wife does not have authority over her own body, but the husband does; likewise, the husband does not have authority over his own body, but the wife does." Here we see a striking "merger" of the structures of this age and the coming one, in which the traditional patriarchal rights of husbands over the bodies of wives are severely curtailed, and yet the bodily intimacy of life in "this age" is deeply affirmed. It is precisely this capacity for living in that new tension that marks the distinctive genius of the New Testament's eschatological vision.

---

17. I recognize that there are a number of features of this text that I have not fully addressed, including the meaning of the "headship" of males, particularly in verse 3, as well as the difficult question of Paul's treatment of the image of God in men and women in 1 Cor. 11:7. As difficult as these questions are, however, I believe that Paul's discussion of them fits within the larger context and dynamics I have been describing. For further discussion of the relevant issues, see Gordon Fee's discussion of this passage in Pierce, Groothuis, and Fee, *Discovering Biblical Equality*, pp. 142-60.

1 Corinthians 14:33b-35

We see dynamics similar to 1 Corinthians 11 in Paul's injunction for women to be silent in the church in 1 Corinthians 14:33b-35. Even though a number of scholars have raised considerable doubt about whether these verses are part of the original text of 1 Corinthians, they can be understood — albeit with some difficulty — within the larger context of the Corinthian correspondence.[18] The central problem in this text is simple to describe, even if it is difficult to resolve. The text declares: "As in all the churches of the saints, women should be silent in the churches. For they are not permitted to speak, but should be subordinate, as the law also says." Yet, as I have just explored, 1 Corinthians 11 assumes that women *are* praying and prophesying, and chapter 11 is concerned only about how their hair looks as they do so. This means that the injunction for women to be silent in chapter 14 cannot be construed as absolute in its scope; it must be qualified in some way. But here is where opinions differ. Those who argue that Paul is teaching male leadership argue that the silence enjoined here is from public and authoritative speech or, more specifically, the oral weighing of prophecies by the leaders in the community.[19] But the text by no means makes this connection clear, nor is it clear that "the others" mentioned in verse 29 who are to "weigh" the prophecies are the leaders in the community rather than simply the other prophets (a group that would, of course, include women).

A more natural interpretation builds on verse 35 in the text: "If there is anything they desire to know (or, more literally, "if they want to learn anything"), let them ask their husbands at home. For it is shameful for a woman to speak in church." This immediate context connects women's speaking not with "weighing" of prophecy, but rather with asking questions. In the culture of the biblical world, the asking of questions can be construed in many contexts as a contest for dominance.[20] This internal contextual clue suggests that the concern here focuses not on public

18. See the extensive discussion of the text-critical problems in Gordon D. Fee, *The First Epistle to the Corinthians,* New International Commentary on the New Testament (Grand Rapids: Eerdmans, 1987).

19. See Donald Carson's argument to this effect in Piper and Grudem, *Recovering Biblical Manhood and Womanhood,* p. 151.

20. Cf. Job 15; 38:3; 40:7; Matt. 21:23ff.; 22:46; Mark 12:34; Luke 20:40; John 20:30. We see a similar concern for women seeking to "learn" by asking questions, apparently in an aggressive and/or wayward manner, in 1 Tim. 2:11 and 2 Tim. 3:7.

speech in general, but on seizing authority in inappropriate ways that challenge or shame others in the congregation. Verse 34, then, would seem to be saying that it is disgraceful for a woman to get up in church and challenge the authority of others publicly. Again, what we see, in context, is a refusal to allow the eschatological vision of Galatians 3:27-28 to be used in ways that disrupt the life of the community or shame others.

1 Timothy 2:8-15

Turning to 1 Timothy 2:8-15, we see a similar pattern: curtailing the behavior of women who are aggressively disrupting the life of the community:

> [8]I desire, then, that in every place the men should pray, lifting up holy hands without anger or argument; [9]also that the women should dress themselves modestly and decently in suitable clothing, not with their hair braided, or with gold, pearls, or expensive clothes, [10]but with good works, as is proper for women who profess reverence for God. [11]Let a woman learn in silence with full submission. [12]I permit no woman to teach or to have authority over a man; she is to keep silent. [13]For Adam was formed first, then Eve; [14]and Adam was not deceived, but the woman was deceived and became a transgressor. [15]Yet she will be saved through childbearing, provided they continue in faith and love and holiness, with modesty.

In the first place, this text warns against the ostentatious display of wealth (braided hair, gold, pearls, and expensive clothes), which was a common way for wealthy women in the Greco-Roman world to establish their public status — but was inappropriate for the Christian community. Reading between the lines, one can sense the longing for status and recognition on the part of women in the Corinthian congregation whom Paul is addressing in this passage.

But we come to the heart of the problem in verses 11-12, with the call to women to "learn in silence with full submission," and the text's further instructions to women not "to teach or have authority over a man." This appears, at first glance, to be a sweeping patriarchal text, grounded in the creation narrative, one that prohibits the instruction of men by women generally. But a closer look reveals a different picture. First, we must consider the call to "silence." The translation "silent" for the Greek word *hēsuchia* is problematic: *hēsuchia* connotes centrally not silence but *calm ness.*[21] The same Greek word *(hēsuchia)* is translated "quietly" in 2 Thessalonians 3:12. The focus is not centrally on the absence of speech, but on calmness, composure, and peaceableness. This suggests that the problem is not that women are speaking at all, but that they are doing so in an aggressive, agitated way — in the context of giving and receiving instruction ("Let a woman learn . . .").[22]

This line of interpretation is confirmed by the word in verse 12 translated as "have authority over" *(authentein).* This is the only place in the entire New Testament corpus where this word occurs, and because it is very rare, its interpretation is much disputed. Two things may be observed about the word. First, its rarity underscores the fact that this is not the normal word used for the exercise of authority in the New Testament.[23] Second, the parallels that we do have outside the New Testament suggest that the word has a negative sense: it connotes aggressiveness or domination. What is being forbidden of women, then, is not the normal exercise of authority in teaching, but an aggressiveness that seeks to dominate men. This coheres with the exhortation, not to silence, but to calmness and peaceableness implicit in the Greek word *hēsuchia,* as noted above. And it is in keeping with the call to modesty and decency *(meta aidous kai sōfrosunēs)* found in verse 9. Therefore, verse 12 could be appropriately paraphrased: "I do not permit a woman to boss around a man or tell him what to do." What Paul has in mind is not the prohibition of formal instruction, but aggressive bids for domination.

A number of scholars have suggested that a pagan cult that involved particular devotion to the goddess Artemis may help to illuminate the context of this instruction.[24] While the Genesis account speaks of the priority of the man in creation, the cult placed the female Artemis as the first being (cf. 1 Tim. 2:13f.) Here we see how the eschatological vision of the New Testament, in which "there is no male and female" may have been blended with the pagan cult of Artemis to create a distorted syncretistic vision that was disrupting the life of the community. The same dynamics seem to be reflected in other concerns reflected in the Pastoral Epistles, in-

21. The Greek word is different from the Greek word calling for silence *(sigato)* in 1 Cor. 14.

22. Note the similarity to the context I discussed in 1 Cor. 14 above, where the issue of asking questions aggressively appeared to be at the center of the problem.

23. The more normal Greek word is *exousia* and related forms.

24. Note the reference to Artemis, in connection with Ephesus ("Great is Artemis of the Ephesians!") in Acts 19:28-37. See also the helpful summary of related issues by Linda Belleville in Pierce, Groothuis, and Fee, *Discovering Biblical Equality,* pp. 219ff.

cluding a fascination with ascetic practices and the avoidance of marriage (1 Tim. 4:3-5; 5:11-12) and the problematic claim that the resurrection has already occurred (2 Tim. 2:18). Again, we see the same pattern: wherever the vision of a new life in Christ is creating conflict and disruption, and the eschatological tension of the gospel is dissolved, Paul gently reins these views in, with the recognition that the church lives with one foot in the age to come, but with the other foot still firmly planted in this world — and thus subject to its structures and roles. One senses this domestic concern in the way the passage ends, with its focus on safety in childbearing and the call for "them" (probably husband and wife together) to "continue in faith and love and holiness, with modesty" (1 Tim. 11:15).

Therefore, in all three of the above texts, which appear to subjugate women to men in patriarchal terms, we see the predominance of pragmatic rather than fundamental concerns. In each case, the text addresses some kind of culturally inappropriate behavior by women — involving hair styles or coverings, expensive clothing, and aggressive confrontations between men and women. Wherever this aggressive and disruptive behavior occurs, the New Testament writers call for restraint, and they base that call on the creation narratives. The church must not assume that it has passed completely from this world into the age to come. It must not dissolve the "already/not yet" tension and assume that the structures of this world are completely done away with. Yet at the same time, where the life of the age to come can be experienced with peaceableness and harmony, it is to be embraced: women lead, teach, pray, prophesy, host churches, and model a new form of equality that stood markedly apart from the prevailing Greco-Roman culture.

The "Household Codes"

We see this same tension expressed in the so-called "household codes," passages that offer instruction to the various members of ancient households — husbands and wives, masters and slaves, and parents and children — in a number of places in the New Testament (e.g., Eph. 5:21-33; Col. 3:18–4:1; 1 Tim. 6:1-2; Titus 2:1-10; 1 Pet. 2:18–3:7). The same pattern of instruction is found frequently in noncanonical early Christian documents as well.[25]

25. E.g., *Didache* 4:9-11; *Barnabas* 19:5-7; *1 Clement* 21:6-9; Ignatius, *Pol.* 4:1–6:1; Polycarp, *Phil.* 4:2–6:3.

These household codes are structured in terms of the essential pairings of the household, which I noted earlier, based on Aristotle's *Politics*. After discussing procreation and rulership, Aristotle goes on to offer the threefold pairing we see in the household codes:

> Now that it is clear what are the components of the state, we have first of all to discuss household management; for every state is composed of households . . . . The investigation of everything should begin with the smallest parts, and the primary and smallest parts of the household are master and slave, husband and wife, father and children; we ought therefore to examine the proper constitution and character of each of these relationships, I mean that of mastership, that of marriage . . . , and thirdly the progenitive relationship.[26]

Aristotle's discussion makes it clear that the household codes found in the New Testament and other Jewish and early Christian literature are using the basic structures of society as they were understood throughout the ancient world, seen in the microcosm of the household. The household codes are thus clearly part of the structures "of this world," and not part of the new creation envisioned in Galatians 3:27-28. Since most of these household codes come from those portions of the New Testament that emerged at a somewhat later period, some scholars see the emergence of this form of instruction as a lapse back from the eschatological vision of earlier New Testament documents into a more "this-worldly" and less radical vision than we see in Galatians 3:27-28.[27]

Though this analysis may contain some truth, however, it is not the whole picture. Even in the household codes, which seem so oriented to the structures of the ancient world outlined by Aristotle, we see countervailing motifs that glimpse a new creation, qualifying and deconstructing an absolute understanding of household role differences and responsibilities. Consider, for example, the most extensive of all the New Testament household codes, found in Ephesians 5:21–6:9. Here we see the classic pairs: husbands and wives (5:22-33), parents and children (6:1-4), and masters and slaves (6:5-9). But the entire code is introduced by 5:21: "Be subject to one another out of reverence for Christ." Hence, a quality of mutuality, flowing directly from the gospel, frames the entire discussion.

---

26. Aristotle, *The Politics*, 1.1253b.

27. See, for example, Johan Christiaan Beker, *Heirs of Paul: Paul's Legacy in the New Testament and in the Church Today* (Minneapolis: Fortress, 1991).

This same tendency toward mutuality is noted in the proportion of instruction given to husbands and wives in this text. Wives receive instruction in three and a half verses (5:22-24, 33b), whereas husbands receive instruction in eight and a half verses (5:25-33a). Moreover, the essence of the instruction given to husbands is to sacrifice their own interests in favor of their wives, and to love them as they love themselves, in imitation of Christ. This proportion of interest in husbands is unprecedented in other household codes outside the New Testament, and it represents a distinctive approach to the life of households: it seeks to introduce into traditional structures something of the new eschatological life ushered in by the gospel. In other words, Aristotle provides the basic framework, but Galatians 3:27-28 provides some of the inner dynamic that begins to transform that framework from within. We see the same pattern in the injunctions given to slaveholders in Galatians 6:9: "And, masters, do the same to them. Stop threatening them, for you know that both of you have the same Master in heaven, and with him there is no partiality." Any rights of masters over slaves are qualified by the recognition that God shows no partiality, and is no respecter of persons, regardless of this-worldly social structures.

It is probably the case that, in the history of Christianity, this internal, deconstructive approach has had the most influence in finally bringing many cultures influenced by Christian faith closer to a fully egalitarian vision for the relationship between men and women. There is something about the call to sacrificial love that finally removes any claim to superiority, any claim to priority in decision-making, any claim to special honor. The same vision finally led, in the nineteenth century, not only to the "humanization" of the slave trade but to the recognition that slavery itself was fundamentally incompatible with the worship of a God who "shows no partiality." Throughout the history of Christianity the eschatological vision of Galatians 3:27-28 has slowly but surely undermined patriarchal structures and relationships, as well as those between masters and slaves, so that more and more, the church has begun to experience in its daily life its destiny as the new creation, where there is "no longer Jew or Greek, no longer slave or free, no longer male and female, for you are all one in Christ Jesus."

Of course, this eschatological vision was not fully realized when the New Testament documents were written. The New Testament writers still had to rein in those egalitarian excesses that disrupted the life of the community and damaged its witness. Such social change takes time — and lots of it. But the capacity of the New Testament writers to embrace this paradoxical existence, with one foot in "this age" and one foot in the "age to come," set in motion powerful forces of social change that finally have undermined the unquestioned hegemony of patriarchy. To recognize this is not to abandon the more qualified approach to patriarchy in the New Testament documents; rather, it is to embrace the inner dynamic that energizes the New Testament itself.[28]

Implications for "Gender Complementarity"

Before concluding this chapter, we must explore the implications of this study for an understanding of "gender complementarity" and reflect, at least briefly, on the implications of our analysis for the debate over same-sex relationships. First, I will turn to gender complementarity as a form of moral logic: To what extent should we understand the Bible to presuppose and assume a hierarchical or patriarchal understanding of gender complementarity as one of its underlying forms of moral logic? The implications of our study should now be clear. There are two countervailing streams with respect to patriarchy in Scripture. One of these streams assumes a patriarchal framework and the concomitant obligations, duties, and responsibilities of husbands and wives within household structures. The other stream flows from texts such as the words of Jesus: "In the resurrection, they neither marry nor are given in marriage" (Matt. 22:30; Luke 20:35), and the words of Paul in Galatians 3:28: "There is no longer Jew or Greek, there is no longer slave or free, there is no longer male and female, for all of you are one in Christ Jesus." One of these streams assumes life in

28. In some more recent expressions of the Christian debate over patriarchy, the focus has shifted somewhat to more pragmatic concerns focusing on the need, in many communities, to find ways of structuring households that will keep husbands more engaged with family life. In some of these cultures, a rediscovery of male headship has been viewed positively. Yet this pragmatic concern fits very well within the framework we have described, under the basic principle that egalitarian visions that are destructive to community must be subjected to critique. In some contexts, it is simply true that clearer delineations of authority are helpful. However, even in such contexts, these differentiations must avoid the disparity in essential value that represents the darker legacy of patriarchy. Nor should these differentiations be assumed to have universal or transcultural applicability, since that would clearly undermine the eschatological tension regarding gender differentiation that we have been exploring in the New Testament. For further discussion, see David Blankenhorn, Don S. Browning, and Mary Stewart Van Leeuwen, eds., *Does Christianity Teach Male Headship? The Equal-Regard Marriage and Its Critics*, Religion, Marriage, and Family (Grand Rapids: Eerdmans, 2004).

this world, shaped by the structures of creation; the other assumes life in the age to come, shaped by the structures of the gospel, lived out in the life, death, and resurrection of Jesus. These two streams cannot simply be equated with each other; rather, they live in dynamic tension throughout Scripture. But even the creation narratives themselves provide a glimpse of the new creation ushered in by Christ. They proclaim, in dramatically countercultural fashion, that both men and women are equally image-bearers of God, equally set apart from the rest of creation for covenant communion with God. Similarly, Paul's assertion that both spouses exercise authority over the bodies of the other (1 Cor. 7:3-4) presents a striking contrast to prevailing patriarchal assumptions, and a glimpse into the transforming influence of this eschatological vision on life in this world.

The overall movement of the moral logic of Scripture with respect to patriarchy is thus away from roles defined by household responsibilities in the ancient world — including the divisions of honor, status, and worth defined along gender lines — and toward a vision of mutuality and equality in which the procreative enterprise of male and female no longer defines human identity at its core. Instead, humans draw their core identity from their union with Christ and their participation in the age to come.

Implications for the Homosexuality Debate

When viewed in a comprehensive canonical context, therefore, hierarchy or patriarchy cannot be construed to be the essence of a normative "gender complementarity" that is allegedly violated by same-sex unions. We might understand gender complementarity in other terms, of course. (In fact, I will explore procreation as a basis for an understanding of gender complementarity in chapter 6.) However, if we are to say that same-sex unions are wrong, we cannot say that they are wrong because they violate a hierarchical understanding of gender complementarity. The Bible, taken as a whole, does not support such a hierarchical vision of gender complementarity as expressive of core Christian identity. Moreover, Paul's insistence in 1 Corinthians 7:3-4 that husbands and wives exercise mutual authority over each other's bodies explicitly removes hierarchical relationships from the sex act itself, where, in Paul's vision, a purely egalitarian structure exists. In this context, any attempt to claim that same-sex eroticism is wrong because it violates a hierarchical understanding of gender complementarity cannot be sustained, even if one might wish to posit, as some interpreters do, a "soft patriarchy," in which some kind of limited or symbolic hierarchical relationship exists between the genders more broadly in marriage.[29]

This insight has one further implication that is important to note here. Almost all studies of homoeroticism in the ancient world recognize that the nearly universal pattern of same-sex erotic relationships in the ancient world (particularly among men) involved status differences between the active and passive partners. An individual male did not assume both active and passive roles in same-sex erotic activity in the ancient world. The dominant, penetrating male was always older versus younger, free versus slave, of higher status versus lower status.[30] We see this same differentiation in the vice list of 1 Corinthians 6:9, in the two words rendered by the NRSV as "male prostitutes" and "sodomites." A number of interpreters see these two terms as reflecting this distinction between the active and passive partners.[31] This connection between higher status and the act of penetration is unquestioned in the ancient world, and it reflects deeply patriarchal assumptions about the relative status of males and females (and by extension, males who play the female role). Because of this, one cannot ignore issues of patriarchy if one wishes to understand the moral logic underlying ancient attitudes toward same-sex erotic relationships.

Similarly, a number of interpreters have suggested that patriarchal assumptions also help to explain the revulsion implicit in the Old Testament texts that address same-sex relationships. For a man, to be penetrated is to be inherently degraded — that is, to be forced to act like a woman instead of a man. It is this degradation that stands behind the assumed offensiveness of the attempted rape of the visitors in the Sodom and Gomorrah story (Gen. 19) and the story of the Levite's concubine in Judges 19. (The offensiveness of this degradation of males is highlighted by the fact that, in both of these ancient stories, the threatened parties offer females as substitutes for the attackers' demand for males. In the ancient world, deeply shaped by patriarchy, the rape of a woman, as horrible as it might be, cannot be compared to the horror of raping, and thereby degrading, another man.) Similarly, interpreters note the seemingly patriarchal assumptions undergirding

29. See, for example, William J. Webb, *Slaves, Women and Homosexuals: Exploring the Hermeneutics of Cultural Analysis* (Downers Grove, IL: InterVarsity, 2001).

30. For extensive documentation of this pattern in Mesopotamian cultures, as well as in the Hebrew Bible, classical antiquity, and Judaism, see Martii Nissinen, *Homoeroticism in the Biblical World: A Historical Perspective* (Minneapolis: Fortress, 1998).

31. See Robin Scroggs, *The New Testament and Homosexuality: Contextual Background for Contemporary Debate* (Philadelphia: Fortress, 1983), pp. 106ff.

the prohibitions of same-sex eroticism in Leviticus 18:22 and 20:13. The wording itself suggests that *treating a man as if he were a woman* is the core problem. Such an activity would have been viewed, given patriarchal assumptions, as inherently degrading. (Of course, this may not be the only reason why the Levitical texts speak against this activity, but it probably is at least part of the motivation underlying these prohibitions.[32])

It is more debated whether assumptions of patriarchy underlie Paul's rejection of same-sex relations in Romans 1:24-27, and we will need to consider that passage under our review of other forms of moral logic, particularly when we examine "nature" and natural law in chapter 11 below. Some interpreters believe that Romans 1:26 refers to female-female erotic unions when the text says, "Their women exchanged natural intercourse for unnatural." If this were true, patriarchy would be ruled out as the moral logic underlying this text, because, in the logic of patriarchy, for a woman to treat another woman as a man is not to degrade her but to elevate her. Yet I will argue in chapter 11 that this "lesbian" interpretation of Romans 1:26 is unlikely, and that a stronger case can be made for understanding Romans 1:26 as referring to noncoital *heterosexual* intercourse, making this a moot point as far as patriarchy is concerned.

However, my survey of patriarchy in Scripture does suggest that at least some of the biblical prohibitions and negative portrayal of same-sex eroticism were clearly linked to assumptions regarding patriarchy: what made such an act wrong, at least in large part in these texts, was that it was regarded as inherently degrading to treat a (higher-status) man as if he were a (lower-status) woman. To the extent that these concerns shape biblical discussions of homosexual activity, they must be subjected to a wider critique, based on the larger biblical movement we have chronicled, away from patriarchy toward a more egalitarian vision. Looked at in its wider context, Scripture does not see women as inherently of lower status than men, and thus it is not inherently degrading to treat a man as if he were a woman. (It may be impolite or unloving to do so, particularly if such treatment is unwelcome, but those are separate issues that do not involve the *inherent* degradation of a person by reducing his status from male to female.) Nor is it true, in the wider biblical view — despite its seemingly un-

---

32. In some ancient contexts, such as pederasty in Greek culture, the status difference between the active and passive males entailed a benevolent and pedagogical concern of the older male for the younger, passive male (see the discussion in Nissinen, *Homoeroticism in the Biblical World,* pp. 65ff.) The status differences of patriarchy are not always viewed negatively, but they are rarely questioned in the ancient world.

questioned acceptance in Genesis 19 and Judges 19 — that the rape of a woman by a man is any less offensive than the rape of a man by another man. There may well be other forms of moral logic underlying biblical texts dealing with same-sex eroticism that have more cross-cultural relevance. But to the extent that biblical texts prohibiting same-sex eroticism are based on patriarchal assumptions, the need for a cross-cultural critique of those passages must be recognized.

Summing Up

- We see the presence throughout Scripture of contrasting patriarchal and egalitarian streams.
- These tensions are best resolved by the eschatological vision of the New Testament, which holds in tension the ways in which we "already" have entered into the new life of the world to come (and thus have left patriarchy behind) and the ways in which we still live in this world, and have "not yet" fully entered into the life of the world to come (and thus are still bound, in some ways, by the structures of society, including — in the ancient world — patriarchal structures).
- But the canonical witness as a whole portrays the egalitarian vision as the eschatological destiny of human life, and invites people to live into that destiny, as long as such life does not disrupt the everyday functioning of the Christian community.
- This means that the hierarchy of the genders cannot be used today as a form of gender complementarity, which is allegedly violated by same-sex intimate relationships.
- However, to the extent that hierarchical assumptions shape the Bible's negative portrayal of same-sex eroticism (and such assumptions are evident in multiple places), these texts may be limited in their ability to speak directly to same-sex relationships today — in a context where such hierarchical assumptions no longer apply.

5

One Flesh

I n my exploration of the meaning of sexuality and gender in Scripture in this book, it has been necessary to clear away some misconceptions before we can move ahead more constructively. Thus chapter 2 was concerned, in large part, with clearing away unhelpful attempts either to use "gender complementarity" in undefined ways or to define such complementarity in terms of the biological differences between male and female. In that chapter I argued that, despite the obvious and subtle biological differences between male and female, Scripture does not use these biological differences as the explicit basis for differentiating roles or identities for male and female. In the next chapter I explored whether the biblical themes of justice and love were sufficient to develop an entire sexual ethic, and I argued that they were necessary but not sufficient in themselves to develop a comprehensive and canonical sexual ethic. In the preceding chapter, I explored whether hierarchy was an appropriate way to characterize a canonical understanding of the relationship between the sexes. While I do recognize a patriarchal stream within the biblical witness, I also acknowledge a powerful countervailing egalitarian stream; and thus in chapter 4, I have concluded that Scripture as a whole tends to take a more pragmatic approach to patriarchy — rather than a fundamental or essentialist view.

Up to this point, then, most of the results of my investigation have been negative. The focus has been on clearing away misconceptions. When we move to the language of "one flesh" in Genesis 2:24, however, we move to a much more foundational and positive form of moral logic that underlies much of what the Bible and the Christian tradition say about the meaning of sexuality and marriage. The entire Christian tradition has tended to speak of marriage under three broad rubrics (with differing levels of emphasis on each, in different parts of the tradition): the *unitive, procreative,* and *sacramental* meanings of marriage. This chapter explores biblical texts that build on the reference to "one flesh" in Genesis 2:24, and in it I shall explore two of these key elements that are deeply established in the Christian tradition: both the unitive and the sacramental understanding of sex and marriage. In short, the language of "one flesh" calls attention to the deep interconnections between marriage, sexual intercourse, and long-term bonding of persons to each other. The same language is used in Paul's letter to the Ephesians to reflect on the mysterious union between Christ and the church. After we explore the contours of the moral logic that shapes these texts, we will conclude with some reflections on the implications of our study for the debate concerning gay and lesbian committed relationships.

"One Flesh" in Genesis 2:18-25

In chapter 2, I discussed the account of the creation of woman in Genesis 2, and concluded there that the reference to "one flesh" in Genesis 2:24 focuses attention on the establishment of a new primary kinship bond, rather than on the overcoming of the incompleteness of male and female by recovering an alleged original unity of the genders. Yet a bit more needs to be said about this passage before we can move on to other biblical texts that refer back to it. It will be helpful to recall the text more explicitly:

> [21]So the LORD God caused a deep sleep to fall upon the man, and he slept; then he took one of his ribs and closed up its place with flesh. [22]And the rib that the LORD God had taken from the man he made into a woman and brought her to the man. [23]Then the man said, "This at last is bone of my bones and flesh of my flesh; this one shall be called Woman, for out of Man this one was taken." [24]Therefore a man leaves his father and his mother and clings to his wife, and they become one flesh. [25]And the man and his wife were both naked, and were not ashamed. (Gen. 2:21-25)

As I have argued in chapter 2, the focus here is not on the *complementarity* of the man and the woman but on the *similarity* between the two. Indeed, it is precisely this similarity that establishes the possibility of a new kinship tie, since kinship is based fundamentally on shared life and experience. One cannot help but feel the sense of discovery and exhilaration that pervades Genesis 2:23. After a series of failures to overcome the isolation of the man, "at last" a helper suitable for him has been found! While the narrative does not suggest that this sense of discovery represents the overcoming of *incompleteness* (as if the problem were the man's gender), it clearly presents the discovery of shared life and meaning as a powerful antidote to the problem with which the story begins: "It is not good that the man should be alone" (Gen. 2:18).

The second important thing to note about this text is that the "one flesh" union flows from sexual union, but is distinct from that sexual union, and is expressed in ways that extend beyond sexual union alone. This is evident already in the use of the word "cling" in Genesis 2:24, which is assumed by many commentators to refer directly to sexual intercourse. The Hebrew word for "cling" here *(dabaq)* is used fifty-four times in the Hebrew Bible, and nowhere else does the word have explicit sexual connotations.[1] Yet Paul's usage in 1 Corinthians 6:16 interprets this word in sexual terms. Paul refers to sex with a prostitute with the Greek word *kollaō*, which is closely related to the Greek word used for "cling" *(proskollaō)* in Genesis 2:24 in the Septuagint, the original Greek translation of the Hebrew Bible. So the "clinging" of Genesis 2:24 can be understood to include sexual intercourse, but it does not refer solely to sexual intercourse. A good parallel text illustrating this broader understanding of the Greek word for "cling" is found in the Old Testament apocryphal text Sirach 13:16: "All living beings associate with their own kind, and people stick close [Greek *proskollaō*] to those like themselves." Here the broader kinship connotation clearly is in focus. But even the "clinging" spoken of in Genesis 2:24 is not the same thing as becoming "one flesh"; rather, the "clinging" *leads* to becoming one flesh. In other words, the language of "one flesh" is not simply a euphemistic way of speaking about sexual intercourse; it is a way of speaking about the kinship ties that are related to the union of man and woman in marriage, a union that includes sexual intercourse. It is important not to overgenitalize or oversexualize this passage.

---

1. The usage that comes closest to a sexual connotation is Gen. 34:2-3, where Shechem rapes Dinah, daughter of Jacob, and subsequently falls in love with her. The text says: "When Shechem, son of Hamor the Hivite, prince of the region, saw her, he seized her and lay with her by force. ³And his soul was drawn [using the same Hebrew word, *dabaq*] to Dinah, daughter of Jacob; he loved the girl, and spoke tenderly to her." Note that here the "clinging" of the soul to Deborah *follows* sexual intercourse, but is quite distinct from it.

For example, the "clinging" spoken of in this text also connotes a sense of *desire*, which may include sexual desire but also clearly extends beyond sexual desire. Ruth "clings" to her mother-in-law after her husband dies, when she is told to return to her own country (Ruth 1:14). This relationship is too precious for her to abandon. "Clinging" in this context connotes the desire to overcome aloneness, the longing for intimacy, to know and to be known, to live one's life with others. It is the desire that finds its fulfillment in the sharing of life and experience together. Genesis 2:24 thus speaks of profound longings that are not merely sexual in character. They are at bottom longings for human community and fellowship, and these longings may express themselves in a variety of forms elsewhere in Scripture, in a variety of gendered relationships.

Yet clearly the "one-flesh" kinship union spoken of in these verses is intended by God to be a uniquely intimate one. This is made clear in Genesis 2:25: "And the man and his wife were both naked, and were not ashamed." This absence of shame clearly precedes the Fall in the overall Genesis narrative. Later, the sense of shame will flow from the Fall in Genesis 3:7: "Then the eyes of both of them were opened, and they realized they were naked; so they sewed fig leaves together and made coverings for themselves." The narrative as a whole leaves unclear whether, apart from the Fall, clothing would have been unnecessary for human society more generally. But it does make clear that, in the original divine purpose for the "one-flesh" union of the man and the woman, shame played no role, and the deep intimacy and bodily knowing that characterizes "nakedness without shame" was assumed as a given of this relationship.[2]

All of this describes what the Christian tradition terms the "unitive" character of marriage. The Genesis text speaks of intimacy, knowing, longing, and sharing. Sexuality is an important part of this picture, but it is not the totality of this picture. Indeed, sexuality and sexual expression find their deepest meanings when viewed against this wider backdrop. The joining of bodies cannot be separated from the joining of lives. As we shall see, particularly when we consider the use of one-flesh language in 1 Corinthians 6, this vision for the link between sex and kinship bonds provides the basic moral logic underlying the Bible's consistent rejection of sexual promiscuity. Sexual union is conceived in the Bible as profoundly

---

2. It is important to note how frequently, in the Hebrew Bible, "uncovering the nakedness" of someone is equivalent to having sexual relations with that person. See esp. the numerous instances of this pattern in Lev. 18, 20.

metaphorical — it points beyond the physical act to the relational connections and intimacy that undergird and surround it. This is why the Bible requires that sexual expression find its meaning against this larger and more comprehensive backdrop emphasizing shared life and kinship.

It is also worth noting, at least in passing, that this entire discussion of one flesh in Genesis (and indeed throughout the Bible) takes place without even a hint of concern with procreation. Although the one-flesh union of man and woman creates a stable kinship bond into which children can be born and raised, the one-flesh union of man and woman as narrated in Genesis 2 is not dependent on children in any essential way; indeed, children are nowhere to be found in Genesis 2 at all. The creation of the woman is not narrated, first of all, as a means for humankind's achieving "fruitfulness," but rather as an antidote to the problem of aloneness. Prior to any discussion of her role in procreation, the woman is created as a "helper" — and the closest companion. This stands in contrast to Pope Paul VI's encyclical *Humanae Vitae,* which quotes the earlier Second Vatican Council in insisting that "[m]arriage and conjugal love are by their nature ordained toward the procreation and education of children."[3] This statement subordinates the unitive meaning of marriage to procreation, which it defines as the true purpose of marriage and conjugal love. But there is nothing of this in Genesis 2. Certainly, procreation is an important purpose of marriage, but there is nothing in the language of "one flesh" anywhere in Scripture that even remotely suggests that this unitive meaning of marriage is subordinated to the purpose of procreation. Indeed, everything about the Genesis 2 text suggests the opposite: the procreative meaning of marriage should, in fact, be subordinated to its more essential unitive purpose.

It is important to explore this relationship between the unitive and procreative meanings of sexuality and marriage in greater detail. Many have noted the close link — in Roman Catholic teaching — between the centrality of procreation and the importance of "natural law" in Roman Catholic moral theology. The interest in natural law helps to explain the importance of procreation in Roman Catholic moral teaching. But the centrality of procreation in Roman Catholic moral teaching springs not only from an understanding of natural law; it also springs from a deeply held conviction that procreation is the point at which human beings exist

---

3. Paul VI, *Humanae Vitae* (1968): http://www.vatican.va/holy_father/paul_vi/encyclicals/documents/hf_p-vi_enc_25071968_humanae-vitae_en.html.

not merely for themselves but for something beyond themselves — the next generation. In this sense, procreation is not merely a biological imperative, but the deepest expression of love that is willing to sacrifice oneself and one's own desires for the other — in this case, for one's children. Paul VI speaks of each marital partner as "the minister of the design established by the Creator."[4] Another Catholic commentator writes: "Since the good of the species is more important to nature than the good of individuals, procreation and rearing of children is a more important end of marriage than mutual help, conjugal love, and the remedy [for excessive desire]."[5] Yet a more sensitive reading of Genesis 2 suggests that this summons to ministry — to live beyond one's own needs and concerns for the purposes of God and for the sake of the other, appears already in the unitive vision for marriage offered in Genesis 2. The man "leaves" the familiarity of father and mother and "clings" to his wife.

Already here, humans are summoned out of isolation, out of familiarity, into a deeper and more mysterious reality that transcends their life as individuals and participates in the divine purpose. Already here, life is called out of itself into something deeper and richer. Procreation is, of course, the natural extension of this movement, but it is not the beginning of this movement beyond the self to the other. That movement already begins in the "one-flesh" union spoken of in Genesis 2, quite apart from any interest in procreation. Before marriage can do anything about bringing a coming generation into existence, it must first form the essential kinship bond that makes shared life possible in any generation. This explains, in essence, why the unitive meaning of marriage is more central than the procreative meaning.

"One Flesh" and Jesus' Teaching on Divorce

This broader "unitive" meaning of "one flesh," focusing on bonding and kinship, is at center stage in the reference to "one flesh" found in the Jesus tradition (Matt. 19:3-12; Mark 10:2-12; cf. Matt. 5:31-32; Luke 16:18). Given the most commonly accepted understanding of the relationship between

---

4. Paul VI, *Humanae Vitae*.

5. John C. Ford and Gerald Kelly, "The Essential Subordination of the Secondary Ends of Marriage," in Charles E. Curran and Julie Hanlon Rubio, eds., *Marriage: Readings in Moral Theology* (New York: Paulist Press, 2009), p. 24.

the Gospels (the "Two Source Hypothesis"), most scholars believe that Mark's Gospel was written and available first, and that the writers of Matthew and Luke made independent use of the text of Mark in constructing their Gospels. Therefore, we turn first to Mark's version as the earliest form of the tradition:

> [2]Some Pharisees came, and to test him they asked, "Is it lawful for a man to divorce his wife?" [3]He answered them, "What did Moses command you?" [4]They said, "Moses allowed a man to write a certificate of dismissal and to divorce her." [5]But Jesus said to them, "Because of your hardness of heart he wrote this commandment for you. [6]But from the beginning of creation, 'God made them male and female.' [7]'For this reason a man shall leave his father and mother and be joined to his wife, [8]and the two shall become one flesh.' So they are no longer two, but one flesh. [9]Therefore what God has joined together, let no one separate." [10]Then in the house the disciples asked him again about this matter. [11]He said to them, "Whoever divorces his wife and marries another commits adultery against her; [12]and if she divorces her husband and marries another, she commits adultery." (Mark 10:2-12)

The fact that Jesus makes the "one-flesh" reference to Genesis 2:24 in the context of a discussion about divorce is noteworthy. Divorce is essentially the severing of kinship ties and obligations. The use of this text in the Jesus tradition thus confirms my argument that the language of "one flesh" has kinship in view. Jesus' words are striking in that, at least in the Markan version of this story, there is no allowance for divorce and remarriage under any circumstances.[6] Matthew's version of the story has some slight but notable differences: in Matthew 19:3, Jesus is asked "Is it lawful for a man to divorce his wife *for any cause?*" The question is no longer whether divorce is permissible at all, but rather how much freedom a man has in divorcing his wife.[7] Jesus' response in Matthew 19:8-9 allows one legitimate ground

---

6. As many scholars have pointed out, the question of remarriage is not separate from the question of divorce; indeed, the essential meaning of divorce grants to both partners the right to remarry. See the discussion in William R. G. Loader, *Sexuality and the Jesus Tradition* (Grand Rapids: Eerdmans, 2005), pp. 61ff.

7. In contrast to the Markan account, Matthew's version assumes that only men can initiate divorce. These differences may reflect a more Hellenistic context in Mark, versus a more Jewish context in Matthew.

for divorce: "Whoever divorces his wife, *except for unchastity,* and marries another commits adultery."

Some scholars believe that the exception clause in Matthew simply renders explicit what was already assumed in the Markan version of the story. They argue that, in a first-century Jewish context, adultery would have made divorce mandatory under any circumstances: they would have understood that the marital bond was already irreparably broken by adultery.[8] Yet the absence of this exception clause from the earliest tradition in Mark cannot be glossed over so easily.[9] The absence of an exception clause in the earliest version of Jesus' prohibition of divorce suggests that the prohibition, on the lips of Jesus, may have had a different quality from the more casuistic discussion in Matthew. One wonders whether the closest analogies are found in other statements of Jesus that are shockingly unqualified: "But I say to you that everyone who looks at a woman with lust has already committed adultery with her in his heart. If your right eye causes you to sin, tear it out and throw it away; it is better for you to lose one of your members than for your whole body to be thrown into hell" (Matt. 5:28-29). Such parallels suggest that Jesus is not setting forth case law here, but rather is pressing to the essential purpose of God and exposing as sinful all departures from that central purpose. Then the later tradition, both in Matthew and in 1 Corinthians 7:10-15, struggled to take Jesus' provocative words and to express them in a form that could provide concrete and tangible guidance to a community wrestling with specific difficult cases. If this analysis is correct, it also suggests that the contemporary church must also hold people accountable to Jesus' costly and categorical vision, while also following the precedent of other New Testament writers in exercising pastoral discernment, recognizing when marriages are irretrievably broken and when the grace of God calls for repentance, forgiveness, and a new beginning.[10]

8. See Loader, *Sexuality and the Jesus Tradition,* p. 85.

9. Note that the "Q" version of this saying in Luke 16:18 also lacks any exception clause. It is likely that Matthew added the same exception clause in Matt. 19:9, as well in Matt. 5:32.

10. See the carefully nuanced discussion in Richard B. Hays, *The Moral Vision of the New Testament: Community, Cross, New Creation; A Contemporary Introduction to New Testament Ethics* (San Francisco: HarperSanFrancisco, 1996), pp. 347-76. The current reading of paragraph 2 of section 24 of the Westminster Confession of Faith in the PCUSA (modified in 1953 by the UPCUSA from the 1646 original) presents a helpful summary of the issues: "2. Because the corruption of man is apt unduly to put asunder those whom God hath joined together in marriage, and because the Church is concerned with the establishment of mar-

As important as these questions concerning the legitimate grounds for divorce may be, however, they are not the central focus of this chapter. Our concern is with Jesus' reference to the "one-flesh" language of Genesis 2:24. Jesus' central concern here is with the bond of marriage, and his conclusion, in addressing that bond, is to declare, "What God has joined together, let no one separate" (Mark 10:9, Matt. 19:6). Frederick Bruner notes three important aspects of the Greek of this text.[11] First of all, the word for "God" includes the definite article in the Greek text, making it all the more emphatic. *God* is the one whose action cannot be violated. Second, Bruner notes that the word rendered "joined together" is more literally translated "yoked together." The image is of a dual yoke, pulling a wagon or plow. The focus falls, therefore, on shared productive labor and service. The "one-flesh" union of marriage is not just about mutual satisfaction but about shared service and ministry: childbearing, mutual care, hospitality, and service to the wider community. Finally, Bruner notes, the tense of the imperative verb for "separate" indicates the call to stop an action that has been going on repeatedly. This places Jesus' words in an ancient Judean context, where the practice of divorce had become increasingly casual, particularly among the nobility.[12] Bruner thus paraphrases the text: "Therefore, what the Great God has yoked together a mere human being must stop tearing apart."

All these are important nuances that we must keep in mind. But I want to focus further attention specifically on the phrase "what God has joined together." The question arises: *In what sense* does God "join together" a husband and wife in the one-flesh union? The Reformer Martin Luther argued that not all marriages were necessarily joined together by God.[13] This assumes that the "joining together" is a direct act of God, and it raises an

---

riage in the Lord as Scripture sets it forth, and with the present penitence as well as with the past innocence or guilt of those whose marriage has been broken; therefore as a breach of that holy relation may occasion divorce, so remarriage after a divorce granted on grounds explicitly stated in Scripture or implicit in the gospel of Christ may be sanctioned in keeping with his redemptive gospel, when sufficient penitence for sin and failure is evident, and a firm purpose of and endeavor after Christian marriage is manifest." (http://www.pcusa.org/oga/publications/boc.pdf).

11. Frederick Dale Bruner, *Matthew: A Commentary*, rev. ed. (Grand Rapids: Eerdmans, 2004), II:254ff.

12. Cf. the story of John the Baptist and Herod Antipas in Mark 6:17-29; Matt 14:3-12; cf. Luke 3:19-20; Josephus, *Ant.* 18:116-19.

13. *Luther's Works* (American edition, 1955-76) 46:275-77, cited in Bruner, *Matthew: A Commentary*, II:254.

uncertainty about whether any given marriage has received this mark of indissolubility by God. However, it would scarcely be faithful to the teaching of Jesus to attempt to argue that a particular marriage, though publicly and solemnly enacted, was not "yoked together" by God, and hence that the partners were free to divorce.[14] It is better to understand "what God has joined together" as a more general *decree*, rather than as a discrete *act* directed toward a specific couple. In other words, Jesus is saying that when a man "leaves father and mother, and clings to his wife," the two — by divine decree — become one flesh, one kinship unit. It is this divine decree that must not be contradicted by human beings. Humans are not free to enter marriage without accepting the binding commitments and responsibilities of the kinship bond decreed by God to accompany marriage. They must not say at one point, with their bodies and their words, what they are unwilling to continue to say with the rest of their lives. This emphasis on divine decree also recognizes that marriage is not necessarily performed only in a church by a direct divine representative; marriage is not accomplished by God in this sense. Rather, human society (as well as the church) recognizes when two persons have solemnly and publicly bound themselves to each other, and society (as well as the church) rightly holds them accountable to fulfill the commitments they have made. To the extent that church and society do this, they honor the God who has decreed that a husband and wife shall become one flesh. This again underscores the unitive character of marriage that we have been exploring throughout this chapter.

But another question still presses forward in any careful reading of this text. It concerns the underlying form of moral logic that gives shape and meaning to this text. *Why* does God decree that the union of husband and wife should be inseparable? What is it about the one-flesh union spoken of in Genesis 2:24 that makes it permanent in God's design and purpose? One can point to practical reasons such as the need for children to have a stable home. Yet such considerations usually begin to fade as children grow up and leave the home. Certainly, questions of economic justice are part of the picture, since divorced wives in the ancient world were particularly cut off from economic support. But Mark's Gospel prohibits women from initiating divorce as well (Mark 10:12), a provision that seems to extend be-

---

14. This is different from the question of annulment, which is quite a distinct issue, since annulment assumes that a marriage was never fully enacted *by law*, not that the requisite divine action failed to occur.

yond merely a concern for economic justice. Hence neither the procreative character of marriage nor considerations of economic justice alone are sufficient in themselves to explain the moral logic underlying this text.

We come closer to a more complete understanding when we recognize that the permanence of the one-flesh union is analogous to all other kinship ties. We never cease to be parents, children, brothers, or sisters, and these identities carry with them certain obligations to others. So why should our identity as spouses, and the attendant obligations to our spouses, be any different? Yet in all these other kinship ties, there are variations that occur throughout life. One's obligations both to parents and to children change over time. And while the character of marital obligations may also evolve over time, it is clear that this text envisions a greater stability in the one-flesh union than in any other kinship tie. Indeed, the Genesis account seems to assume that the one-flesh union is the foundation of every other kinship bond. So even though the analogy of kinship is helpful, it is not entirely adequate to explain the permanence of the one-flesh union, because it explains the deeper, one-flesh bond by analogy with the lesser kinship ones. It does not yet explain the nature of the deeper bond itself.

To understand this deeper bond in its own nature, we must return to the Old Testament texts that use the husband-wife relationship as an analogy of the covenant relationship between God and Israel. Malachi 2:14 speaks of one's wife as "your companion and your wife *by covenant.*" This language picks up a theme that we see in earlier texts as well, particularly the prophet Hosea's enacted oracle in which he marries a prostitute as a mirror reflecting Israel's unfaithfulness to its God (see esp. Hos. 2:19). Jeremiah 3:1–4:4 and Ezekiel 16 both develop the same metaphor of marriage into an extended history of God's covenantal relationship with Israel. Jeremiah speaks of Israel as God's "bride," or of God as Israel's "husband" (2:2; 3:20; 31:32; cf. 9:2), and Isaiah uses marital imagery in speaking of God's covenant relationship with Israel (50:1; 54:5ff.; 62:5). Yet it is important to understand the nature of the analogy between marriage and God's covenant with Israel. Marriage is not understood intrinsically as a covenant in the cultures of the Ancient Middle East. Human marriage itself is only rarely spoken of in the Old Testament as a covenant (Mal. 2:14 is the only unambiguous text that speaks this way).[15] Apparently, it was the prophetic

---

15. It is possible that Prov. 2:17 speaks of marriage as a covenant, though the text is not entirely clear, whether the "covenant of her God" which is forgotten by the adulterous woman is the covenant of marriage, or the Sinai covenant, which forbids adultery.

tradition that began to use marriage as a metaphor for God's covenant with Israel, deepening Israel's understanding of what marriage itself meant by using marriage as an image for divine faithfulness. I shall explore below a similar analogy between Christ's covenant relationship to the church and marriage in Ephesians 5:25ff.

This analogy, emerging from the prophetic tradition, between divine covenant and human marriage is an important element in our understanding of the permanence of the one-flesh union. It is precisely in the context of speaking of marriage as a covenant in Malachi 2:14 that God declares, "I hate divorce." Similarly, Hosea's extended meditation on the analogies between the unfaithfulness of Israel and his own unfaithful wife ends with the affirmation that God will not abandon this "marriage," despite Israel's unfaithfulness (Hos. 14:4-7). In the same way, the extended meditation on Israel's waywardness as sexual unfaithfulness in Ezekiel 16 ends with words of divine faithfulness: "I will establish my covenant with you, and you shall know that I am the LORD in order that you may remember and be confounded, and never open your mouth again because of your shame, when I forgive you all that you have done, says the Lord GOD" (Ezek. 16:62-63).

Indeed, it may well be that these Old Testament analogies between God's covenant with Israel and marriage led Jesus to see in Genesis 2:24 a vision for the permanence of marriage. God had not sent Israel away forever, despite Israel's adulterous pursuit of other gods. The faithfulness God expects of marriage thus finds its ultimate grounding in God's own character. God's faithfulness to Israel is the norm and ground of all relational bonds that give structure and meaning to human existence. And just as God's faithfulness knows no limits, so Jesus insists that marriage — the foundational kinship bond — must be marked by similar faithfulness that knows no limits.[16] Thus the one-flesh union intended by God must not be sundered by human unfaithfulness. This again underscores the originality of Mark's version of Jesus' prohibition on divorce, which admits no exceptions whatsoever.

One final issue needs to be mentioned before we conclude our explora-

---

16. This indirectly confirms my previous assertion that the original form of Jesus' prohibition of divorce lacked any "exception clause" for adultery, and that these case-law considerations were added later. Indeed, to the extent that God's history with Israel is in view, even Israel's *adultery* cannot destroy God's covenant faithfulness. By analogy, then, one could argue that Jesus intends to say that even marital adultery does not *necessarily* destroy the marriage covenant. Jesus is not seeking to define case law, but attempting to illuminate fundamental principles underlying marriage, grounded in the faithfulness of God.

tion of Jesus' use of the "one-flesh" language. Many scholars have noted that Jesus' words prohibiting divorce and remarriage in Matthew 19:9 and Mark 10:11 presuppose that a man may not be married to more than one woman at the same time (polygyny). In a polygynous society, a man does not commit adultery against one wife by marrying another, whether or not the first wife is divorced from him. But if Jesus' words are true, that "whoever divorces his wife and marries another commits adultery against her [the first wife]," how much more would it be the case that marrying another *without* divorcing the first wife would be considered adultery! Jesus' words, therefore, reflect the assumption that one cannot be married to more than one person at the same time. Of course, this was not the case in much of the Old Testament, where polygynous marriage is commonly attested. Jesus' words thus represent a deepening and a focusing of the moral logic underpinning marriage in Scripture. They also represent a deepening emphasis on the singularity and significance of the one-flesh union spoken of in Genesis 2:24.

"One Flesh" in Ephesians 5:21-33

The link that I have already noted in the Jesus tradition between marriage and God's covenant with Israel receives further development and a more focused christological exposition in Ephesians 5:21-33. Here marriage is no longer an analogy for God's relationship with Israel, as we saw in texts from Jeremiah, Isaiah, Malachi, Ezekiel, and Hosea; instead, the focus is more specifically on the analogy between marriage and Christ's relationship to the church. After citing Genesis 2:24, Ephesians 5:32 says: "This is a profound mystery — but I am talking about Christ and the church." This raises a complex but important question: In what sense is the union between Christ and the church analogous to the one-flesh union of husband and wife?

Some interpreters attempt to interpret the text allegorically. Aquinas expresses the perspective of much of the ancient church when he interprets Christ as the new Adam, who in the incarnation "leaves his father [i.e., the first person of the Trinity] and his mother [i.e., the synagogue, or, in other interpreters, the New Jerusalem], and he shall cleave to his wife [the church]."[17] But it is unlikely that the details of the text should be

17. Thomas Aquinas, *Aquinas Scripture Series,* trans. Matthew L. Lamb (Albany, NY: Magi Books, 1966), vol. 2, p. 225.

pressed in this way, particularly since the first half of Genesis 2:24 is not discussed at all in Ephesians 5:21-33. Rather, the focus throughout the Ephesians text seems to fall on the last part of the Genesis text cited in Ephesians 5:31: ". . . the two will become one flesh."

This connection already appears in the instructions to wives in Ephesians 5:22-24:

> [22]Wives, be subject to your husbands as you are to the Lord. [23]For the husband is the head of the wife just as Christ is the head of the church, the body of which he is the Savior. [24]Just as the church is subject to Christ, so also wives ought to be, in everything, to their husbands.

We can see the linkage between head and body — parts of the one flesh — linked to the relationship between Christ and the church.[18] But where does this text get the idea that the husband is the "head" and the wife is the "body" in this one-flesh union? This is not found in any sense of the Genesis text itself. We get a clue as to the writer's logic in Ephesians 5:23, which speaks of the church as "the body of which he is the Savior." Clearly, husbands are not the spiritual or religious saviors of their wives. Only Christ can fulfill that function.[19] But in the ancient world, husbands were "saviors" of their wives in a more general meaning of that word: the providers and source of security for the households that were dependent on them. It is probably in this sense that the text speaks of husbands as "heads": the emphasis is on connectedness, care, and provision.[20] Therefore, throughout this section we see the reciprocal relationship between provision and care of the head, on the one hand, and submission of the body, on the other. It is obvious that in a modern context, where husbands are no longer the sole source of provision and care, this framework needs to be re-

18. Ephesians seems to use "flesh" and "body" interchangeably throughout this passage; cf. similar Pauline usage in Rom. 8:13; 1 Cor. 6:16; Col. 2:11.

19. Interestingly, Paul can speak of how wives may possibly "save" their unbelieving husbands, as well as husbands "saving" their unbelieving wives, by positively influencing them in marriage (1 Cor. 7:16). The call to be "savior," at least in this derivative, but more specifically religious sense, belongs equally to husbands and to wives.

20. We see the same focus on connectedness, care, and provision in other uses of the word "head" in Ephesians. In Eph. 1:22, the fact that Christ is "head over all things for the church" is directly related to the way in which Christ "fills all in all." In Eph. 4:15, the same emphasis occurs, where Christ is spoken of as the head "from whom the whole body, joined and knit together by every ligament with which it is equipped, as each part is working properly, promotes the body's growth in building itself up in love."

considered and "retranslated."[21] Yet the same dynamics should continue to apply: wherever one partner takes the lead in providing for the family unit, the other partner needs to be graciously receptive to such provision, recognizing the deep interconnectedness of the one-flesh union. In this sense, there are moments when both husbands and wives represent Christ — in varying circumstances — to each other.

The "one-flesh" metaphor receives further exposition in the instructions given to husbands in the following verses from Ephesians 5:25-30:

> [25]Husbands, love your wives, just as Christ loved the church and gave himself up for her, [26]in order to make her holy by cleansing her with the washing of water by the word, [27]so as to present the church to himself in splendor, without a spot or wrinkle or anything of the kind — yes, so that she may be holy and without blemish. [28]In the same way, husbands should love their wives as they do their own bodies. He who loves his wife loves himself. [29]For no one ever hates his own body, but he nourishes and tenderly cares for it, just as Christ does for the church, [30]because we are members of his body.

We see here again an analogous relationship between husbands/wives and Christ/the church. The text argues that humans have an instinctive and natural drive to care for their own bodies; therefore, husbands (who are "one flesh" with their wives) should recognize the natural imperative to care for their wives as they care for themselves. This is also illustrated by analogy in the care that Christ exercises on behalf of the church. But this is also where we see limitations to the analogy. Husbands are not told to "cleanse" their wives, nor to make them "holy and without blemish." Husbands do not "present" wives "to themselves" as Christ presents the church to himself (Eph. 5:27). These functions, like the full meaning of "savior" in Ephesians 5:23, are unique to the relationship between Christ and the church, and they are not part of the one-flesh union between husband and wife.

In other words, the analogous relationship between husbands/wives and Christ/the church is not a symmetrical one. The relationship of husbands and wives is a partial reflection of the deeper reality seen in the relationship between Christ and the church. Just as we saw in Jesus' words on divorce, the paradigmatic faithfulness of God to Israel (or in this case, the

---

21. In the ancient world, especially in Jewish contexts, there was great aversion to women taking the role of provider. The Old Testament apocryphal text Sirach 25:22 declares: "There is wrath and impudence and great disgrace when a wife supports her husband."

faithfulness of Christ to the church) becomes the purpose to which human marriage must aspire — the norm that must shape the way human marriages seek to find their meaning and identity. I believe that this is what the text is getting at when, after citing Genesis 2:24, Ephesians 5:32 declares: "This is a profound mystery — but I am talking about Christ and the church." In the book of Ephesians, "mystery" always refers to something previously unknown, which is now revealed in Christ (cf. 1:9; 3:3, 4, 9; 6:10). The writer of Ephesians seems to be taking his cue from the texts in Malachi, Ezekiel, and Hosea that we have already explored, and then taking this form of reasoning a step further. Jews had previously known that the faithfulness of marriage was intended as a pointer to the greater faithfulness of God to Israel. Now, in the faithfulness of Christ to the church we see a deepening and widening vision of the way in which marital faithfulness, love, and care point beyond themselves toward the newly revealed secret of Christ's redemptive relationship to the people of God — now including not only Jews, but Gentiles as well (Eph. 1:10). As in Jesus' teaching on divorce, the one-flesh language here is taken far beyond its original connotations of shared kinship, and it is drawn into a vision of the divine life, in which God's steadfast love and faithfulness embodied in Christ's love for the church does not mirror human faithfulness but serves as the fountain of light, reflected — even if only dimly — in the faithfulness and care of husbands and wives who live out the one-flesh union day to day.

This widening vision helps to inform the debate in the church over whether marriage should be understood as a sacrament. And this text in Ephesians is central in that debate, because the Vulgate, the early translation of the New Testament into Latin, translated the Greek word *mustērion* ("mystery") in Ephesians 5:32 with the Latin word *sacramentum* ("sacrament"). The Greek and Latin words overlap significantly, but the Latin word *sacramentum* took on the broader ecclesiastical meaning of a special rite of the church that functions as a distinctive means by which divine grace is communicated to humans. Most scholars agree that the writer of Ephesians does not have this wider meaning in mind. Already in the Reformation, Calvin observed that Ephesians 5:31 does not apply the word "mystery" or "sacrament" to marriage, but rather to Christ and the church: "This is a profound mystery — but I am talking about Christ and the church."[22]

---

22. John Calvin, *The Epistles of Paul the Apostle to the Galatians, Ephesians, Philippians and Colossians*, ed. David W. Torrance and Thomas F. Torrance, trans. T. H. L. Parker, Calvin's Commentaries (Grand Rapids: Eerdmans, 1965), p. 210.

Marriage is not a sacrament either in the sense that it is ordained by Christ or in the sense that its outward form uniquely conveys an inward and spiritual grace. But marriage can be understood to be "sacramental" in a more general sense. That is, the call to live as "one flesh" can be the school in which we learn more deeply "what is the breadth and length and height and depth, and to know the love of Christ that surpasses knowledge, so that you may be filled with all the fullness of God" (Eph. 3:18-19). In seeking to imitate the pattern of Christ's faithfulness to us in the context of marriage, we are forced, again and again, to die with Christ to our selfish ways and our self-centered identity, and to rise with Christ to a deeper expression of love and faithfulness in union with another.[23] In this wider "sacramental" sense, marriage — like many forms of human community — becomes the context in which we learn and live out our union with Christ and enter more deeply into its riches.

Sex and One Flesh: 1 Corinthians 6:12-20

The last reference to "one flesh" in Scripture is found in 1 Corinthians 6:15-17:

> [15]Do you not know that your bodies are members of Christ? Should I therefore take the members of Christ and make them members of a prostitute? Never! [16]Do you not know that whoever is united to a prostitute becomes one body with her? For it is said, "The two shall be one flesh." [17]But anyone united to the Lord becomes one spirit with him.

The first and most striking thing to notice in this passage is that Paul seems to think that the one-flesh union spoken of in Genesis 2:24 is created even by casual sex with a prostitute. But even though this is more than sufficient grounds for rejecting sex with prostitutes, based on this text, it would be a distortion of Paul's interpretation of the Genesis 2:24 text to assume that everything intended in Genesis 2:24 is fully brought into reality by having sex with a prostitute. Sex with a prostitute is a parody and distortion of a true one-flesh union, and is thus to be avoided. It doesn't give us, in itself, a full account of what such a one-flesh union means.

23. See the wide-ranging exploration of this sacramental meaning of marriage and community, embracing straight couples, gay couples, and celibate communities, in Eugene F. Rogers, *Sexuality and the Christian Body: Their Way into the Triune God,* Challenges in Contemporary Theology (Oxford: Blackwell, 1999).

Paul's point acquires deeper meaning when we draw the larger context into view. Paul's deeper point is that the body is important, and what Christians do with their bodies is important. This becomes clear when we single out the view that Paul is trying to correct, the assumption that "food is meant for the stomach and the stomach for food, and God will destroy both one and the other" (1 Cor. 6:13a). Paul is probably quoting a slogan of the Corinthians here, which in their minds meant that bodily functions (including both eating and sex) were matters of indifference to Christians. Paul disagrees, offering his own corrective summary response: "The body is meant not for fornication but for the Lord, and the Lord for the body. And God raised the Lord and will also raise us by his power" (1 Cor. 6:13b-14). In the place of the Corinthians' rigid dichotomy between the physical and the spiritual — and thus their indifference to all things pertaining to the body — Paul speaks of the offering of bodies to God in worship, and the resurrection of the body, a fact that assigns a deep value to bodily existence. His point is clear: "For you were bought with a price; therefore glorify God *in your body*" (1 Cor. 6:20).

Hence, while on the one hand, it would be overreading this passage to conclude that those who have sex with a prostitute should consider themselves to be married to that prostitute, it is also true, on the other hand, that the bodily act of sexual union with a prostitute puts the Christian in an impossible position of being united both to holiness and to uncleanness. Here the basic kinship background we have already seen is evident in Paul's reference to "one flesh." Sexual union is intended to create a shared and continuing social reality. The Corinthians ignore this, and in so doing they fail to understand the conflicting relationships in which they have placed themselves. As we have noted, Paul's use of Genesis 2:24 exposes the core form of moral logic that underlies the problem with sexual promiscuity. We cannot say with our bodies what we will not say with the rest of our lives. Bodies are not indifferent, and what we do with our bodies is not indifferent. Sexual union is deeply metaphorical, and when we strip sexual union of the wider metaphorical kinship meaning intended by Genesis 2:24, we cease to live in the "real world" governed by God's purposes and decrees.

Paul's discussion in 1 Corinthians 6 thus focuses attention on the significance of embodiment and sexuality. Bodies are not neutral, nor are they matters of indifference. Rather, we communicate with bodies (not only with our words), and we bring relationships into existence that were not there before with our bodies. Sexual relations are thus a sort of bodily language in which meaning is enacted and conveyed. Christians need to ensure that this communication has integrity and that it coheres with their overall Christian calling and identity. Rowan Williams reflects on this communicative aspect of sexuality in a remarkable lecture entitled "The Body's Grace," given long before he became Archbishop of Canterbury:

> *Any* genuine experience of desire leaves me in this position: I cannot of myself satisfy my wants without distorting or trivializing them. But in *this* experience we have a particularly intense case of the helplessness of the ego alone. For my body to be the cause of joy, the end of homecoming, for me, it must be there for someone else, must be perceived, accepted, nurtured. And that means being given over to the creation of joy in that other, because only as directed to the enjoyment, the happiness, of the other does it become unreservedly lovable. To desire my joy is to desire the joy of the one I desire: my search for enjoyment through the bodily presence of another is a longing to be enjoyed in my body. As Blake put it, sexual partners "admire" in each other "the lineaments of gratified desire." We are pleased because we are pleasing.[24]

Williams's remarkable words underscore the profound connection between sexual union and the wider one-flesh union we have been exploring. Sex is not simply about the satisfaction of desire. To make such a simplistic claim would be the equivalent of the Corinthians' claim, "Food for the belly and the belly for food." Sexual desire is, in this sense, radically different from other bodily desires, such as hunger, for example. If I am hungry, I can find food on my own and satisfy my hunger. Sexual desire, on the other hand, requires another person, and if sex is to achieve what the body most deeply longs for, one must enter into deep communion with the other — the kind of communion that the Bible speaks of as a one-flesh union. In that union, one relinquishes self-determination, and one's own happiness is bound up in the happiness of the other. Paul points to a similar reality in 1 Corinthians 7:4: "For the wife does not have authority over her own body, but the husband does; likewise the husband does not have authority over his own body, but the wife does." Indeed, sexual desire — the coincidence of the longing to experience joy, and to be joy to another

---

24. Charles C. Hefling, *Our Selves, Our Souls, and Bodies: Sexuality and the Household of God* (Cambridge, MA: Cowley Publications, 1996), pp. 60-61; italics in original. Williams's lecture was originally given on July 2, 1989, as the tenth Michael Harding Memorial address.

— is what drives us to this union and sustains and strengthens this union. Our bodies know, sometimes more deeply than our minds can acknowledge, what Genesis 2:18 declares: It is not good for us to be alone. This is not to deny the legitimacy of the calling to celibacy, whether this is a temporary calling for some or a lifelong calling for others. But even celibacy cannot be fully lived out in isolation, and the language of the body is not limited to sexual union alone. The language of the body — whether it may be a touch, a hug, or in some cases full sexual intimacy — is a language that we cannot and should not avoid. Our faithfulness as Christians depends in no small part on what we say with our bodies.

To think of sexual relations as a language brings with it another important corollary. Sex can bring with it an incredibly wide range of meanings. We may use sex to express compassion, hope, playfulness, dominance, consolation, competition, submission, exploration of new roles — the list goes on and on. To speak of sex as a language is to recognize that there is not one single meaning of mystic union that is conveyed by the language of "one flesh." Rather, the one-flesh union is the place where human creativity expresses itself: the creativity that results in endlessly diverse cultural forms, both for good purposes and for less admirable ones. Thus Christian faithfulness has only begun when it recognizes that full sexual intimacy belongs in one-flesh kinship unions. The following steps are equally, if not more, important: learning the bodily language for giving and receiving love and using that language to create a space of beauty and love where both partners become more fully the persons God intends them to be.

Implications for the Debate over Gay and Lesbian Relationships

Among the questions at the center of the church's debate over same-sex unions lies a simple but contentious one: Can the Bible's vision for one-flesh unions be understood in a way that can also encompass committed same-sex unions? For traditionalists, the answer is clearly no. They point out, first of all, that whenever the Bible uses the language of "one flesh," it is referring, usually explicitly, to unions between a male and a female. Yet this unanimity of the biblical witness, even though it carries substantial weight, is not necessarily the end of the discussion. The reason is simple, though it is difficult to discern in the midst of controversy. Over the course of human history we have encountered questions that take us beyond the assumptions and problems envisioned by the biblical writers themselves, and these new questions and problems have forced us to reread the text and to probe more deeply for answers. The fact that the Bible uses the language of "one flesh" to refer to male-female unions *normally* does not inherently, and of itself, indicate that it views such linkages *normatively*.

For example, the Bible everywhere assumes that the sun moves around the earth. Yet the "Copernican revolution" forced the church to change its understanding of the normative meaning of statements such as "The world is firmly established; it shall never be moved" (1 Chron. 16:30; Ps. 93:1; 96:30). When we encounter questions and issues not contemplated by the biblical writers, we must not allow the limitations of the experience of the biblical writers to be used to deny the truths that evidently lie before us. The same principles emerge outside the scientific arena, for example, in the moral arena — surrounding the question of the Bible and slavery. The Bible never envisions the elimination of the practice of slavery in society. The Bible does, of course, call for a "humanization" of the institution of slavery. It appeals to slave owners to treat their slaves justly and compassionately (Eph. 6:9; Col. 4:1), and, in the case of Philemon, it even calls for the freedom of an individual slave (vv. 15-16). But nowhere does the Bible even envision the possibility that slavery itself would or could be banished from society — that is, prior to the return of Christ. Without exception, the Bible urges slaves to obey their masters. These sorts of arguments were made vigorously by slaveholders in the American South against the abolitionists during the middle of the nineteenth century.[25] But the silence of the Bible on issues never envisioned by the Bible (such as the abolition of slavery) is, in and of itself, not a compelling argument. What is normal in Scripture is not necessarily also normative.

How might these principles apply to the debate over same-sex relationships? Some Christians argue that the biblical writers never imagined that two people of the same sex might seek to be united in a lifelong bond similar to marriage. To the extent that this is true, it remains an open question whether the *consistent* reference to male and female in discussion of the one-flesh union in Scripture should be interpreted in *exclusive* terms. In order to answer that question, we must inquire into the moral logic that shapes the Bible's discussion of one-flesh unions, just as Christians in the

---

25. See the fuller documentation in texts such as Willard M. Swartley, *Slavery, Sabbath, War, and Women: Case Issues in Biblical Interpretation*, The Conrad Grebel Lectures 1982 (Scottdale, PA: Herald Press, 1983); Jack Bartlett Rogers, *Jesus, the Bible, and Homosexuality : Explode the Myths, Heal the Church* (Louisville: Westminster John Knox, 2006), pp. 18-25.

abolitionist debate had to reread the Bible's texts on slavery in order to discern the deeper and more basic principles at work there. This is in keeping with one of the overall theses of this book: that is, that the commands and prohibitions of Scripture must be understood in light of their underlying forms of moral logic. So the question must be put in a more focused way: Is there anything inherent in the moral logic that shapes the Bible's discussion of one-flesh unions that not only *assumes* but also *requires* that such unions take place only between a male and a female?

Here again, the debate is joined. Traditionalists often appeal to the complementarity of the genders as an essential component of the one-flesh union. Yet we have already encountered the problems with this argument. We have already seen that there is no reference to a physical or biological understanding of gender complementarity either in the Genesis account or in any of the other "one-flesh" passages. We have also observed that any concern with procreation is completely absent from the texts dealing with "one flesh," eliminating that way of understanding gender complementarity as a window into the meaning of one-flesh unions. It is true that the text from Ephesians 5 assumes a patriarchal frame of reference: the husband is the "head" of the wife, and this might be construed as a form of gender complementarity that is intrinsic to the one-flesh union. Yet here also I have suggested that this imagery is driven more by pragmatic than essentialist concerns, and that the wider biblical vision portrays a movement away from patriarchy and toward a more egalitarian vision.[26] In all of these cases, then, there is reason to doubt that gender complementarity, construed in the sense of either biological differences, procreation, or patriarchy, represents an essential characteristic of one-flesh unions that would necessarily exclude same-sex unions.

Moreover, there are some arguments that might suggest that same-sex unions could be understood as one-flesh unions. The first and most important of these focuses on the link between kinship and one-flesh unions. As I have already observed, the language of "one flesh" is the language of kinship. When the man meets the woman in Genesis 2:23, he declares, "This at last is bone of my bones and flesh of my flesh." In Genesis 29:14, Laban recognizes his kinship bond to Jacob, and says, "Surely you are my bone and my flesh!" In 2 Samuel 5:1, as the tribes of Israel move to make David their king, they declare to him, "Look, we are your bone and flesh" (similar examples can be found in Judg. 9:2; 2 Sam. 19:12f.; and 1 Chron.

---

26. See chapter 4 of this volume.

11:1). In all these cases, gender distinctions play no role; the focus is entirely on kinship, shared culture, experience, and identity — the same focus that I argued is present in Genesis 2. Furthermore, the use of the word "cling," used in Genesis 2:24 to describe the relationship of the man and the woman, does not carry sexual connotations in any other usage, but reflects the desire for association and connection that is characteristic of kinship.

To the extent that kinship marks the heart of the one-flesh union (and I have argued that it is a very important element in that union), one cannot exclude other unions that involve long-term commitments to shared life from being considered under this rubric. However, our discussion has also made clear that kinship is not the only form of moral logic underlying Scripture's treatment of one-flesh unions. Indeed, I have observed that no other kinship relationship in Scripture has the permanence required of the one-flesh union described between male and female. Kinship is part of Scripture's one-flesh union, but it is not the totality of what Scripture means when it speaks of "one flesh."

Here is where our discussion of 1 Corinthians 6 helps to shed further light. This text makes a clear and explicit connection between sexual union and becoming "one flesh." This same sense of intimacy is reflected in the observation made in Genesis 2:25, at the end of the narrative that describes the creation of woman: "And the man and his wife were both naked, and were not ashamed." The one-flesh union entails the giving and receiving of bodily love, a love that is intended by God to forge two people into a permanent shared life at the most intimate level. In the ancient world, such ongoing permanent relationships between persons of the same sex are never documented in the extant literature of the period. When the texts that actually describe same-sex erotic relationships are evaluated, these relationships in the period during which the New Testament was being written were always marked by differences in social rank and status, and they were always described as episodic rather than permanent.[27] They did not involve the mutual accountability described by Paul in 1 Corinthians 7:4: "For the wife does not have authority over her own body, but the husband does; likewise the husband does not have authority over his own body, but the wife does." Rather, they were consistently unilateral, with the subordinate partner serving the sexual needs of the dominant partner. Such relationships are inherently incapable of bearing the deep bodily communion

27. See the extended discussion in Martti Nissinen, *Homoeroticism in the Biblical World: A Historical Perspective* (Minneapolis: Fortress, 1998).

implicit in the language of "one flesh," and it is not surprising, therefore, that Scripture never even considers such relationships when speaking about becoming one flesh.

But what about loving, committed, long-term, mutual same-sex unions today? Are they inherently incapable of being considered under this rubric? What if such relationships are marked by the recognition of deep kinship obligations, the presence of mutual love, the cultivation of a deep bodily form of communion and self-giving, and the desire for a life of fruitfulness, hospitality, and service to the wider community? Does the fact that Scripture never countenances such relationships mean that they can never exist? Or is it the case that the sexual ethics of Scripture may have a wider applicability than their original scope and focus? Our exploration in this chapter suggests an opening for further dialogue about the meaning of the one-flesh union — and the place of same-sex unions in such an understanding. It suggests that same-sex committed unions might have a strong analogical similarity to heterosexual one-flesh unions, particularly when the underlying forms of moral logic are clearly considered. Obviously, this is not the last word from Scripture, because one flesh is not the only form of moral logic that Scripture brings to bear on sexuality and the moral life. But a reasonable case can be made, under this rubric, for a wider consideration of the kinds of intimate relationships that might fulfill the deepest intents of the divine purpose, which decreed, "It is not good that the man should be alone," and "The two shall become one flesh."

Such a position continues to affirm the vital connection between sexual intimacy and lifelong bonding. It thus affirms a powerful cross-cultural argument against sexual promiscuity of any kind. It continues to summon all Christians to a vision of committed love that reflects and draws on the covenant faithfulness of God. It continues to summon all Christians to ensure that what they say with their bodies fully expresses the deep commitments and values that shape their lives as a whole. It calls for holiness, self-restraint, and sacrificial love in the cultivation of one-flesh unions. Moreover, such a position continues to affirm that the normal experience of the vast majority of Christians not called to celibacy should be that the one-flesh union consists of one man and one woman in the bond of marriage. However, where Christians find the longings of their hearts and bodies directed toward those of the same sex, and where celibacy is clearly not God's calling, this position invites them to use the bodily language of love to nurture lifelong bonds of faithfulness and allegiance. It also invites these Christians to learn to love each other as Christ loved the church and gave himself for the life of the church. This is not always an easy path, for either gay or straight Christians. But it is the path that Scripture clearly marks out for sexual expression in the body of Christ.

Summing Up

- The context and overall language of Scripture suggests that the one-flesh bond spoken of in Genesis 2:24 is essentially a lifelong *kinship* bond.
- The prophetic tradition in the Old Testament deepens the Bible's understanding of this bond by speaking of God's faithfulness to Israel as a marriage bond, emphasizing grace and lifelong faithfulness.
- This emphasis on kinship and bonding is reflected in each New Testament text that refers back to Genesis 2:24.
- The biblical usage suggests that this emphasis on bonding ("one flesh") constitutes the essence of marriage, even where the procreative meaning of marriage cannot be fulfilled.
- This focus on the bonding implicit in becoming one flesh is the basis for the Bible's categorical rejection of all forms of sexual promiscuity. People are not to say with their bodies what they cannot or will not say with the whole of their lives.
- It is clear that Scripture *assumes* that this one-flesh bond only takes place between a man and a woman. Yet there is nothing inherent in the biblical usage that would necessarily exclude committed gay or lesbian unions from consideration as one-flesh unions, when the essential characteristics of one-flesh unions as kinship bonds are held clearly in view.
- Therefore, what is *normal* in the biblical witness may not necessarily be *normative* in different cultural settings that are not envisioned by the biblical writers.

6

Procreation

We come now to a form of moral logic that has been a central concern in the ethics of sex and marriage throughout much of the
church's history. For Saint Augustine, "the procreation of children belonged to the glory of marriage" from its very beginning.[1] Indeed, for Augustine and many other ancient theologians of the church, procreation
was not only the central purpose of marriage; it was the *only* God-
ordained reason for married people to have sexual relations at all. In this
understanding of sexuality, the will should reign supreme, and people
should have sexual relations only for the rationally directed purpose of
raising up children. Saint Ambrose, for example, rejects sexual intercourse
as immoral even between husband and wife while the wife is pregnant,
since such an act cannot be procreative.[2] The modern Roman Catholic
Church has softened this position, allowing married couples to intentionally plan for sexual intercourse during infertile periods with the intention
of avoiding conception. Yet the Catholic Church continues to teach that all
marriages, and all acts of sexual intercourse within marriage, must be
open to procreation; therefore, all forms of birth control, beyond simply

---

1. Augustine, *Concerning the City of God against the Pagans*, Penguin Classics (London:
Penguin Books, 2003), bk. XIV, chap. 21, p. 583.

2. Saint Ambrose writes: "God does the marvels of creation in the secret sanctuary of
the mother's womb, and you dare to desecrate it through passion! Either follow the example
of the beasts or fear God." *Expositio Evangelii secundum Lucam*, liber I, Migne *PL* 15, 1552 (as
cited by Bernard Häring, "The Inseparability of the Unitive-Procreative Functions of the
Marital Act," in Charles E. Curran and Richard A. McCormick, eds., *Dialogue about Catholic
Sexual Teaching*, Readings in Moral Theology, 8 [New York: Paulist Press, 1993], p. 154).

avoiding sex during fertile periods, are considered immoral. The reason is that the Catholic Church still conceives of procreation as the chief end or purpose of marriage. To engage in sex within marriage — while willfully refusing procreation — is to deny the essential purpose of both sex and marriage itself.

The Protestant church has taken a somewhat different view of the importance of procreation, but these differences from the Roman Catholic position did not appear until the twentieth century, when birth control began to be more effective and more widely used.[3] While recognizing that procreation is an important purpose of marriage, most Protestant Christians emphasize the importance of conjugal love and faithfulness as most basic to marriage. Because love and faithfulness are seen as most central to marriage, avoiding pregnancy through contraception is not regarded as inherently sinful or destructive of the purpose of marriage itself. In the Reformed tradition, marriage is often viewed essentially as *covenantal,* focusing on the promises that form the basis for lifelong communion. In the Lutheran and Anglican traditions, the focus shifts to *commonwealth,* understanding marriage as the most basic building block of human society.[4] But in almost all Protestant traditions, procreation no longer is understood to comprise the essence of marriage. Even among Protestants who want to keep procreation as part of the basic meaning of marriage, the unitive purpose of marriage, emphasizing conjugal love and faithfulness, is just as important as the procreative purpose of marriage. Therefore, in Protestant discussions, contraception is generally considered a practical matter of stewardship that does not inherently compromise the primary and essential purpose of marriage itself.[5] Despite this overall Protestant

3. The first clear and unambiguous public statement by Protestants allowing the use of contraception comes from the Anglican Church, stemming from the Lambeth Conference of 1930. Within a year of this statement, the Roman Catholic Church came out with its definitive statement opposing the use of contraception: Pope Pius XI's encyclical *Casti connubii.*

4. See John Witte, *From Sacrament to Contract: Marriage, Religion, and Law in the Western Tradition,* The Family, Religion, and Culture (Louisville: Westminster John Knox, 1997). Witte goes on to point out how, in many modern secular contexts, thinking about marriage has shifted to a focus on marriage as a *contract* between two individuals, where procreation plays no significant role at all.

5. The Eastern Orthodox position tends to focus on marriage as a *sacrament,* and is less systematic about the essential role of procreation. See Stanley S. Harakas, "Covenant Marriage: Reflections from an Eastern Orthodox Perspective," in John Witte and Eliza Ellison, eds., *Covenant Marriage in Comparative Perspective* (Grand Rapids: Eerdmans, 2005), pp. 92-123.

consensus on birth control, however, there remain differences, even among Protestants, regarding how procreation fits into an overall theology of marriage. I shall explore these differences later in this chapter.

Important as these debates regarding birth control may be, however, they are not this book's focus. Rather, its focus is on the procreative character of marriage that has become a major issue in today's debates about same-sex relationships — and the possibility of same-sex marriages. Some traditionalists argue that, because same-sex unions inherently lack procreative capacity, these unions cannot be considered marital unions (and thus same-sex sexual activity may not, under any circumstances, be accepted as morally legitimate). This challenge will shape the focus of this chapter, and I will need to explore what Scripture says about the relationship between procreation and marriage; I will also probe some differing emphases regarding procreation and marriage that emerge in different parts of the biblical witness. The goal is to explore the extent and way in which procreation shapes the moral logic undergirding what Scripture has to say about marriage — and sex within marriage. After exploring this biblical witness in more detail, I shall return to the question of same-sex unions and procreation.

The Procreation/Marriage Link

Everywhere in Scripture, marriage is presumed as the context in which children are to be brought into the world; conversely, the birth of children outside of married households is viewed negatively everywhere in Scripture.[6] But when we press further, and ask why this is so, the picture becomes more complicated. In our modern context we immediately tend to think of the rights of children. We assume that children should be born into intact households so that they can be adequately provided for. Although a concern for the welfare of children is present in Scripture in many places, this concern for the rights of children is not the primary reason Scripture itself uses to explain why children should be born into married households. Instead, the emphasis in the Old Testament falls on the *father's name:* one of the central purposes of children was to carry on their father's name. Therefore, children had to be born into a household whose

---

6. Even in the story of the birth of Jesus, Joseph is portrayed as a "righteous" man when he plans to dismiss his fiancée Mary quietly after he has learned that she has become pregnant before their marriage (Matt. 1:19).

name they could carry on. Closely related to this concern was the need for the orderly transmission of inheritance, particularly the land, which was normally passed on to sons, with the oldest son receiving a double portion (Deut. 21:17). Keeping procreation within married households ensured the orderly transmission of the land given by God through the coming generations. One of the central blessings promised in many places in the Old Testament is the hope of many descendants (see Gen. 15:5; Exod. 32:13; Deut. 1:8; 4:40; 30:19; 1 Sam. 22:51, etc.). Keeping sexual intercourse and childbirth within marriage ensured that the descendants would truly belong to the patriarch whose name they carried on and whose legacy they inherited.

This also helps to explain why brides must be virgins (e.g., Lev. 21:13; Deut. 22:14-21) in Scripture, and why adultery is consistently viewed as a great sin. In both cases, a woman who has sexual relations outside of marriage violates the father's or husband's rights. But even more troubling than this denigration of the father or husband is the danger that the children born within the patriarchal household may not actually be the children of the head of the household.[7] If not, then they cannot carry on the father's name or inherit the father's legacy. This importance of inheritance and carrying on the father's name is further underscored by one of the marital customs in the Old Testament that is strangest to us in the modern world: the practice of levirate marriage. In this practice, a childless wife whose husband dies is to marry her husband's brother, "so that his [the original husband's] name may not be blotted out of Israel" (Deut. 25:6). Indeed, this mandate to carry on the father's name is so important that, in the case of the story of Judah and Tamar (Gen. 38), Tamar is deemed "more righteous" than her father-in-law, Judah, because she acted according to the levirate obligations, even though, in doing so, she also acted deceptively as a prostitute and committed incest with her father-in-law (Lev. 18:15) because her father-in-law had failed to fulfill his obligations under the levirate marriage law. Here we get a fascinating glimpse into the ranking of different forms of moral logic. In this context, deceit, prostitution,

---

7. In the Old Testament, adultery always means having sex with another man's wife or fiancée. It is a violation of the rights of the husband or fiancé. For a married man to have sex with an unmarried woman is viewed in Scripture as immoral, but it is not considered adultery, since it is a violation of the rights and dignity of the unmarried woman's father, not her husband (cf. Exod. 22:16-17; Deut. 22:28-29). The adultery laws in the Old Testament do not give exclusive sexual rights to the wife over her husband, though Paul later affirms these mutual rights in 1 Cor. 7:4-5 (but Paul does not derive this injunction from adultery laws directly).

and incest all are pardonable offenses, because they are done in the pursuit of raising up children to carry on the name and receive the inheritance of the deceased husband.[8]

Yet it was not only husbands who were interested in the procreative aspect of marriage in the Old Testament. Wives also had an important stake in the bearing of children, especially male children. For a wife, children were the source of her security in old age, particularly if her husband should die. Male children were also status symbols for their mothers, conferring on them special dignity in the culture of the biblical world. This desire for children powerfully motivates wives in the biblical narratives. In the Judah-Tamar story, Tamar is driven both by a concern for her deceased husband but also by her own desire for progeny. Earlier in the Genesis narrative, when Sarai, the wife of Abram, is unable to conceive, she offers her slave girl to Abram as a concubine so that she can acquire children through her slave (Gen. 16:2). Here the urgency of procreation displaces the exclusivity of Sarai's one-flesh union with Abram (note a similar action by Rachel in Gen. 30). The biblical characters not only assume the importance of procreation within marriage; they are willing at times to sacrifice other values related to marriage so that they may achieve the goal of procreation. Indeed, if one looks overall at the Old Testament, we see a small, imperiled people, struggling to receive and then to hold on to their land and their identity, surrounded by powers much greater than themselves, forced into radical reliance on their God. It is not surprising that they longed to "be fruitful and multiply," that they understood their marriages to be directed particularly to this end, and that they were willing to make significant sacrifices and even to bend other moral principles in order to achieve that end.

Is Procreation the *Essence* of Marriage?

Accordingly, procreation in Scripture always assumes and requires the context of marriage. Despite the fact that our culture may not structure households in the same patriarchal way as we find in the Old Testament,

---

8. There are limits, however, beyond which the Bible does not condone the desire for procreation. The daughters of Lot make their father drunk and have sex with him as the only possible way for them to bear children in Gen. 19:31-38; but the text views this very negatively — as the origin of the corrupt Moabites and Ammonites.

and despite the fact that the need for procreation may not be felt so acutely today, there is no good reason to set aside the consistent assumption of Scripture that procreation belongs in the context of marriage. The good order of society and the care of children both suffer significantly when this value is lost. Hence we come to an important basic form of scriptural moral logic that applies across many cultures, times, and places: procreation belongs in the context of marriage.

But the inverse question is neither that explicit nor that clear: Does marriage always assume and require the purpose of procreation in order for marriage itself to be valid or to fulfill its purpose? Some argue that this is so, and they point to the procreative command found in Genesis 1:27-28: "So God created humankind in his image, in the image of God he created them; male and female he created them. God blessed them, and God said to them, 'Be fruitful and multiply. . . .'" Here the creation of humanity as male and female and the call to fruitfulness are directly linked with each other. However, though this fact may support the notion that procreation in Scripture always assumes and requires the context of marriage, it does not speak directly to whether marriage always assumes and requires the purpose of procreation. Indeed, several exegetical observations call into question whether Genesis 1 is directly asserting that the necessary purpose of marriage is procreation — without which marriage ceases to fulfill its divinely intended purpose.

First, the command to "be fruitful and multiply" is not given merely to the man and the woman. It is also given to the animals (Gen. 1:22), and is thus not a directive given uniquely to human marriage. This in itself calls into question whether the essence of marriage is in view here, or whether the focus should be more generally on the divine blessing given to the creation. This leads to a second observation: the words "be fruitful and multiply" are more properly understood as a *blessing* rather than as a *command*.[9] In fact, every usage of the phrase "be fruitful and multiply" in Scripture occurs in the context of divine blessing (see Gen. 8:17; 9:1, 7; 35:11; Lev. 26:9; Jer. 23:3; Ezek. 36:11). To use technical language, procreation in all these contexts is not spoken of as the *esse* (essence) of marriage, but rather as the *bene esse* (well-being) of marriage and of society as a whole. Scripture regularly speaks of a good marriage as one that has children, but marriage does not cease to exist in the absence of procreation, nor is a marriage

9. Note the language of blessing in Gen. 1:22 and 28. In both verses, the command "be fruitful and multiply" is preceded by the words, "God blessed them . . ."

without children always portrayed in a negative light. For example, in 1 Samuel 1, Hannah, one of the wives of Elkanah, is unable to bear children. Yet the text states that Elkanah gave to Hannah a double portion of the sacrificial offerings, "because he loved her, though the Lord had closed her womb" (1 Sam. 1:5). Clearly, the text intends to portray the marriage as exemplary even though it is barren.

As I have already noted in the preceding chapter on one-flesh unions, Genesis 2, which explores the one-flesh marital bond in detail, does not mention procreation at all. Here, if anywhere in Scripture, the essence of marriage is clearly in view — and procreation is never mentioned. The command to "be fruitful and multiply" is noticeably absent from this chapter, even though marriage is in central focus. Similarly, the most extended meditation on sexual love in the entire Old Testament, the Song of Songs, makes no mention of issues related to procreation at all, focusing entirely on the delights of physical love. If procreation is the essential purpose of sex and marriage, one is hard-pressed to explain its absence from this entire book of the Bible that is devoted to sex and marriage.

When we move to the New Testament, we find even more extended discussions of marriage that do not mention procreation at all — or that relativize its value. Jesus' prohibition of divorce, discussed in the preceding chapter, must be understood, at least in part, as forbidding husbands to divorce barren wives in the pursuit of descendants. In this context, and indeed throughout Scripture, childlessness is never a justifiable reason to dissolve a marriage. The covenantal obligations of love and loyalty alone are sufficient to constitute a permanent marriage, even if children are absent. Yet the "exception clauses" in Matthew 5:32 and 19:9 recognize that adultery — the violation of the unitive, or one-flesh, meaning of marriage — is sufficient grounds for divorce. With adultery, we are talking about something more essential about marriage than procreation.

In other contexts, Jesus also seems to limit the central importance of procreation. In his eschatological discourse, he says, "Woe to those who are pregnant and to those who are nursing infants in those days!" (Mark 13:17; cf. Luke 21:23; Matt. 24:19). Luke 23:29 expresses a similar sentiment: "For the days are surely coming when they will say, 'Blessed are the barren, and the wombs that never bore, and the breasts that never nursed.'" In the apocalyptic upheaval expected by the early church, procreation could be understood more as a burden than as a blessing. We should not too quickly discount the significance of this apocalyptic perspective. The New Testament church did not expect that its progeny would inhabit and fill the land for many generations. It did not understand itself any longer to be directed primarily by the mandate given in creation to "be fruitful and multiply; fill the earth and subdue it" (Gen. 1:28). Rather, that community's call was to "make disciples of all nations" (Matt. 28:19), even if that meant forgoing marriage and becoming "eunuchs for the sake of the kingdom of heaven" (Matt. 19:12).[10] Similarly — and even somewhat shockingly to us — Jesus, in Luke 18:29, promises a reward to those who have "left house or wife or brothers or parents or children for the sake of the kingdom of God." Paul insists that "the appointed time has grown short; from now on, let even those who have wives be as though they had none" (1 Cor. 7:29). Soon the resurrection would come, in which the joining of male and female would be no more (Matt. 22:30; Luke 20:35; Gal. 3:28). In this "interim" period, marriage continued to be valid, but procreation moved to the periphery of the meaning of life in general — and thus of marriage in particular.

We see this most clearly in Paul's discussion of marriage earlier in chapter 7 of 1 Corinthians. Here Paul is confronting some in the Corinthian church who are encouraging people to avoid marriage, or to avoid sex within marriage, probably claiming that they have already begun to participate in resurrection life, where "there is no longer male and female" (Gal. 3:28). In the most extended discussion of marriage in the New Testament, Paul rejects the complete avoidance of marriage by Christians, and he insists that those who cannot exercise self-control in celibacy should get married. But marriage, in this context, has as its purpose not the bearing of children but the exercise of mutual care and the avoidance of uncontrolled lust (1 Cor. 7:2-9). Here one might naturally expect Paul to argue quite differently, insisting that Christians must not avoid marriage but exercise their divine responsibility to raise up godly offspring (cf. Mal. 2:15). Yet we see none of this here. Marriage is still important, but the purpose of procreation plays no role in Paul's discussion of marriage. Rather, Paul focuses on mutual care and fellowship (as we saw in Gen. 2 and the Song of Songs) — as well as the need to control lust.

Even in the Pastoral Epistles, some of the most traditional discussions of marriage in the New Testament, procreation is important but not essential. The text inveighs against those who "forbid marriage and demand ab-

---

10. Note the contrast between the central value of procreation and the core value in Jesus' ministry, which is based instead on hearing the word of God, in Luke 11:27-28: "While he was saying this, a woman in the crowd raised her voice and said to him, 'Blessed is the womb that bore you and the breasts that nursed you!' [28]But he said, 'Blessed rather are those who hear the word of God and obey it!'"

stinence from foods, which God created to be received with thanksgiving by those who believe and know the truth" (1 Tim. 4:3). Careful provision is made for widows in the community (1 Tim. 5:3). But younger widows are denied inclusion in the list of those widows cared for by the community (v. 11), not because they should be bearing children but because they may later want to marry, violating their pledge of celibacy (v. 12). Instead, the younger widows are encouraged to marry and bear children (v. 14), reflecting a high but scarcely essential view of the relationship between procreation and marriage. Similarly, the household codes found in various places in the New Testament and other early Christian literature provide instructions to parents and children, thereby assuming procreation as one of the meanings of marriage (e.g., Eph. 5:21-33; Col. 3:18–4:1; Titus 2:1-10). But in all the instructions about the husband-wife relationship in these codes, we never see any discussion of procreation at all. The focus is entirely on the quality of the relationship between husband and wife, particularly in Ephesians 5, where the husband-wife relationship is compared to the relationship between Christ and the church — a relationship that is never spoken of as procreative in Scripture.

The moral logic of the Bible is thus fairly clear on this subject; procreation is an important purpose of marriage, and marriage is the sole context where procreation should happen, but marriage has something more than procreation as its essential reason for being. When we consider some of the most extensive discussions of marriage in Scripture, including Genesis 2, Song of Songs, Ephesians 5:21-33, and 1 Corinthians 7, procreation is entirely absent from the discussion, and the focus falls on kinship, sharing, mutual support, self-control, and intimacy. And nowhere in Scripture is the absence of children a justification for dissolving the marriage bond itself.

Of course, the modern development of contraception has complicated this picture for us today. It is now possible, as it never was in the biblical world, to choose to engage in a regular sexual relationship within marriage (or outside of marriage) without ever having to deal with pregnancy and childbirth. Sex no longer unavoidably includes the possibility of procreation. Thus we are able to distinguish and separate the unitive from the procreative meanings of marriage in a way that was not possible until the twentieth century. According to Roman Catholic thought, this path opened up by medical technology represents a dangerous temptation that may ultimately lead to the destruction of marriage as God intended it. Most Protestant theologians also warn against wrong motives that may use contraception in the pursuit of an overly self-centered marriage. For example, Protestant ethicist Kathryn Blanchard urges caution in the wholesale and uncritical Christian use of contraception within marriage.[11] For her, the question is not whether Christians *should* use contraception, but the *reasons* they choose for doing so. She calls for a recovery of the deeply biblical notion, reaffirmed by both John Calvin and Karl Barth, that children are a gift from God (Ps. 127:3). For Christians, decisions about whether or not to bear children — and how many children to bear — should be driven not merely by utilitarian economic and "lifestyle" considerations, but by a deep discernment of the gifts that God offers and how they are best received. To say that procreation is not essential to marriage is not to say that it is irrelevant to marriage, or that it is merely another consumer-oriented "option" for married couples, despite some currents to that effect in modern society. Yet, within this framework, most Protestants stop short of claiming that all couples capable of bearing children are required or expected by God to do so.

Moreover, the whole church — both Catholic and Protestant — is united in its affirmation that the inability to bear children, either through advanced age or through physical limitation, cannot be used as a reason to forbid marriage between a man and a woman. Here again, the overall pattern we saw in Scripture applies: the unitive purpose of marriage (i.e., conjugal love and faithfulness) is sufficient, not just to preserve but also to establish a marital bond, even when the procreative purpose of marriage cannot or should not be fulfilled. In this clear sense, the unitive purpose of marriage is primary, and the procreative purpose is secondary. The unitive purpose is essential, because, without it, marriage cannot exist; the procreative purpose is important, but not essential, because marriage can exist without fulfilling it.

Implications for the Debate over
Gay and Lesbian Relationships and Marriage

All of this has clear and important implications for the debate over gay and lesbian unions and the related issues of sexual ethics. In Roman Catholic thought, opposition to homosexuality and gay or lesbian marriages flows directly from Catholic teaching that procreation is the essence of marriage.

---

11. See Kathryn D. Blanchard, "The Gift of Contraception: Calvin, Barth, and a Lost Protestant Conversation," *Journal of the Society of Christian Ethics* 27, no. 1 (2007): 233ff.

Roman Catholic teaching argues that homosexual activity, in addition to violating divinely intended gender complementarity, is not

> able to transmit life; and so it thwarts the call to a life of that form of self-giving which the Gospel says is the essence of Christian living. This does not mean that homosexual persons are not often generous and giving of themselves; but when they engage in homosexual activity they confirm within themselves a disordered sexual inclination which is essentially self-indulgent.[12]

In other words, because same-sex relations are unable to transmit life, the inclination to engage in these activities is "essentially self-indulgent." Such an inclination serves the desires of the self rather than the purposes of God. But this argument only makes sense if one also rejects the use of any form of contraception. By the same logic that shapes this argument against homosexual relations, it would also be true that married couples who have sex while the woman takes a birth-control pill also are avoiding precisely the same "form of self-giving" that is avoided in same-sex relations. Because these forms of sexual activity are not "able to transmit life" due to consciously chosen contraception, they must also be considered "essentially self-indulgent." The same argument would apply to other forms of heterosexual intimacy, such as mutual masturbation. This may make sense within the broader assumptions of Catholic social teaching on contraception, even though a significant number of Catholics do not accept the church's prohibition of birth control in their own lives or work.[13]

But even in the context of this conservative form of Catholic social teaching — opposed to both homosexual relations and to artificial forms of contraception — one must wonder about coherence and consistency. Indeed, one might just as readily argue that *any* inclination to engage in sex

---

12. "Pastoral Care of Homosexual Persons (1986)," Congregation for the Doctrine of Faith, reprinted in Curran and McCormick, *Dialogue about Catholic Sexual Teaching*, pp. 300-301.

13. According to a 2005 survey reported by the Religion News Service, 87.5 percent of 327 self-described Catholic physicians said that they would "prescribe birth control to any adult patients that request them and for whom they are medically appropriate": http://www.encyclopedia.com/doc/1G1-132420289.html. A PBS report concluded that "by 1970, two-thirds of all Catholic women and three-quarters of those under 30 were using the Pill and other birth control methods banned by the Church": http://www.pbs.org/wgbh/amex/pill/peopleevents/e_humvit.html.

while even attempting or hoping to avoid procreation represents a self-indulgent expression of sexual desire. The Catholic argument thus assumes that the only legitimate purpose of sex is procreation. Recent Catholic sexual teaching has softened this stance a bit, so that sexual relations must be "open to procreation," even though it may be lawful for married partners to engage in sex without intentionally seeking procreation. Yet one wonders whether this softened stance is compatible with the rejection of same-sex relationships in the quote above. Indeed, given the argument above, any act of heterosexual intercourse could be construed as immoral, precisely to the extent to which the partners hope to use even natural means to avoid bearing children and thus to avoid fulfilling the purpose for which God has created sex in the first place. If the purpose of sex is simply procreation, then any form of sexual intercourse that does not yield in procreation is deficient, and any attempts to have sex that are directed to such a deficient goal are self-indulgent and thus immoral, even if they use "natural" means. This is the older Catholic position, but the modern attempts of the Roman Catholic Church to soften that position do not square with the logic used by the same church to condemn homosexual relations.[14]

But the exploration of Scripture in this chapter exposes a deeper problem with this approach. Roman Catholic social teaching assumes that the central and essential purpose of marriage is procreation, a conclusion that the biblical texts themselves simply do not confirm. Instead, the study of texts in this chapter leads to the conclusion that the unitive purpose of marriage (i.e., conjugal love and faithfulness) is essential, and the procreative purpose of marriage, while important, is not essential in the same way to marriage itself. If this is true, one cannot say that either the inability to procreate or the avoidance of procreation necessarily represents a denial of the essential purpose of sex or marriage itself. Most Protestant ethicists, and many Catholics as well, recognize that sexual relations exercise a powerful and important role in bonding people to each other, quite apart from their reproductive function, and that this unitive meaning of sexuality is not "self-indulgent"; rather, it is an entirely appropriate and God-given aspect of human sexuality.[15] If this is true for heterosexual couples, it raises the question of whether it should also be true for same-sex unions.

14. Recall Ambrose's rejection of sex during pregnancy; see note 2 above.
15. See a careful and comprehensive Protestant critique of the Augustinian position that sex is only for procreation in Gilbert Meilaender, *The Way That Leads There: Augustinian Reflections on the Christian Life* (Grand Rapids: Eerdmans, 2006), pp. 117-41.

Procreation and Gender Complementarity

These considerations must inform how we evaluate the significance of procreation as a means of defining gender complementarity in Scripture. Scripture clearly assumes what continues to be essentially true (despite many medical options and alternatives today): that the only way children come into the world is through the coming together of sperm from a human male and an egg from a human female. Indeed, it may be that part of Paul's claim that same-sex relations are "contrary to nature" in Romans 1 is based on this procreative relationship of male and female, a relationship that is absent in same-sex relations. (I will explore this question in more detail in chapter 11 below, which deals with nature and natural law.)

Nevertheless, the fact that procreation does not play, strictly speaking, an essential role in Scripture's discourse about marriage is important to consider and to ponder. The scriptural texts we have explored make it clear that the identities of husband and wife, male and female, are not based essentially or ultimately on their capacity to procreate. Not only is human life more than procreation; maleness and femaleness are about more than procreation. Barren wives, celibate men and women, and even eunuchs have a place in God's kingdom. If this is true — that is, that neither marital identity nor gender identity is *essentially* concerned with procreation — it raises the question about whether it is right for gay or lesbian marriagelike unions to be rejected simply because they are incapable of procreation. If my argument holds — that procreation is important but not essential to marriage and gender identity — then "gender complementarity," understood as procreative complementarity, may well be a *normal* part of one-flesh unions in Scripture, but the witness of Scripture as a whole suggests that it cannot be a *defining*, or essential, aspect of such unions. What is "normal" cannot simply be assumed to be "normative." Here again, when we press for greater precision about what we mean by gender complementarity, the shape of the discussion shifts significantly.

The Social Argument

To recapitulate the central argument of this chapter: if one accepts in any cases the possibility of intentional contraception in Christian marriage, it means that the unitive meaning of sexual relations is entirely sufficient to sanction sexual intercourse within marriage, quite apart from the purpose of procreation. To the extent that this is true, it is impossible to sustain the argument that forms the heart of Roman Catholic social teaching, that homosexual acts are inherently self-indulgent because they cannot be procreative.[16] But this is not the end of the debate. There is another form of the procreation argument that is often implicit in Protestant arguments about homosexuality and gay or lesbian marriages. This argument focuses on the place of marriage in society as a whole. It underlies the often-heard claim that gay or lesbian marriages "undermine the meaning of marriage itself."[17] In our modern context, this argument usually focuses on the rights and needs of children and goes something like this: Because God intends for procreation always to take place in the context of heterosexual marriage, and because society should ensure the safety and well-being of children, therefore heterosexual marriage should occupy a unique place in society as a whole. Laws supporting marriage exist for this purpose. Therefore, gay or lesbian marriages should not be granted the same societal protections and privileges as heterosexual marriages, because they are inherently incapable of procreation.

This argument recognizes and affirms some principles with which the biblical texts studied in this chapter would agree. Scripture clearly teaches that God intends for procreation to take place within marriage rather than outside of marriage. Moreover, it is impossible for same-sex couples to be procreative — without help from beyond the couple itself. Insofar as heterosexual marriage exists for the purpose of procreation, therefore, it deserves special support from any society that seeks to conduct itself according to the will of God. This much seems supported by the exploration in this chapter.

But the key phrase in the previous paragraph is: "Insofar as heterosexual marriage exists for the purpose of procreation. . . ." Our study in the previous chapters and this one suggests that heterosexual marriage does not exist solely or even essentially for the purpose of procreation. Marriage exists as a context where deep bodily joy is received, given, and celebrated as a gift (Song of Songs). It is a school of Christian living and a means of grace, as two persons learn to live with each other and to deepen their love

16. In chapter 2 above, I have addressed the other claim cited in Catholic social teaching: that same-sex relationships violate a form of gender complementarity that reflects "the inner unity of the creator."

17. See, e.g., the 2004 comments of then President George W. Bush, calling for a constitutional amendment defining marriage in the United States "as a union of a man and woman as husband and wife": http://usgovinfo.about.com/od/rightsandfreedoms/a/bushvgays.htm.

over the long haul, discovering more deeply the love and faithfulness of God in their relationship with each other (Eph. 5). It exists as a graceful means of preventing promiscuity and strengthening sexual self-control (1 Cor. 7). It provides a more diversified and stable economic base for society, where differentiation of labor and responsibilities allow more focused productivity of individuals in society as a whole (Eccles. 4:9-12). These diverse benefits of marriage to society as a whole are reflected in the diverse ways in which American society provides particular support for the institution of marriage. Indeed, many of the benefits American law provides to married couples have little to do with procreation: tax benefits, hospital visitation rights, inheritance rights, decision-making rights in the case of incapacity, and so on.[18]

Thus, even though society has a clear interest in the procreative character of marriage, and should, according to Scripture, provide particular support and encouragement to couples in their raising of children, this procreative interest is not the only concern, and certainly not the exclusive concern society has in fostering stable marriages. In fact, society is strengthened in a wide range of ways by encouraging its members to enter into stable, long-term, committed relationships, both heterosexual and same-sex unions, regardless of whether those unions produce children or not. Health rates improve; reported happiness increases; and economic stability is strengthened.[19] Given these realities, it seems that society has little to fear from broadening the number or type of lifelong unions supported and encouraged by law. In keeping with the results of our study up to this point, if such unions are to fulfill the biblical vision for one-flesh unions, they should be exclusive, lifelong, intimate, loving, and fruitful in the broad sense of the word. But they need not necessarily bring children into the world, or even be capable of bringing children into the world; not even all heterosexual marriages have this capability. One can affirm wholeheartedly the importance of procreation within marriage and still support some marriages, both heterosexual and same-sex, that contribute in other recognizable ways to the good of society as a whole, and that embody and exemplify the faithful love of God for the whole creation.

But some may still object that same-sex unions cannot provide appro-

18. For more extensive discussion, see William Stacy Johnson, *A Time to Embrace: Same-Gender Relationships in Religion, Law, and Politics* (Grand Rapids: Eerdmans, 2006) pp. 159ff.

19. For more extensive discussion, see David G. Myers and Letha Scanzoni, *What God Has Joined Together: A Christian Case for Gay Marriage* (San Francisco: HarperSanFrancisco, 2005).

priate parenting for children, and thus same-sex unions should not be given the societal benefits that are given to marriages that are capable of providing such parental oversight. Yet we should be cautious, first of all, in assuming that parenting strategies in the modern world resemble those of the biblical world. Parenting patterns differ markedly in different cultures and different epochs. It is also self-evidently true in many cultures that when more than one adult assists in parenting, the flourishing of children improves. But what about gay or lesbian parents in particular? Though research into parenting in same-sex households is still in its early stages, some conclusions already seem clear. David Myers and Letha Scanzoni cite the conclusions of a 2004 briefing paper for the American Psychological Association, which affirms that children raised by gay or lesbian parents are no more likely to become gay or lesbian themselves than others in the general population. Moreover, the paper concludes, "not a single study has found children of lesbian or gay parents to be disadvantaged in any significant respect relative to children of heterosexual parents."[20] Finally, one might also note that an important way in which many same-sex couples acquire children is through adoption, providing vital support and care for those children most gravely in need of a loving home.

It is difficult to see, therefore, how the biblical treatment of the relationship between procreation, sexuality, and marriage precludes gay unions from consideration as marital unions. As I have already observed, this is not the only argument in the debate over homosexuality and gay marriage. But the conclusion on this question seems clear: Unless one stands with the Roman Catholic Church (against the witness of Scripture) in insisting that procreation is the essential purpose for sexual relations in marriage (and therefore that contraception is always morally wrong), it is difficult to use procreation as an argument to bar gays and lesbians from marriage or marriagelike unions without also barring from marriage those heterosexual couples who are incapable of bearing children. If God still loves and blesses childless heterosexual couples, we cannot say that God refuses to love and bless gay and lesbian couples simply because they cannot bear children. And if society still has good reasons for encouraging the lifelong bonds of heterosexual couples, even when they cannot or do not bear children, we can say that society has good reason to encourage such lifelong bonds among gay and lesbian couples as well.

20. Charlotte J. Peterson, "Lesbian and Gay Parents and Their Children: Summary of Research Findings," cited in Myers and Scanzoni, *What God Has Joined Together*, p. 122.

Summing Up

- In contrast to the Roman Catholic Church, whose official teaching states that procreation defines the essential purpose of marriage, most Protestant churches emphasize instead that the unitive meaning of marriage defines its essence.
- Therefore, though procreation always assumes and requires the context of marriage in Christian ethics, marriage does not require procreation in order to be valid, and the inability to bear children is never a sufficient reason to dissolve a marriage.
- Society's interest in supporting marriage is based in part on its desire to provide for the care of children, but this does not by any means make up the only reason why marriage receives legal benefits in modern societies. Society benefits in a wide variety of ways when people live together in long-term committed unions.
- If this is true, then the lack of procreative capacity cannot of itself be a sufficient reason to deny the legitimacy of stable gay or lesbian marriages or marriagelike relationships.

7

Celibacy

A comprehensive view of what the Bible has to say about marriage and sexuality will not be complete without an exploration of when and why the Bible envisions people saying no to marriage and/or sex within marriage. Hence, my focus in this chapter is on celibacy, the decision to abstain from marriage, or, in some cases, the decision of married couples to refrain from sexual intercourse — even though marriage and sex within marriage are permitted and affirmed by the biblical witness. Why does the Bible, which clearly affirms marriage and procreation, also at times affirm the avoidance of marriage or sex within marriage? This question about the meaning of celibacy is also relevant to the debate about gay unions and homosexuality. Traditionalists argue that Scripture offers no inalienable right to marriage; they contend that those who cannot with integrity enter into heterosexual marriage are called by God to a life of chastity in celibacy. Revisionists counter that celibacy is a gift that is not offered to all, and thus that gay and lesbian unions or same-sex marriages provide an appropriate context for the chaste expression of sexuality in committed relationships for those gays and lesbians who are not called to celibacy. I will not settle this debate in this chapter. However, I will focus here on what Scripture says about celibacy, why Scripture envisions some choosing a life of celibacy, and how the answers to these questions may impact the way we think about whether all gays and lesbians who cannot change their sexual orientation are *necessarily* called to a life of celibacy.

The Old Testament and Celibacy

A small number of Old Testament passages envision the occasional avoidance of sexual intercourse, even by married couples. In Exodus 19:15, Moses prepares the people to meet God at Mount Sinai, and he tells them, "Do not go near a woman." Meeting God face-to-face and recent sexual intercourse are, in some way, incompatible. In 1 Samuel 21:1-6, David and the men with him are permitted by the priest Ahimelech to eat the "bread of the Presence," special bread offered to God, but only if "they have kept themselves from women" (v. 4). Again, sex and holiness stand in some tension. Abstinence from sex sometimes accompanied the practice of "holy war" (e.g., 2 Sam. 11:11). We see a similar tension between sex and holiness in the book of Leviticus, which outlines a number of forms of ritual impurity related to sexual intercourse and emissions of semen or menstrual flow (Lev. 15); but the purification processes are fairly simple. The book of Ezekiel places tighter restrictions on whom a priest may marry than the strictures applying to the rest of Israel: it forbids priestly marriages to widows of nonpriests, divorced women, or anyone else who is not an Israelite virgin (Ezek. 44:22). In all these cases, marriage is never forbidden or even discouraged, but sex within marriage is viewed as potentially in conflict with an encounter with the holy God, and thus it requires careful regulation. Any close proximity of sexual relations with worship in the temple or tabernacle is generally discouraged, perhaps partly to distance Israel from the fertility cults of surrounding nations. But nowhere in the Old Testament is the avoidance of marriage altogether envisioned as a possible religious duty or vocation. Sex within marriage is avoided for brief periods, at most, when one is to encounter holiness most directly. But celibacy — in the sense of a lifelong commitment to singleness — does not appear in the Old Testament.

The New Testament and Celibacy

In the New Testament, however, the picture changes. Jesus himself remained unmarried throughout his life. In Matthew 19:12 he speaks positively of some who "have made themselves eunuchs for the sake of the kingdom of heaven." Similarly, he declares in Luke 18:29-30, "Truly I tell you, there is no one who has left house or wife or brothers or parents or children, for the sake of the kingdom of God, who will not get back very much more in this age, and in the age to come eternal life." In other words,

Jesus models in his own ministry an urgent and comprehensive divine call that displaces the normal responsibilities of marriage and family, commending this way of life to at least some of his followers as well.

Paul takes up the same question in more detail in 1 Corinthians 7, addressing one of the slogans of the Corinthians: "It is well for a man not to touch a woman" (7:1). Paul responds in a complex and nuanced fashion, instructing married couples not to avoid sexual relations for extended periods, and to avoid divorce if at all possible (7:2-7, 10-16). Despite this apparent endorsement of marriage, however, Paul also invites (but does not require) single people to follow his example and remain unmarried (v. 8), both "in view of the impending crisis" (v. 26), and so that they may be more single-hearted in their devotion to the Lord (vv. 32-35). Apparently, Jesus' commendation of those who "have made themselves eunuchs for the sake of the kingdom of heaven" (Matt. 19:12) was a source of some controversy in the early church, and some of this controversy is reflected in the problems Paul addresses in 1 Corinthians 7. Reflecting somewhat similar controversies, 1 Timothy 4:3 speaks against those who "forbid marriage and demand abstinence from foods." Likewise, Hebrews 13:4 urges: "Let marriage be held in honor by all," suggesting perhaps that some early Christian circles may have looked on marriage with some suspicion — or even disdain.

In order to understand what the New Testament says about celibacy, we must explore these controversies in more detail. Therefore, this chapter will seek to understand the character and focus of Jesus' teaching on marriage and celibacy, and to discern why that teaching became controversial in the early church. It is only when we read these texts in their original contexts that we can see accurately the forms of moral logic that give shape to their commands and prohibitions, and thus accurately and helpfully apply them to contemporary life.

Stoic-Cynic Debates on Marriage

These New Testament controversies must be understood in part against the backdrop of a wider discussion of marriage in the Hellenistic world, particularly an ongoing debate between two philosophical schools, the Stoics and the Cynics, regarding the place of marriage in society as a whole and the relative importance of getting married.[1] In this context, the pri-

1. Much of the following discussion is drawn from Will Deming, *Paul on Marriage and*

mary concern in the debate surrounding marriage focused not so much on sexual activity but on the responsibilities involved in marriage, child-rearing, and household management. The Stoics held to the view that humans were by nature political beings, and because the household was understood as the basic and foundational building block of the city-state, it was the responsibility of all men to marry and to take their part in building the wider social order of the world.[2] Some Stoics recognized, however, that there might be specific cases where other duties and responsibilities outweighed this responsibility to marry — at least for some people. Marriage thus found its place in society as an important civic responsibility that most people, under most circumstances, were obliged to fulfill.

The Cynics, by contrast, emerged during a somewhat later period, when the city-state was in decline after the conquests of Alexander the Great, and the connections between the wider political world and individual households seemed much more distant and tenuous. The Cynics denied the importance of the Greek city-state; instead, they promoted a radical cosmopolitanism. Marriage in their view was a humanly constructed institution that did not in itself express a divine purpose implicit in nature. Instead, the basic responsibility faced by all people focused on individualism, self-sufficiency, and the pursuit of philosophy. The Cynic vision of freedom entailed specifically freedom *from* marriage and the responsibilities that marriage entailed.[3] Cynics believed that human life, devoted to the pursuit of philosophy, required free time — time that the responsibilities of marriage would too easily crowd out.

As these debates continued, various thinkers blended elements from both of these visions. Some affirmed the value of the single life in pursuit of philosophy as a special calling for some, while they commended marriage for others. But what is striking in this debate about marriage, which spanned approximately four centuries, is the lack of concern about sexual activity itself. The Stoic-Cynic debate on marriage focused almost entirely on the relative importance of the responsibilities of household management, compared to other responsibilities, including the call to the philosophical life. But one does not encounter any concern that sex itself is de-

---

Celibacy: The Hellenistic Background of 1 Corinthians 7, 2nd ed. (Grand Rapids: Eerdmans, 2004).

2. Cf. the preceding discussion of Aristotle's view of the relationship between households and the state in chapter 4 above.

3. Deming, *Paul on Marriage and Celibacy,* p. 57.

filing in these wider Hellenistic discussions. Indeed, both philosophical schools viewed the sex act as entirely natural, and though the Stoics in particular viewed excessive sexual desire as a problem, this concern did not extend to sexual intercourse within marriage itself. Stoics believed that the pleasure of sex should not be pursued apart from reason, but it could be enjoyed in its proper and natural place.[4] The entire Stoic-Cynic discussion concerning marriage operates at a highly pragmatic level, focusing on the relative importance of various responsibilities in the good life.

"Eunuchs for the Sake of the Kingdom of Heaven" (Matt. 19:12)

Given this wider context, it is entirely plausible to suggest that some early Christians may have heard the words of Jesus regarding "eunuchs for the sake of the kingdom of heaven" in terms of this Stoic-Cynic debate concerning marriage. Indeed, the context of these words in Matthew 19 suggests that these concerns and questions lie in the background. Jesus' commendation of "eunuchs for the sake of the kingdom of heaven" is preceded by his forbidding divorce for any reason except for sexual immorality (Matt. 19:9). In response, the disciples say, "If such is the case of a man with his wife, it is better not to marry" (Matt. 19:10). In other words, the disciples see Jesus' intensified prohibition of divorce as an infringement on human *freedom,* an ideal highly valued in the Cynic perspective. Marriage, in this Cynic view, is an intrusive and unnecessary entanglement. Therefore, the disciples suggest to Jesus that his prohibition of divorce tilts the bias toward the Cynics' negative view of the relative importance of marriage. One must forgo marriage for the higher calling, not of philosophy as the Cynics understood it, but rather for the higher calling of the kingdom of heaven. Jesus' response, however, would sound to many in the ancient world like a modified Stoic view: he allowed that, in some cases, the avoidance of marriage might well be appropriate. Yet Jesus makes it clear that the path of celibacy is not for all: "Not everyone can accept this teaching, but only those to whom it is given" (Matt. 19:11). This coheres with the modified Stoic vision that marriage is a general responsibility, unless cir-

---

4. See, for example, Seneca, *Epistles* 116: "For after I have issued my prohibitions against the desires, I shall still allow you to wish that you may do the same things fearlessly and with greater accuracy of judgment, and to feel even the pleasures more than before; and how can these pleasures help coming more readily to your call, if you are their lord rather than their slave."

cumstances make it unwise in certain cases. Yet it is also not difficult to sense in Jesus' words at least a modest commendation of those who may choose the path of being "eunuchs for the sake of the kingdom of heaven," not because of the inherent superiority of avoiding sex and marriage, but because of the sacrifice and devotion to God that this path requires — a sacrifice implicit in the use of the shocking word "eunuch" to describe those who forgo marriage for the sake of service to God.

The background of the Stoic-Cynic debates concerning marriage, as well as the specific unfolding of this story in Matthew 19, both suggest that Jesus' commendation of "eunuchs for the sake of the kingdom of heaven" arose not because of any negative view of sex itself, but rather out of pragmatic concerns related to Jesus' call to missionary proclamation. Jesus recognized that the demands of his own calling did not allow him to marry, and he also recognized, in this passage, that some of his followers might face similar demands, requiring them to forgo marriage as well. Yet in such cases Jesus promises not only an eternal reward but also benefits that are received in this life as well: "Truly I tell you, there is no one who has left house or wife or brothers or parents or children, for the sake of the kingdom of God, who will not get back very much more in this age, and in the age to come eternal life" (Luke 18:29-30). Therefore, even though marriage is commendable (the Stoic view), it may not be the appropriate path for everyone (the Stoic adaptation to the Cynic view), and the unmarried life may bring its own rich rewards (the Cynic view). But in all of this, there is not a hint of concern with the defiling nature of sex, the need to control lust, or debates about whether sexual relations compromise one's holiness. In other words, what we see here is not a form of sexual *asceticism,* in which the center of concern is the avoidance of sex; instead, we see a form of *celibacy,* where the focus falls on the avoidance of the responsibilities of marriage for pragmatic reasons.[5]

Celibacy and Marriage in 1 Corinthians 7

When we turn to Paul's discussion of marriage in 1 Corinthians 7, however, the picture becomes more complex. This is evident already in the Corinthian slogan that Paul quotes at the beginning of the chapter: "It is well for a

5. Of course, one may embrace a life of celibacy that is motivated by sexual asceticism, but celibacy does not inherently require this motive. Indeed, in most of the Stoic-Cynic debate regarding marriage, as in this passage from the Gospels, the motivations are pragmatic and have little to do with sexual asceticism.

man not to touch a woman" (7:1). Here the focus falls more on sexual contact than on marriage.[6] The next few verses make it clear that the Corinthians are interpreting this slogan in a way that discourages sexual relations, not only generally, but even *within marriage,* since Paul goes on to instruct married couples not to permanently refuse to have sexual relations with their spouses (7:3-5). This raises an important question: Does the focus in this slogan, "it is well for a man not to touch a woman," fall on avoiding the obligations and responsibilities of marriage in general, or on the need to avoid the potential defilement of sexual relations in particular?

Of course, these two emphases cannot always be completely separated, since sexual relations often result in pregnancy and the accompanying responsibilities and obligations of childrearing. In fact, there is some evidence that women in the Corinthian church were particularly attracted to this sex-free vision of marriage, precisely because it would free them from gender-related obligations and free them to a deeper spiritual freedom that included public prayer and prophesying (1 Cor. 11) and other "freedoms" that Paul interpreted as disruptive to the community in 1 Corinthians 14:34-35. Given the fact that Paul speaks in a particular way to women who are praying and prophesying in 1 Corinthians 11, it might also be the case that women were seeking to avoid sex in marriage in order to maintain the ritual purity required for such public religious acts.[7] Therefore, both practical and religious motivations for avoiding sex within marriage may have been at work among women in that community.

Given the larger frame of the Stoic-Cynic debates on marriage, however, there is no reason to restrict the interest in sex-free marriages to women alone. Men may also have been attracted to a form of marriage that entailed freedom from the traditional responsibilities of providing for an ever-growing family. Various articulations of the Cynic position in the ancient world underscore the attractiveness of such an option. Moreover, the obvious interest of the Corinthians in spiritual gifts (1 Cor. 1:7; 12:1; 14:1, 12) and their questions surrounding the resurrection of the body (1 Cor. 15:12-22) may suggest a "spiritualizing" aspect to the community's faith that ren-

---

6. The sexual meaning of the Greek verb is well attested (see *A Greek-English Lexicon of the New Testament and Other Early Christian Literature,* 3rd ed., ed. W. Bauer, F. W. Danker, W. F. Arndt, and F. W. Gingrich [Chicago: University of Chicago Press, 2000], *haptō,* §4), and is confirmed by the subsequent discussion, which focuses on whether married persons should avoid sexual relations.

7. For further exploration of this hypothesis, see Antoinette Clark Wire, *The Corinthian Women Prophets: A Reconstruction through Paul's Rhetoric* (Minneapolis: Fortress, 1990).

dered bodily activities such as sexual intercourse inherently suspect in their eyes, or perhaps irrelevant to authentic Christian existence.

All of these possible reasons may help to explain why the Corinthians might have been inclined to avoid marriage — or to avoid sex within marriage. But a closer look at 1 Corinthians 7 may provide a clearer and more direct sense, growing from Paul's words, regarding how Paul at least perceives the problem — as well as the solutions he proposes to address it.

Paul Addresses the Corinthians' Motivations for Avoiding Sex and Marriage

One of the motivations for avoiding marriage and/or sex within marriage that Paul seems to be concerned about is the desire for greater freedom. This longing for freedom is an essential foundation of the Cynic critique of marriage, and it is reflected in Paul's words in a variety of ways. Paul's insistence that husbands and wives exercise authority over each other's bodies (1 Cor. 7:3-4) may be an indirect way of restraining an excessive emphasis on freedom. This suggests that one of the Corinthians' motivations for avoiding sex and marriage was greater control and authority over their own bodies. This longing for freedom may also be reflected in Paul's words disallowing divorce within the Christian community (1 Cor. 7:8-16). It may well be that members of the community sought to disentangle themselves from marriages that they had entered before they became Christians. This problem gets quite a bit of attention in verses 12-15. Paul's language in verse 15 may also reflect this desire to avoid "enslavement." The Greek word used in the NRSV's translation "in such a case the brother or sister *is not bound*" could be more literally translated, "in such a case, the brother or sister is not *enslaved*."[8] Paul insists that, despite Jesus' prohibition of divorce, marriage is not a form of slavery and it should not be regarded as such by the Corinthians. All of this suggests that part of the motivation of the Corinthians — both men and women — for avoiding marriage and/or sex within marriage was a longing for freedom.

---

8. The Greek work *dedoulōtai* is not the normal word for being legally "bound." That word *(deō)* occurs several times in this text, for example, in vv. 27 and 39. But here Paul addresses an extreme case of abandonment by an unbelieving spouse, and he concedes in this case that marriage is not a form of slavery. It may be that the Corinthians were using this argument even more broadly than Paul uses it here (see further discussion in Deming, *Paul on Marriage and Celibacy*, pp. 145ff.).

That desire for freedom may also have had a more specific focus: freedom for devotion to prayer and spiritual things. Such devotion to prayer may have been viewed as competing with married life for the use of one's time (more time raising children meant less time to pray). But at a deeper level, some may have longed for freedom from sex so that they could be more holy in their devotion to prayer. In this view, sex and prayer stand at least in some tension with each other. As we have seen, a similar view holding sex and holiness in some tension is also echoed in a number of Old Testament texts. Paul seems to accept something like that view, at least to some extent, in 1 Corinthians 7:5: "Do not deprive one another except perhaps by agreement for a set time, to devote yourselves to prayer, and then come together again, so that Satan may not tempt you because of your lack of self-control." Here Paul seems to grant some credence to the notion that devotion to prayer might be a legitimate reason to avoid sexual relations. His only concern is that such disciplines in prayer should be temporary, rather than permanent, because of the danger of the loss of self-control. But these instructions only make sense if the desire for prayer was already regarded by the Corinthians as standing in some tension with marriage and sex. It may well be that for Paul and the Corinthians, a temporary avoidance of sex was regarded as similar to the Jewish practice of fasting. Both seem to be viewed as disciplines related to an intensified prayer life for a particular period of time. In this case, Paul's only argument with the Corinthians seems to be whether this practice should be permanent or temporary for married couples.

This concern about holiness leads to yet another concern that may have been on the minds of at least some of the Corinthians when they proposed avoiding marriage and sex within marriage: the avoidance of defilement or pollution, particularly defilement that came about via marriages to unbelievers. Paul addresses this problem explicitly in 1 Corinthians 7:10-16, where he reaffirms Jesus' command not to divorce. After a brief summary of that prohibition in verses 10-11, Paul spends more time speaking of the applicability of this command in the case of mixed marriages between a believer and an unbeliever. Paul refuses to permit divorce in these cases, if the unbelieving partner consents to continue in the marriage. He gives his rationale in verse 14: "For the unbelieving husband is made holy through his wife, and the unbelieving wife is made holy through her husband. Otherwise, your children would be unclean, but as it is, they are holy." Paul apparently reverses the more commonly assumed direction of the "stream of contagion," by which holy things are defiled through contact with common things. In this case, Paul says, the stream flows in the other direction: the holiness of the believing partner makes the unbelieving partner holy. Most commentators do not interpret this "holiness" to mean saving grace, since the salvation of the partner is only considered a possibility in verse 16. Rather, the problem that he seems to be addressing is the potential defilement of the believing partner. Should believing spouses get out of marriages to unbelievers so that they can remain holy? Paul's answer is clear: Believing spouses will not be defiled by their unbelieving partners; in fact, they may "sanctify" their nonbelieving spouses, and may even "save" them (1 Cor. 7:16): "Wife, for all you know, you might save your husband. Husband, for all you know, you might save your wife." All this discussion makes sense in a context in which the Corinthians were seeking to remove themselves from marriages to unbelievers in order to maintain holiness.

It is difficult to be precise in determining the relative weight of these different motivations, but the overall thrust of Paul's rhetoric seems fairly clear. He understands the Corinthians' desire to avoid sex and marriage to be motivated by three distinct but interrelated concerns: (1) the desire for greater freedom; (2) the longing to enter more deeply into holiness and prayer; and (3) a concern about avoiding the perceived pollution of a marriage to an unbeliever.

Paul's Response to the Corinthians' Concerns

Some of Paul's response to these concerns is already evident in the discussion to this point. Paul insists that avoidance of sex within marriage should only be temporary and by mutual consent, and that both husbands and wives have rights over the bodies of the other (a striking articulation of mutuality not commonly seen in the ancient world). He forbids divorce, and he urges believers to remain in marriages with consenting unbelievers, assuring them that they will not be defiled by these marriages, but that their spouses will be sanctified — and may even be saved.

But Paul's concern in 1 Corinthians 7 is not simply to answer questions; it is also to question the answers that the Corinthians take for granted.[9] We do not get a full picture of Paul's understanding of celibacy simply by reconstructing the concerns of the Corinthians; we also have to

---

9. See Wire, *The Corinthian Women Prophets*, p. 80.

look further at what Paul himself says about marriage, singleness, and sexuality in this chapter. One of the major issues that Paul injects into the conversation is his concern about sexual immorality *(porneia)* and the need for self-control *(enkrateia)* to fight against sexual immorality. Paul has already devoted extensive attention to this subject in 1 Corintians 5 and 6, where he addresses both the problem of incest and sex with prostitutes. The same concerns with immorality and self-control surface in chapter 7. It is because of the temptation to sexual immorality that people should be married (7:2, 9), and the same concern underlies Paul's warning that married couples should not refuse each other sexually for extended periods of time (7:5). We see the same concern with both self-control and sexual immorality elsewhere in Paul's writings, for example, in 1 Thessalonians 4:3-8.

This concern with sexual immorality and self-control brings to focus an issue that arises to some extent in the larger Stoic-Cynic debates about marriage, but emerges with much greater force in both Jewish and Christian contexts. In these Jewish and Christian settings we can see a heightened concern, not only with the responsibilities associated with sex and marriage (the dominant theme in the Stoic-Cynic debates over marriage) but also with the immorality of sex outside of marriage (a dominant theme in early Jewish and Christian texts on sexuality and marriage). For Paul, one of the central purposes of marriage is that it can channel sexual energy constructively and thus help people avoid sexual immorality. "It is better to marry than to be aflame with passion," he says in 1 Corinthians 7:9. Sexual immorality is a much higher-priority issue for Paul than for the Cynic and Stoic debates on marriage.[10]

In fact, Paul's statement is sometimes seen as a somewhat grim and repressed understanding of marriage merely as an outlet for uncontrollable sexual passions. Indeed, Dale Martin argues that Paul believed that the truly fulfilled human life is one in which all sexual desire is simply extinguished. He argues that, for Paul, marriage is simply a second-best mechanism for the extirpation of desire.[11] Will Deming counters this argument by noting that, for Paul, the goal was not the *absence* of desire but the ability to restrain an *excess* of desire — a problem addressed in other Stoic lit-

10. Yet Stoics also speak extensively about the need for self-control, even though their writings on marriage do not portray it as a means to greater self-control.

11. See Dale Martin, "Paul without Passion: On Paul's Rejection of Desire in Sex and Marriage," in Martin, *Sex and the Single Savior: Gender and Sexuality in Biblical Interpretation* (Louisville: Westminster John Knox, 2006), pp. 65-76.

erature.[12] In fact, any view that regards sexual desire in marriage only negatively wrests Paul's statement from the larger context of his teaching generally, which recognizes and affirms a wider positive meaning for marriage. In the immediately preceding verses, Paul has just spoken of the mutual authority exercised by husbands and wives over each other's bodies in their sexual relationships (vv. 3-4), a powerful image of marriage and sex as a context for mutuality and sharing, and not merely as a "pressure relief valve" for passions that are out of control. Likewise, Paul's claim that the unbelieving partner is "sanctified" through the marriage (v. 14), and may be "saved" by the witness of the believing spouse (v. 16), suggests that marital love can be a powerful channel for God's grace. The concern to avoid sexual immorality is not Paul's only interest in marriage, and the subsequent Pauline tradition greatly expands on his more constructive interests.[13]

But it would also be a grave mistake to fail to recognize the practical insight embodied in Paul's words "it is better to marry than to be aflame with passion." Implicit in these words is the recognition that marriage is normal. Sexual desire is normal: it is a powerful God-given drive. In 1 Corinthians 7, Paul argues that a cavalier and overly hasty or naïve avoidance of marriage will set up many people for problems in their sexual lives. Marriage is not just about duties and responsibilities; it is about drives and longings. Paul is concerned that the Corinthians' understandable desire for freedom, prayer, and purity may lead them astray if they do not reckon with the power of passion and desire, and if they are not realistic about their own capacity for self-control.

This same concern is clearly reflected in Paul's advice to unmarried people in this chapter. Paul offers two (perhaps related) practical reasons why single people should consider not becoming married — if they are able to exercise self-control. In 1 Corinthians 7:26, Paul speaks about an "impending crisis" that may make it prudent for single people to remain unmarried (other translators render the phrase "present crisis"). Some commentators believe that this refers, at least in part, to a famine that may have struck the environs of Corinth at the time Paul wrote this letter.[14] To

12. Deming, *Paul on Marriage and Celibacy,* p. 45.

13. The household code in Col. 3:18-22 is thought by some scholars to be written by Paul himself; cf. the wider attention to issues in marriage in Eph. 5:21-33 and in the Pastoral Epistles.

14. For a summary of the discussion, see Anthony C. Thiselton, *The First Epistle to the Corinthians: A Commentary on the Greek Text,* New International Greek Testament Commentary (Grand Rapids: Eerdmans, 2000), p. 573.

the extent that this is true, the decision to avoid marriage is an eminently practical one that was based on contemporaneous circumstances.

But most scholars recognize that there is also an eschatological dimension in this reference to an "impending crisis," focusing not merely on short-term problems but on the return of Christ and the end of the world as we know it. This eschatological focus is more clearly articulated later — in 1 Corinthians 7:29-31:

> [29]I mean, brothers and sisters, the appointed time has grown short; from now on, let even those who have wives be as though they had none, [30]and those who mourn as though they were not mourning, and those who rejoice as though they were not rejoicing, and those who buy as though they had no possessions, [31]and those who deal with the world as though they had no dealings with it. For the present form of this world is passing away.

Here the imminence of Christ's return comes into central focus, and with it the expectation that normal married life will not continue much longer for anyone. Indeed, if a local famine is what Paul is referring to by the "impending crisis" of verse 26, he probably viewed such a crisis as simply a prelude to the eschatological vision articulated in verses 29-31. This concern to avoid marriage because of a coming eschatological upheaval is cut from the same cloth as Jesus' lament for those who are pregnant and nursing in the last days (Matt. 24:19; Mark 13:17; Luke 21:23). In this context, then, Paul's suggestion that unmarried people should remain single if possible is a pragmatic decision based on his understanding of their circumstances, not based on a negative view of marriage or sexuality. This is also reflected in Paul's expressed desire that his readers avoid unnecessary trouble and anxiety by remaining single (1 Cor. 7:28-29).

Yet Paul also acknowledges that remaining single has spiritual benefits. He recognizes in 1 Corinthians 7:32-35 that unmarried men and women can be more concerned about the affairs of the Lord since they need to be less concerned about the needs of their spouses and the logistics of family life. Paul commends unmarried women, whose situation allows them to be "holy in body and spirit" (1 Cor. 7:34). This may be another reference to the connection between prayer and the avoidance of sexual intercourse noted earlier (1 Cor. 7:3-4); but it may also simply reflect the capacity of unmarried women to devote their bodies to the work of the Lord in a wider context, rather than devoting them to the demands of pregnancy, childbirth, and childrearing. But counterbalancing all these benefits of singleness that Paul affirms stands the danger of sexual immorality and the need for self-control. Thus he repeatedly urges single people to marry if they cannot exercise self-control in singleness (1 Cor. 7:9, 36).

Celibacy as Gift and Calling

There is one more theme that I need to explore in this chapter if we are to gain a comprehensive understanding of Paul's vision for marriage and celibacy. That is the concern with God's gift and call. Paul introduces these categories in 1 Corinthians 7:7: "I wish that all were as I myself am. But each has a particular gift from God, one having one kind and another a different kind." Paul seems to pick up an analogous theme later, in 1 Corinthians 7:17, when he says, in speaking not only of marriage but also of one's identity as slave or free, Jew or Gentile, "Let each of you lead the life that the Lord has assigned, to which God called you."[15] Here Paul seems to echo the words of Jesus in Matthew 19:11: "Not everyone can accept this teaching, but only those to whom it is given." Celibacy is "given" by God to some, but not to all.

Although some commentators read the "gift from God" named in 1 Corinthians 7:7 to refer only to celibacy, this interpretation cannot be sustained by a close reading, since Paul refers to multiple gifts that differ from each other in that verse: "Each has a particular gift from God, one having one kind and another a different kind." Luther is thus probably correct when he says, "Marriage is just as much a gift of God, St. Paul says here, as chastity is."[16] This interpretation is confirmed by a broader look at 1 Corinthians, in which Paul repeatedly feels the need to broaden the Corinthians' understanding of the diversity of spiritual gifts given by God (cf. 12:4-11, 14). Here also, the Corinthians see only one gift, one good: "It is well for a man not to touch a woman" (7:1). But they fail to recognize that marriage, too, is a gift given by God, and that different gifts are given to different people. Paul seeks not to contradict them but to broaden their awareness of the issues involved and the diversity of God's grace.

15. Note that the same categories appear in these verses that are enumerated in Gal. 3:28: "There is no longer Jew or Greek, there is no longer slave or free, there is no longer male and female; for all of you are one in Christ Jesus."

16. Luther, *Works* vol. 28, Amer. ed. (St. Louis: Concordia, 1973), p. 16, as cited in Thiselton, *The First Epistle to the Corinthians*, p. 513.

Implications for the Debate about
Gay or Lesbian Committed Unions

What is striking, in the context of 1 Corinthians 7, is that the particular kind of "gift" one has received, relative to marriage and celibacy, is determined by the extent to which one is able to exercise self-control (7:9, 36-40). Paul clearly recognizes that there are quite a few unmarried people whose "gift" is not the calling to celibacy but the calling to marriage, and he urges them to get married. Paul also implicitly recognizes that simply admonishing these people to avoid sexual immorality will not always be sufficient. Instead, the divinely given calling for them is marriage, and the failure to follow that call will likely result in sexual immorality. Paul's comment "it is better to marry than to be aflame with passion" presupposes that, for many people, these will be the only realistic options that they have. Celibacy in this context represents a third way, beyond either marriage or "burning" with passion. It involves not merely sufficient willpower to restrain sexual impulses but also the capacity to live in a focused and undistracted way apart from marriage. To use more modern categories, this means not the *absence* or *repression* of sexual desires but the capacity to *sublimate* and *channel* those desires and energies into focused and disciplined service to God.

Of course, all people are called to exercise sexual self-control for periods of time in their lives, both before marriage and during those periods in marriage when sex isn't possible or appropriate. But this is not the same as celibacy. Celibacy is a lifelong discipline that involves not only the avoidance of sexual relations but also the capacity to sustain faithful discipleship without the deep intimacy and mutual support and care established by sexual relations with a lifelong partner. Celibacy means more than simply going without sexual relations for a period of time. It entails constructing one's whole life apart from sexual intimacy.

Here we confront the central dilemma for gay and lesbian Christians. Most Christians on both sides of the homosexuality debate now recognize and acknowledge that sexual orientation is very resistant to efforts to change. Even an evangelical group like Exodus International, which opposes all forms of same-sex sexual activity, now focuses its mission not on seeking to change the sexual orientation of all gays and lesbians so that they become heterosexuals, but on helping gays and lesbians to live lives of chastity and self-control. Exodus International optimistically believes that 30 percent to 50 percent of gay men and women can enter into heterosexual marriage through a variety of forms of support and therapy.[17] A recent traditionalist document arising from theological dialogue in the Episcopal Church makes much more modest claims, arguing that "10-15 percent of those with same-sex attraction can achieve noticeable change," though what constitutes "noticeable change" is not clearly defined.[18] Most academic studies are also considerably less promising. Wilson and Rahman report on a study of 200 gay and lesbian persons who were highly religious and highly motivated to change their sexual orientation from same-sex to heterosexual. In this study, "only 11 per cent of the males and 37 per cent of the females reported a complete change to heterosexuality."[19] Yet even here, Wilson and Rahman note methodological problems that make this study a "best case" scenario; they suggest that results under more normal circumstances may show significantly less success.

For the purpose of this chapter, however, it is not necessary to adjudicate this entire debate. Even the most optimistic traditionalist reading of the research data suggests that more than half of all gay men should *not* be expected fully to change their sexual orientation, and should instead focus on changing their behavior.[20] Other studies peg the number of gays whose orientation is not subject to change at much higher levels, and some studies call into question whether sexual orientation can be completely changed under any circumstances, regardless of whether some gays may learn how to live effectively in heterosexual marriages.[21] In 2009, the American Psychological Association revised its guidance to therapists working with gay and lesbian clients. It said that, though it can be appropriate for therapists to assist gay and lesbian clients who have religious convictions against homosexual activity to move toward a responsible celi-

17. From the Exodus International website: "Some former homosexuals marry and some don't, but marriage is not the measuring stick; spiritual growth and obedience are" (http://www.exodusinternational.org/content/view/43/87/).

18. John E. Goldingay, Grant R. LeMarquand, George R. Sumner, and Daniel A. Westberg, "Same-Sex Marriage and Anglican Theology: A View from the Traditionalists," in "Same-Sex Relationships in the Life of the Church," p. 36. Published at: http://www.collegeforbishops.org/assets/1145/ss_document_final.pdf.

19. Glenn D. Wilson and Qazi Rahman, *Born Gay: The Psychobiology of Sex Orientation* (London: Peter Owen, 2005), p. 40.

20. Chapter 8 below will address the question of whether orientation and behavior can be as easily distinguished as is assumed in many traditionalist readings. See esp. pp. 176ff.

21. See the chapter on "Changing Sexual Orientation" in David G. Myers and Letha Scanzoni, *What God Has Joined Together: A Christian Case for Gay Marriage* (San Francisco: HarperSanFrancisco, 2005), pp. 69-83.

bate life, it is not ethical for therapists to work with clients to attempt to change their sexual orientation, since such goals are not supported by current research. They conclude: "Efforts to change sexual orientation are unlikely to be successful and involve some risk of harm."[22] This question thus remains for the church: What should the church say to the substantial majority of gays and lesbians whose sexual orientation is not amenable to change? All sides of the debate acknowledge that this group includes *at least* 70 percent of all gay men and a majority of lesbian women.

Encouraging heterosexual marriage in such cases is fraught with peril. It is morally and ethically problematic to marry a partner who expects to be fully desired, both personally and sexually, when a person is not able fully to meet those expectations. Even when partners hope that a change in their sexual orientation will allow them to be faithful partners, such hopes often end in difficulty or disaster. Already, many marriages fail because one partner finally acknowledges that his or her sexual orientation is not compatible with heterosexual marriage. Encouraging marriages that are likely to end in divorce is not Christian faithfulness.

But here is where the paradox emerges. Traditionalists insist that, for those gays and lesbians who cannot change their orientation, chastity in celibacy is the only alternative. But this counsel sounds remarkably akin to the slogan of the Corinthians: advising or demanding complete abstinence from sex. Paul rejects that counsel, encouraging even single persons to get married if they are not able to exercise self-control. But can we assume that all gays and lesbians who cannot change their sexual orientation are gifted by God to exercise such self-control, and thus are called to a life of celibacy? If not, wouldn't it be consistent with Paul's moral logic in this chapter of Corinthians to encourage these gay and lesbian persons not called to celibacy to live lives of faithful commitment in gay or lesbian marriages or marriagelike relationships?

Traditionalists are quick to respond that all Christians are called to exercise self-control outside of marriage, and that both Scripture and the Christian tradition have always understood marriage as between one man and one woman. Thus Christian morality requires self-control and chastity as the only faithful response outside of heterosexual marriage. And if it is true that the one-flesh union of marriage can only be heterosexual in character, such an argument certainly applies. It is well beyond the purpose of this chapter to resolve this debate in its entirety, but the previous

22. http://www.apa.org/pi/lgbt/resources/sexual-orientation.aspx.

discussion of one-flesh unions in chapter 5 certainly must inform that discussion. In any case, however, it is important to note here that this traditionalist way of framing the issue of celibacy stands in some tension with Paul's discussion in 1 Corinthians 7. Paul clearly states that those who have not received the calling and gift of celibacy should get married. He thus implicitly recognizes that some Christians are clearly not called and gifted by God for a life of singleness. However, the traditionalist position requires us to assume that *all* gay and lesbian Christians who cannot change their sexual orientation are called and gifted for a life of celibacy — an assumption that stands in some tension with Paul's view articulated here.

Paul realizes that asking Christians not called to celibacy to remain unmarried is opening the door to sexual immorality: the use of prostitutes, sex outside of marriage, and other even more distorted expressions of sexuality. This is why he qualifies the Corinthians' statement "it is well for a man not to touch a woman." It seems unavoidably the case that the same problems will be true for gay and lesbian persons as well. Indeed, one could argue that this is precisely what is happening in American culture. Given the absence of more constructive and stable channels for gays and lesbians to express their sexual lives, we are seeing far too much distorted sexuality in the use of prostitutes, promiscuity, one-night stands, and the like. Indeed, it does not take much moral imagination to realize that, even if one may not fully embrace the morality of committed gay and lesbian unions, such unions may represent a substantial moral improvement over anonymous and unrestrained sexual activity.

Whether such "moral improvement" should be sanctioned and embraced by the church continues to be a source of controversy within the church. The late evangelical theologian and ethicist Lewis Smedes argued in a 1999 article that committed gay unions should be viewed in light of the history of the church's wrestling with the question of divorce and remarriage. He claimed that even though gay marriage may not fully reflect God's purpose seen in heterosexual marriage (just as remarriage after divorce is not God's intention), committed unions may be an appropriate expression of sexual life for gays and lesbians who find that their sexual orientation leaves them no other options.[23] Even some Christians who cannot find grounds fully to bless gay or lesbian marriages thus recognize

---

23. Lewis B. Smedes, "Like the Wideness of the Sea," *Perspectives*, May 1999; cf. Smedes, *Sex for Christians: The Limits and Liberties of Sexual Living*, rev. ed. (Grand Rapids: Eerdmans, 1994), pp. 238-44.

that Paul's reasoning in 1 Corinthians 7 may call for greater tolerance and accommodation toward gays and lesbians in committed relationships. For gays and lesbians as well, it may be "better to marry than to be aflame with passion."

Conclusions

Without fully resolving these tensions between tolerance/accommodation and full support for gay marriage, we can see that some aspects of Scripture's approach to celibacy are clear. Scripture as a whole tends to take a fairly pragmatic approach to marriage and celibacy. Celibacy is recognized as an important vocation for which some are gifted and called. Temporary avoidance of sex, even by married couples, may be useful as a spiritual discipline, and all Christians are called to exercise sexual self-control at various points in their lives. But Jesus makes it clear that the calling to lifelong celibacy is not for all (Matt. 19:11), and Paul explicitly urges those who cannot exercise self-control to get married. This should not be viewed as a "second-best" option, but merely as an expression of the diversity of gifts given by God. If the traditionalist case is correct, we must assume that God calls all gays and lesbians whose sexual orientation is not subject to change to a life of celibacy, regardless of evidence that many of these people may not have received this gift and call. This stands in some tension with Paul's recognition that marriage is the natural God-given answer to deep and persistent sexual longing.

On the other hand, if the revisionist case is to stand, and committed gay unions are to be understood as a fitting solution for gay and lesbian Christians not called to celibacy, we must explore further the ethics of same-sex relations and discern more clearly the moral logic by which Scripture speaks about them.

Summing Up

- While the Old Testament envisions occasional short-term avoidance of sex for the purposes of holiness, it does not envision celibacy as a lifelong calling.
- The ancient world generally tended to view the question of whether to marry or remain single as a pragmatic matter. Marriage was considered

primarily in terms of the responsibilities and duties required to sustain a household. Cynics and Stoics differed on the relative importance of marriage for the fulfilled life.

- Jesus, in his commendation of those who have "made themselves eunuchs for the sake of the kingdom of heaven" (Matt. 19:12), recognized that God calls some, but not all, to a single life.
- Paul addresses this question extensively in 1 Corinthians 7 in a carefully balanced way, recognizing some circumstances under which married people might avoid sex for brief periods of time, but discouraging married people from avoiding sex altogether. Paul invites single people to remain unmarried, but clearly recognizes that not all people are gifted with lifelong celibacy.
- The modern awareness of the persistence of sexual orientation thus raises an important question: Are all gay and lesbian Christians whose sexual orientation is not subject to change *necessarily* called to a celibate life? If so, then this stands in some tension with the affirmation — of both Jesus and Paul — that lifelong celibacy is a gift for some but not for all.

PART III

Exploring the "Boundary Language" of Romans 1:24-27

8

Lust and Desire

I n the next four chapters I wish to shift the focus, at least to some extent. Whereas the previous chapters focused on identifying central themes and values that lie at the heart of the biblical vision for sexuality, the next four chapters focus on the boundaries that distinguish an emerging biblical vision for sexuality from a variety of distortions and corruptions. The subjects I will cover are *lust, honor/shame, purity,* and *natural law.* In each case I will explore the nature of this boundary language, its cultural particularity, and its transcultural significance. These four categories are all drawn from the language of Romans 1:24-27:

> [24]Therefore God gave them up in the *lusts* of their hearts to *impurity,* to the *degrading* of their bodies among themselves, [25]because they exchanged the truth about God for a lie and worshiped and served the creature rather than the Creator, who is blessed forever! Amen. [26]For this reason God gave them up to *degrading passions.* Their women exchanged *natural* intercourse for *unnatural,*[27]and in the same way also the men, giving up *natural* intercourse with women, were *consumed with passion* for one another. Men committed *shameless* acts with men and received in their own persons the due penalty for their error.

Paul characterizes the sexual behavior in these verses as lustful ("lusts," "passions," "consumed with passion"), as impurity, as shameful ("degrading," "shameless"), and as "unnatural." In each case, we must explore why Paul speaks in this way, and what is the more specific moral and rhetorical force of his comments. This close examination of negative ethical language illuminates the forms of moral logic that shape and undergird Paul's discussion here, and they help us discern the underlying forms of moral logic that shape the Bible's treatment of same-sex eroticism in general. In this chapter we turn first to Paul's understanding of lust and desire.

The Larger Context of Paul's Letter to the Romans

Before exploring lust and desire more specifically, however, it is important to get an accurate picture of the overall flow of Paul's thought in this opening of his letter to the Romans. These verses are part of a larger section of Romans (1:18–3:20), and the overall goal of this larger section is to demonstrate the universal sinfulness of humanity and the universal need of humanity for the salvation that is found in Paul's gospel (1:16). Paul concludes this larger section beginning in Romans 3:9 by saying, "We have already charged that all, both Jews and Greeks, are under the power of sin." He follows with a long list of Scripture quotations affirming the universality of human sinfulness. Within this larger section, Romans 1:18-32 focuses on the sinfulness of Gentiles who are "without excuse" (1:20) in their sinfulness and their refusal to worship the true God, even though they have not received the law. Paul argues that the truth about God — God's eternal power and deity — is plain to them in the created order (1:20). The core Gentile problem is idolatry: it is their refusal to worship the true God and instead their devotion to "images resembling a mortal human being or birds or four-footed animals or reptiles" (1:23). This practice of idolatry constitutes rebellion against God, and as a result God hands them over "in the lusts of their hearts to impurity, to the degrading of their bodies among themselves" (1:24). The verses following verse 24 depict a cascading and intensifying montage of evil and corruption that culminates in a list of twenty-one separate vices in Romans 1:29-31.

Yet this is not the end of Paul's argument. As Richard Hays has argued, Paul engages here in a "homiletical sting operation." Hays writes:

> The passage builds a crescendo of condemnation, declaring God's wrath upon human unrighteousness, using rhetoric characteristic of Jewish polemic against Gentile immorality. It whips the reader into a frenzy of indignation against others: those unbelievers, those idol-worshipers, those immoral enemies of God. But then the sting strikes

in Romans 2:1: "Therefore you have no excuse, whoever you are, when you judge others; for in passing judgment on another you condemn yourself because you, the judge, are doing the very same things."[1]

Hays's point is an important one. Paul's argument assumes that his readers will agree with him entirely in Romans 1, and will applaud and join him in his outrage against such wickedness. This rhetorical ploy helps Paul expose the more subtle but no less deadly sins of judgmentalism and selfish ambition in the second chapter of Romans.[2]

But the rhetorical turn of Romans 2:1 only raises a further question. What does Paul mean when he says, "For in passing judgment on another you condemn yourself because you, the judge, are doing the very same things"? A literal meaning of "the very same things" makes no sense. If Paul's Roman readers are engaging in the same licentious and unlawful behaviors that Paul describes in chapter 1, they are not likely to be responding in judgmentalism but rather in defense of their actions. Why would anyone be outraged over the same behavior in which he or she is also engaged? The whole movement of Paul's argument is based on the expectation that his readers will join him in rejecting the litany of specific sins described in Romans 1, and that these readers are at least trying to avoid living in this way. So what does Paul mean when he says in 2:1, "You, the judge, are doing the very same things"?

Two answers seem evident from the text. The first answer appears in Romans 2:1: "Passing judgment on another" is the sin that is equated with the licentiousness, greed, and lust portrayed in 1:18-32. The posture of judgmentalism entails essentially the same sin described in the previous chapter. But this only raises the further question: What does out-of-control lust have in common with judgmentalism? In both cases, what Paul seems to have in mind is the attempt to advance one's own honor, sta-

---

1. Richard Hays, *The Moral Vision of the New Testament: Community, Cross, New Creation; A Contemporary Introduction to New Testament Ethics* (San Francisco: HarperSanFrancisco, 1996), p. 389.

2. Douglas Atchison Campbell argues, in fact, that Paul speaks in the voice of a Jewish teacher whom he opposes in Rom. 1:18-32, and then exposes the problems with this voice in the following chapters (Campbell, *The Deliverance of God: An Apocalyptic Rereading of Justification in Paul* [Grand Rapids: Eerdmans, 2009]). Whether this more ambitious hypothesis can be sustained remains to be seen; regardless, Paul's rhetorical turn in Rom. 2:1 has the clear effect of saying, "Yes . . . but . . ." to the intensifying rhetoric of judgment and condemnation found in Rom. 1:18-32.

tus, and will at the expense of others. This interpretation is confirmed by a second piece of evidence found a bit later in the passage, in Romans 2:8, where Paul characterizes those who are subject to divine judgment as "those who are self-seeking and who obey not the truth but wickedness." The Greek word translated here as "self-seeking" *(eritheia)* is an uncommon word and somewhat difficult to translate. But most interpreters follow the lexicon's suggestion of "selfishness" — or, even better, "selfish ambition." What is at stake here is the thirst for honor, status, and prestige that is so prevalent in the ancient world.[3] Hence, as Paul sees it, what lustful pagans have in common with self-righteous judgmental Christians is that both are driven by the thirst for their own agenda — their own way, their own status, their own honor — while ignoring the concerns of everyone around them, particularly those of the living God. At the root of all sin is the will to power that resists the posture of humble gratitude and trust that marks human life as God intends it.

Indeed, as Robert Jewett has argued in his recent magisterial commentary on Romans, this is the discovery that marked Paul's own conversion: the realization that his zeal for the law was in reality selfishly driven by his own longing for status and honor. In commenting on Romans 7:7 ("I would not have known what it is to covet if the law had not said, 'You shall not covet'"), Jewett defines the core problem driving covetousness as "the sin of asserting oneself and one's group at the expense of others."[4] Jewett notes how this includes both Gentile competition for honor, as well as the Jewish desire for superior status through law observance. Such analysis also links with our discussion of Romans 1 and 2. The word for "covet" here in Romans 7:7 *(epithumeō)* comes from the same root as the word translated as *"lusts* of their hearts" *(epithumiais)* in Romans 1:24. Covetousness, out-of-control lust, and judgmentalism are all manifestations of the same root problem: "the sin of asserting oneself and one's group at the expense of others." These are "the very same things" (Rom. 2:1) that all sinners do. Later, in Romans 13:8-10, Paul will state the same case more positively, arguing — in keeping with the words of Jesus — that loving one's neighbor as oneself represents the fulfillment of the law. This stands over

---

3. *A Greek-English Lexicon of the New Testament and Other Early Christian Literature,* 3rd ed., ed. F. W. Danker, W. Bauer, W. F. Arndt, and F. W. Gingrich (Chicago: University of Chicago Press, 1999). For further discussion, see chapter 10 below on honor and shame.

4. Robert Jewett, Roy David Kotansky, and Eldon Jay Epp, *Romans: A Commentary,* Hermeneia: A Critical and Historical Commentary on the Bible (Minneapolis: Fortress, 2007), p. 449.

against the many varieties of self-seeking that lie at the core of all human sinfulness and idolatry. Jewett argues that this concern for mutuality and cooperation among Christians lies at the heart of Paul's overall agenda in writing Romans: urging the competing factious and disparate Roman tenement and apartment churches to welcome each other (15:7) and to unite together in support of Paul's planned gospel mission to Spain (15:22-24).

Passion and Lust in Romans 1 — and in the Larger Historical Context

This larger rhetorical context helps to illuminate Paul's discussion of passion and lust in Romans 1. In contrast to some streams of Hellenistic Judaism, Paul is not writing as a Christian philosopher, preaching about the irrationality of lust and the supremacy of reason informed by the law, as we see in some early Jewish texts like 4 Maccabees, which declares, "Devout reason is sovereign over the emotions" (1:1). Indeed, for Paul, the unredeemed *mind* is every bit as problematic as the *flesh*. Romans 1:28 not only speaks of the "lusts of the flesh" as a result of idolatry, but also describes how God "gave up" idolaters to a "debased mind." The consequences of idolatry encompass the entire person. Hence, for Paul, the central conflict is not between reason and lust but between the "lusts of the flesh" and the renewing of the Holy Spirit (Gal. 5:16-17). What is centrally wrong about lust is not that it is irrational, or that it takes over and controls people's lives (though Paul would certainly agree that lust does these things — and that that is a problem). Rather, the central problem with lust in Romans 1 is that it is an expression of idolatry in a specific sense: lust involves serving one's own self-seeking desires rather than worshiping the one true God.[5]

Ironically, however, such self-seeking results in the loss of self-control. Paul speaks in Romans 1:26 of "dishonorable *passions*." The word for "passions" in Greek *(pathē)* comes from a root that literally means "to suffer," or "to be passive." In the Greek language and the thought forms influenced by the language, emotional states were conceived as states of passivity in which the will and the higher powers of reason lost control over the per-

---

5. Note the same connection between lust, greed, and idolatry in Col. 3:5: "Put to death, therefore, whatever belongs to your earthly nature: sexual immorality, impurity, lust, evil desires and greed, which is idolatry."

son. Here is the central paradox that Paul describes in Romans 1: seeking to avoid their appropriate worship and service to God, and to establish their own agendas and their own independent purposes, humans end up enslaved to lustful passions instead, passions that control their lives and lead them to disgrace and corruption. Seeking greater autonomy, they lose control over their lives.

But Paul is not talking about just any ordinary kind of lust in this passage. The flow of the rhetoric makes it clear that the whole range of behaviors Paul describes in Romans 1, including same-sex eroticism, is for him an extraordinarily powerful and excessive manifestation of lust. We see a similar connection between idolatry and excessive lust and perversion in the Wisdom of Solomon, a Jewish apocryphal text dating from a period not long before Paul's writings.

> [12]For the idea of making idols was the beginning of fornication, and the invention of them was the corruption of life. . . . [23]For whether they kill children in their initiations, or celebrate secret mysteries, or hold frenzied revels with strange customs, [24]they no longer keep either their lives or their marriages pure, but they either treacherously kill one another, or grieve one another by adultery, [25]and all is a raging riot of blood and murder, theft and deceit, corruption, faithlessness, tumult, perjury, [26]confusion over what is good, forgetfulness of favors, defiling of souls, sexual perversion, disorder in marriages, adultery, and debauchery. [27]For the worship of idols not to be named is the beginning and cause and end of every evil. (Wisdom 14:12, 23-28)

It was a commonplace of Jewish rhetoric to link idolatry with excessive perversion and corruption, a "raging riot" of every form of evil. But we also find more specific references to same-sex eroticism as an expression of insatiable lust in Greco-Roman sources. The Roman orator Dio Chrysostom, for example, who wrote shortly after Paul's time, speaks of same-sex eroticism as the manifestation of insatiable lust:

> The man whose appetite is insatiate in such things, when he finds there is no scarcity, no resistance, in this field, will have contempt for the easy conquest and scorn for a woman's love, as a thing too readily given — in fact, too utterly feminine — and will turn his assault against the male quarters, eager to befoul the youth who will very soon be magistrates and judges and generals, believing that in them he will find a kind of pleasure difficult and hard to procure. His state

is like that of men who are addicted to drinking and wine-bibbing, who after long and steady drinking of unmixed wine, often lose their taste for it and create an artificial thirst by the stimulus of sweating, salted foods, and condiments.[6]

The early Jewish philosopher-theologian Philo, writing a bit earlier than Paul, makes a similar equation between same-sex eroticism and self-centered lust that refuses any boundaries. He comments on the story of Sodom and Gomorrah:

The land of the Sodomites, a part of the land of Canaan afterwards called Palestinian Syria, was brimful of innumerable iniquities, particularly such as arise from gluttony and lewdness, and multiplied and enlarged every other possible pleasure with so formidable a menace that it had at last been condemned by the Judge of All. The inhabitants owed this extreme license to the never-failing lavishness of their sources of wealth, for, deep-soiled and well-watered as it was, the land had every year a prolific harvest of all manner of fruits, and the chief beginning of evils, as one has aptly said, is goods in excess. Incapable of bearing such satiety, plunging like cattle, they threw off from their necks the law of nature and applied themselves to deep drinking of strong liquor and dainty feeding and forbidden forms of intercourse. Not only in their mad lust for women did they violate the marriages of their neighbours, but also men mounted males without respect for the sex nature which the active partner shares with the passive; and so when they tried to beget children they were discovered to be incapable of any but a sterile seed.[7]

Note that in all of these contemporaneous texts we see a clear echo of the language we find in Romans 1:27, which speaks of men who, "giving up" (or, to translate more accurately, "leaving behind") natural intercourse with women, "were consumed with passion for one another." What Paul has in mind here is not the modern concept of homosexual orientation, that is, the notion that some people are not sexually attracted to those of the opposite sex at all, but instead are inclined to love those of the same

6. Dio Chrysostom, *Dio Chrysostom*, trans. J. W. Cohoon and H. Lamar Crosby, Loeb Classical Library (London/New York: W. Heinemann/G. P. Putnam's Son's, 1932), 7:152, vol. 1, p. 373.
7. *De Abr.* 133-135; cited from Philo, *Philo*, trans. F. H. Colson, 9 vols., Loeb Classical Library (Cambridge, UK: Cambridge University Press, 1935), 6:69f.

sex. Such a perspective is found nowhere in the literature of Paul's day. Instead, in that literature, whenever same-sex eroticism is viewed negatively, particularly in sources contemporaneous with Paul, it is regarded as a particular manifestation of self-centered lust, one that is not content with women alone but is driven to ever more exotic and unnatural forms of stimulation in the pursuit of pleasure. It represents the pinnacle of wanton self-indulgence at the expense of others. It is entirely reasonable to assume that this is the kind of image that Paul's language in Romans 1 would have stirred up in the minds of his original readers.[8] Of course, this also raises questions about how this text should be applied to committed gay and lesbian unions today, questions that I will address in more detail below.

A Possible Allusion to the Roman Imperial House?

But there may well have been something even more specific that Paul intended to refer to with his words about sexual excess in Romans 1. Neil Elliott has called attention to the striking similarities between Paul's language and the incredible greed, violence, and sexual excesses of Gaius Caligula, an emperor who reigned in a period not too long before Paul wrote Romans.[9] First of all, Gaius is closely linked to the practice of idolatry. The Roman writer Suetonius reports how Gaius "set up a special temple to his own godhead, with priests and with victims of the choicest

---

8. Robert Gagnon attempts a counterargument by declaring: "It is misleading to argue as if Jewish Christian writers had nothing but negative images from which to base their judgment of homosexuality." He goes on to cite texts from the fourth century BCE and the third century CE that portray same-sex eroticism favorably (but, notably, nothing contemporaneous with Paul!). The implication, of course, is that Paul would have condemned nonlustful examples of same-sex eroticism as well (Gagnon, *The Bible and Homosexual Practice: Texts and Hermeneutics* [Nashville: Abingdon, 2001], pp. 350ff.). But such an argument is entirely speculative and runs counter to the actual evidence. Whether Jewish-Christian writers had access to more positive portrayals of homosexuality — and how they would assess such portrayals — is a question that is difficult or impossible to answer. What we can say with some clarity is that the actual portrayal of same-sex eroticism in Jewish and Christian writers in Paul's day is entirely negative, and one of the assumptions at the heart of this negative portrayal is the view that such behavior is a manifestation of insatiable lust. Whether this assumption was ever entirely valid, or whether it continues to be valid today is, of course, an entirely different question.

9. See Neil Elliott, *The Arrogance of Nations: Reading Romans in the Shadow of Empire*, Paul in Critical Contexts (Minneapolis: Fortress, 2008), pp. 79ff.

kind."[10] Another Roman writer, Dio Cassius, comments negatively on how Gaius was the only emperor to claim to be divine and to be the recipient of worship during his own lifetime.[11] Gaius also tried at one point to erect a statue of himself in the Temple in Jerusalem; he was dissuaded only by a delegation from Herod Agrippa.[12] Hence the link between Gaius and idolatry would have been well-known indeed, particularly in Jewish circles. But Gaius also serves as "Exhibit A" for out-of-control lust. Suetonius reports how Gaius "lived in perpetual incest with all his sisters, and at a large banquet he placed each of them in turn below him, while his wife reclined above" (24). He records gruesome examples of Gaius's arbitrary violence, vindictiveness, and cruelty. Later, Suetonius chronicles Gaius's sexual liaisons with the wives of dinner guests, raping them in an adjoining room and then returning to the banquet to comment on their performance. Various same-sex sexual encounters between Gaius and other men are similarly recounted (36). Finally, a military officer whom he had sexually humiliated joined a conspiracy to murder him, which they did less than four years into his reign. Suetonius records that Gaius was stabbed through the genitals when he was murdered (58). One wonders whether we can hear an echo of this gruesome story in Paul's comments in Romans 1:27: "Men committed shameless acts with men and received in their own person the due penalty for their error."[13] Gaius Caligula graphically illustrates the reality of which Paul speaks in Romans 1: the movement from idolatry to insatiable lust to every form of depravity, and the violent murderous reprisal that such behavior engenders. Interestingly, Elliott notes how the Jewish writer Philo writes in similarly scathing terms of the evils of Gaius

---

10. Suetonius, *Suetonius,* trans. J. C. Rolfe, Loeb Classical Library (London/New York: Heinemann/Harvard University Press, 1920), sec. 22, p. 437 (subsequent citations by section number alone).

11. Cassius Dio, *Roman History* LIX.26-28.

12. See Philo's *Legatio ad Gaium* ("Embassy to Gaius") for historical details.

13. Commentators generally struggle with this line in Rom. 1:27, frequently alluding to a line in the Jewish book of Wisdom (11:16), which says, "One is punished by the very things with which he sins." Other commentators suggest that this refers to the bodily damage done by anal intercourse (Jewett, Zahn). But both of these allusions are vague at best, and they both assume that the same persons are involved, both actively in penetrating others and in being penetrated themselves. Yet research by Nissinen and Scroggs strongly suggests that such a reversal of active and passive roles was not the norm in same-sex male intercourse in the ancient world, rendering this interpretation problematic. On the other hand, if there is an allusion to the death of Gaius Caligula in Rom. 1:27, its rhetorical force would be substantial and memorable!

Caligula, interpreting his depravity as the result of his refusal to honor God, and his death as a manifestation of divine justice.[14] This suggests that Gaius's excesses and the divine judgment incurred by them were a common theme that would have been familiar to many Jews in the ancient world.

These contemporary parallels from the Wisdom of Solomon, Dio Chrysostom, Philo, and Suetonius give a clearer sense of the kinds of linkages and associations that Paul's readers would have made as they read his words in Romans 1. Paul is speaking of sinfulness in its extreme and most obvious forms here. His goal is to clearly delineate the essence of the human problem and to secure the unambiguous agreement of the Roman Christians in condemning such outrageousness. That "sets them up" for the rhetorical "sting operation" in 2:1. But in Romans 1, Paul is not directly describing, as some claim, the behaviors of Roman Gentile Christians before they were converted.[15] The twenty-one vices recounted in Romans 1:29-31 recount the full depth and breadth of human corruption, the sort of outrageous conduct that could be seen in Gaius Caligula. Paul's intent to elicit agreement and outrage is evident at the end of his discourse, in verses 29-31, with his climactic use of alliteration in the Greek text, which is reflected in the English translation in the NRSV as well:[16]

14. Elliott, *The Arrogance of Nations*, p. 81. See esp. Philo's *Legatio ad Gaium* ("Embassy to Gaius").

15. See Gagnon, *The Bible and Homosexual Practice*, p. 276. Gagnon cites Rom. 6:19-21: "For just as you once presented your members as slaves to impurity and to greater and greater iniquity, so now present your members as slaves to righteousness for sanctification. [20]When you were slaves of sin, you were free in regard to righteousness. [21]So what advantage did you then get from the things of which you now are ashamed? The end of those things is death." Gagnon claims that Paul is referring back to the sins mentioned in Rom. 1. Yet such an argument fails to consider the rhetorical force of Rom. 1 and its intention to stir up feelings of judgmentalism in its Christian hearers (see Rom. 2:1). Moreover, Rom. 2:1 states that those who judge are *doing* (present tense) the very same things described in chapter 1. This conflicts with Rom. 6, where Paul speaks of sinful behavior as part of the *past* of the Roman Christians. Moreover, Paul never speaks of sin as slavery in Rom. 1, as he does in Rom. 6. If Paul were describing the previous behavior of Roman Christians in Rom. 1, the rhetoric would be completely ineffective, stirring up in his readers shame rather than pride and judgmentalism. Paul is not beyond reminding his hearers of their past sins in other letters (cf. 1 Cor. 6:11), but he is usually explicit when he does so. That is not the case with Rom. 1, which speaks entirely in the third person, to congregations whom he has never met personally (which would also make it unlikely that he is speaking of their past behavior).

16. All the words in v. 31 begin with the Greek letter *alpha*, the equivalent of the English prefix *un-*.

²⁹They were filled with every kind of wickedness, evil, covetousness, malice. Full of envy, murder, strife, deceit, craftiness, they are gossips, ³⁰slanderers, God-haters, insolent, haughty, boastful, inventors of evil, rebellious toward parents, ³¹foolish, faithless, heartless, ruthless.

Neil Elliott writes of this long list:

> As a description of conventional Gentile morality, the passage is an inexcusable exaggeration (which Christian commentators occasionally recognize and seek to excuse nonetheless by referring to Paul's "radical" and "apocalyptic" perspective). As a description of the horrors of the imperial house, however, Paul's words actually seem restrained.[17]

If Elliott is correct, Paul's allusion to the emperor can be understood as an indictment of the Gentile world through the behavior of its leaders, who embody and typify the people as a whole. But even if the allusion to Gaius would not be perceived by all of Paul's readers, the rhetoric of Romans 1 makes it clear that Paul is not picking out "typical" sinners, but the most extreme forms of sinfulness. (As is also true today, same-sex eroticism was not nearly common enough in the ancient world to be considered "typical" of all Gentiles.) He does this so that he can elicit from his Roman Christian readers the feelings of superiority and judgmentalism. He hopes to bring these feelings to the light of day in order to convey his larger theological conviction of the universality of sinfulness, and the mercy and graciousness of God to all — to the most dissolute Gentiles and to the proudest and most pious Jews and Christians.

Romans 1:26 is sometimes cited as a counterexample to this form of argument, particularly when Paul says, "Their women exchanged natural intercourse for unnatural." Paul appears to be speaking here not only of men in power who were abusing that power, but also of women having sexual relations with other women. In such a case, the argument seems to focus less on the lustful abuse of power, since women in the ancient world were not in positions of power. If this argument has merit, it may shift the locus of the problem in these verses away from the centrality of excessive lust, and focus more on how same-sex eroticism is "against nature."

Many commentators recognize that this is a difficult verse. Discussions

---

17. Neil Elliott, *Liberating Paul: The Justice of God and the Politics of the Apostle*, The Bible and Liberation (Maryknoll, NY: Orbis Books, 1994), p. 195.

of lesbian sexuality were fairly rare in the ancient world.[18] Yet one cannot gloss over Paul's recurring emphasis on the centrality of passion and lust — even in this text. The discussion of women giving up "natural relations" in Romans 1:26 begins with the words "God gave them up to degrading passions." So whatever Romans 1:26b may have in mind in the sexual behavior of women, it is presented as an expression of excessive and degrading passion, just as male-male sex is described in the following verse as "consumed with passion." But here is where Elliott's suggestion of an allusion to Gaius Caligula may also be helpful. As noted above, Gaius "lived in perpetual incest with all his sisters, and at a large banquet he placed each of them in turn below him, while his wife reclined above."[19] Such behavior would certainly qualify on several counts as an example (in Rom. 1:26b) of how "their women exchanged natural intercourse for unnatural." Similarly, the reference to "their women" suggests that women are still being thought of in relationship to men in this context.[20] While we may not be able to know definitively what Paul had in mind here, it is clear that it is intended to be part of an overall picture of over-the-top lust, self-centeredness, and greed.

What holds Romans 1:24-27 and its description of sexual excess together with Romans 1:29-31 and its description of moral corruption is, therefore, *self-seeking desire,* unrestrained by obedience to God. Paul's expression "worshiping and serving the creature rather than the creator" (Rom. 1:25) is thus absolutely crucial. Humans are restless, desiring creatures, and when that desire is attached to something or someone other than God, all hell breaks loose. Misdirected desire — not in the sense of homosexual desire, but desire for God that is not expressed in true worship — becomes distorted and excessive desire, which runs out of control and is destructive. In this sense, the sexual excesses and the violence and injustice of the Roman Empire are all threads that are part of the same fabric. In Romans 1, Paul portrays the tendency of such desire to express itself

18. For a comprehensive discussion, see Bernadette J. Brooten, *Love between Women: Early Christian Responses to Female Homoeroticism,* The Chicago Series on Sexuality, History, and Society (Chicago: University of Chicago Press, 1996).

19. Suetonius, *Suetonius,* section 24.

20. For arguments and evidence that noncoital (i.e., oral or anal) heterosexual intercourse is what Paul has in mind in Rom. 1:26, rather than same-sex eroticism between women, see James Miller, "The Practices of Romans 1:26: Homosexual or Heterosexual?" *Novum Testamentum* 37 (1995). For counterarguments that same-sex eroticism between women is in view, see Brooten, *Love between Women,* pp. 248-49, n. 99. See also the further discussion of these issues in chapter 11 below.

in increasingly extreme and destructive ways as a manifestation of the justice of God, as self-seeking desire collapses under the weight of its own relentlessness and insatiability.[21]

Lust in Romans 7

But there is also another sense in which lust appears in Paul's letter to the Romans, and we will not gain a comprehensive picture of lust and desire without considering this sense as well. Paul speaks in Romans 7 of a particular way in which the law is related to lust and desire. In this passage, the Greek word translated "covet," or "covetousness" *(epithumeō, epithumia),* is the same Greek word that is translated in Romans 1 as "lust."

> [7]What then should we say? That the law is sin? By no means! Yet, if it had not been for the law, I would not have known sin. I would not have known what it is to covet if the law had not said, "You shall not covet." [8]But sin, seizing an opportunity in the commandment, produced in me all kinds of covetousness. Apart from the law sin lies dead. [9]I was once alive apart from the law, but when the commandment came, sin revived [10]and I died, and the very commandment that promised life proved to be death to me. (Rom. 7:7-10)

Here we see a somewhat different manifestation of the truth and justice of God. The extreme lust Paul speaks of in Romans 1 manifests itself by its own excessiveness and ultimately self-destructive character. But the "covetousness" that Paul speaks of here (using the same Greek word) is only discovered when it is exposed by the law. This raises a basic and important question: Why is it that lust is exposed quite apart from the law in Romans 1, simply by its self-evident excesses, but "covetousness" is only exposed by the law in Romans 7?[22]

---

21. For further exploration of the notion of lust as insatiability — with extensive citations from Greco-Roman literature — see David E. Fredrickson, "Natural and Unnatural Use in Romans 1:24-27," in David Balch, ed., *Homosexuality, Science, and the "Plain Sense" of Scripture* (Grand Rapids: Eerdmans, 2000).

22. There is an extensive and somewhat unresolved exegetical debate among scholars concerning the exact identity of the "I" who speaks in these verses. Various commentators interpret it as either Adam, Israel, humanity in general, or Paul prior to his bar mitzvah. Each theory has its own difficulties. References to Adam seem unlikely, since the language about sin "reviving" in v. 9 would make no sense in the context of the Adam story. Further-

Paul seems to be speaking about two different levels of lust or covetousness in these two passages. There is a general sense in which extreme human lust and self-centeredness manifests itself in ways that are obvious to all and need no further explication. That is the sense of lust that Paul is talking about in Romans 1. But Romans 7 speaks of more subtle manifestations of lust and covetousness, which may not be visible at all. In this context one is reminded of Jesus' words in Matthew 5:27-28: "[27]You have heard that it was said, 'You shall not commit adultery.' [28] But I say to you that everyone who looks at a woman with lust has already committed adultery with her in his heart." Here a deeper manifestation of self-seeking lust is being exposed. The obvious forms of lust that manifest themselves in adulterous behavior are not the end of the problem. The commandment that one not covet his neighbor's wife (Exod. 20:17; Deut. 5:21), following after the commandment not to commit adultery (Exod. 20:14; Deut. 5:18), drives the command deeper, focusing not only on external behaviors but on the disposition of the heart. Here is where both Jesus and Paul focus the spotlight, recognizing the toxic power of lust and covetousness long before it may manifest itself in destructive behaviors. In this sense, when Israel receives the law, it does not *solve* the problem of lust and covetousness that is so self-evident in human history; it only *magnifies* the problem, driving the divine command into the depths of the heart, calling not only for an end to the self-destructive behaviors narrated in Romans 1, but also for a purity of heart that only deepens and increases one's awareness of the depths of one's own sinfulness. This, for Paul, is why the law cannot save us and why the gospel of grace in Jesus Christ is the only answer to the human predicament.

Indeed, for Paul, union with the crucified and risen Christ brings about a transformation that the law alone could never achieve. Because Christians have been united to Christ in baptism (Rom. 6:3-4), they must consider themselves "dead to sin and alive to God in Christ Jesus" (Rom. 6:11). Therefore, Paul tells his readers, "Do not let sin exercise dominion in your mortal bodies to make you obey their passions" (Rom. 6:12). Paul says in Galatians that "those who belong to Christ Jesus have crucified the flesh

---

more, autobiographical interpretations encounter the difficulty of Paul's claim to be "blameless" according to the law in Phil. 3:6. A more generic reference to Israel or Jewish experience in general seems most likely because of Paul's use of "I" here. Yet for our purposes, these issues may not make much difference, since our concern is the relationship between lust/covetousness and the law, regardless of whose experience it may be.

with its passions and desires" (5:24). This should not be construed as a moral accomplishment of Christians but rather as a gift of God, which is given in the believers' union with Christ by the Holy Spirit. For Paul, the reality of union with Christ and the gift of the Spirit implants a new dynamic into the lives of Christians, a new power that displaces the self-seeking lusts and overwhelming passions of the flesh with the power of the Spirit and manifests itself in "faith working through love" (Gal. 5:6). This new power is the antidote for both the toxic, self-destructive manifestation of lust narrated in Romans 1 and for the paralyzing inward crisis of the self-seeking heart narrated in Romans 7.

Is Sexual Desire Itself Evil?

This exploration of lust and covetousness in Romans raises one further question: Is desire itself (sexual or more generally) the problem? Does Paul's citation of the Tenth Commandment against covetousness in its absolute form in Romans 7:7, without his listing of the forbidden objects of that coveting (e.g., one's neighbor's house, wife, etc.), mean that, for Paul, desire itself lies at the heart of human sinfulness?[23] There certainly were other ancient writers who seemed to move in that direction. Stoicism identifies lust *(epithumia)* as one of the four chief passions that must be subdued.[24] The Tenth Commandment against lust/covetousness is similarly summarized in 4 Maccabees 2:6 — absolutely without qualifiers. Philo speaks of lust/covetousness as the "source of all evils" and as the "original evil" lying at the bottom of all human sinfulness.[25] Dale Martin has argued that something like this is close to Paul's view, at least with respect to sexual desire. Martin claims that Paul believes that sexual desire is inherently evil and that the goal of Christian life, whether married or celibate, is the extirpation of sexual desire.[26] One can point to other New Testament texts that seem to take a similar categorically negative view of desire. James 1:14-

---

23. See the same absolute quotation of the Tenth Commandment without listing the coveted objects that are forbidden in Rom. 13:9.

24. Lust *(epithumia)*, grief *(lupē)*, fear *(phobos)*, and envy *(phthonos)*. See Büchsel's article on *thumos* and related words in *TDNT* III:167ff.

25. Philo, *De Specialibus Legibus* 4:84, 85.

26. Dale Martin, "Paul Without Passion: On Paul's Rejection of Desire in Sex and Marriage," reprinted in Martin, *Sex and the Single Savior: Gender and Sexuality in Biblical Interpretation* (Louisville: Westminster John Knox, 2005), pp. 65-76.

15 declares: "But one is tempted by one's own desire, being lured and enticed by it; then, when that desire has conceived, it gives birth to sin, and that sin, when it is fully grown, gives birth to death." Similarly, 2 Peter 1:4 says: "Thus he has given us, through these things, his precious and very great promises, so that through them you may escape from the corruption that is in the world because of lust, and may become participants of the divine nature."

Yet Paul can also speak of desire positively: he uses the same word that is here translated as "lust" *(epithumia)* positively in texts such as Philippians 1:23 ("I am hard pressed between the two: my desire [*epithumia*] is to depart and be with Christ, for that is far better") and 1 Thessalonians 2:17 ("As for us, brothers and sisters, when, for a short time, we were made orphans by being separated from you — in person, not in heart — we longed with great eagerness [*epithumia*] to see you face to face").[27] It is not desire itself that Paul opposes, but excessive desire, which directs itself toward what is not rightly ours, overcoming self-control and obedience to God. Paul's thinking is probably shaped by the Tenth Commandment, which does not forbid desire itself but only desire that is directed toward what belongs to the neighbor. Even in 1 Corinthians 7, where Paul says, "It is better to marry than to be aflame with passion" (7:9), he instructs the married Corinthian believers: "Do not deprive one another except perhaps by agreement for a set time, to devote yourselves to prayer, and then come together again, so that Satan may not tempt you because of your lack of self-control" (7:5). Martin writes that Paul envisions such sexual union in marriage as occurring "only in the absence of sexual passion and desire."[28] But if there is no sexual passion or desire within marriage, why would married people need or want to have sex at all? Desire itself is not the problem; it is desire that is out of control.[29] The opposite of lust for Paul is not the absence of passion *(apatheia)* but the presence of self-control *(enkrateia)* (see 1 Cor. 7:9; 9:25; Gal. 5:23; cf. Titus 1:8; 2 Pet. 1:6). For Paul, marriage exists not to extinguish desire, but rather — among other things — as the di-

27. Martin claims that it is only *sexual* desire that Paul regards entirely negatively, but this requires more precise understandings than the Greek text allows. The simple fact is that Paul does not always use these words for desire negatively.

28. Martin, *Sex and the Single Savior*, p. 66.

29. This is the conclusion of an extensive study on this subject by J. Edward Ellis, *Paul and Ancient Views of Sexual Desire: Paul's Sexual Ethics in 1 Thessalonians 4, 1 Corinthians 7, and Romans 1*, Library of New Testament Studies, 354 (London/New York: T & T Clark, 2007).

vinely ordained means for satisfying sexual desire that otherwise would be out of control and lead to sin.

Indeed, from a wider, canonical perspective, it is impossible to claim that the Bible as a whole views sexual desire itself negatively, particularly in light of the extended celebration of desire that we find in the Song of Songs. The fact that the later tradition perceived in these canticles the love between God and Israel, between Christ and the church, or even between the individual soul and God, should not overwhelm the plain sense of the Song of Song's words, which express a profound celebration of the beauty of sexual desire itself. In the light of this book, no canonical interpretation of sexual desire can ever claim that desire itself is evil. The Psalmist declares to God, "You open your hand, satisfying the desire of every living thing" (145:16). If this is true, desire itself cannot be intrinsically evil. In fact, the desire to love and to be loved is one of the deepest and most profound markers of the fact that we belong to God and exist for relationship with God. Augustine's quote at the beginning of the *Confessions* rightly declares, "You have made us for yourself, O Lord, and our heart is restless until it rests in you." Human love and desire, including sexual desire (if we consider the long tradition of metaphorical and allegorical readings of the Song of Songs), always points beyond itself. The drama of loving and being loved, desiring and being desired, is an echo and foretaste of the deeper drama in which our hearts find their deepest home in communion with God, the fountain and source of all love, who himself *is* love (1 John 4:8). The one who abides in love abides in God (1 John 4:16). Such love is quite different from self-seeking desire, but in the strange providence of God it is the desires of body and heart that draw us into such relationships, where true love can be experienced most deeply. Our desires — particularly our sexual desires — can readily lead us astray, but such desires are not inherently evil. In fact, they can draw us into marital relationships that, according to Ephesians 5, reflect and point to the deeper love between Christ and the church.

Implications for the Homosexuality Debate

What are the implications of the understandings of lust and desire that we have explored in this chapter for interpreting Romans 1:24-27, which describes same-sex eroticism, in part at least, as a manifestation of "the lusts of their hearts" (Rom. 1:24), as characterized by "degrading passions"

(Rom. 1:26), or as "consumed with passion" (Rom. 1:27)? We must begin by recognizing that when we explore lust, we are only looking at one of the forms of moral logic found in this passage. In fact, most of the contemporary debate about this passage has focused, not on lust, but on Paul's characterization of same-sex sexual activity as "unnatural" in Romans 1:26-27. (I will explore this debate more fully in chapter 11 below.) Nevertheless, it will be helpful to pause here to consolidate the learnings and questions that have emerged from our exploration thus far. In many discussions of this passage, lust is not given the attention it deserves.

The first point to observe is one that I have already noted earlier in this chapter. Writers in the first century, including Paul, did not look at same-sex eroticism with the understanding of sexual orientation that is commonplace today. Rather, as we can see from a variety of ancient sources contemporaneous with Paul, same-sex eroticism was consistently portrayed by those who opposed this behavior as a manifestation of a form of insatiable lust that, not content with heterosexual relations, was driven to increasingly exotic and perverse forms of sexual behavior that were intended to satiate sexual appetites that had become grotesque through ever-expanding self-indulgence. The specific example of Gaius Caligula explored above illustrates this dynamic powerfully, as this monstrous self-serving ego knew no boundaries and violated virtually every sexual taboo known to humanity. According to Paul, this is the archetypal manifestation of human idolatry, sinfulness, and rebellion against God.

If this connection between Romans 1 and Gaius Caligula has merit, this text becomes, at one level, completely noncontroversial. In every age and in every time — including our own time — Christians readily agree with Paul here, rightly regarding the kind of outrageous behavior of Gaius Caligula as the manifestation of human sinfulness and the just judgment of God. (And in every age and time, Christians will need to heed Paul's warning in Rom. 2:1 that the posture of judgment that we find so tempting can all too easily blind us to our own patterns of self-seeking that are equally resistant to God's purposes.) Even if one doubts that there is an explicit reference to the imperial house in Romans 1, the parallels in Philo and Dio Chrysostom that I noted above clearly suggest that Paul is speaking of extreme sexual excess and self-indulgence. But precisely because Paul speaks in Romans 1 of human desire in its *extremity*, it becomes more complicated to discern the implications of this passage in cases where desire seems directed, not toward self-seeking lust that demeans the other and advances one's own agenda, but toward loving gay or lesbian relationships that seek to honor the other and to express something of divine love to the other. Are such relationships inherently and necessarily "lustful," regardless of the level of passion or self-seeking that may or may not be expressed in them?

Where Does the Focus Lie when Paul Speaks of "Lust"?

As I noted in chapter 6 in the discussion on procreation, the Roman Catholic Church currently takes such a view. Because same-sex eroticism cannot be procreative, Catholic teaching says that persons who engage in homosexual activity "confirm within themselves a disordered sexual inclination which is essentially self-indulgent."[30] I have already observed (in chapter 6 above) the difficulties that are involved in attempting to apply such reasoning consistently, particularly when most Protestant churches accept the use of artificial forms of contraception by heterosexual couples, and many Catholic marriages routinely ignore the church's teaching on contraception. But for the discussion in this chapter, it is important to remember that there is some discrepancy between the range of meaning implied in the English word "lust" and the Greek word *epithumia,* commonly translated as "lust." In English, the word "lust" always has a negative connotation: it refers to a strong desire that is misdirected, excessive, or self-seeking. The Greek word *epithumia,* however, has a wider range of meaning. There are numerous New Testament passages where the word (along with its related cognate verb *epithumeō*) have either neutral or positive meanings, indicating, for example, strong desire or longing.[31] The root meanings of the Greek words *epithumia* and *epithumeō* focus on the *intensity* of desire. Most translators render the Greek word only as "lust" when the context is clearly a negative one.

This means that one cannot ignore the level of passion when a pattern of behavior is characterized by the word *epithumia,* "lust." If such behavior

30. Congregation for the Doctrine of the Faith, "Letter to the Bishops of the Catholic Church on the Pastoral Care of Homosexual Persons (1986)," printed in Charles E. Curran and Richard A. McCormick, *Dialogue about Catholic Sexual Teaching,* Readings in Moral Theology, 8 (New York: Paulist Press, 1993), p. 301.

31. The following New Testament uses of the Greek noun *epithumia* carry neutral or positive connotations: Luke 22:15; Phil. 1:23; and 1 Thess. 2:17. The following New Testament uses of the cognate Greek verb *epithumeō* have the same neutral or positive sense: Matt. 13:17; Luke 15:16; 17:22; 22:15; 1 Tim. 3:1; Heb. 6:11; and 1 Pet. 1:12.

is not marked by a strong intensity of desire, it may indeed be morally wrong, but it cannot be characterized as "lustful," given the meaning of the Greek word. What seems clear, then, in our exploration of Romans 1 is that, when Paul describes same-sex eroticism as "consumed with passion" (1:27) and as an expression of the "lusts of their hearts" (1:24), he has in view an expression of *intense* or *excessive* desire, which he regards also as "unnatural" and thus *misdirected*. It is because lust is inherently and centrally excessive, driven by a self-seeking will to power that it also manifests itself in misdirected desire, as unrestrained desire burns itself out in destructive patterns. This, according to Paul, is the manifestation of the just judgment of God, who "hands us over" to our own excesses.

But what would Paul say to a gay couple who wish to enter a marriage or marriagelike relationship in order to discipline their desire by the constraints of mutual commitment, self-giving love, and communal accountability — "for better and for worse, for richer and for poorer, in sickness and in health, to love and to cherish until we are parted by death"? What if their love is not excessive or self-indulgent but rather reflects divine love? Must such a desire for a lifelong union still be called "lust" because it is misdirected and "essentially self-indulgent," regardless of the amount of compassion, self-giving, and good will that may accompany it? I think it is fair to say that Paul's language never directly envisions such a possibility. Moreover, I am not aware of any discussions in the ancient world more generally that would characterize such a disposition as "lustful." In the ancient world, moderated and disciplined desire (even if it might be considered wrong or misdirected) simply was not referred to as "lust" *(epithumia)*, because such circumstances lack the intensity of desire that stands at the root of the meaning of the Greek word *epithumia*, which, in its ancient usage, always takes on the connotation of strong intensity of desire, whether positive, negative, or neutral. We are left to speculate about what Paul *might* have said or thought, but the evidence before us may not be adequate.

My exploration suggests that, while such a desire might still be characterized as "unnatural" by Paul (I will explore this further in chapter 11 below), it would probably not be appropriate to speak of this kind of desire for long-term gay unions as "lust," since it lacks the intensity and excessive self-seeking and self-centered drive that lies at the heart of Paul's understanding of sinful lust. For Paul — and in his world — whenever same-sex eroticism was viewed negatively, it was characteristically understood as an expression of insatiable lust that "leaves behind" the natural use of the opposite sex, not content with "normal" sexual satisfaction and driven to self-destructive excess (Rom. 1:27).

This is also reflected in the rest of Paul's discourse in Romans 1. In verse 27, Paul speaks of men engaged in same-sex eroticism as "consumed with passion for one another." This is not merely the portrayal of an "objective" problem; this is a portrayal of out-of-control desire, the same kind of desire recounted in the parallel texts we have observed. The word translated as "consumed" in Romans 1:27 *(ekkaiō)* literally means "to kindle or burn." The focus is not on objective behavior but on passions that are running out of control and threaten to "consume" one's better judgment.[32] It could be that Paul regards such same-sex erotic behavior as "objectively" wrong as well, but this "objective" perspective is not what he has in mind when we consider the language of lust and passion. With these words, the emphasis falls on the interior, subjective side of sinfulness. The essence of lust *(epithumia)* lies in its intense passion *(thumos)*. To the extent to which Paul's rejection of same-sex eroticism is based on his assumption that such behavior is inherently lustful, marked by passions that are out of control, we must recognize a gap between what Paul is describing and the modern experience of gay couples seeking marriage or marriagelike unions. Such a gap requires further conversation about the nature of our sexuality and sexual desires and the proper conditions that best prevent lust and encourage healthy desires in all Christians. We may agree with Paul that whenever same-sex (or heterosexual) eroticism is driven by excessive lustful passion and manifests itself in self-centered and destructive behavior, we see the manifestation of divine judgment. At the same time, we may also recognize that some gay or lesbian Christians seek to form loving same-sex bonds that are not characterized by excessive, self-centered, and destructive behavior. It is simply out of keeping with the biblical meaning of words to characterize such behaviors as "lustful" and "consumed with passion." To the extent that this is true, it may call into question whether a text like Romans 1:26-27 is speaking directly to the contemporary experience of gay Christians who long to sanctify their relationships in the bonds of marriage or marriagelike covenants, at least insofar as these verses see same-sex eroticism through the lens of lustful desire.

---

32. Paul also refers to "burning" with a different Greek word *(puroō)* in 1 Cor. 7:9, where he says, "It is better to marry than to be aflame with passion." Here again, the focus is on impulses that are out of control.

On Distinguishing "Orientation" and "Behavior"

This distinction between looking at same-sex eroticism "objectively" and "subjectively" raises a further issue that we must explore before completing our study of lust and desire. The issue concerns the distinction, made in many traditionalist approaches to same-sex eroticism, between a homosexual *orientation* and homosexual *behavior*. This distinction is, of course, a modern one that would make little sense in the ancient world, where the notion of sexual orientation was absent. Most scholars agree that the ancient world thought simply of sexual drives, which could manifest themselves either in heterosexual or in same-sex forms of eroticism. The modern category of sexual orientation that comes closest to the ancient view is probably the notion of bisexuality: the form of sexuality that finds both same-sex and opposite-sex forms of eroticism pleasurable and decides between them based on a variety of other factors.[33] But modern research today recognizes that true bisexuality is quite rare among men (though somewhat more common among women).[34]

So, when we seek to bring ancient discussions into our modern context, we run into some problems. In the ancient world we see almost no interest at all in the question of sexual orientation, particularly among critics of same-sex behavior. Rather, we see the kinds of discussion found in Romans 1 focusing on two problems: the *subjective* problem of excessive lust and the *objective* problem of behavior that is regarded as "contrary to nature." Yet when these discussions are translated into a modern context, the question of lust tends to recede into the background, because, as we have seen, it seems irrelevant to the question of committed gay unions. Instead, the focus falls on the objective problem that same-sex eroticism is "contrary to nature." Traditionalists generally are far more comfortable talking about sexuality "objectively" than in dealing with the inner and subjective aspects of sexual orientation. This is true in no small part because the Bible does not envision the category of sexual orientation; it only addresses the problem of *excessive* desire.

The result is an odd state of affairs that was never quite envisioned in the biblical world. Most contemporary traditionalist churches want to ex-

---

33. See the argument to this effect in Mark D. Smith, "Ancient Bisexuality and the Interpretation of Romans 1:26-27," *Journal of the American Academy of Religion* 64, no. 2 (1996).

34. See chapter 6 above, pp. 141ff., for discussion of the extent to which sexual orientation is subject to change.

press a welcoming posture toward gay and lesbian *persons* while expressing disapproval of gay and lesbian *behavior*. Such a posture is expressed paradigmatically in Stanley Grenz's title for his book on homosexuality, *Welcoming but Not Affirming*.[35] Yet when we speak of gay and lesbian persons today, we mean something a bit different from what Paul was referring to in 1 Corinthians 6:9, when he spoke of *malakoi* ("softies," or "effeminate ones") or *arsenokoitai* (literally "man-bedders," probably those taking the active role in same-sex eroticism, in contrast to the *malakoi*).[36] When Paul speaks of vices in general, he is referring to people who experienced sinful *inclinations* (e.g., lust) that led them to engage in particular forms of sinful behavior (e.g., sexual immorality). The remainder of this list in 1 Corinthians 6 includes fornicators, idolaters, adulterers, thieves, the greedy, drunkards, revilers, and robbers. All of these address not only inclinations but also behaviors, and Paul says that those who do these things "will not inherit the kingdom of God" (1 Cor. 6:10). When Paul goes on to say, "this is what some of you used to be" (1 Cor. 6:11), he is speaking of the *combination* of inclination and behavior that characterized the former lives of the Corinthian Christians. These inclinations and behaviors (including, for Paul, those of *malakoi* and *arsenokoitai*) were not affirmed by the church, even though the church was called to welcome sinners. But most importantly, when the Corinthian Christians ceased to engage in these behaviors, they no longer were "fornicators, idolaters, adulterers . . . *malakoi* or *arsenokoitai*." In Paul's world, if the inclination ceased to express itself in behaviors, that inclination no longer characterized the person at all.

But here is where our modern notions of identity complicate matters. For us today, being gay or lesbian is not first of all a question of behavior but rather of sexual orientation, a concept that ancient moralists, particularly those who opposed same-sex erotic behavior, did not recognize or ac-

---

35. Stanley J. Grenz, *Welcoming but Not Affirming: An Evangelical Response to Homosexuality* (Louisville: Westminster John Knox, 1998).

36. The NRSV's translation of *malakoi* as "male prostitutes" is highly interpretive, and is probably overly precise and restrictive. Similarly, the NRSV's translation of *arsenokoitēs* as "sodomite" is even more problematic, representing an archaizing term that bears little connection to thought forms or usage in the ancient world. The scholarly debate about the precise meaning of these terms is extensive, and it lacks full resolution. For an interesting and important discussion that sees *malakos* ("soft") referring not to the passive role in male-male eroticism but rather to a general vice focusing on the absence of self-control, see Fredrickson, "Natural and Unnatural Use in Romans 1:24-27," pp. 219-20.

knowledge. We recognize today that even though gay or lesbian persons may avoid the kinds of genital contact that traditionalists consider sinful behavior, they usually still experience attraction, interest, love, desire, or special affection toward people of the same sex. In other words, in our modern context, people are still "gay" or "lesbian" if they experience same-sex attraction, whether or not they act on those attractions, and whether or not those attractions manifest themselves as out-of-control lust or as calm and pleasurable interests that are fully under control. We define the words "gay" and "lesbian," not first of all by behavior, but by sexual orientation; this is not at all the same thing as lust, which is understood as excessive desire. Nor is this merely an artificial verbal distinction; it arises from the actual experience of gay and lesbian persons, experience that went largely unrecognized in the ancient world.

So here is the paradox. In the ancient world, if a man ceased engaging in same-sex erotic behavior, or ceased engaging in prostitution, or no longer was involved in cultic activity, or simply avoided sexual vice (depending on one's specific interpretation of the relevant terms), he was no longer a *malakos* or an *arsenokoitēs*. But in our context, the same kind of change may not happen, even if behavior changes. As long as individuals experience same-sex attraction, they are understood to be "gay" or "lesbian," regardless of whether or not they act on that attraction by engaging in same-sex erotic behavior or other more specific behaviors. Moreover, as I have noted earlier, such same-sex attraction, in the vast majority of cases, is stable, enduring, and resistant to change. It is one thing to refrain from explicit, genitally focused, erotic behavior; it is quite another to cease finding others of the same sex attractive, interesting, and sexually desirable.

When the church speaks of "welcoming but not affirming," it claims to welcome gay and lesbian persons who experience same-sex attraction, but it simply refuses to affirm same-sex erotic behavior. Such a posture, however, may not be as welcoming as it seems. In fact, many such churches not only refuse to affirm same-sex erotic behavior; they also refuse, either implicitly or explicitly, to affirm same-sex *attraction* in gay and lesbian people, and they call such people to reject those impulses that are part of their experience. From that perspective, all those attractions are lustful because they represent disordered desire, even when that desire is not excessive or out of control. As a result, even when gay and lesbian Christians who accept this message are able to refrain from same-sex erotic behavior, they still face ongoing struggles with their own sexual orientation: their own impulses to be with others of the same sex are constantly placed under question and suspicion. They thus face relentless reminders of their own "disordered" state. For many gay and lesbian Christians, this internal conflict creates the unhappy reality of "the closet," a secret life that is revealed to few people — if it is revealed to anyone at all. Gay Christians often live lives of public composure and private anguish.[37] It is not surprising that attempted suicide rates among gay youth are higher than those of the general population.[38] For others, the internal conflict is simply too great, and they become part of the growing "ex-ex-gay" movement of gay and lesbian Christians who have found that the denial of their sexual orientation gives them no integrated basis for becoming whole persons.[39]

Other traditionalist churches recognize the difficulty of an approach that attempts to say both "we welcome you" and "we do not welcome the way you function at the emotional level." These churches take a different approach, but one fraught with different problems. This approach distinguishes homosexual orientation from behavior, and declares that, though homosexual behavior is forbidden for Christians, there is nothing sinful about a homosexual orientation. As long as Christians keep their behavior under control, their attractions to others of the same sex should not be the occasion of guilt and self-hatred. Rather, they should rest in the accepting grace of God with respect to their emotional processes, learn to accept themselves the way God has accepted them, and find ways to live responsibly with their given emotional makeup, albeit avoiding same-sex erotic behavior. Hence, Michael R. Saia says:

> As one man put it, "I feel as if God is always breathing down my neck." If, no matter how pure his life is, he has to feel guilty for his attractions, then there is never any relief from guilt. "How would you feel," another man said, "if you had to feel guilty every time you become hungry?" Hunger is not gluttony, and preference is not homo-

37. For a similar critique, see the discussion of the "tolerationist" position in Johnson, *A Time to Embrace: Same-Gender Relationships in Religion, Law, and Politics*, pp. 53-61.

38. While data on "successful" suicide attempts is difficult to gather (given the problem of determining motives for suicide after people have died), the rates of suicidal ideation and attempted suicide among lesbian, gay, or bisexual youth are significantly higher than in the overall population. In a range of studies, LGB youth are 1.5 to 3 times more likely to have experienced suicidal ideation, and 1.5 to 7 times more likely to have attempted suicide (Suicide Prevention Resource Center, "Suicide Risk and Prevention for Lesbian, Gay, Bisexual and Transgender Youth" [Newton, MA: Education Development Center, Inc., 2008]).

39. See the website: http://www.beyondexgay.com/.

sexual sin. But the confused Church has often equated preference and homosexual acts (sin) and held people responsible for something that is not actually a moral issue.[40]

It is easy to recognize both the deep compassion and the moral intuition that undergirds this statement. In any construal of Christian ethics and morality, the temptation to engage in a sinful act does not carry the same weight as the actual performance of a sinful act. Scripture itself declares that Jesus was tempted, yet did not engage in sin (Matt. 4:1-11; Mark 1:13; Luke 4:2; Heb. 15). Temptation in Scripture often has the neutral connotation of "testing," rather than a negative sense of a manifestation of internal sinfulness.[41] Yet the Bible does not regard impulses to sin that arise from within oneself in the same neutral way. Instead, it views these inner impulses as manifestations of an inward sinful nature. This is seen most clearly in Jesus' Sermon on the Mount in Matthew, where Jesus declares that looking at a woman with lust is the same as adultery (Matt. 5:28); he also likens the inner experience of anger toward one's brother to murder (Matt. 5:21-22). Similarly, James 1:12-15 declares:

> [12]Blessed is anyone who endures temptation. Such a one has stood the test and will receive the crown of life that the Lord has promised to those who love him. [13]No one, when tempted, should say, "I am being tempted by God"; for God cannot be tempted by evil and he himself tempts no one. [14]But one is tempted by one's own desire, being lured and enticed by it; [15]then, when that desire has conceived, it gives birth to sin, and that sin, when it is fully grown, gives birth to death.

Here as well, inner evil impulses are a manifestation of one's sinful nature which, if it is not resisted, will lead to sinful acts, and eventually to death. In all these verses that speak of inward impulses, the neutral sense of "testing" doesn't provide an adequate understanding. Such impulses are seen in

40. Michael R. Saia, *Counseling the Homosexual* (Minneapolis: Bethany House, 1988), p. 23, as cited by Grenz, *Welcoming But Not Affirming*, pp. 122-32.

41. The same Greek words *(peirazō, peirasmos)* can have either neutral (testing) or negative (temptation) connotations. The more neutral meaning is probably intended in the phrase in the Lord's Prayer that we commonly recite as, "Lead us not into temptation," but whose more precise meaning is: "Do not put us to the test." Other neutral usages include Luke 22:28; John 6:6; Acts 15:10; 20:19; 1 Cor. 10:9, 13; 2 Cor. 13:5; Gal. 4:14; Heb. 2:18; 11:17; James 1:2, 12; 1 Pet. 1:6; 4:12; Rev. 2:10.

Scripture as manifestations of a sinful nature and are to be resisted in the same way that sinful actions are to be avoided (see Matt. 26:41; Mark 14:8; Luke 22:40, 46; 1 Cor. 7:5; Gal. 6:1; 1 Tim. 6:9).

These New Testament texts call into question the adequacy of the orientation/behavior distinction in addressing gay and lesbian Christians. If same-sex erotic acts are always morally wrong, then the impulse to engage in those acts is also a manifestation of a disordered and sinful inner state. Focusing on behavior alone — and regarding as neutral the "preference" or inclination toward such behaviors — simply cannot be justified from Scripture, particularly from the teaching of Jesus in the Sermon on the Mount. If the acts are sinful, all inclinations to such acts are to be understood as manifestations of a sinful nature, and are to be resisted as such.

Certainly, from the perspective of social ethics, the moral distinction between inclination and action is essential. We cannot discern each other's hearts, and wrong actions do far more social damage than sinful inclinations. We are not accountable to each other for our thoughts in the same that we are for our actions. Yet, if we take the teaching of Jesus and the rest of Scripture seriously, such distinctions between impulse and action don't carry the same importance in the presence of God, who searches the heart (see 1 Chron. 29:17; Ps. 139:23; Jer. 17:10). Before God, if an action is wrong, the inward impulse toward that action is equally culpable. Anger is the same as murder, lust the same as adultery. Unless divine grace transforms us throughout, we cannot find wholeness before God.

This means that the attempt by some traditionalists to bracket sexual orientation and to focus only on sexual behavior is ultimately untenable, even if it may seem necessary or benevolent from a pastoral point of view. Where does one draw the line? Where does the sinful impulse begin? Is it when gay or lesbian persons experience a desire for friendship with others of the same sex, admiration for another's physical beauty, the tendency to frequently think about another person, the persistent desire to be with another person, the desire to be touched by another, the desire to kiss or be kissed, or the desire for still more intimate sexual contact? For most gay and lesbian persons, these desires are part of the same continuum, and they cannot always be readily distinguished from each other. Of course, in any given instance, even for those who affirm the morality of a same-gendered sexual orientation, some of these desires may or may not be appropriate, given the context and the character of the relationship. The same is true in heterosexual ethics. Some of our sexual impulses will lead us astray from the will of God, and they must be resisted. But it is one thing to interpret the appropriateness of one's sexual desires based on relationships and context, and it is quite another when the whole continuum of desires that are part of sexual orientation are placed under suspicion — that is, as a manifestation of a distorted and sinful nature. With these assumptions, determining when the sinful nature begins to express itself will require an endless and exhausting practice of introspective vigilance — with no clearly discernible lines for guidance. A focus merely on genital acts will be no more helpful with gay and lesbian persons than it is with heterosexual persons, when sexual intercourse is divorced from a wider vision of one's sexuality encompassing the entire fabric and character of relationships. When we add to this the conclusion of a wide range of studies — that sexual orientation is stable, enduring, and resistant to change, even when that change is religiously motivated — we have a recipe for deep frustration.[42]

Many traditionalists sense this problem, and they attempt to resolve the tension by critiquing the whole notion of sexual orientation. Stanley Grenz, for example, joins social constructivists in objecting to the notion of sexual orientation as a transcultural phenomenon, saying: "By using the language of orientation, we risk transposing a construction of contemporary society into indelible scientific fact."[43] He, along with many others, points to the ambiguity in current research concerning the causes of homosexual orientation as evidence of this social construction.[44] But the increasingly "indelible scientific fact" that all sides of the debate are being forced to recognize is the resistance of sexual orientation to change, particularly among males, regardless of whether that orientation may be socially constructed or not. The increasingly established scientific fact cannot be evaded or avoided: a substantial majority of people who experience same-sex desires will not be able to change their sexual orientation even if they attempt to do so, regardless of the extent to which they can control their behavior. The distinction between orientation and behavior will probably condemn those gay and lesbian Christians who embrace traditionalist teaching to a lifetime of inner turmoil and tension, even if they control their behavior, and even if they do not regularly experience overwhelm-

---

42. See the preceding chapter, pp. 141ff., for a discussion of the extent to which sexual orientation is subject to change.

43. Grenz, *Welcoming But Not Affirming*, p. 123.

44. For contrasting perspectives, see Stanton L. Jones and Mark A. Yarhouse, *Homosexuality: The Use of Scientific Research in the Church's Moral Debate* (Downers Grove, IL: InterVarsity, 2000); Glenn D. Wilson and Qazi Rahman, *Born Gay: The Psychobiology of Sex Orientation* (London/Chester Springs, PA: Peter Owen, 2005).

ingly lustful thoughts. Still, they will probably experience a persistent same-sex orientation, which will for them also be a persistent reminder of their "disordered" nature, casting its shadow over every relationship with others of the same sex.

However, all these dilemmas represent problems that are vastly different from those described in Romans 1:26-27, with its focus on insatiable lust. Unfortunately, most traditionalist readings of Romans 1 are so focused on the claim that same-sex acts are inherently and objectively "contrary to nature" that the interior emotional gap between the lustful world of Romans 1 and the world of contemporary gays seeking the church's blessing on long-term same-sex unions is completely ignored. Moreover, the emotional burden imposed explicitly or implicitly by traditionalists on contemporary gays and lesbians — not just to avoid same-sex behavior but to renounce their own persistent impulses and desires, even when those desires are not excessive, simply because they are "objectively" disordered — creates a profoundly difficult and duplicitous message of acceptance interlaced with rejection.

Despite all this contemporary controversy, however, the simple fact remains: Romans 1, like other ancient Roman, Jewish, and Christian texts that oppose same-sex eroticism, views this behavior as the manifestation of out-of-control lust, as "consumed with passion." If, in the contemporary debate over long-term gay relationships, we are confronting a desire for sexual bonding and communion that is *not* driven by out-of-control lust nor "consumed with passion," then we must recognize that we are in a new situation, a situation that Paul does not directly address in Romans 1. In itself, this does not answer the question about whether such unions are appropriate in the church; however, it does discourage us from rejecting such unions because they are inherently and unavoidably "lustful." It also cautions us against avoiding or minimizing the importance of the inner, subjective experience of gay and lesbian persons in favor of purely "objective" considerations, and it calls for clearer criteria for evaluating that inner experience. Moreover, the discoveries in this chapter invite us to think more deeply about other principles and forms of moral logic that shape our ethics.

Summing Up

- Paul clearly expects his readers to join him in outrage over the sexual behavior he describes in Romans 1:24-27 as an expression of excessive, self-centered desire. He describes this behavior as an expression of "lusts" (1:24), as driven by "passions" (1:26), and as "consumed, or "burning," "with passion" (1:27).

• This is in keeping with the general perception of same-sex relations in the ancient world: that they were driven by insatiable desire, not content with more normal sexual relationships. Jews and Christians opposed to same-sex eroticism show no awareness of the modern notion of sexual orientation.

• In Romans 1:24-27, Paul may be alluding to the notorious excesses of a former Roman emperor, Gaius Caligula, whose idolatrous patterns and sexual excesses — including same-sex eroticism — were well known, and whose murder by being stabbed in the genitals markedly echoes Paul's words in Romans 1:27: "receiving in their own persons the due penalty for their error."

• Paul does not regard sexual desire itself as evil; it is only when desire gets out of control that it becomes lust and leads to sin.

• Many traditionalist interpreters of this passage focus on the "objective" disorder of same-sex relationships, but when Paul speaks of these behaviors as "lustful," the focus falls on their excessive nature: out-of-control, self-seeking desire.

• Modern attempts to differentiate between same-sex orientation and same-sex behavior tend to minimize Paul's concern with out-of-control lust in this text, focusing instead on the "objective" disorder of same-sex intimacy. Yet this move leaves gay and lesbian Christians with little help in wrestling with their "subjective" sexual orientation, which is in most cases highly resistant to change.

• Ultimately, Scripture does not sanction a sharp split between sinful acts and the inclination toward sinful acts. If an act is sinful, the inclination to that act is also a manifestation of one's sinful nature. This calls into question whether the orientation/behavior dichotomy in many traditionalist approaches to homosexuality is theologically and ethically viable.

• But if we keep Paul's focus in Romans 1:24-27 on out-of-control desire firmly in focus, we will recognize that these concerns may not be reflected in committed gay or lesbian relationships, opening up the possibility that these relationships may not be "lustful" and thus not directly addressed by Paul's polemic in Romans 1.

9

Purity and Impurity

W hen Paul speaks of the sexual excesses into which God "hands over" idolatrous people in Romans 1, he speaks not only of "lust" but also of "impurity." Romans 1:24 declares: "Therefore God gave them up in the lusts of their hearts to *impurity*, to the degrading of their bodies among themselves." This association between sexual misbehavior and impurity is a fairly common one in the writings of Paul, as well as the later Pauline tradition.[1]

I have noted in the preceding chapter how Paul understands lust to be excessive desire that runs amok and becomes self-defeating. His use of the term "licentiousness" *(aselgeia)* carries much the same connotation: it refers to a disposition that accepts no boundaries or limits and thus gives a free and unrestrained scope to the passions in sexual excess, violence, and

---

1. In 2 Cor. 12:21, Paul links "impurity" *(akatharsia)* with "sexual immorality" *(porneia)*, as well as "licentiousness" *(aselgeia)*. In this passage, Paul speaks of all three of these as previous sinful behaviors or dispositions practiced by some of the Corinthian Christians. Paul fears they have not repented of these sins. The same three words ("impurity," "sexual immorality," and "licentiousness") occur at the beginning of a list of the "works of the flesh" in Gal. 5:19. Similarly, 1 Thess. 4:7 also speaks of "impurity" in the context of a discussion about sexual behavior, speaking of it as the result of "lustful passion." The same associations are found in other Pauline writings whose authorship is disputed. Col. 3:5 links together "fornication" (or "sexual immorality," from the same Greek word, *porneia*), "impurity" *(akatharsia)*, "passion" *(pathos)*, "evil desire" (or "evil lust," from *epithumian kakēn*), and "greed" *(pleonexia)*. Similar linkages between impurity and "fornication/sexual immorality," "licentiousness," and "lust" are found in Eph. 4:19ff. and Eph. 5:3-5. Clearly, Paul uses "impurity" to speak broadly about sexual misbehavior.

outrageous behavior.[2] It is thus licentiousness (lack of self-restraint), working together with lust and passion (excessive desire), that gives rise to "fornication/sexual immorality" *(porneia,* a rather generic word Paul uses for a wide range of sexual misbehaviors). But where does "impurity" fit into this picture? What is the moral logic underlying this word, and how should we understand its significance?

Getting a clear answer to this question is more complicated than it might initially appear, especially when we attempt to keep the whole canon of Scripture in view. This becomes evident when we recognize that the New Testament as a whole exercises a remarkable freedom in removing, for Gentiles, much of the purity legislation found in the Old Testament, particularly those laws dealing with dietary restrictions and circumcision. A quick survey of this larger canonical movement is necessary to set a framework for understanding Paul's language about sexual purity in particular.

Larger Canonical Treatment of Purity and Impurity

Many of the laws dealing with purity in the Old Testament are found in the book of Leviticus, particularly the so-called Priestly Code of Leviticus 11–16 and the Holiness Code of Leviticus 17–26. The Priestly Code focuses on the practical matters of how various forms of impurity are contracted and dealt with in their respective priestly purification rites; by contrast, the Holiness Code focuses not on the practical matter of cleansing various forms of impurity but on the broad command to the people of Israel to avoid all behavior that would lead to impurity, and to expel all impure persons from Israel, so that the people might dwell in the holy land God has given them. Failure to do so will cause the land to "vomit out" the people of Israel, just as it did to the Canaanites before them (Lev. 18:28; 20:22). Other passages of Scripture have regulations governing purity as well, especially the books of Exodus through Deuteronomy.

The purity codes in Scripture deal with a wide range of behavioral requirements: extensive lists of different foods that may or may not be eaten (Lev. 11; Deut. 14); extensive purity laws having to do with leprosy and other skin ailments (Lev. 13–14); and laws governing contact with dead bodies, which was seen as particularly defiling (Num. 19:11-22; Lev. 21:11).

---

2. Interestingly, 2 Pet. 2:7 also links licentiousness *(aselgeia)* to the Sodom and Gomorrah story.

There are elaborate discussions of a variety of forms of impurity related to reproductive and sexual issues: purification after childbirth (Lev. 12); purification after bodily discharges of blood or semen (Lev. 15); careful definitions of incestuous relationships (Lev. 18:6-18; 20:17-21; Deut. 27:20-23); the prohibition of a man "lying with a man as with a woman" (Lev. 18:20; 20:13) and of humans having sex with animals (Lev. 18:23; 20:15-16); and the prohibition of adultery (Exod. 20:10; Lev. 18:20; 20:10; Deut. 5:18). In these and related purity codes, there is a wide range of additional material dealing with a host of subjects, ranging from stealing (Lev. 19:11) to skin rashes (Lev. 13–14), from the detestable nature of lobster (Lev. 11:12) to the abominations of unjust weights (Deut. 25:15-16) and cross-dressing (Deut. 22:5).

What is perhaps most striking about the purity codes, at least from the perspective of modern Western Christians, is that they seem to be a collection of a wide range of laws that use very diverse forms of moral logic. For example, the New Testament repeatedly tells us[3] that Leviticus 19:18 offers one of the greatest commandments of all: "You shall not take vengeance or bear a grudge against any of your people, but you shall love your neighbor as yourself; I am the LORD." Here we see an extremely lofty ethical principle, embodying the moral logics of justice, compassion, forgiveness, and love. Yet the following verse is as strange to us as the prior verse is compelling. Leviticus 19:19 declares: "You shall keep my statutes. You shall not let your animals breed with a different kind; you shall not sow your field with two kinds of seed; nor shall you put on a garment made of two different materials." In a single verse, the entire moral framework shifts. Discerning the moral logic underpinning this requirement is a much more challenging task.

Distinguishing "Ceremonial" from "Moral" Law?

For many Christians, sorting through this remarkable diversity involves making a distinction between the "ceremonial law" and the "moral law" (or, as some designate it, the contrast between "ritual law" and "moral law").[4] According to this distinction, the ceremonial (or ritual) law is done

---

3. Matt. 5:43; 19:19; 22:39; Mark 12:31; cf. Rom. 13:9; Gal. 5:14; Jas. 2:8.
4. Later rabbinic Judaism also spoke of "ritual" laws concerning purity as tied directly to Temple worship — and irrelevant outside of the Temple. Yet a recent article by John C. Poirier

away with in Christ, but the moral law continues to express the will of God for all human beings of all times. But this distinction between moral and ceremonial law is never explicitly made within Scripture itself. In fact, Paul (whose writings form the very heart of a Christian understanding of the law) rarely distinguishes some aspects of the law from others. He tends to speak of the law in its totality. Accordingly, he speaks of a righteousness of God that is revealed "apart from the law" (Rom. 3:19); he insists that Christians are justified by faith "apart from works of the law" (Rom. 3:28); Christians are not "under law" but "under grace" (Rom. 6:14); the "just requirement" of the law is fulfilled by those who walk according to the Spirit (Rom. 8:4). In all of this, there is never any parsing out of "ceremonial," "ritual," or "moral" aspects of the law. Paul treats the law in its totality as a unity, a unity that no longer fundamentally determines the relationship to God of those who are "in Christ." The moral versus ceremonial/ritual distinction is thus a distinction of later interpreters, those attempting to differentiate between aspects of the law that have continuing relevance and aspects that do not. This distinction between moral and ceremonial is not in the text of Scripture itself, despite the fact that the New Testament sets aside the relevance of some Old Testament laws for Gentiles.

Moreover, at many points during the history of the church's reading of Scripture, the distinction between moral and ceremonial/ritual is exceedingly blurry and contentious. For example, consider the Sabbath commandment: it stands not only in Leviticus (23:3) but also appears as one of the Ten Commandments in Exodus 20, where it receives a longer exposition than any other commandment, with the possible exception of the prohibition of idolatry. The fact that the Sabbath commandment also explicitly prohibits work done by slaves or employed aliens (Exod. 20:10) suggests that powerful considerations of morality and justice are in play here: even slaves deserve a day of rest. The Sabbath commandment is explicitly rooted in the creation story itself: "For in six days the LORD made heaven and earth, the sea, and all that is in them, but rested the seventh day; therefore the LORD blessed the sabbath day and consecrated it" (v. 11). This sounds very much like a universal requirement of moral law. Yet Jews

---

has persuasively argued that purity laws in the Second Temple period were not restricted to Temple worship alone. The exclusive linkage between purity laws and Temple worship arose later, after the Temple was destroyed, and rabbis sought a diminishment of the rigors of purity legislation. For further details, see John C. Poirier, "Purity Beyond the Temple in the Second Temple Era," *Journal of Biblical Literature* 122, no. 2 (2003).

never understood this commandment to apply to Gentiles outside of Israel, and Paul writes to the Romans about Sabbath observance in remarkably indifferent terms: "Some judge one day to be better than another, while others judge all days to be alike. Let all be fully convinced in their own minds" (Rom. 14:7). This makes the Sabbath commandment sound more like a ceremonial law — that is, no longer universally binding on Christians — than a moral law, despite its obvious moral functions in the Old Testament. Distinguishing ceremonial laws (those no longer binding on Christians) from moral laws is no easy task, and disputes over proper Sabbath observance, for example, have cropped up on numerous occasions in the history of the church.[5] Indeed, the entire distinction between the ceremonial (bad and irrelevant) and moral (good and binding) probably gains more of its energy today from low-church Protestantism than it does from anything in the New Testament itself.

Setting the Context: Purity and Impurity in the New Testament

Rather than using the moral versus ceremonial/ritual distinction, we will be better served and will make more progress if we look at the way the New Testament itself regards those aspects of the law that are not binding on Gentile Christians. In the New Testament, those laws that are no longer applicable to Gentiles in Christ have to do with the contrast between what is "pure" or "clean" *(katharos)* and what is "profane/common" *(koinos)* or "unclean/impure" *(akathartos)*. When Peter speaks of the vision that led him to welcome Gentiles without requiring them to eat kosher or to be circumcised, he tells how the voice from heaven told him, "What God has cleansed, you must not call common *[koinos]*" (Acts 10:15). Peter later declares: "God has shown me that I should not call anyone profane *(koinos)* or unclean *(akathartos)*" (Acts 10:28). Similarly, Paul says, with respect to food laws: "I know and am persuaded in the Lord Jesus that nothing is unclean in itself; but it is unclean for anyone who thinks it unclean" (Rom. 14:14). In one sentence Paul simply sets aside (for Gentiles) the entire system of kosher food laws laid out in great detail in Leviticus 11 and Deuteronomy 14.

This radical reassessment of what is clean and unclean finds its roots in

---

5. For a concise exploration of these controversies, see Willard M. Swartley, *Slavery, Sabbath, War, and Women: Case Issues in Biblical Interpretation*, The Conrad Grebel Lectures, 1982 (Scottdale, PA: Herald Press, 1983).

the church's memory of Jesus' own ministry. Jesus himself seemed remarkably indifferent to many concerns about purity. In the Gospels he seems unconcerned about physical contact with lepers, which is forbidden in Leviticus (14:45-46; see, e.g., Matt. 8:2ff.; Mark 1:40-41). When he is touched by a woman with a flow of blood (Mark 5:25-34) — rendering him impure according to Leviticus 15:19 — he seems entirely unconcerned about himself, and he reassures the woman that her faith has saved her. Mark records an even more explicit teaching of Jesus on the subject, and he supplies his own interpretation of its meaning (Mark 7:18-19): "'Do you not see that whatever goes into a person from outside cannot defile, since it enters, not the heart but the stomach, and goes out into the sewer?' (Thus he declared all foods clean.)."

It seems clear, therefore, that although the New Testament does not use linguistic distinctions between ceremonial and moral laws, it does obviously address those laws that deal with purity: from the perspective of Jesus' ministry and the life of believers in Christ, many of those laws are no longer binding on Gentile Christians in the same way that they were binding on the Jews of the Old Testament period. But this only raises the more pressing question: What is the moral logic underlying the purity laws, and why does the New Testament set that form of moral logic aside in guiding the moral responsibility of Gentile Christians? Once we are clear on that question, we can return with greater clarity to the original question of this chapter: Why does Paul characterize the excessive sexual behavior in Romans 1 as "impurity," and what are the implications of this characterization for sexual ethics today?

The Meaning of Purity in the Old Testament

At one level, the language of purity represents an internalized, "gut-level" form of moral discernment. The need to avoid being "dirty" — and the equation of "dirty" with "bad" — is one of the earliest lessons we learn as children. In fact, we find an extraordinary concentration of emotional, visceral language when the Bible deals with questions of purity. In the NRSV translation of Leviticus, we see the word "abomination" ten times, the word "detestable" nine times, and the language of "abhorrence" seven times. The language of purity encompasses not only the mind, but the heart and the stomach as well. To say that something or someone is "unclean" evokes an immediate visceral reaction that shapes attitudes and behavior. Purity thus represents a different way of socializing communities into shared commitments, values, and behaviors. It involves an appeal to the emotions as much as to the mind and will. Purity regulations direct the social formation of the emotional response of disgust. Most of the forbidden conditions and behaviors in the purity codes of Leviticus and elsewhere in the Old Testament are designed to identify very clearly for Israel what they should regard as disgusting and abhorrent — in food, dress, use of bodies, social roles, and relationships.

This helps to explain why the purity codes seem to us to embody such a disparate collection of different forms of moral logic. Leviticus wants the people of Israel to abhor dishonest weights and injustice just as much, and with the same intensity, as they instinctively and viscerally abhor bestiality, leprosy, contact with corpses, or "unclean" foods. Hence the purity codes are a wide and varied collection of materials. Yet when Leviticus uses the language of "clean" and "unclean" more specifically, we can begin to discern a distinct grouping of materials within this larger collection that seems to have its own underlying logic and assumptions. It is to this more specific range of material that we now turn.

One theorist whose work has been helpful in clarifying the underlying forms of moral logic that shape the purity codes is Mary Douglas.[6] Douglas begins with the simple observation that "dirt" is simply "matter out of place." Soil in the garden is normal, and we don't call the garden "dirty." But when soil comes in on the carpet, we say that the carpet is "dirty," or even "filthy." Purity is thus essentially concerned with the orderliness of the world, and whether everything is in its proper place. Defilement is therefore fundamentally a state of some sort of disorder. Douglas goes on to discuss the concept of holiness as it appears in Leviticus, and identifies three distinct ideas that recur over and over. First of all, holiness means *separateness*. Holy things are kept separate and distinct from "ordinary" things. In fact, the word often translated "profane" literally means "common" or "ordinary." Holiness means separation from "common" life. But Douglas goes on to note the close association between holiness and the ideas of wholeness and completeness. She notes that "much of Leviticus is taken up with stating the physical perfection that is required of things presented in the temple and of persons approaching it."[7] This wholeness and

---

6. See esp. Douglas's groundbreaking work, *Purity and Danger: An Analysis of Concepts of Pollution and Taboo* (London: Routledge & Kegan Paul, 1966).

7. Douglas, *Purity and Danger*, p. 51.

completeness must characterize bodies. Hence skin disruptions, which blur the boundaries of the body, or the emission of fluids from the body (especially blood and semen) render the body unclean, in that the wholeness and completeness of the body is undefined and indistinct.

But what about food? Why are some foods unclean and others permitted? Here Douglas points out that many of the forbidden foods have something ambiguous about them. For example, Leviticus requires that animals that come from the water should have scales and fins, and that anything from the water lacking scales and fins is "detestable" (Lev 11:9-12). Even though shrimp are a tasty dish, they have legs and live in the water. Thus they are ambiguous creatures, reflecting both life on land and life in water. Because they blur boundaries, they are unclean. We see this same concern over inappropriate blurring of boundaries in the prohibitions of mixtures. Leviticus 19:19 declares: "You shall not let your animals breed with a different kind; you shall not sow your field with two kinds of seed; nor shall you put on a garment made of two different materials." Wholeness, completeness, and distinctness are the marks of purity; ambiguities and mixtures are unclean.

Douglas argues that this vision is grounded in the creation story, where God creates the world by *separating* light from darkness (Gen. 1:4), the waters above from those below (Gen. 1:6), the waters from the dry land (Gen. 1:9), and then *filling* each separate place with its own appropriate beings, from lights in the heavens to fish in the sea, birds in the air, and animals on the ground. In this sense, the purity laws call Israel to live in accordance with the original meaning of creation, maintaining appropriate distinctions and keeping everything in its proper place. Douglas summarizes her argument clearly:

> If the proposed interpretation of the forbidden animals is correct, the dietary laws would have been like signs which at every turn inspired meditation on the oneness, purity, and completeness of God. By rules of avoidance holiness was given a physical expression in every encounter with the animal kingdom and at every meal. Observance of the dietary rules would thus have been a meaningful part of the great liturgical act of recognition and worship which culminated in the sacrifice in the Temple.[8]

Douglas's framework is helpful in discerning the underlying form of moral logic that shapes much of the purity codes. However, her framework

8. Douglas, *Purity and Danger*, p. 57.

does not address everything in the purity codes. Two additional observations may help round out the picture. Jacob Milgrom, in his analysis of Leviticus, has placed great emphasis on the relationship between the purity codes and the stewardship of life.[9] Hence, despite the fact that urine and excrement far more commonly come out of the body than does blood or semen, the purity codes in Leviticus concern themselves almost exclusively with the latter. Blood represented life (Lev. 17:11-14), and semen was the "seed" of new life. Because the stewardship of life belongs ultimately to God, Israel was required to pay special attention to that stewardship, and to hedge that stewardship with appropriate boundaries and safeguards. This perspective also helps to explain why contact with corpses was so defiling (Lev. 21:11; Num. 21:11ff.).

Finally, many scholars have noted the way the purity codes attempt to differentiate Israel from its surrounding cultures. Indeed, from a simple literary point of view, this is the most obvious form of moral logic that explicitly shapes Israel's understanding of purity. Emphatically, the priestly and holiness codes urge the people of Israel to avoid behaving like the Egyptians or Canaanites (Lev. 18:3). The pagan worship of Molech is specifically singled out, and its practices forbidden (Lev. 18:21; 20:2-5). In this sense, the holiness that the purity codes require is specifically a holiness that is directly related to their occupation of the promised land.[10] Because God drove out the nations who lived there, and gave the land to Israel, Israel must not act as the other nations do, but must keep itself distinct. Otherwise, the land will "vomit out" the people of Israel just as it did the former inhabitants (Lev. 18:28; 20:22).

Purity in Second Temple Judaism and Christianity

It is this last aspect of purity — the importance of keeping Israel separate from the surrounding nations — that begins to dominate Jewish thinking after Israel's return from exile. The urgency of keeping Israel separate is

9. See his three-volume commentary on Leviticus in the Anchor Bible Commentary series; or, for a more concise treatment, see Milgrom, *Leviticus: A Book of Ritual and Ethics,* Continental Commentaries (Minneapolis: Fortress, 2004).

10. It is worth noting that the first five books of the Bible seem to assume that the purity codes were not in force prior to the giving of the law at Sinai. The book of Genesis seems unconcerned that Abraham married his half-sister (Gen. 20:12, forbidden by Lev. 18:9) and Jacob married the two sisters Rachel and Leah (Gen. 29:16, forbidden by Lev. 18:18).

seen, for example, in Ezra's requirement that all foreign wives must be sent away (Ezra 10:11-14). Here we see an intensification of the earlier legislation on marriage that does not entirely forbid intermarriage with other peoples.[11] During the Second Temple period, the primary practical function of purity codes, particularly dietary restrictions, was to keep Jews separate from other people in their ordinary lives, whether or not they were living in Palestine. Indeed, the literal meaning of the Aramaic word *perushim*, from which the word "Pharisee" is derived, is "distinct or separated ones." The Pharisees wanted to keep Israel pure and separate from her neighbors, and they sought to deepen the sense of Israel's holiness and distinctness in all of life, not merely in worship at the Temple in Jerusalem.

Yet it is precisely this sense of holiness as separateness, and the dominant concern to avoid defilement, that distinguished the Pharisees from Jesus. The Pharisees derisively called Jesus a "friend of tax collectors and sinners" (Matt. 9:11; 11:19; Mark 2:16; Luke 5:30; 7:34). Jesus is accused of failing to keep himself appropriately separate, both from the dominating Roman occupiers and from those who defile themselves by scorning the law. He failed, in their view, to honor the boundaries of wholeness and distinctness that underlay the holiness codes of Leviticus.

But it would not be accurate simply to say that these concerns of holiness, wholeness, and distinctness had no meaning for Jesus, and that he simply rejected this form of moral logic entirely. The Gospels record several occasions in which Jesus healed lepers and restored them to a state of ritual purity. These healings are called "cleansings," an implicit recognition that purity, and not merely illness, is at stake (Matt. 8:2-4; 10:8; 11:5; Mark 1:40ff.; Luke 5:12-13; 7:22). In general, however, Jesus sought to focus attention concerning purity, not primarily on external behaviors, but on internal states. I noted above the statement of Jesus on this issue in Mark 7:18-19: "'Do you not see that whatever goes into a person from outside cannot defile, since it enters, not the heart but the stomach, and goes out into the sewer?' (Thus he declared all foods clean.)." The same text goes on to describe what real "defilement" consists of: "It is what comes out of a person that defiles. For it is from within, from the human heart, that evil inten-

---

11. Moses himself had married a non-Israelite (Num. 12:1). Note the instructions for marrying foreign women captured in battle in Deut. 21:10ff. The book of Ruth eulogizes Boaz for his willingness to marry a foreigner under the rules of levirate marriage. See also Jer. 29:6, which seems to encourage intermarriage during the exile. But notice the contrast in Josh. 23:12, which regards intermarriage with other nations as falling away from God. Priests are forbidden to marry outside their own kin in Lev. 21:14.

tions come: fornication, theft, murder, adultery, avarice, wickedness, deceit, licentiousness, envy, slander, pride, folly. [23]All these evil things come from within, and they defile a person" (Mark 7:20-23). Therefore, purity of the heart mattered greatly to Jesus, and such purity should, in his view, characterize the whole of life — both inside and outside.

An important part of Jesus' ministry involved driving out "unclean" spirits (Matt. 10:1; 12:43; Mark 1:23, 26-27; 3:11, 30; 5:2, 8, 12-13; 6:7; 7:25; 9:25; Luke 4:33, 36; 6:18; 8:29; 9:42; 11:24). Jesus directed a leper who was cured to "offer for your cleansing what Moses commanded" (Mark 1:44). Moreover, the early church regularly spoke of the work of Christ on their behalf as a "cleansing" (Acts 10:15; 11:9; 15:9; Eph. 5:26; Heb. 10:22; 2 Pet. 1:9; 1 John 1:7ff.). This kind of language suggests that concerns of purity did not simply cease to be relevant to early Christians.

It is in this light that we need to consider Paul's repeated characterization of sexual misbehavior as "impurity." Paul is not simply being inconsistent here with his statement in Romans 14:14: "I know and am persuaded in the Lord Jesus that nothing is unclean in itself; but it is unclean for anyone who thinks it unclean." Impurity still exists and must be avoided, but distinguishing clean from unclean requires new, gospel-centered criteria. In what follows, I will attempt to delineate three basic movements that mark the New Testament's reinterpretation of purity and impurity in light of the life, death, and resurrection of Jesus.

Three Basic Movements in Redefining Purity in the New Testament

First, we see a movement away from defining purity *externally* toward defining purity in terms of the motives and dispositions of the *heart and will.* We see this in Jesus' Sermon on the Mount, where he equates inner hatred with murder and inner lust with adultery (Matt. 5:21-30). The same theme occurs in the text from Mark 7:21 quoted above: "It is what comes out of a person that defiles. For it is from within, from the human heart, that evil intentions come." Jesus criticizes the Pharisees as "whitewashed tombs" that look fine externally but are filled with internal corruption (Matt. 23:27). Paul also rejects the disposition to "boast in outward appearance and not in the heart" (2 Cor. 5:12). He insists in Romans 14:14 that some foods are indeed unclean for someone who *thinks* that they are unclean, even if this property of uncleanness is not inherent in the food itself. This concern with inward disposition is also reflected in Paul's use of the language of impurity for sexual misbehavior. As we have noted above, Paul regularly links the language of sexual impurity with references to lust *(epithumia)* and licentiousness, or lack of self-restraint *(aselgeia)*. Despite the fact that the New Testament sets aside much of the purity legislation of the Old Testament, it continues to call for inner purity of heart, mind, and will, and to reject excessive desire and the absence of restraint as "impurity," particularly in sexual matters.

Second, we see in the New Testament a movement away from *defensiveness and separateness* toward *confidence and engagement* in matters of purity and impurity. One of the unwavering assumptions of the purity codes in the Old Testament is that holy things and holy persons become unclean and impure by contact with unholy things and unholy persons. Impurity is conceived of as contagious. This is why separation from impurity is such a critical part of the purity codes. Simply touching someone who is unclean makes you unclean. But in the ministry of Jesus, this "flow of contagion" is reversed. In repeated instances in Jesus' ministry, his own holiness and power drive out impurity. Jesus does not regard himself as contaminated when he touches the lepers; instead, the lepers become clean. Jesus doesn't worry about himself when the woman with a flow of blood touches him; his concern is entirely about proclaiming the gospel to her (Matt. 9:20-22). Underlying this confidence is Jesus' conviction that his holiness and relationship to God are not jeopardized by contact with uncleanness. Instead, in the reign of God, holiness drives out impurity. We see the same understanding in Paul's instructions to those Christians who are married to unbelievers in 1 Corinthians 7:14, where he says, "For the unbelieving husband is made holy through his wife, and the unbelieving wife is made holy through her husband. Otherwise, your children would be unclean, but as it is, they are holy." Again, we see that holiness expels impurity, rather than impurity defiling holiness.

Why this change in the "flow of contagion"? The New Testament writers were convinced that the Spirit of God had been poured out on the church in a dramatically new way. It was the work of the Spirit that persuaded Peter in Acts 10 that Gentiles were also included in the people of God, apart from observance of purity laws (cf. Acts 15:8-9). Similarly, Paul appeals to the gift of the Spirit, received apart from the observance of the law, to persuade the Galatians not to impose circumcision and dietary restrictions on the Gentiles (Gal. 3:1-5). In the new reality unfolding in the pages of the New Testament, the posture of the people of God was not one of huddled separateness and defensive self-protectiveness. Instead, the church understood itself to be sent to all nations, bringing holiness and purity where there was only impurity before. The powerful new gift of the Holy Spirit is the underlying reality that gives the church confidence where there was only defensiveness before. It is the Holy Spirit who reverses the flow of contagion, and who makes holiness contagious rather than making impurity contagious.

Third, we see a shift in defining purity, away from a backward look to the old creation to a forward look toward the new creation. We have already noted how many of the purity codes are grounded in an understanding of the creation narratives in Genesis. Purity codes attempt to conform life to the original intention of God in the creation stories. Dietary restrictions exclude animals whose bodies are not "proper" to the place God created for them. Sabbath observance attempts to replicate God's action in resting after the creation of the world. Likewise, all imperfections, blurrings, and deviations from the original boundaries of the created order are summarily excluded from holiness. Because God is the life-giver, any contact with corpses renders one unclean. Imperfections, rashes, and breaks in the skin render the body impure, and they exclude one from the presence of the Lord. Indeed, the requirements of Leviticus are sweeping and clear:

> [17]No one of your offspring throughout their generations who has a blemish may approach to offer the food of his God. [18]For no one who has a blemish shall draw near, one who is blind or lame, or one who has a mutilated face or a limb too long, [19]or one who has a broken foot or a broken hand, [20]or a hunchback, or a dwarf, or a man with a blemish in his eyes or an itching disease or scabs or crushed testicles. (Lev. 21:17-20)

All of this is done, not from a motive to oppress and exclude unfortunate people, but rather from a vision of the purity and perfection of the original creation, from a desire to replicate and re-create that original purity and perfection, as much as possible, in the community's life before God.

But in the New Testament we see a different movement, perhaps nowhere more clearly portrayed than in the story of the conversion of the Ethiopian eunuch in Acts 8:26-40. The purity laws on this subject are clear: "No one whose testicles are crushed or whose penis is cut off shall be admitted to the assembly of the Lᴏʀᴅ" (Deut. 23:1). Eunuchs were sexually ambiguous, incapable of transmitting life, and they provoked deep purity concerns over their lack of wholeness, completeness, and fittedness to their proper type and kind. They stood outside of the purposes and categories of the original creation. Yet Philip is directed specifically by the angel of the Lord to encounter this man (Acts 8:26). Philip grants the eunuch's request to be baptized, and the eunuch "goes on his way rejoicing." Something powerfully new begins here, already anticipated in Jesus' surprising commendation of those who "have made themselves eunuchs for the sake of the kingdom of heaven" (Matt. 19:12).

Similarly, we see a movement in the New Testament away from the Sabbath commandment, focusing on the original creation, to worship on "the Lord's day" (Rev. 1:10) — the day of resurrection, the day of the dawn of the new creation. Paul sums up this entire line of thinking when he declares in 2 Corinthians 5:17: "So if anyone is in Christ, there is a new creation: everything old has passed away; see, everything has become new!" Paul connects this "new creation" to the radical reframing of the purity laws even more specifically in Galatians 6:15: "For neither circumcision nor uncircumcision is anything; but a new creation is everything!"

Of course, this shift of focus from the old creation to the new creation cannot and must not be absolutized, as if the original creation narratives no longer have anything to teach us. Paul refers back to the creation narratives on a number of occasions, as do many other New Testament writers. It was the later Gnostic heresies that regarded the original creation as a tragedy, something from which the new creation delivers us. In contrast, the message of Scripture, broadly considered, is that the new creation fulfills what is best and most true about the original creation. But this fact must not obscure the "newness" of the new creation as it is narrated in the New Testament. The new creation is not simply a return to a pristine past but rather an opening of a new and unexpected future, a place where they will neither marry nor be given in marriage (Mark 12:25). On the last day, "there will be no night; they need no light of lamp or sun, for the Lord God will be their light, and they will reign forever and ever" (Rev. 22:5). It is precisely this kind of new creation where, according to Acts 8 and Matthew 19:12, even eunuchs find their place — a place unimaginable in the orders of the original creation as interpreted by the Old Testament purity codes. Thus the creation narratives must always be read in the light of Christ, the "second Adam," who fulfills and teaches us the true meaning of the life of the first Adam, and who directs our attention to a new and coming kingdom where the final word is: "See, I am making all things new" (Rev. 21:5).

These three basic movements help us understand what the New Testament is doing with the Old Testament purity codes. We see a movement away from a preoccupation with externals to a concern for the inner origins of behavior, focusing on the heart and the will. We see a movement away from defensiveness and separation toward confidence and mission, empowered by the Holy Spirit. Finally, we see a movement away from the attempt to replicate the original creation to a forward-looking expectation of a new creation, which fulfills — but also transforms — the old creation in surprising ways.

Why, Then, Does Paul Still Speak So Negatively about Sexual Misbehavior as "Impurity"?

In the midst of these transformations in the way that purity is envisioned, however, we also see lines of continuity. The same book of Revelation that records the words of the risen Jesus, "See, I am making all things new," also says, in reference to this new Jerusalem, "Nothing unclean will enter it, nor anyone who practices abomination or falsehood, but only those who are written in the Lamb's book of life" (Rev. 21:27). Despite all the reframing and reinterpretation of the Old Testament purity codes, several themes from those codes remain, deeply embedded in the New Testament's vision for a godly and holy life. These remaining themes help explain why Paul continues to use the language of "impurity" in reference to sexual misconduct (as I explored at the opening of this chapter).

The New Testament retains a deep concern that the life of the Christian community must be *ordered* and *disciplined*. All purity codes are predicated on a sense of order that must not be violated. What is "dirty" is what is out of its proper place. And clearly for Paul, there are many behaviors and dispositions that are "out of place" within the Christian community: "Fornication, impurity, licentiousness, idolatry, sorcery, enmities, strife, jealousy, anger, quarrels, dissensions, factions, envy, drunkenness, carousing, and things like these" (Gal. 5:19b-21a). These are the "works of the flesh," and Paul declares that those who do these things "will not inherit the kingdom of God" (Gal. 5:21b). Though "impurity" is only one item on the list, the list in its entirety reflects the assumption that disordered life is not regulated and normed by the Spirit of God. It is striking, in this regard, to notice how commonly Paul links licentiousness or lack of self-restraint with impurity (2 Cor. 12:21; Gal. 5:19; cf. Eph. 4:19). A large part of what makes sexual misbehavior "impure" is its lack of restraint and order, its wanton excess. In this regard, note also the linkage between impurity and lust (or greed) in Paul (Rom. 1:24; 1 Thess. 4:4-7; cf. Eph. 4:19; 5:3; Col. 3:5). The order of God's kingdom in Christ is an order marked by love, mercy, service, and community; and that order is torn apart by unrestrained greed and desire. Therefore, such things are, even in the New Covenant, "impure."

In short, the life to which Christ calls us, and the life that the Spirit empowers in us, is a life ordered by faith, hope, and love. The New Testament expects Christians to conform their internal dispositions, as well as their external behaviors, to this gracious order empowered by the Holy Spirit through our union with Christ. The failure to do so is "impurity," a disordered life where things are not in their proper places. Paul's reference to sexual misbehavior with the term "impurity" must be understood in this larger context.

But it is also important to note *how* the New Testament writers hope to achieve the orderly state marked by purity in its best sense. They generally move away from focusing on the purity or impurity of external behaviors alone, and toward a deepening focus on purity of the heart and the will. The purity of the life to which the New Testament directs us is not primarily measured by the externals of our behavior but by the disposition of our hearts. It is interesting to note, in this regard, that most New Testament writers, including Paul, spend fairly little time giving detailed descriptions of permitted and forbidden behaviors. The closest we get to this is the "household codes" found in the later New Testament literature: those provide more detailed instructions to household members. But Paul's more general tendency is to speak in broad categories. In particular, we never find in Paul a detailed definition of exactly what "sexual immorality" *(porneia)* means, even though the range of Paul's use of the word indicates that its scope is quite broad. Paul uses the word in reference to incest violations (1 Cor. 5), sex with a prostitute (1 Cor. 6), and adultery and any sex outside of marriage (1 Cor. 7; 1 Thess. 4:3). Yet we never get a clear definition; Paul seems to assume that people will understand what he is talking about, at least in general terms. Paul's preferred rhetorical device for ethical instruction is a list of vices and/or virtues. These lists do not provide detailed criteria; instead, they paint with broad strokes the types of behaviors to emulate or avoid. Rather than legislating Christian behavior in detail, Paul is content to appeal to broad categories and to encourage Christians to avoid the life of the flesh while aspiring to life in Christ. Even when Paul speaks specifically about sexual misbehavior, he tends to use words with very broad ranges of meaning: "lust," "licentiousness," "sexual immorality," and "impurity."

This concern with broad categories rather than detailed requirements and proscriptions is accompanied by a strong focus on internal attitudes and dispositions rather than on external behaviors. It is particularly worth noting how many of the "works of the flesh" in Galatians 5:19-21 address inner attitudes and dispositions: Paul refers, among other things, to licentiousness, enmities, strife, jealousy, anger, quarrels, dissensions, factions, envy, and drunkenness. Similarly, the "fruits of the Spirit" are likewise tilted, not toward specific behaviors, but toward attitudes and dispositions: love, joy, peace, patience, kindness, generosity, faithfulness, gentleness, and self-control. This is entirely in keeping with the broader movement in the New Testament away from focusing on externals and toward a concern with the heart and the will. Such a focus on internals does not exclude a more objective approach to certain behaviors as acceptable or unacceptable — we see that kind of discourse as well. But it does suggest an approach to the good order of the Christian community that relies more on the work of the Spirit and the transforming impact of relationships than on written codes and specific behavioral requirements. All of this reflects, in clear and important ways, the teaching of Jesus himself.

This focus on internals is also reflected in Paul's use of the language of impurity with reference to sexual ethics. The fact that Paul regularly associates "impurity" with "licentiousness" and "lust" makes it clear that "impurity" in sexual matters is primarily the result of excessive desire and a lack of self-restraint. The wrongness of the behavior is linked primarily to the attitude or disposition with which the behavior is carried out. We also see this in the larger context of the end of Romans 1. After describing the details of sexual impurity in Romans 1:24-27, Paul goes on in verses 29-31 to catalog a list of sins, most of which concern internal dispositions and attitudes, including covetousness, malice, envy, strife, deceit, and craftiness; he goes on to speak of those who are God-haters, insolent, haughty, or boastful; and he concludes with a sweeping reference to those who are "foolish, faithless, heartless, ruthless." In all this we see a tendency to frame ethical requirements in terms of attitudes and dispositions rather than behaviors. Therefore, when Paul speaks of sexual misbehavior as "impurity," the focus falls on the attitudes and dispositions that result in a disordered life and a disordered community. Those attitudes and dispositions, if we consider the general pattern of Paul's usage, focus on lust (excessive desire) and licentiousness (lack of self-restraint). Therefore, I disagree with

L. William Countryman when he attempts to argue, in reference to Romans 1, that "[the same-sex eroticism described in Rom. 1] was not in itself sinful, but had been visited upon the Gentiles as recompense for sins — first and foremost the sin of idolatry but also those additional sins of social disruption listed in verses 29-31."[12] The language in Romans 1:24, with its references to both lust and impurity, points to a disordered inner state that can only be described as sinful, both in light of Paul's usage and of the larger New Testament witness. Whether this inner state accurately describes the inner state of all gay men and lesbians today is quite another matter, however, to which we shall return later in this chapter.

But when Paul uses the language of impurity with respect to sexual misbehavior in Romans 1, does he also intend to say that impurity represents an "objective" disorder and not simply the "subjective" excesses of lust and licentiousness? This is a question raised by many traditionalist interpreters. But if Paul does intend an "objective" reference when he speaks of impurity here, we must recognize that such usage would stand as a single exception to the overall approach to purity language we find throughout the rest of the New Testament, particularly Paul's own usage. Paul speaks in Romans 6:19 of how Christians once were "slaves to impurity," a usage that sounds much more as though impurity is conceived as a controlling subjective disposition (i.e., lust and licentiousness) rather than an objective state. Moreover, Paul's own statement in Romans 14:14, "I know and am persuaded in the Lord Jesus that nothing is unclean in itself," speaks clearly and powerfully against an "objective" understanding of uncleanness and impurity. This "subjective" interpretation of impurity is also required by an interesting use of the word in 1 Thessalonians 2:3: "For our appeal does not spring from deceit or impure motives [literally "impurity"] or trickery. . . ." Even though the Greek text says nothing explicit about "motives," the context and accompanying words in this verse make a subjective interpretation the only possible one and render the NRSV translation an accurate one. "Impurity" here speaks of motives, not actions. In the same way, the close linkage between lust and impurity in Romans 1:24 also speaks to the subjective orientation of this verse.

I conclude that it is entirely fair and judicious to declare that, in the New Testament, without exception, the language of "impurity" and "uncleanness" is reframed — away from an "objective" approach that regards

---

12. Countryman, *Dirt, Greed, and Sex: Sexual Ethics in the New Testament and Their Implications for Today*, rev. ed. (Minneapolis: Fortress, 2007), p. 116.

impurity simply as a "dirty" action or bodily state. The call to purity drives deeper in the New Testament, toward a "subjective" approach that sees purity and impurity as qualities of one's attitudes or dispositions. Purity of heart has replaced bodily and external forms of purity, and it is the central and operative meaning of "purity" throughout the New Testament. The absence of any exceptions to this pattern in Paul's usage strongly suggests that the same understanding of impurity as disordered attitude and disposition should also apply here.[13] Impurity is thus marked in Romans 1:24, as it is everywhere else in Paul, by excessive lust and lack of self-restraint, which in turn leads to sexual immorality.

Implications for the Debate over Gay and Lesbian Unions

I noted in the preceding chapter how Paul regards same-sex eroticism as the manifestation of out-of-control lust that is insatiable: not content with "normal" sexual relations with the opposite sex, it is driven to more and more exotic and bizarre forms of gratification. The Roman emperor Gaius

---

13. There is one possible exception to this "subjective" pattern of references to impurity in Paul, but the verse is a source of some controversy and dissension among scholars. In 2 Cor. 6:17, the text cites Isa. 52:11 by way of saying, "Therefore come out from them and be separate, says the Lord. Touch no unclean thing, and I will receive you." In this passage uncleanness is something that can be "touched," reflecting more the "objective" understanding of impurity common in the Leviticus codes. However, many scholars question whether this particular passage (2 Cor. 6:14–7:1) is part of the original letter, and some even question whether Paul actually wrote it, since it seems to disrupt the argument that precedes and follows it. Furthermore, the call to avoid "unequal yokes" (2 Cor. 6:14) with unbelievers stands in some tension with Paul's advice (in 1 Cor. 7:12-13) that Christians married to unbelievers should not divorce them — that is, if the unbeliever consents to remain married. But even if one accepts that Paul wrote these words (whether they may be a separate Pauline fragment or originally part of 2 Cor.), we must keep in mind the overall thrust of this specific text. The passage in its entirety is concerned about the dangers of alliances and relationships with unbelievers — and the potential damage that such relationships may inflict on believers. Note the language of relationships in vv. 14-16: "For what *partnership* is there between righteousness and lawlessness? Or what *fellowship* is there between light and darkness? What *agreement* does Christ have with Beliar? Or what does a believer *share* with an unbeliever? What *agreement* has the temple of God with idols?" (italics added) The call to "touch nothing unclean," in its context, does not refer to ritual defilement as Leviticus envisions it, but to entangling relationships that may lead one away from Christ. Here the question of *influence* far outweighs any "objective" issue of physical contact. Even this passage is thus finally concerned with the integrity of the heart and the will of believers.

Caligula provides a compelling Exhibit A of such excessive lust and its self-destructive end. Our exploration of impurity has moved in a similar direction. In the New Testament generally, and in Paul's writings in particular, purity is primarily a matter of the heart and one's internal disposition. The fact that Paul in Romans 1:24 links "the lusts of their hearts" with "impurity" confirms the connection between these two ideas in this passage in particular.

Today, many Christians who argue in favor of a greater openness in the church to gay and lesbian relationships would readily join Paul in regarding any form of either heterosexual or homosexual sexuality that is driven by out-of-control lust and a lack of self-restraint as "impurity." Indeed, in our culture today, a great deal of both gay and heterosexual eroticism is marked by promiscuity, an absence of self-restraint, and the dominance of lust. Life in Christ invites us to a deeper form of life, which is located in relationships with others, where desires are sanctified by the Spirit to lead us more fully into life in Christ rather than into self-defeating grasping after our own gratification.

But the question remains: Can same-sex intimate relationships be a context in which desires can be disciplined and sanctified, where the restraint of selfish impulses can be learned, and where the interplay of sacrifice and self-giving with the surprising reception of unmerited love may create a dance of the Spirit, drawing couples into the triune life of love? It is certainly true that same-sex friendships are often such a context of learning and sanctification in Scripture and in widespread Christian experience. Might not even more intimate same-sex relationships be capable of bearing such a work of the Spirit? Might not such relationships be capable of leading us more deeply into the pure life of Christ? Or are such relationships *inherently* "impure," incapable of reflecting divine life and love?

If purity is focused on the restoration of the clearly demarcated roles and distinctions of the original creation (to the extent these can be clearly discerned in the creation narratives), there may well be no place for such relationships of same-sex intimacy, just as there was no place for the eunuch in the assembly of God's people in the Old Testament. But if purity in the New Covenant means the transformation of hearts and wills by the love of Christ, in anticipation of the new creation, then the question remains today about whether God may use long-term committed gay or lesbian unions to cleanse gay and lesbian persons and to draw them into divine love, just as heterosexual marriages may serve as a means of grace to achieve the same ends for heterosexual men and women. In any case, if we are to face such an issue honestly and objectively, we must consider the actual experience and testimony of gay and lesbian Christians. If God is sanctifying such relationships, drawing them past lust and licentiousness and into the love of Christ, the church must sit up and pay attention. To the extent that this is happening, the church today will have to wrestle again with the same shocking instruction that Peter received long ago: "What God has cleansed, you must not call profane" (Acts 10:15).

Of course, this presupposes that same-sex intimacy is capable of being cleansed — and capable of being a means of grace. Many traditionalists believe that this is impossible. Robert Gagnon points to the prohibitions of incest in Leviticus as a counterexample.[14] He argues that incestuous relationships are inherently and objectively wrong and disordered, regardless of the amount of love or concern that might characterize them. They will never be capable of being a means of grace; even though some such relationships might conceivably have moments of kindness, they must simply be avoided. Hence, if both incest and "lying with a man as with a woman" receive the death penalty in Leviticus 20:11-13, should not both offenses be understood as "objective" disorders and not merely as expressions of lust and licentiousness?

Paul clearly accepted the Leviticus prohibitions of incest, at least in general terms (though we cannot know if he embraced all the detailed parameters of Leviticus 18 and 20).[15] He assumes that a man "having" his father's wife is inherently wrong in 1 Corinthians 5, a behavior he describes as *porneia* ("fornication/sexual immorality"). He calls for the immediate expulsion of the man from the Christian community, without any kind of inquiry into his motives or passions (1 Cor. 5:3-5). But he does not characterize this incestuous behavior as "impurity." The exploration in this chapter helps to explain why this is so. If, as I have argued, "impurity" in Paul's usage focuses on the excesses of passion and the absence of self-restraint, it only makes sense that, in this context, such factors are not the most relevant. Incest is clearly "objectively" wrong in Paul's view, so an appeal to

14. Dan Otto Via and Robert A. J. Gagnon, *Homosexuality and the Bible: Two Views* (Minneapolis: Fortress, 2003), pp. 48ff.

15. The specific boundaries of incest vary from one culture to another, even though all cultures prohibit sexual relationships with immediate family members. Leviticus allows marriage between first cousins, for example, though such marriages are prohibited in many states in the United States. Moreover, Paul says nothing of the death penalty required in Leviticus 20:11 for a man having sex with his father's wife. He simply requires their expulsion from the community.

subjective factors such as lust and licentiousness is less critical and could overly complicate what appears to Paul as a clear case.

For us today, there are many good reasons why we should continue to regard incest as "objectively" disordered. It wreaks havoc with the stable, deeper intimacy of household life in general; it violates important power, status, and role differentials; and it makes the true mutuality of "one flesh" impossible to achieve. It often exposes vulnerable children to abuse. In terms of the creation narrative, it fails to fulfill the meaning of the narrative that speaks of a person's leaving father and mother and clinging to one's spouse. Modern discoveries of the genetic problems of inbreeding only compound the obvious disorder that is present in these relationships.

Yet we cannot assume that all same-sex intimacy falls under the same form of moral logic as the prohibitions of incest until we explore in more detail how specific same-sex relationships actually function, both in the ancient world and in the modern world. Robert Gagnon suggests two commonalities between incest and same-sex intimacy. Both incest and same-sex intimacy involve people who are "too much alike"; and both are wrong "because of the disproportionately high incidence of scientifically measurable, ancillary problems."[16] We have already seen that Gagnon's theory of gender complementarity is not sustainable as a reading of the Genesis narratives. Nowhere does Scripture say — or even suggest — that "too much sameness" is the reason one should avoid same-sex eroticism.[17] Moreover, the notion that what is wrong with incest is simply that people are too much alike ignores the actual reasons for the incest prohibitions that we find in Leviticus: incest is often described as a violation of the rights of another male in the household (18:8, 12, 15, 16; 20:11, 20, 21). In other cases, the argument is simply that "she is your mother" (18:7) or "she is your sister" (18:11). In all these cases, the issue identified in the text

16. Via and Gagnon, *Homosexuality and the Bible*, p. 48.

17. Gagnon attempts to make this case by appealing to Lev. 18:6, where prohibited incestuous relationships are characterized as relations with the "flesh of one's flesh." Gagnon declares: "Scripture avoids the twin extremes of too much structural identity between sex partners (same-sex intercourse and incest) and too little (bestiality, sex with prepubescent children)" (Via and Gagnon, *Homosexuality and the Bible*, p. 48.) But this argument is unsustainable when we bring forward analogous texts. The man in Gen. 2:23 speaks of the newly created woman as "flesh of my flesh." How can "flesh of my flesh" denote appropriate gender complementarity in Gen. 2:23, but an almost identical phrase connote "too much structural identity" in Lev. 18:6? These problems suggest that this entire line of reasoning ("too much" or "too little" difference) is foreign to the logic of Scripture itself. In both cases, the issue is not the ratio of similarity and difference, but the recognition of kinship bonds.

itself is not too much "sameness" but the crossing of inappropriate boundaries by which people are connected to each other in the household — and the "too much alike" theory thus fails to account for both sets of prohibitions.

Gagnon's second argument, appealing to contemporary research, can hardly qualify as an exegetical argument. Moreover, such an approach fails to distinguish between those forms of same-sex intimacy that are driven by promiscuity, out-of-control lust, and licentiousness, and those relationships in which love is disciplined by long-term commitment. Incest, by contrast, is wrong not because ancillary problems are "disproportionately high" in such cases, but because problems are nearly inevitable with incest. Gagnon has by no means proved that the same is true in all cases of same-sex intimacy, particularly in long-term committed relationships. Hence the analogy of incest cannot be used to prove that same-sex intimate relationships are inherently incapable of being sanctified. There is no relevant analogy between the two questions — beyond the fact that both concern sexuality (which explains their concurrence in Lev. 18 and 20).

I have not finished my exploration of Paul's understanding of same-sex intimacy, and thus I am not yet prepared to make comprehensive statements about Paul's "objective" view of same-sex intimacy. I will explore the Levitical prohibitions against same-sex eroticism in more detail in coming chapters, as well as Paul's claim that same-sex eroticism is contrary to — or in excess of — "nature." I want to return to the question of whether this behavior is "objectively" disordered in those chapters. But the focus of this present chapter has been on "purity," particularly as this concept appears in the New Testament generally — and in Paul's letters in particular. We have seen that Paul and the rest of the New Testament writers consistently reframe their discussions of purity as away from "objective" considerations and toward an exploration of attitudes and dispositions.

This movement toward matters of the heart, mind, and will is critical in Romans 1. Paul's larger thesis here is that the core of human sinfulness is first of all an inward problem. He introduces this entire section (in Rom. 1:21) by initially focusing on the mind: "They became futile in their thinking, and their senseless minds were darkened. Claiming to be wise, they became fools." The failure to worship the one true God and to desire God above all else results in the distortions of heart, mind, and desire that Paul describes in Romans 1. Consequently, a more "subjective" interest dominates in Romans 1. This is why we see here the language of "impurity," which places the emphasis on matters of the heart and the will. In short, the language of "impurity" focuses attention, not on the supposed "objective" disorder of same-sex eroticism, but on its obvious "subjective" problems in the ancient world, that is, its excesses of self-seeking passion and its lack of self-restraint.

In the New Testament, purity moves from being a matter of externals to a matter of the heart and the will; it moves from an anxious defensiveness to a confidence in God's cleansing power, at work in the most unexpected places; and it moves from an attempt to restore the original structures of the old creation to an anticipation of the new creation. The kind of same-sex eroticism that Paul had in mind in Romans 1 was indeed "impure" in the sense in which that word is understood in the New Testament, that is, marked by lust and licentiousness. But given the way the New Testament (and particularly Paul) speaks of purity and impurity, we cannot categorically reject all same-sex intimacy as "impure" until we discern the extent to which God may indeed be disciplining and sanctifying these relationships as one means by which gay and lesbian persons may move, as all Christians must move, beyond self-seeking desire and lack of self-restraint into the love of God. Moreover, the New Testament's movement in speaking of purity, away from a focus on the original creation and toward the new creation, at least opens the possibility that gays and lesbians might find the same kind of new place in the Christian community that the Ethiopian eunuch found in Acts 8.

Summing Up

- Because Paul speaks of same-sex eroticism as "impurity" in Romans 1:24-27, an exploration of the moral logic underpinning these verses must grapple with the notions of purity and impurity.
- The Old Testament defines purity in three broad ways: conforming to the structures of the original created order; safeguarding the processes by which life is stewarded; and emphasizing Israel's distinctness from the surrounding nations.
- In the New Testament we see three movements with respect to the Old Testament purity laws:
  - away from defining purity *externally* toward defining purity in terms of the motives and dispositions of the *heart and will;*
  - away from defensiveness and separation toward confidence and mission, empowered by the Holy Spirit;

- ○ away from the attempt to replicate the original creation, to a forward-looking expectation of a new creation that fulfills but also transforms the old creation in surprising ways.
- These movements clarify that, for Paul, the core form of moral logic underlying his characterization of sexual misconduct as "impurity" focuses on internal attitudes and dispositions, particularly lust (excessive desire) and licentiousness (lack of restraint).
- Because Paul characterizes the same-sex eroticism of Romans 1:24-27 as "impurity," and therefore understands it as characterized by excessive passion and a lack of restraint, it raises the question concerning whether committed gay and lesbian unions, which seek to discipline passion and desire by means of lifelong commitment, should still be characterized as "impurity."

10

Honor and Shame

The sexual excesses described in the latter part of Romans 1 are characterized not only as "lustful" and "impure" but also as "degrading" (or "shameless").

> [24]Therefore God gave them up in the lusts of their hearts to impurity, to the *degrading* of their bodies among themselves, [25]because they exchanged the truth about God for a lie and worshiped and served the creature rather than the Creator, who is blessed forever! Amen. [26]For this reason God gave them up to *degrading* passions. Their women exchanged natural intercourse for unnatural, [27]and in the same way also the men, giving up natural intercourse with women, were consumed with passion for one another. Men committed *shameless* acts with men and received in their own persons the due penalty for their error. (Rom. 1:24-27; italics added)

Two related Greek words that are translated here as "degrading" literally mean "dishonoring" or "dishonorable." References to things that are "dishonorable" or "shameless" represent part of a larger cultural reality that scholars describe using the language of "honor and shame." If we are to understand these words and the moral force and logic that undergirds them, we need to learn about how the dynamics of honor and shame operated in the ancient world.

Anthropological/Cultural Perspectives on Honor and Shame

Anthropologists characterize a number of cultures, both ancient and modern, as "honor-shame" cultures. In these cultures, sensitivity to the dynamics of honor and shame is one of the centrally defining values that shape all social interactions. In these contexts, "honor" represents a claim to worth or value, along with the social acknowledgment of that worth or value. One can have *ascribed* honor, as a result of the family into which one was born, or the wealth one has inherited. One of the major purposes of genealogies in the Bible is to set out a person's claim to ascribed honor by virtue of his or her ancestry. One doesn't need to do anything to have ascribed honor; one is simply born with it. However, there is also *acquired* honor, which one gains by excelling in social interactions with others: these interactions are called *challenge and riposte,* in which a conflict and competition for honor results in one person's gaining honor and the other person's losing it.[1] In honor-shame cultures, honor plays the role that money plays in most Western cultures. One of the important words in Greek for both money and value is the same word; it is often translated "honor."[2] If you have honor in honor-shame cultures, you can accomplish what you set out to do. People will cooperate with you and do what you ask — because they honor you. On the other hand, if you lack honor, all of life will be difficult. The presence or absence of honor in these cultures is roughly equivalent to the presence or absence of wealth in North American culture. Honor brings with it both power and value.

This brief introduction must define one more basic element in honor-shame cultures. Honor and shame are not absolute realities; instead, honor and shame are defined by how others treat and regard you. In every public interchange where honor and shame are in play, it is the observers who determine who receives honor and who is shamed. Anthropologists speak of these observers as the Public Court of Reputation (often abbreviated as PCR). Consider, for example, the story of Jesus' healing of the woman who was unable to stand up straight in Luke 13:10-17. Jesus heals the woman on the Sabbath. Immediately, the leader of the synagogue is indignant and publicly rebukes Jesus for performing the healing on the Sabbath. Jesus re-

---

1. Bruce J. Malina, *The New Testament World: Insights from Cultural Anthropology,* rev. ed. (Louisville: Westminster John Knox, 1993), pp. 31-34.

2. See the following texts, where the Greek word *timē,* usually translated "honor," is rendered as "price" or "money": Acts 4:34; 5:2-3; 7:16; 19:19; 1 Cor. 6:20; 7:23.

sponds to the challenge by pointing out the inconsistency of practice on this issue, where Jews were permitted to care even for their animals on the Sabbath. His riposte concludes with a rhetorical flourish in Luke 13:16: "And ought not this woman, a daughter of Abraham whom Satan bound for eighteen long years, be set free from this bondage on the Sabbath day?" Luke then narrates the result of this challenge and riposte: "When he said this, all his opponents were put to shame; and the entire crowd was rejoicing at all the wonderful things that he was doing" (Luke 13:17). Jesus thus gains in honor in the Public Court of Reputation, and his critics are shamed for their criticism of Jesus.

Scholars describe the society of the ancient Mediterranean world in which the Bible was written as an honor-shame culture. Certainly, in every human culture, dynamics of honor and shame do operate to some extent. But when anthropologists speak of an "honor-shame culture," they are speaking of those cultures in which these dynamics are much more central to social interactions, particularly among males. Honor-shame cultures also treat honor as a *limited good*. That is, if someone gains in honor, someone else must lose honor. This injects the competitive challenge-riposte dynamic into a great many public social interactions. Modern cultures that can be characterized as honor-shame cultures include Japan, some other Asian cultures, and some Arab societies, as well as subcultures like those of gangs in many North American urban settings.

Gender also plays an extremely important role in honor-shame cultures. Public competition for honor happens mainly — but not exclusively — among males, who, in terms of gender, embody honor. Females are thought to embody shame. Shame here is considered a positive quality: it is sensitivity to what other people think and the willingness to adapt one's behavior and demeanor to publicly accepted values. We might describe this sort of shame by using the word "modesty." Modesty and sexual purity are considered the essential virtues for females in an honor-shame culture. The early Jewish text Sirach 4:21 declares: "There is a shame that leads to sin, and there is a shame that is glory and favor." Shame can thus be construed very positively. The opposite of this positive sense of shame is *shamelessness*, a disposition in which one's public behavior shows obliviousness or lack of concern for what other people may think.

Finally, it is important to note that the honor of females is bound up with the honor of the males who are responsible for them, usually the patriarchal heads of the households in which wives and daughters reside. If women act shamelessly — by failing to maintain sexual purity or public modesty, for example — the male head of the household is shamed. Sirach 22:4-5 says: "A sensible daughter obtains a husband of her own, but one who acts shamefully is a grief to her father. An impudent daughter disgraces father and husband, and is despised by both." Honor-shame cultures are thus collectivist cultures where males are the clear heads of households.

Interpreting Romans 1 in an Honor-Shame Cultural Context

When viewed through the honor-shame lens, some different and commonly ignored aspects of Romans 1:26 tend to emerge more clearly. One is the reference to "their women" in Romans 1:26: "For this reason God gave them up to degrading passions. Their women exchanged natural intercourse for unnatural." What we can see here is not simply the shaming of women, but also the shaming of the men in whose households these women reside. In an honor-shame culture, just about any kind of sexual impropriety on the part of females would be considered shaming the male head of household. Such shame is clearly what the writer has in mind here, particularly when we note that there is not a parallel reference to "their men" in the following verse. Whatever the "dishonorable passions" referred to in Romans 1:26 might be, the effect of this behavior is to bring shame, not only on the women themselves, but on the heads of their households as well. This suggests some kind of public disgrace — and not merely a private act. Again, the outrageous public sexual behavior of the women in the household of Gaius Caligula explored above (in chapter 8) fits this description perfectly.

Yet this interpretation is not universally embraced. Some scholars think that Romans 1:26 refers to female same-sex eroticism; others believe that Paul has in mind other forms of heterosexual misbehavior between men and women, either oral/anal intercourse or simply a failure to act in sexually proper ways. Yet, despite the opinion among some commentators that Romans 1:26 refers to lesbian sexual behavior, such an interpretation of that verse appears nowhere in the early church prior to Chrysostom in the East, and Ambrosiaster in the West, in the late fourth century. In other words, the "lesbian" reading of Romans 1:26 is completely unattested in the early church in the first 300 years of its life, despite fairly common discussion of this text among the patristic commentators. For example, both Clement of Alexandria and Augustine interpret Romans 1:26 as referring to oral or anal intercourse between women and men.[3] Jeramy Townsley notes that, while there is a close connection between male same-sex activity and idolatry in the ancient world — specifically in the widespread Magna Mater, or Cybele, cult — there are no associations anywhere in the ancient world between female same-sex eroticism and idolatry, making such a linkage less likely in the context of Romans 1, where the larger question in view is clearly the consequences of idolatry (Rom. 1:22-23).[4]

Therefore, there is good reason to question the contemporary assumption that Romans 1:26 refers to lesbian sexual behavior. By referring to "their women," this passage ties the sexual misbehavior of women more closely to the men with whom they live. But when we apply the lens of honor-shame to this entire passage, what emerges more clearly is the relationship between the female sexual misbehavior referred to in verse 26 and the male sexual misbehavior of verse 27. The symmetrical references to "males" and "females" in these two verses (and the balanced use of the Greek particle *te* in both verses) suggest that there is some sort of analogy between the sexual misconduct of the two verses. As we have noted, it has often been assumed that what is analogous between the two verses is that both refer to same-sex eroticism. Yet what is stated explicitly in the text is something a bit different. Both of these forms of sexual misbehavior are explicitly identified as "degrading" or "shameless." The "dishonoring" of bodies is first introduced in verse 24, and then repeated again in the reference to "degrading passions" in verse 26 and in the reference to "shameless acts" in verse 27. The text makes it clear that at least one thing these behaviors have in common is that they all violate ancient Mediterranean understandings of honor and shame.[5]

For women, the honor-shame codes are violated by engaging in any kind of sexual impropriety, and violating such codes brings shame on both the woman and the head of the household in which she resides. For men,

---

3. See Clement's "Discussion on Procreation" (*Paedagogus* 10), and Augustine's "On Marriage and Desire," bk. II, chap. 35. For further discussion, see James Miller, "The Practices of Romans 1:26: Homosexual or Heterosexual?" *Novum Testamentum* 37 (1995): 1-11.

4. Jeramy Townsley, "Paul, the Goddess Religions and Queers: Romans 1:23-28," *Journal of Biblical Literature*, forthcoming.

5. Of course, the behaviors of both men and women in this passage are also said to be "contrary to" or "in excess of" nature. I will explore the meaning of that phrase in the next chapter. See also note 1 in the next chapter, which explores how the discussion of female sexual misbehavior in Rom. 1:26 and male actions in Rom. 1:27 are parallel in that they both "exchange" proper behavior for improper.

the relationship between honor, shame, and sexual impropriety is a bit more complicated. In the ancient world generally, men would lose honor if they violated the rights of another man by having sex with his wife or daughter. But for a man to have sex with his female slave or a female captured in war was not considered dishonorable; this was the man's right.[6] In the wider Greco-Roman culture, it was not even regarded as shameful for a man to make sexual use of male slaves, as long as the master was not himself penetrated.[7] However, for a man to play the role of a woman and to be penetrated was clearly a violation of honor: it was considered inherently degrading.[8]

Yet the biblical writers also qualify in important ways the common ancient assumption that only the passive partner in male-male sex was degraded or culpable. In the Levitical prohibitions of male-male sex (18:22; 20:13), no moral distinction is made between active and passive partners; indeed, both are subject to the death penalty (20:13). Likewise, Romans 1:27 makes no distinction between the active partner and the passive partner in its negative portrayal of male-male sex. Some traditionalist interpreters argue that this means that violations of honor-shame are not operative in these passages and that the core moral logic here focuses instead on violations of gender complementarity. But Romans 1:27 is explicit in describing male-male sex as a "shameless act," and in invoking the categories of honor and shame in condemning this behavior. Honor-shame codes are clearly applicable here, even though the passive partner is not singled out for special reproach.

6. The book of Leviticus addresses the problem of a man having sex with a female slave who is pledged to another man (19:20-22). Such a case is considered a sin, since the man to whom the slave was pledged is harmed; but the penalty is notably milder (scourging) than that required by other forms of sexual misconduct. The case is clearly not considered equivalent to adultery or rape. Leviticus is notably lacking in any legislation against a man having sex with a slave who is not pledged to another man. This was considered a man's right, apparently even in ancient Israel. Note also the clear instructions given about marrying a woman captured in war in Deut. 21:10-14. A man may marry such a woman, and if she is not pleasing to him, he may set her free. The only restriction on the otherwise typical practice in the ancient world is that, after sleeping with her, the man may not sell her as a slave. Cf. Num. 31:18 for a similar practice with even fewer restrictions.

7. See the extended discussion, along with relevant texts, in Martti Nissinen, *Homoeroticism in the Biblical World: A Historical Perspective* (Minneapolis: Fortress, 1998), pp. 57-88. See also the discussion of these issues in William Stacy Johnson, "Empire and Order: The Gospel and Same-Gender Relationships," *Biblical Theology Bulletin* 37, no. 4 (2007).

8. See the discussion of this issue near the end of chapter 4 above, pp. 82-83.

This apparent quandary is resolved by way of a wider consideration of the biblical writers in their context. Because the active role in male-male sex is portrayed so negatively in the stories of Sodom and Gomorrah (Gen. 19) and the Levite's concubine (Judg. 19), we see very early in the biblical witness a resistance to sanctioning this kind of behavior, whether or not it might have been accepted elsewhere in the ancient world. It was too closely linked to violence of the worst kind and inhospitality toward the most vulnerable. In addition, given the fact that male-male sex is associated with cultic prostitution in the ancient world generally, and in the area surrounding Israel in particular, there were also religious reasons for rejecting both the active and passive roles in male same-sex behavior, particularly since the active role belonged to those making use of cultic prostitution.[9] The biblical writers clearly do not accept the common ancient assumption, documented above, whereby a male could make sexual use of other males (particularly slaves and social inferiors) as long as he himself was not penetrated. To degrade others in this way was to violate deep biblical values: the call to love one's neighbor as oneself, as well as the call to justice and hospitality. You cannot violate the honor of another and also love that person. Hence, the fact that Leviticus 18:22 and 20:13, as well as Romans 1:27, do not single out the passive partner for special blame does not negate the dynamics of honor-shame that operate in these passages. To treat a man like a woman is still seen as a negative act that necessarily degrades the passive partner. Honor-shame codes are still at work. But the summons to justice, love, and religious faithfulness are also deeply embedded in the biblical witness, rendering the active partner equally culpable (see a further discussion of the Levitical prohibitions in chapter 12 below).

While these values surrounding honor and shame for men are clearly documented elsewhere in Scripture and throughout the ancient world, Paul also clearly links the shamefulness of the behavior described in these verses with its excessive passion. Romans 1:26 characterizes all the sexual misbehavior of these verses as "degrading passions," underscoring the close link between shame and passion in Paul's mind, a link echoed in verse 27, where shamelessness and passion are again closely linked. For men, being overcome by passion was losing control over their own lives — and thus being subject to shame.

We see the same linkage between honor-shame codes and gender identities in 1 Corinthians 11, where the problem focuses on length of hair and/

9. See Nissinen, *Homoeroticism in the Biblical World*, pp. 37-56.

or head coverings. I have already explored Paul's qualified endorsement of patriarchal household relationships in this passage in chapter 4 above. But for our present focus, 1 Corinthians 11:14-15 is particularly noteworthy: "Does not nature itself teach you that if a man wears long hair, it is degrading to him, but if a woman has long hair, it is her glory?" Here we see the same juxtaposition of the language of honor-shame and references to "nature" that we find in Romans 1:26-27. I shall explore these shared references to "nature" in more detail in the next chapter. But for our present purposes, it is important to note the close linkage between the blurring of gender distinctions and the loss of honor in the world in which Scripture was written. To present oneself in a way that conforms to gender expectations was considered honorable; to violate those gender expectations was shameful. This confirms the understanding of the moral logic implicit in the honor-shame language of Romans 1:26-27. The sexual misbehavior described here, in addition to being characterized as "lustful" and "impure," is considered "degrading" or "shameless" for a particular reason: such behavior violated established social expectations of the time regarding gender — and regarding behaviors that are appropriate to males and females. For females, such dishonor arose from any kind of sexual behavior outside marriage, as well as the failure to maintain the appropriate passive or submissive role within marriage. For males, dishonor or shame was more particularly a result of either actively degrading others into the female role or shamefully adopting the passive female role for oneself. This shame also expressed itself in the irrationality of excessive passion (associated in the ancient world with the feminine).

Evaluating Honor-Shame as a Form of Moral Logic in Cross-Cultural Settings

Although the Bible was written in an honor-shame culture, most Christians in the Western world do not live in this kind of cultural setting. We do not regard all public interactions among males as contests where honor is either gained or lost. Western cultures are not (at least not entirely) patriarchal; males no longer play the unquestioned role as the head of all households. Moreover, most Western cultures have become much more flexible on the question of gender roles more broadly as well. In most Western cultures, women play important and active roles in public life. We no longer think that it is shameful for women to wield economic power, in contrast with the ancient perspective articulated in Sirach 25:22: "There is wrath and impudence and great disgrace when a wife supports her husband." Similarly, forms of dress, by both men and women, vary dramatically from one culture to another. Nineteenth-century missionaries were shocked by bare-breasted women in some tropical cultures; most people in the ancient world would have been equally scandalized by clothing patterns in modern Western cultures. What is "shameful" in matters of dress or hairstyle is highly specific to the norms of the culture in which one finds oneself.

This raises the larger hermeneutical question: In what way, if at all, is the biblical discussion of honor and shame relevant in cultures where honor and shame are understood quite differently? It is tempting simply to say that all these discussions of honor and shame in Scripture are simply irrelevant to us because we live in a cultural setting vastly different from the ancient world. Yet there are many honor-shame texts that seem to make important claims that continue to be relevant to contemporary life in a wide range of cultural settings. Most Christians believe that the command "honor your father and mother" is still relevant to contemporary life, even if the fulfillment of this command may express itself somewhat differently in different cultural settings. Likewise, Paul's injunction to "outdo one another in showing honor" (Rom. 12:10) represents a broadly compelling way in which the gospel subverts competitiveness into concern for others. Similarly, the polemic in the Epistle of James against those who "dishonor the poor" (James 2:6) continues to speak powerfully across a wide range of cultures and settings.

Moreover, the emotional dynamics of honor and shame are universal in the human species, despite the fact that the specific definitions of what may be honorable and shameful are widely disparate in different cultures. In every culture, people long to be praised and honored by others. Every culture knows and abhors the feeling of embarrassment. In every culture, a flushed face, a downcast look, and drooping shoulders mark the universal response of shame when someone feels embarrassed or disgraced. In almost every culture, a raised face, bright eyes, and a smile denote the feeling of pride. The relative importance and means of allocation of honor and shame may vary from one culture to another, and the context by which we define honor and shame is culturally specific. But the emotions of pride and embarrassment are universal.

In light of this, what seems relevant across all cultures, from a biblical and theological perspective, is that people have an inherent worth that should be recognized in social interactions. The call to honor one another is always relevant, regardless of the cultural setting, because all humans are created in God's image and thus have an intrinsic worth that must be recognized and affirmed. What seems subject to significant cultural variation, however, is the delineation of specific relationships that mark out the boundaries of honor and shame. The text of 1 Timothy 6:1 requires slaves to "consider their masters worthy of full respect" (*pasēs timēs,* literally "worthy of complete honor"). In the ancient world this seemed self-evident; in the modern world, we now recognize the master-slave relationship as inherently disordered and in violation of the implications of the gospel that attributes incalculable value to each person. In our contemporary context, therefore, this command for slaves to honor their masters makes no sense at all. The summons to give appropriate honor is relevant cross-culturally; but the specific delineation of who should receive honor and who should give it is marked by cultural particularity and is not necessarily cross-culturally relevant.

Moreover, we must recognize the close linkage between ancient honor-shame codes and ancient understandings of gender roles in their limited cultural particularity. Most modern cultures no longer restrict the public role of women in the way that was practiced in the ancient world. The attributes of submissiveness or passion in men — or aggressiveness in women — are no longer regarded with universal suspicion. In Western cultures, it is not shameful for a woman to speak in public, or even to argue or debate with men. This makes the appropriation of texts such as 1 Corinthians 14:35 ("It is shameful for a woman to speak in church") much more problematic in our contemporary settings.

What is vitally important to recognize here is the simple fact that, even in the ancient world, honor and shame were culturally defined and socially governed realities rather than absolute and transcendent concepts. What was honorable was, quite simply, what most people thought honorable, and shameful things were defined by the negative reaction that most people had to those things. Honor and shame were simply part of the collectivist social world in which the Bible was written. Therefore, honor and shame have little to do with transcendent meaning: rarely are exhortations using the language of honor and shame justified by an appeal to God's will in the Bible. Such appeals are unnecessary because we learn honor and shame from our youngest years, and we internalize them in ways that seem completely self-evident to us. Honor-shame conventions find their content, meaning, and justification in the concrete fabric of specific social interactions and relationships. Honor and shame constitute one important means by which the larger values of a society get lived out in the specifics of day-to-day interactions.

Honor-shame codes, therefore, do not have a privileged, culture-transcending status, despite the fact that, in most specific cultural settings, they are considered normative. In fact, at many points the New Testament also challenged the honor-shame codes of its day. Its proclamation of a crucified Messiah implied a radical revision of what should be considered honorable and shameful. Jesus repeatedly pushed the boundaries of honor-shame codes, associating with tax collectors and sinners, allowing himself to be touched by a menstruating woman, and to be publicly kissed by a woman known to be a sinner (Luke 7:36-50). Paul repeatedly declares that he does not worry when others regard his behavior as shameful, because he is confident that he will be vindicated (i.e., honored) by God (e.g., 1 Cor. 1:27; 4:10; 2 Cor. 6:8; Phil. 1:20). In other words, wherever the honor-shame codes in the ancient world were felt to contradict core values of the gospel, they were readily and quickly challenged or set aside. Paul was quite willing to be considered a fool in the wider culture in order to be faithful to Christ (2 Cor. 11). A large part of learning to live by the gospel in the New Testament entails learning to relinquish both true and false shame, to give up worldly honor, and to relearn the meaning of honor and shame, in light of the overwhelming love of God revealed in Christ.

This capacity to live counterculturally, to reframe prevailing codes of honor and shame in light of the gospel, has continued in various ways throughout the life of the church. In the early church the martyrs shocked the empire by their peaceful and purposeful devotion to Christ, in the midst of a world bent on violently shaming them. Their witness converted a dying empire, radically altering its understandings of honor. During the Middle Ages, the practice of celibacy challenged the assumption that patriarchal heads of households were the only truly honorable positions in society. Figures like the desert fathers and Saint Francis of Assisi embraced poverty, critiquing the unquestioned honor granted to the wealthy and the powerful. In the nineteenth century, the abolitionist movement persuaded the world that the institution of slavery made it impossible to obey the biblical command to "honor everyone" (1 Pet. 2:17). Likewise, in the twentieth century, most Western cultures came to realize that traditional gender roles failed to fully use and honor the gifts of women given by God, and gender roles were revised in dramatic ways, resulting in a much more active role for women in society. The ongoing critique and revision of honor-shame codes in and through the church has continued throughout its history.

Implications for the Homosexuality Debate in the Churches: The Meaning of Shame

And now the church faces the question of shame, particularly in its engagement with the gay, lesbian, bisexual, and transgendered persons in its midst. In almost all societies, it is particularly in the area of sexuality that shame wields enormous power. As in the ancient world, shame can be both positive and negative. James Fowler speaks eloquently of the positive role of shame in our lives:

> Spiritually, shame is related to the deepest places of truth in our souls. Shame cuts to the heart. In its healthy forms, it helps to form and inform the heart. Shame provides the primary foundation for conscience and for the instinctive sense of what is worthy or unworthy, right or wrong. Shame, as an emotion, relates to the sensitive feelings touched in love and deep communion with others. Shame protects the intimacy of our closest relations with friends, lovers, spouses, or children. It surrounds our relation with the Holy or the domain of what is sacred to us. Shame, in its positive influence, is the caretaker of our worthy selves and identities. When we listen attentively to the voice of our healthy shame, we speak and act from our "center."[10]

A healthy sense of shame is vital to our humanity. But precisely because our sense of shame is socially constructed, it can also be the place where we internalize the prejudices, fears, anxieties, distortions, and hatred of those around us, particularly those closest to us. Moreover, it is in the area of shame that the traditionalist approach to gay and lesbian persons becomes fraught with deep problems. The typical slogans clearly express the ambivalence: "Welcoming, but not affirming"; "Hate the sin, but love the sinner." On the surface, the gay or lesbian person is welcomed into the traditionalist fellowship; but the desires and the emotional orientation or disposition of the person's sexuality are shunned. Ironically, in this context, the more

---

10. James W. Fowler, *Faithful Change: The Personal and Public Challenges of Postmodern Life* (Nashville: Abingdon, 1996), p. 92.

deeply the gay or lesbian person is welcomed and loved by the fellowship, the more profound the problem of shame becomes. The internalized message becomes something like this: "These people love me so much, they must be right when the say that my sexual orientation is a manifestation of sinful brokenness. Therefore, I must resist this part of myself all the more insistently." Sometimes such a process is effective in helping a person who is confused about his or her sexual orientation to move toward embracing the wider norms of society in his or her sexuality. But research shows that such change happens only in a small minority of relevant cases. And when this attempt to embrace the dominant society's perspective on sexuality is unsuccessful, when desires for others of the same sex persist, the result is a deeply internalized sense of shame, frustration, and self-loathing. The self is divided, and shame becomes toxic. Shame always becomes toxic when it is constructed out of double messages (e.g., "We love you, but we abhor the way you operate emotionally"). These conflicting messages create divided souls, and those inner conflicts, precisely because they are so shameful, powerfully resist the light of day. They remain submerged, manifesting themselves in depression, scapegoating, sickness, anger toward others, or even suicide.

It is important to emphasize, in this context, the difference between shame and guilt. Guilt is specific. When we feel guilty, we condemn ourselves for specific things we have done wrong. In a Christian context, guilt can be addressed by repentance and the receiving of forgiveness. But shame is not so easily dealt with. Shame quickly becomes all-encompassing: it defines the self in its entirety. Guilt says that we have done bad things; shame says that we are bad. In a traditionalist context, homosexual *acts* may incur guilt, but a homosexual *orientation* causes shame.

As Fowler notes, release from shame involves not only the acknowledgment and exposure of the defect or lack to a trusted other or others, but also the undertaking of substantial change in one's way of being a self.[11] Guilt can be healed through forgiveness, but the healing of shame cannot happen apart from a dramatic alteration in the basic way we understand and relate to our very selves. Twelve-step programs recognize this, and they provide powerful and persistent support for people seeking to redefine themselves in the most basic ways. Unfortunately, attempts to replicate this strategy with gays have been much less fruitful. Since sexual orientation is so deeply embedded in the fabric of our experience of the world, such at-

11. Fowler, *Faithful Change*, p. 107.

tempts to dramatically alter one's self-understanding and self-definition most commonly end in failure — only deepening the sense of shame.[12]

Pastoral Responses to Shame

Of course, merely describing such painful dilemmas does not in itself solve the problem. Traditionalists are quick to point out that other Christians find themselves needing to wrestle throughout their lives with shameful addictions or temptations to sexually abuse children. It does not help these unfortunate people to tell them that there is nothing shameful about addiction or pedophilia. Instead, they simply need the support of the church as they seek to resist these shameful urges. The church rightly stands with them when it welcomes them but does not affirm their impulses to sinful behavior. It does this as an expression of love. We do not love someone when we affirm behaviors or dispositions in them that will lead to disastrous consequences. We love them when we help them resist such shameful impulses, whether or not they are able to fully eradicate these impulses themselves from their lives.

But it is at this point that greater precision is important. No one disputes that the shame over addiction or child abuse is healthy and appropriate. The negative and ultimately disastrous consequences of these dispositions are evident to all. The deep reformulation of the self that is required to move beyond this shame is extremely difficult, but it is absolutely necessary work, and the church is right to do all it can to assist in that arduous task. But the parallels with the shame attached in many cultures to gay, lesbian, bisexual, or transgendered experience seem much more strained, at least when one considers the consequences of actions. Of course, gays and lesbians may, like heterosexuals, experience sexual addiction or impulses to pedophilia, and these addictions and impulses should certainly be resisted with the church's help. (Despite common prejudices, however, gay men are no more likely to be pedophiles than straight men are.)[13] But when these excesses are excluded, a wide range of loving, com-

12. See the discussion of change in sexual orientation in chapter 7 above.

13. See the helpful review article by Gregory M. Herek on this topic at: http://psychology.ucdavis.edu/rainbow/html/facts_molestation.html. His conclusion: "The empirical research does *not* show that gay or bisexual men are any more likely than heterosexual men to molest children. This is not to argue that homosexual and bisexual men never molest children. But there is no scientific basis for asserting that they are more likely than heterosexual

passionate, same-sex desire may remain, untainted by these more specific problems. Should these desires be painted with the same brush of shame?

What Exactly is Shameful in Romans 1:24-27?

This requires a closer look at Romans 1. More specifically, the links between shame and the sexual excesses portrayed there need to be made a bit clearer. Everything depends on how we interpret Paul's references to "degrading" and "shameless" behavior. Traditionalists argue that what is degrading or shameless is "homosexuality," or same-sex eroticism in general. Whenever sexual contact takes place between two people of the same gender, regardless of the amount of love, mutuality, or self-giving that might be present, shame is always the result. But as I have repeatedly noted, broad and generic concepts like "homosexuality" did not exist in the ancient world; and it is considerably less than clear that Romans 1:26 even envisions same-sex eroticism between women. Our explorations in this chapter and the previous two chapters suggest a different perspective: What is degrading and shameless about the behavior described in Romans 1:24-27 is that it is driven by excessive, self-seeking lust, that it knows no boundaries or restraints, and that it violates established gender roles of that time and culture, understood in terms of masculine rationality and honor. Such behavior is, in the context of the ancient world, incapable of expressing love, incapable of being a vehicle by which compassion, kindness, self-giving, and mutual service might find expression. You cannot love someone at the same time that you are dominated by self-centered passion, and are in the process violating his or her honor or the honor of the household in which that person resides.

By this reading, revisionists can claim that Paul is exactly correct in what he affirms. Indeed, whenever either heterosexual or same-sex behavior is driven by lust and licentiousness, whenever it violates the boundaries of an ordered community, and whenever such behavior violates the honor and dignity of persons as that dignity is understood and expressed in a particular cultural setting, such behavior *should* be regarded as shameful. In these cases, the deep work of repentance and reformulation of the self is required, empowered by the light of the gracious and transformative gos-

---

men to do so. And . . . many child molesters cannot be characterized as having an adult sexual orientation at all; they are fixated on children."

pel of Christ. But in these cases, the disciplining of the affections is clear: the direction for healing involves relinquishing excessive desire, learning self-restraint, honoring communal boundaries, and respecting the honor of others. These are deep values about which there is no disagreement. It is quite another matter, however, when the desire to love and to be loved by someone of the same sex is shamed. Here it is not a matter of disciplining the desire; traditionalists believe that same-sex desire must simply be eradicated. Here it is not a matter of recognizing the destructive nature of what one desires (as in the case of addictions or child abuse); rather, it is a matter of renouncing a desire to love and to be loved by another in an intimate relationship. To insist that moderated, loving same-sex desires are incapable of being sanctified is to attempt to make equivalencies between same-sex desires and more toxic relationships where they simply do not exist. The toxic and destructive impact of child abuse and addiction is obvious to all. To make the same claim about all committed gay or lesbian relationships is completely unwarranted — both by experience and by a careful reading of the way the language of shame is used in Romans 1 and related texts from the ancient world. In the ancient world, male same-sex eroticism is regarded as shameful not because there is "too much sameness," as some attempt to argue, but rather because the ancient world thought it was an expression of excessive self-centered passion, and because they believed it was inherently and unavoidably degrading for a man to play the role of a woman and be penetrated by another man. There is no reason to read the references to dishonor and shamelessness in the Romans text as assuming anything different from this overall ancient consensus.

What is at stake here is the distinction between healthy and toxic shame. Healthy shame can always name the deep values that are being violated — a simple task in the case of addictions or child abuse. Toxic shame, by contrast, is almost always vague about the deep values that are violated. The worst of traditionalist rhetoric resorts to mere Bible-thumping and proof-texting, consigning gays and lesbians to the shadows under the weight of unquestionable divine authority and refusing even to countenance any questioning of this dogmatic assurance. Other traditionalist strategies attempt to be more compassionate, but they remain almost as vague. Gay men, for example, are told that they have not developed adequate non-sexual friendships with other men or that their relationship with their father is "wounded." Simply fix these things, it is said, and desire will return to its proper object. But it is precisely such vagueness that allows shame to persist in the darkness. Moreover, the ineffectiveness of "reparative therapy" that is based on these questionable assumptions has led professional groups such as the American Psychological Association to explicitly rule out such therapeutic approaches because they don't work, and they only compound shame and frustration on the part of the client. If shame cannot be clearly named, and its destructive elements cannot be clearly identified, it is toxic shame, and the deeper call of the gospel is not to reinforce such shame but to expose its deceptiveness by the light of Christ.

A number of traditionalist writers have attempted to focus the shamefulness of male-male erotic relationships somewhat differently — on the physical and psychological health risks that such behavior allegedly involves. Thomas Schmidt's analysis is the most extensive and graphic in his depiction of a wide range of health problems associated with male homosexual practice in the United States.[14] What is clear in his discussion, however, is that almost all the health problems he describes are associated with sexual promiscuity and the use of multiple sex partners. There is every reason for Christians to agree on this: sexual promiscuity of any kind — homosexual or heterosexual — violates the purpose of God. Scripture clearly links sexual expression with "one-flesh" unions that establish lifelong, stable kinship ties. *Eros* is intended to lead to *agapē*; desire finds its transformative end in mutuality and self-giving. Christians should not say with their bodies what they are unable or unwilling to say with the rest of their lives. The failure to respect this divinely intended purpose for sexuality results in multiple destructive consequences. Shame attached to promiscuity of any kind is healthy shame, not toxic shame. But again the question arises: Should committed, long-term gay relationships be painted with the same brush?

Consider as an analogy the way the writings of the New Testament confront heterosexual brokenness. As the gospel confronted the Gentile world, early Christian leaders encountered all sorts of sexual problems, sin, and distortion. The New Testament is full of exhortations about such things, often reiterating its call to holy living. If the New Testament writers had access to an ancient survey on sexuality, they might well have felt that their cause was hopeless, given that so many heterosexuals did not live according to the will of God. But they pressed on, confident in the sanctifying and healing power of the Spirit, moving people to greater sexual wholeness

---

14. See Thomas E. Schmidt, "The Price of Love," in Schmidt, *Straight and Narrow? Compassion and Clarity in the Homosexuality Debate* (Downers Grove, IL: InterVarsity, 1995), pp. 99-130; cf. Robert A. J. Gagnon, *The Bible and Homosexual Practice: Texts and Hermeneutics* (Nashville: Abingdon, 2001), pp. 471ff.

and integrity. For centuries the church has consigned gay and lesbian sexuality to the shadows and to the closet. Is it really surprising that, banished from the clear light of Christian teaching and the supportive context of redemptive communities, some serious problems have emerged? Again, we see the importance of clear light when shame is healthy. But when we insist that all homosexual relations are shameful because they are *necessarily* unhealthy, we move again from clear light into the shadows. In fact, research shows no significant health-related issues among lesbians at all, and the failure to differentiate between committed partners and bar-cruising one-night stands will not illuminate a helpful direction for Christian ethics. It is entirely reasonable and appropriate for the church to ask gay and lesbian couples to express their love to each other in ways that do not damage each other's bodies. The same expectation should stand with heterosexual couples. Why not simply take this approach rather than claiming that all same-sex love is inherently unhealthy?

The church will stay on much stronger and clearer footing — and remain more closely linked with its Scripture — if it approaches honor and shame more clearly in the light of deeper and more sustainable scriptural principles. What is honorable is what contributes to a form of life and dignity that is permeated by the gospel of Christ. What is shameful is any impulse or behavior that diminishes life and dignity, as that life and dignity is portrayed in the gospel of Christ. The missionary character of the gospel makes it clear that this new life and dignity will take a somewhat different shape in different cultures and settings — and in different times and places. As the gospel of Christ delves more deeply into these various cultural settings, honor-shame codes may continue to undergo deeper transformation — in light of the gospel. It remains to be seen whether the inclusion of gays and lesbians in committed relationships will be one of those places where honor-shame codes undergo a deeper transformation in the life of the church. However, the history of the church suggests that, if that happens, it won't be the first time or the last time that such transformation takes place.

Summing Up

- Paul's characterization of the sexual misbehavior in Romans 1:24-27 as "degrading" and "shameless" requires that we understand this form of moral logic.

- This language must be understood in the context of an honor-shame culture in which public esteem is valued very highly, and where male and female roles are clearly and sharply delineated.
- In this context, the reference to "their women" in Romans 1:26 probably does not refer to same-sex activity but to dishonorable forms of heterosexual intercourse. The reference to degrading acts between men probably refers both to the ancient assumption that same-sex eroticism is driven by excessive passion, not content with heterosexual gratification, and also to the general assumption in the ancient world that a man was inherently degraded by being penetrated as a woman would be.
- Although the need to honor others is a universal moral mandate, the specific behaviors that are considered honorable and shameful vary dramatically from one culture to another.
- In the past, the church has often contributed to the toxic shame of gay and lesbian persons by the ambivalent response, "We welcome you, but we abhor the way you operate emotionally."
- What is shameful about the sexual behavior described in Romans 1:24-27 is the presence of lust, licentiousness, self-centeredness, abuse, and the violation of gender roles that were widely accepted in the ancient world.
- The church must wrestle with whether all contemporary gay and lesbian committed relationships are accurately described by Paul's language. If not, then perhaps this form of moral logic does not apply to contemporary committed gay and lesbian relationships.

11

Nature

Nothing has been more central to the debates over homosexuality in
the churches than Paul's language regarding "nature" in Romans 1.
The claim that same-sex intimacy is "unnatural" or "contrary to nature"
constitutes the heart of most traditionalist opposition to any move toward
the acceptance of these relationships in the life of the church. The importance of the references in this passage to "nature" becomes evident when
the recurring use of the language of "exchange" is noted in Romans 1: verse
23 speaks of how sinful humans "exchanged *[ēllaxan]* the glory of the im-
mortal God for images resembling a mortal human being or birds or four-
footed animals or reptiles." Verse 25 uses the same verb in a slightly modified form, speaking of how these godless people "exchanged *[metēllaxan]*
the truth of God for a lie and worshiped and served the creature, rather
than the creator." The last "exchange" is noted in verse 26: "Their women
exchanged *[metēllaxan]* natural intercourse for unnatural," and similarly,
men "giving up natural intercourse with women, were consumed with
passion for one another" (Rom. 1:27). These polarities are summarized in
the table on page 224. In this context, "natural" aligns with divine glory
and truth, and "unnatural" aligns with idolatry, deception, and all-
consuming passion. Paul links departure from the worship of God to a departure from what is "natural."[1] In this light, one can readily understand

---

1. For further explication of these parallels from a traditionalist perspective, see Ulrich
Mauser, "Creation, Sexuality, and Homosexuality in the New Testament," in Choon-Leong
Seow, ed., *Homosexuality and Christian Community* (Louisville: Westminster John Knox,
1996).

1:23	They *exchanged*	the glory of the immortal God	for images resembling a mortal human being or animals.
1:25:	They *exchanged*	the truth of God	for a lie.
1:26:	Their women *exchanged*	natural intercourse	for unnatural.
1:27:	In the same way also the men, giving up	natural intercourse with women,	were consumed with passion for one another.[2]

traditionalist concern about the approval of homosexual behavior. Given these parallels, such an endorsement appears to be essentially equivalent to the endorsement of idolatry, deceit, and out-of-control lust.

Paul certainly does equate what is "unnatural" with what is wrong; but to recognize this is only the beginning of the interpretation of this passage. We have not yet discerned *why* the sexual behavior described in these verses is wrong — what, more precisely, makes such behavior "unnatural." Until we do so, we will not be able to discern clearly whether all contemporary "homosexual behavior" should be equally described as "unnatural" in the sense that Paul is using the word in this passage. For example, as I have noted in the preceding chapter, the reference to "their women's" sexual

2. This way of framing this text makes it clear that "in the same way" *(homoiōs)* in Rom. 1:27 recalls not only the "unnatural" sexual behavior of women in Rom. 1:26, but all the "exchanges" that precede this verse. This weakens the contention of many interpreters that the sexual misbehavior of women in Rom. 1:26 *must* refer to the same kind of same-sex eroticism we see in v. 27. The usual argument that Rom. 1:26 is speaking of lesbian sexual expression claims that the phrase "in the same way" in Rom. 1:27 (which clearly addresses same-sex eroticism between men) places this verse in direct parallel with the prior reference to women abandoning the "natural use." In reality, however, Paul probably uses "in the same way" in Rom. 1:27 to make it clear that the behavior of these males is another "exchange," like the *three* already narrated, even though Rom. 1:27 uses a different verb. What Rom. 1:27 shares most significantly with Rom. 1:26 is not that they both necessarily refer to same-sex eroticism, but that they both, like Rom. 1:23 and 25, are "exchanges" of something good for something bad. At the same time, there is a more qualified parallel between Rom. 1:26 and 27 in that both deal with sexual issues that are "natural" or "unnatural," and the two verses deal in contrasting ways with males and females. This lesser parallelism/contrast is evident in the repeated use of the Greek particle *te* in these two verses, a common device in Greek for making comparisons or contrasts. For a very extensive discussion of the use of "in the same way" *(homoiōs)* in a wide range of Greek literature, and its implications for reading this text, see Jamie A. Banister, "Ὁμοιως and the Use of Parallelism in Romans 1:26-27," *Journal of Biblical Literature* 128, no. 3 (2009). She also argues, on a somewhat different basis, that the wider syntactical usage of *homoiōs* does not suggest that the meaning of Rom. 1:26 should be limited by Rom. 1:27.

misbehavior in Romans 1:26 was not interpreted as same-sex eroticism in the first three centuries of the church's life, but as noncoital or non-procreative forms of *heterosexual* intercourse. This suggests that "unnatural" in the ancient world connoted a wider range of sexual misbehavior than same-sex eroticism alone. This also suggests that the violation of "gender complementarity" may not stand at the heart of the claim that these sexual behaviors are "unnatural," as traditionalists often claim, since some of these "unnatural" behaviors may also occur in sexual relations between men and women. Clearly, greater clarity is needed in order to determine exactly what Paul means by "natural" and "unnatural." Hence this chapter is devoted to discerning the moral logic, scope, and force of appeals to "nature" in Scripture as a whole, and in Romans 1 in particular.

The Greek word that Paul uses here for "nature" *(phusis)* never occurs in the Septuagint's translation of the Hebrew Bible into Greek.[3] That is, the concept of "nature" in the sense that Paul uses it in Romans 1 is not found explicitly in the Hebrew Bible. In this sense, "nature" is not an inherently Jewish concept, and it plays no role in either Hebrew or Aramaic Jewish literature. But "nature" appears very often in later Jewish texts that were written in Greek, from about 200 BCE onward. These later texts use the term especially in efforts to bring Jewish understandings of ethics and the law into a dialogue with Hellenistic philosophy, particularly Stoicism, the dominant philosophical and ethical framework in the Greco-Roman world. The concept of nature plays a very significant role in Stoicism. Appeals to nature by Jews thus represent an attempt to find a common language and frame of reference with Gentiles, those who might otherwise find the Jewish law and Jewish ethics strange and incomprehensible.[4]

It is not surprising, then, for Paul to make an appeal in Romans 1 to nature, or what is natural. Paul is speaking in this chapter of the universality of human sinfulness apart from the law. (Paul will turn to sinfulness *under* the law later — in Romans 2.) In this context, the revelation of the will and purpose of God in nature assumes critical significance, because Paul is ad-

---

3. *Phusis* does, however, occur in some later apocryphal Greek texts that are part of the Septuagint but are not included in the Hebrew canon. These texts are Wisdom (7:20; 13:1; 19:20); 3 Maccabees (3:29); and 4 Maccabees (1:20; 5:8, 9, 25; 13:27; 15:13; 16:3).

4. The writings of the Alexandrian Jewish philosopher-theologian Philo contain more than 1400 references to "nature" and related words. We also see many references in the Jewish historian Josephus, the Jewish apologist Pseudo-Phocylides, the apocryphal Wisdom of Solomon, the third and fourth books of Maccabees, and other early Jewish texts engaging the Greco-Roman world.

dressing the sinfulness of persons who have never heard the will of God as it is laid out in the Jewish law. If Paul can appeal to commonly held notions of what is natural, notions embraced by both Jews and by Gentiles, he can make his case that all are "without excuse" — whether or not they have received the full revelation of God's will in the law — because they have all failed to live in accordance with what is natural.

Because the concept of *nature* was so useful for both Jewish and Christian apologetic purposes, the word takes on a fairly wide range of meaning in different early Jewish and Christian texts. Not all of these usages may be directly relevant to interpreting Romans 1. Instead, this chapter proceeds with the assumption that the first place to look, in discerning the meaning of "nature" for Paul, is Paul's own use of this word elsewhere in Romans and in his other letters, as well as the word's usage in the rest of the New Testament. Once we have surveyed Paul's use of the word and the wider canonical range of meaning, we can turn to other early Jewish texts to confirm the patterns we detect in the New Testament's and Paul's own usage.

"Nature" as "What Comes Naturally": The Place of One's Individual Nature in the Wider World

If we look at the references to "natural" and "unnatural" immediately following those in Romans 1:26-27, we find that the next reference to "nature" *(phusis)* in the text of Romans occurs in the next chapter, Romans 2:14. In contrast to Romans 1, which speaks of Gentiles who do not act in accordance with nature, Romans 2:14 speaks of those who do: "When Gentiles, who do not possess the law, do instinctively [*phusei*, literally "by nature"] what the law requires, these, though not having the law, are a law to themselves." Clearly, there is some sense of rhetorical balance and contrast between those Gentiles who violate nature in Romans 1:26-27 and those Gentiles who live by nature in Romans 2:14. Here, the phrase "by nature" seems to be a way of saying "what comes naturally," or "what is in accord with one's own nature or identity" — hence the NRSV translation, "instinctively." The focus in this usage in Romans 2:14 is not first of all on behavior that is aligned with the wider natural world, but rather on the inner disposition (i.e., individual nature or identity) of some Gentiles, who do naturally what the law requires. This inner focus is clear in Paul's comment that follows, that these, "though not having the law, are a law to themselves. They show that what the law requires is written on their hearts." The focus is thus not on conformity with some *external* nature in the visible world, but on living in conformity with *their own* nature — what is already "written on their hearts." It is this pattern of behavior that shows that they are a "law to themselves." We see a similar usage in Galatians 4:8: "Formerly, when you did not know God, you were enslaved to beings that by nature are not gods." Here again, "nature" does not refer to a universal reality but to the particular reality of beings that, by their own specific nature, are not gods.

This meaning of "natural" as "what comes naturally" — or with reference to a specific nature or disposition — is attested in other New Testament passages as well, passages that view "what comes naturally" negatively rather than positively. In the later Pauline tradition, Ephesians 2:3 speaks of nature: "All of us once lived among them in the passions of our flesh, following the desires of flesh and senses, and we were by nature [*phusei*] children of wrath, like everyone else." Here "nature" cannot mean "the will of God revealed in creation as a whole." Instead, the clear reference is to the individual nature of those who, simply by doing what came naturally to them, were "children of wrath."[5]

We see the same kinds of references to nature as "what comes naturally" or "what is in accord with one's own nature or identity" in other early Jewish texts. Wisdom 13:1 declares: "For all people who were ignorant of God were foolish by nature [*phusei*]." Again, one's individual nature, rather than universal nature, is the subject here. In a similar vein, Philo suggests in one text that the inability to beget male children arises from the individual nature of the father, which is lacking in justice and virtue:

> And no unjust man at any time implants a masculine generation in the soul, but such, being unmanly, and broken, and effeminate in their minds, do naturally [*ek phuseōs*, literally "from nature"] become the parents of female children; having planted no tree of virtue, the fruit of which must of necessity have been beautiful and salutary, but only trees of wickedness and of the passions, the shoots of which are womanlike.[6]

---

5. Outside the Pauline tradition, 2 Pet. 2:12 derides sinful scoffers as "like irrational animals, mere creatures of instinct *(phusika)* born to be caught and killed." Similarly, Jude 10 speaks of "irrational animals" who "know by instinct" *(phusikōs)*. In all these cases, references to what is natural convey the sense of what comes naturally or what is in accord with one's own individual nature or identity, whether that individual nature is positively or negatively portrayed.

6. Philo, *On the Giants* 1:4.

"What comes naturally" here to the man whose life is characterized by injustice and the absence of virtue is daughters, rather than sons! For our purposes here, we can pass over the obvious sexism in the passage, as well as the ancient ignorance and superstition about the process of conception, and simply note the specific nuances in the use of "nature," in accordance with the usage we have already seen. For the good person, "what comes naturally" or instinctively is good, as we saw in Romans 2:14; for the evil person, what comes naturally is evil or deficient in ways that match the deficiency of the evil person's nature (in the case of this quote from Philo, the birth of female offspring).

This notion of one's individual nature as determinative for identity is also deeply embedded in Stoic thought. Diogenes Laertius, in his *Lives of the Eminent Philosophers,* points out how Stoic philosophy considers the way in which animals "naturally" act in accord with their own best interests. He says: "We must assert that nature has bound the animal to itself by the greatest unanimity and affection for by that means it repels all that is injurious, and attracts all that is akin to it and desirable."[7] To act in accordance with nature is thus to act in accordance with one's own individual nature, to do what comes naturally — that is, what is in one's own best interest in the larger scheme of things.

Nature as Individual Disposition in Romans 1

One revisionist interpreter who has focused particularly on this interpretation of "nature" in Romans 1 is John Boswell. He says: "A possessive is always understood with 'nature' in Pauline writings: it is not 'nature' in the abstract, but *someone's* 'nature,' the Jews' 'nature' or the Gentiles' 'nature' or even the pagan gods' 'nature.'" Boswell goes on to conclude:

> It cannot be inferred from this [i.e., Rom. 1:26-27] that Paul considered mere homoerotic attraction or practice morally reprehensible, since the passage strongly implies that he was not discussing persons who were by inclination gay and since he carefully observed, in regard to both the women and the men, that they changed or abandoned the "natural use" to engage in homosexual activities.[8]

7. Laertius, *Lives of the Eminent Philosophers,* 7:52.
8. Boswell, *Christianity, Social Tolerance, and Homosexuality: Gay People in Western Eu-*

In other words, Boswell claims that when Paul describes men as acting "against nature" by engaging in sex with other men in Romans 1:27, Paul is envisioning heterosexual men who act against their *own* nature and disposition. Boswell thus concludes that this passage says nothing about homosexual men, because their same-sex behavior is in accordance with — and does not violate — their own nature or inclination.

There is certainly textual evidence in Romans 1 to back up at least some of Boswell's claim. This entire discussion of human sinfulness is introduced by the claim that humans "suppress the truth" that they already, in some sense, know (Rom. 1:18). Paul speaks of how women "exchanged natural intercourse for unnatural," and how men "gave up" (*aphentes,* literally "left behind") "natural intercourse with women" and "were consumed with passion for each other." It is impossible to imagine how one can "exchange" something that one does not, in some sense, already possess. Similarly, one cannot "give up" or "leave behind" something that is not already in one's possession or nature. Therefore, "nature" in Romans 1 must include, to some extent, the sense of one's own nature or disposition. In this sense, it is clear that Paul is not operating with the modern sense of sexual orientation here. Rather, he speaks of those who "leave behind" what he regards as their own true nature, which should direct them to relationships with those of the opposite sex. It would probably be inscrutable to him to speak of people who were "naturally" attracted to others of the same sex. This understanding of nature with respect to a same-sex sexual *orientation* is unattested in early Jewish and Christian discussions of same-sex behavior.

Such an awareness of a "natural" orientation toward same-sex relations is attested in some Greek and Roman sources. The myth of human origins presented in Plato's *Symposium* (189C-193D) assumes such a view: Aristophanes recounts how some humans long to be reunited with their "other half" of the same sex, from whom they were divided by the gods in the beginning.[9] However, the absence of such perspectives in early Jewish and Christian sources suggests that these Jews and Christians did not recognize even the possibility that persons might be naturally inclined (in terms of their own true nature) toward desiring others of the same sex. To concede such a possibility would allow a construal of nature that violated

---

rope from the Beginning of the Christian Era to the Fourteenth Century (Chicago: University of Chicago Press, 1980), pp. 110-12.

9. See other sources documented in Robert A. J. Gagnon, *The Bible and Homosexual Practice: Texts and Hermeneutics* (Nashville: Abingdon, 2001), pp. 384-85; see also n. 52.

their understanding of divine law, and thus it would be understood as un-acceptable a priori. Jewish and Christian references to "nature" were more apologetic in character than expressive of the more fundamentally philo-sophical approach to ethics we find in Stoicism. For early Jews and Chris-tians, the true meaning of "nature" could only be discerned in the ways that "nature" converged with the will of God revealed in the Torah. If this analysis is correct, however, it also suggests that the whole modern concept of sexual orientation and the contemporary evidence of its deeply rooted persistence, both in some humans and in some animals, represent an im-portant range of empirical data about the natural world that was not con-sidered by the ancient Jewish or Christian writers.[10]

Most traditionalists agree that Paul does not have the modern notion of sexual orientation in mind when he speaks of same-sex eroticism as "against nature." However, in a variety of ways they tend to minimize the emphasis, in Romans 1:26-27, on nature as one's personal nature or dispo-sition. For example, Robert Gagnon says: "Paul is speaking in corporate terms of the sweep of history, not the experience of each and every indi-vidual practitioner of same-sex intercourse."[11] Similarly, Thomas Schmidt writes: "Paul is describing not individual actions but the *corporate* rebel-lion of humanity against God and the kinds of behavior that result."[12] I must confess that I find this argument inscrutable. Romans 1:27 speaks of specific men who "leave behind the natural use of women" and instead en-gage in sex with other men. It is difficult to see how the focus on corporate rebellion clarifies the text in any way.

Richard Hays is more precise and more helpful when he argues that Boswell underestimates the importance of the broader Stoic background underlying the concept of "nature" as Paul uses it here.[13] We do not grasp Paul's understanding of nature here if we reduce it to one's personal dispo-sition or "nature" alone. Indeed, the whole point of Stoic ethics is to dis-

---

10. For a summary of modern research into the "natural" causes and occurrence of sex-ual orientation, see Glenn D. Wilson and Qazi Rahman, *Born Gay: The Psychobiology of Sex Orientation* (London/Chester Springs PA: Peter Owen, 2005); see also Simon LeVay, *Gay, Straight, and the Reason Why: The Science of Sexual Orientation* (Oxford: Oxford University Press, 2011).

11. Gagnon, *The Bible and Homosexual Practice*, p. 389.

12. Thomas Schmidt, *Straight and Narrow? Compassion and Clarity in the Homosexuality Debate* (Downers Grove, IL: InterVarsity, 1995), p. 78.

13. Hays, "Relations Natural and Unnatural: A Response to J. Boswell's Exegesis of Rom. 1," *Journal of Religious Ethics* 14, no. 1 (1986): 184-215, 196.

cover the convergence between one's own deepest disposition and the structures of the wider human community and the world as a whole. Stoicism is centrally concerned with assisting the individual to find his or her rightful place and function within this larger frame of reference.[14] Therefore, in Stoic thinking, nature has a wide range of meaning, encompassing both one's individual disposition and the larger structures of the community and cosmos as a whole. Paul never imagines nor envisions an individual nature (at least when nature is conceived positively) as divorced from the patterns of nature manifested in the human community as a whole, and in the wider cosmos.

Therefore, Boswell's attempt to read "nature" in Paul to refer *only* to one's individual disposition, without reference to these wider realities, is finally unsatisfactory. When Paul speaks of same-sex eroticism as "unnatural" in Romans 1, he probably assumes that same-sex eroticism violates both the deepest "nature" of the individuals involved and the wider structures of community and cosmos, evident in the differentiation of human beings into male and female, along with their respective roles and functions within the human community.

To note Boswell's reductionist error of excluding the communal and cosmic dimensions of what is natural, however, is not to endorse the traditionalists, who also attempt, with strikingly parallel reductionism of the opposite kind, to eliminate any reference in Romans 1:27 to the individual and personal nature or disposition of those who engage in same-sex eroticism. Boswell is correct — and stands on a strong exegetical basis — when he notes that one's individual nature or disposition is an important *part* of what Paul means when he says that same-sex eroticism is unnatural. Paul clearly intends to convey that when sinful humans act unnaturally they deny not only the "objective" nature evident in the wider human community and the visible world; they also deny their own "subjective" nature. They "leave behind" their own deepest and most natural inclinations and dispositions. For Paul, sinful behavior thus places humans out of sync with both the cosmos as a whole and with the deepest and truest aspects of themselves as persons. To act "unnaturally" is to fail, in the deepest sense, both to be yourself and to find your rightful place in the wider world.

Although this insight is powerfully true in wide areas of human experience, it encounters problems when it is used to interpret the experience of

---

14. For a comprehensive attempt to interpret Paul in light of this Stoic vision, see Troels Engberg-Pedersen, *Paul and the Stoics* (Louisville: Westminster John Knox, 2000).

many gay and lesbian persons. For them, the attempt to live in accordance with normal or "natural" societal expectations, or to embrace the "natural" union of male and female in marriage, often leads to a profound dislocation with respect to their own deepest inclinations and desires. Rather than achieving the harmony between the external natural and social world and their own internal nature and disposition, such attempts by gays and lesbians to live in heterosexual marriages are wrapped in deep conflict, sometimes resulting in the fracture of those marriages, which were intended by God to last for a lifetime, as both partners remain deeply frustrated and unsatisfied by the absence, often despite heroic efforts, of mutually compatible sexual desires. In my own limited experience, I have seen several families walk through this pain and heartache. By contrast, many gay and lesbian couples bear witness to a profound sense of integration and wholeness when they enter into committed relationships with those of the same sex, and when those relationships are recognized and embraced by the wider community. This convergence between internal disposition and communal acceptance can be deeply transformative, despite its apparent conflict with the "natural" differentiation of the world into male and female, and the more normal practice of heterosexual marriage.

It is beyond the scope of the discussion at this point in the chapter to attempt to resolve these dilemmas, but it is important to take note of them. We must reckon with the fact that what we are confronting here is a dimension of human experience that is unaddressed and unanticipated by the biblical writers — Jews or Christians — in the ancient world: we now know that there is a disparity between the deeply personal nature of gay and lesbian persons and the norms and assumptions of the wider human community — along with the apparent structures of the natural world. At the end of this chapter I shall return to this question and explore attempts to resolve this dilemma.

Nature as Communal Well-Being: The Social Dimensions of What Is Natural

In modern understanding, what is natural stands directly opposite to what is social. Nature refers to biology — over against culture. "Contrary to nature" means "contrary to biological structures and processes" rather than "contrary to the good order of society." Modern people generally conceive of the natural world as what exists prior to and apart from human influence, either individual or social. This sort of dichotomous thinking between the natural and the social simply did not exist in the ancient world. Rather, as Troels Engberg-Pedersen has argued, the essential Stoic movement toward living in accordance with nature also entailed a movement from the "I" to the "we," from an individualized notion of human existence to a transformed self-understanding in which the individual no longer sees himself or herself in isolation, but as part of a wider community, as well as part of larger natural processes and structures, including those defined both by society and by biology (in the modern sense of that term). Living in accordance with biological nature and living in accordance with other humans in an ordered society were conceived of as two sides of the same coin. As Engberg-Pedersen puts it, "It is a crucial idea in Stoicism that these two specifications [i.e., 'life in accordance with nature' and 'moral virtue and virtuous acts'] amount to the same thing."[15] He cites Cicero, a prominent expositor of Stoic teaching, who makes this connection between nature and the social good:

> [Human beings] believe that the universe is governed by divine will, and that it is a sort of city and state shared by men and gods, and that each of us is a part of this universe; from which it follows *by nature* that we set the common advantage before our own. For just as the laws set the safety of all before the safety of individuals, so a man who is good, wise, law-abiding, and conscious of his civic duty will care for the advantage of all more than of some single individual — or himself.

If we do not grasp clearly the way in which society is included in ancient understandings of nature, we will not fully understand what Paul means when he speaks, in Romans 1:26-27, of sexual acts that are "unnatural." This claim concerns not only biology but also social order. Life "in accordance with nature" entails a movement from "I" to "we." Note, for example, the way Cicero locates the "naturalness" of marriage, not only in biology, but in the "natural" social disposition of human beings, including politics and government:

> Again, since we see that man is designed by nature to safeguard and protect his fellows, it follows from this natural disposition, that the Wise Man should desire to engage in politics and government, and

15. Engberg-Pedersen, *Paul and the Stoics*, pp. 34ff., 58-59.

also to live in accordance with nature by taking to himself a wife and desiring to have children by her.[16]

This introduces a second major debate concerning the interpretation of "nature" in Romans 1. A number of revisionist interpreters suggest that when Paul says that same-sex eroticism is unnatural, what he means is that it violates normal societal conventions. By this argument, "contrary to nature" simply refers to what is "unusual" or "unconventional." For example, Jack Rogers writes: "For Paul, 'unnatural' is a synonym for 'unconventional.' It means something surprisingly out of the ordinary."[17] When this line of interpretation is pursued, attention is often focused on another reference to "nature" found in 1 Corinthians 11:14-15: "Does not nature itself teach you that if a man wears long hair, it is degrading to him, but if a woman has long hair, it is her glory? For her hair is given to her for a covering." Here "nature" appears very much like "social convention." Victor Paul Furnish summarizes the perspective of many on this text — and its relevance for interpreting Romans 1: "No such 'creation theology' as that alleged for Rom. 1:26-27 is evident in any of Paul's other references to what is 'natural' or 'unnatural' . . . . In [1 Cor. 11:14-15] his appeal to what 'nature itself' teaches is nothing more than an appeal to social convention — to the practice with which he himself is familiar and that he thus regards as self-evidently 'proper.'"[18] Interestingly, even traditionalist interpreter Richard Hays identifies this passage (1 Cor. 11:14-15) as an "isolated instance" of an understanding of nature as merely "convention as understood by me."[19]

Another traditionalist interpreter, Robert Gagnon, senses the difficulty posed by this more socially oriented understanding of nature for his approach, which focuses instead almost entirely on nature as the realm of biology and anatomy. He appeals to a neo-Platonist philosopher, Synesius of Cyrene, who argued in about 400 CE that, since men go bald much more commonly than women do, short hair is more "natural" for men than long hair.[20] Hence, Gagnon argues, even 1 Corinthians 11:14-15 is not making an

16. Cicero, *De Finibus* III:64 (italics added); III: 68.

17. Jack Bartlett Rogers, *Jesus, the Bible, and Homosexuality: Explode the Myths, Heal the Church* (Louisville: Westminster John Knox, 2006), p. 74; cf. Martti Nissinen, *Homoeroticism in the Biblical World: A Historical Perspective* (Minneapolis: Fortress, 1998), p. 105.

18. In Jeffrey S. Siker, *Homosexuality in the Church: Both Sides of the Debate* (Louisville: Westminster John Knox, 1994), p. 30.

19. Hays, "Relations Natural and Unnatural," p. 196.

20. Gagnon, *The Bible and Homosexual Practice*, pp. 373ff.

appeal to "social convention" but to processes discernible in the natural (i.e., biological) world. But the piece that Gagnon quotes is a lighthearted and humorous piece, not a serious discussion, and even if one takes it as a serious argument, it doesn't explain Paul's language, which focuses not on the honorable state of baldness (the concern of Synesius), but rather the dishonorable state of long hair. Paul claims that nature teaches that it is "degrading" for a man to wear long hair. Nature (understood as biological processes) might indeed conceivably teach that the absence of hair is honorable in men, since it is associated with older and respected men, but it is a purely human convention to come to the parallel conclusion, that long hair is degrading for men. It is difficult to see how nature, understood as anatomy and biology, teaches this, particularly since almost all younger men are not bald, and apart from human intervention, will indeed grow long hair. Does nature really teach that all men who are not bald are degraded? (Though such an argument has a certain appeal to a very bald person like me, I remain unconvinced!)

Moreover, if Gagnon is correct, then Paul's words here must clearly be universally binding: the biology of aging hasn't changed (some older men still go bald), and thus long hair is always, by this logic, disgraceful for men. Yet this seems to be contradicted by other passages in Scripture itself. The Nazirite vow in Numbers 6 regards uncut hair as a sign of special devotion to God — hardly something shameful. The story of Samson (Judg. 13–16) is another memorable account in which the cutting of hair represents a loss of God-given, manly strength. Moreover, the notion that long hair is always disgraceful for men is a perspective that has not been sustained through long stretches of the church's life and history in a variety of cultural settings, where that perspective simply doesn't make sense. It's far more realistic to suppose that Paul uses nature here more in the sense that we would speak of convention, or what occurs normally in human life. "Nature," in this sense, refers to those normal social conventions that we simply take for granted as self-evidently true. Such conventions may have echoes in the biological realm, but they are essentially socially constructed perspectives.

Yet Paul's usage here is not an isolated instance in ancient understandings of "nature." Particularly when gender roles are the subject (as they are in 1 Cor. 11), we find many Jews and Christians referring to nature to establish what appear, from a modern perspective, to be merely conventional ancient assumptions about the meaning of gender. Thus Philo writes, for example: "But the passions are female by nature, and we must study to quit them, showing our preference for the masculine characters of the good dispositions."[21] An entire ancient philosophical tradition, from Aristotle through the Stoics, sets on one side what is feminine, subservient, and controlled by passion, and on the other side what is masculine, dominant, and controlled by reason. This tradition views these distinctions as completely "natural," grounded in the creation (or nature) itself. For men to violate these distinctions is not only to violate nature, but to act disgracefully, that is, in conflict with established social conventions of propriety. This is true whether these violations occur when men act in ways that are dominated by passion, or when they allow themselves to be sexually penetrated by another male, or when they simply fail to distinguish themselves clearly from females in the way they dress or wear their hair.

Interestingly, we see the juxtaposition of these concerns in both 1 Corinthians 11:13-14 and Romans 1:24-27. In both of these texts we see a concern with the blurring of gender distinctions and the confusion of gender roles. In both texts this behavior is spoken of as "degrading" or "dishonorable," and in both texts the focus falls on a failure to conform one's behavior properly to "nature." Hence, the linkage between nature and the idea that long hair is degrading to a man is not an "isolated instance," as Hays has argued, but instead represents part of a broad consensus in the ancient world, a consensus that nature provides a pattern that directs and shapes not only the biological but also the social order. To designate this usage as "merely conventional" may represent a modern perspective, according to which these attitudes toward female subservience and long hair seem quaint at best — and hardly self-evidently "natural." From the perspective of the ancient world, however, these connections are all part of the basic fabric of nature and are not distinguished from each other in meaningful ways at all.

In this light we can see more clearly the convergence of the themes I have been exploring in this chapter and the preceding three chapters. It is not coincidental that Romans 1:24-27 speaks of same-sex relations as a manifestation of passion and lust, as shameful, and also as a violation of nature. The three chapters in this volume speak of the same reality from three different vantage points; but it is a single social reality that is portrayed as compromised in these verses. That social reality is marked by male rationality (subverted by "the lusts of their hearts," "degrading passions," and men who are "consumed with passion"), male dominance (subverted by "their women," who no longer have "natural" sexual relations and men who "re-

---

21. Philo, "De Eo Quod Deterius Potiori Insidiatur," 1:29.

ceive in their own persons the due penalty for their error"), and male honor (subverted by "degrading passions" and "shameless acts").

Of course, recognizing that ancient assumptions about gender are thoroughly interwoven with the understanding of nature in these texts poses some difficult challenges for those interpreters who still seek to be taught by Scripture. We shall return to these questions at the end of this chapter. But for now it is sufficient to note that, when Romans 1 speaks of acts that are "unnatural," it is speaking not only of individual natures; it is also speaking of what we would call "social" realities, including widely held social understandings of the meaning of gender, with fairly clear assumptions about the nature of men and women and their respective roles in society. To put it simply, men having sex with other men was considered unnatural, at least in part, because it violated established gender roles, forcing men to play the role of women, upsetting the normal hierarchy of the genders that went unquestioned in the ancient world. If we find it difficult today to directly appropriate a worldview with such assumptions, it suggests that we must grapple with some larger hermeneutical questions in our use of the concept of nature as it is found in this passage. I will return to this question later in this chapter.

Nature, Biology, and Anatomy

Whereas revisionist interpreters tend to emphasize the first two aspects of nature we have already explored — nature as individual character or disposition and nature as a communal, shared reality — traditionalist interpreters tend to strongly emphasize nature as biology and anatomy. Robert Gagnon speaks repeatedly of "anatomical and procreative complementarity" as the essence of "nature," which is violated by same-sex eroticism.[22] Ulrich Mauser speaks of the importance of terms implying gender differentiation in strongly naturalistic terms: "Being male or female is a reality prior to law and morality, and prior to individual choices."[23] Thomas Schmidt quotes with approval an earlier article by David Wright, which

22. Gagnon writes: "Given the meaning of 'contrary to nature' *(para phusin)* and comparable expressions used by Jewish writers of the period to describe same-sex intercourse, the meaning of the phrase in Paul is clear. Minimally, Paul is referring to the anatomical and procreative complementarity of male and female" (Gagnon, *The Bible and Homosexual Practice*, p. 254).

23. Mauser, "Creation, Sexuality, and Homosexuality in the New Testament," p. 48.

declares, "Male and female were created for each other with complementary sexualities grounded in the distinctive constitutions of their sexual organs."[24] Richard Hays comments in similar terms:

> In the same way, the charge that these fallen humans have "exchanged natural relations for unnatural" means nothing more nor less than that human beings, created for heterosexual companionship as the Genesis story bears witness, have distorted even so basic a truth as their sexual identity by rejecting the male and female roles which are "naturally" theirs in God's created order.[25]

Earlier in this chapter I have explored how "male and female roles" in the ancient world contained assumptions that most modern Western Christians do not share, regardless of how natural those roles may have appeared to Paul and others of his day. As we have seen, the boundary between nature and social convention in the ancient world was a blurry one. But biology and anatomy are not subject to the same kind of cultural variation. It will be important, therefore, to discern as precisely as possible whether the "unnaturalness" of same-sex eroticism was considered by Paul to be a violation of nature envisioned as anatomical and/or procreative complementarity. How much — and in what way — did ancient understandings of anatomy and biology inform Paul's characterization of sexual misbehavior as unnatural in Romans 1:26-27?

One kind of answer is evident in the ancient sources. Many ancient writers — Jewish, Christian, and pagan — spoke of procreation as the "natural" purpose of sexual relations. Therefore, any form of sexual relations that was not directed toward the purpose of procreation was understood to be unnatural. The ancient Jewish historian Josephus spoke typically of many Jews when he said: "What are our marriage laws? The Law recognizes no sexual connections, except the natural *[kata phusin]* union of man and wife, and that only for the procreation of children."[26] Note the explicit connection of nature, heterosexual marriage, and procreation. We see a similar juxtaposition of these concerns in a passage where Philo treats same-sex eroticism directly, declaring that it is against nature because it is nonprocreative:

24. David F. Wright, "Homosexuality: The Relevance of the Bible," *Evangelical Quarterly* 61 (1989): 295, cited in Schmidt, *Straight and Narrow?* pp. 79-80.

25. Hays, "Relations Natural and Unnatural," p. 200.

26. Josephus, *Against Apion* 2.199.

And let the man who is devoted to the love of boys submit to the same punishment, since he pursues that pleasure which is contrary to nature, and since, as far as depends upon him, he would make the cities desolate, and void, and empty of all inhabitants, wasting his power of propagating his species.[27]

Elsewhere, Philo speaks of marriage as "the cause of the procreation of children."[28] For Philo, this linkage between sex and procreation is definitive, and it shapes all that he has to say about sex. For example, Philo berates men who marry barren women, or who seek to have sex with their wives during infertile periods.[29]

These examples could be multiplied many times from a variety of ancient sources. It was a commonplace in the ancient world that what was "natural" about sex was its purpose of procreation, the continuation of the species.[30] Moreover, understanding the "nature" of sex in a way that was linked to procreation fit in perfectly with the overall tendency, in Stoicism and more generally in ethical deliberations in the ancient world, to evaluate the morality of behaviors in terms of the "ends" or goals toward which they were directed.[31] The Stoics, who prided themselves on living in accordance with nature, also believed that good actions were those actions that were directed toward goals or ends that were in accordance with nature, and bad actions were directed toward goals that were incompatible with nature. Stoics defined the morality of actions in terms of the goals toward which those actions are directed. In this framework, sex was good when practiced within marriage (so that the children conceived in sexual relationships could be properly cared for) and when it was directed toward the generation of children. Sexual behavior was bad when it was not directed toward these goals, but was instead driven only by passion (the desire for self-gratification). All of this would have been immediately clear — even self-evident — to Paul's readers. Because the same-sex eroticism of

---

27. Philo, *Special Laws* 3:39.

28. *On the Unchangeableness of God* 1:87.

29. *Special Laws* 3:34.

30. For further exploration of the link between sex and procreation in the ancient world, see Margaret Davies, "New Testament Ethics and Ours: Homosexuality and Sexuality in Romans 1:26-27," *Biblical Interpretation* 3 (1995).

31. Aristotle begins his *Nicomachean Ethics* with these words: "Every art and every inquiry, and similarly every action and pursuit, is thought to aim at some good; and for this reason the good has rightly been declared to be that at which all things aim" (I.i.1, 1094a.1-3).

Romans 1:27 is "consumed with passion" and cannot fulfill the procreative purpose of sex, it is necessarily "unnatural."

Of course, Paul can also speak of other purposes for marriage, beyond merely procreation. Hence, in 1 Corinthians 7, Paul speaks of marriage as a means for bringing sexual desire under control, and in that context he does not speak of procreation at all. In this sense, Paul's understanding of the purpose of marriage and sexuality is broader than we saw in Philo, where the purpose of sex was restricted to procreation alone.[32] But the presence of such a broader vision in 1 Corinthians 7 does not diminish the obvious interpretation that Paul's hearers would have made, in Romans 1:26-27, of the claim that same-sex relations are "unnatural." They would have understood those sexual misbehaviors as unnatural precisely because they were nonprocreative, because they could not be directed toward the "end" that nature intends — the generation of children. This perspective is amply attested in multiple sources. Paul may indeed have had a broader understanding of marriage than only what nature teaches; but in Romans 1, because he is speaking of Gentile sinfulness apart from the giving of the law, he is making his argument on the more limited basis of nature — as it was commonly understood in the ancient world. In the ancient world generally, nature was understood to teach that sex was for the purpose of procreation. There is no reason to think that the references to nature in Romans 1 assume any other frame of reference. Indeed, the assumption in ancient patristic writers such as Clement and Augustine that Romans 1:26 refers to nonprocreative forms of heterosexual intercourse as "unnatural" confirms the same perspective.

But many traditionalist interpreters are not quite content with understanding nature only in terms of procreation. Rather, as we have seen, many traditionalist interpreters think that nature teaches not only the procreative purpose of sex but also gender complementarity, or, even more specifically, *anatomical* complementarity. This represents a second kind of argument based on biology and anatomy, which moves in a different direction from the argument linking nature and procreation. Robert Gagnon has been the most forceful proponent of this view. In his work he repeatedly refers to "anatomical and procreative complementarity" as the essential teaching of nature that is violated by same-sex eroticism. But clearly, for Gagnon, procreative complementarity takes second place to anatomical complemen-

---

32. See the prior discussion in chapter 6, which argues that Scripture more broadly does not restrict its understanding of marriage to procreation alone.

tarity as the central teaching of "nature" with respect to sexual expression.[33] For Gagnon, what "nature" teaches most centrally about sex is "the anatomical fittedness of the male penis and the female vagina."[34]

Gagnon attempts to establish this understanding of nature first of all by his reading of Romans 1:19-20:

> [19]For what can be known about God is plain to them, because God has shown it to them. [20]Ever since the creation of the world, his eternal power and divine nature, invisible though they are, have been understood and seen through the things he has made. So they are without excuse.

Gagnon argues that this text focuses on what is visible, or "plain." Therefore, what is contrary to nature about same-sex eroticism must focus on plain or visible differences between men and women.[35] But this reading confuses Paul's meaning. What Paul actually says in these two verses is that what can be known about God is plain or visible in the creation, specifically God's eternal power and divine nature. The focus here is not on knowledge of human things, but on the knowledge of God. The text goes on to say that when this knowledge of God is suppressed through idolatry, the consequences are that God "hands over" idolatrous humans to lust and the degrading of their bodies (Rom. 1:24). Gagnon confuses the initial revelation about God suppressed by idolatrous humans (which focuses on visible things) with the later "handing over" of humans into depravity (which focuses on lust, shame, and the violation of what is "natural"). Romans 1 says nothing particular at all about the "visible" quality of nature

When we consider Paul's other uses of the word "nature," it does not appear that he focuses particularly on the visible aspects of nature. For example, Paul speaks in Romans 11:24 of wild olive branches that, contrary to

---

33. Gagnon thinks that "Paul's opposition to same-sex intercourse was not based primarily on its nonprocreative character" (Dan Otto Via and Robert A. J. Gagnon, *Homosexuality and the Bible: Two Views* [Minneapolis: Fortress, 2003], p. 86).

34. Gagnon, *The Bible and Homosexual Practice, passim,* esp. p. 169.

35. Gagnon writes: "In essence Paul is arguing in Rom 1:26-27 that if one did not have access to Genesis or Leviticus one could still recognize in nature that God designed the male-female union alone to be a complementary sexual fit." Via and Gagnon, *Homosexuality and the Bible,* p. 79. I agree that Paul is saying that, apart from Genesis or Leviticus, nature by itself shows that the sexual excesses he depicts are wrong. However, there is nothing in the passage that even suggests that the reason "nature" regards such practices as wrong is the absence of a "complementary sexual fit."

nature, are grafted into a cultivated olive tree. It is hard to see how this text focuses on visual elements with any particular emphasis at all. Furthermore, references to nature in the ancient world more broadly cannot all be squeezed into the "visible" kind of interpretation that Gagnon attempts here. For example, many ancient writers reflect on the relationship between nature and a range of virtues and vices. Thus Philo:

> Last of all, the divine legislator prohibits covetousness, knowing that desire is a thing fond of revolution and of plotting against others; for all the passions of the soul are formidable, exciting and agitating it *contrary to nature,* and not permitting it to remain in a healthy state, but of all such passions the worst is desire.[36]

Such discussions of things "contrary to nature" necessarily focus on what is not immediately or directly visible.[37] Gagnon's equation of "nature" with "what is visible" is unsustainable, especially in Romans 1, but also in the wider references to nature in Paul and the rest of the Greco-Roman world.

Gagnon also attempts to support this interpretation of nature focusing on complementary sexual organs by appealing to a range of early Jewish texts. However, almost none of the texts cited by Gagnon to support his notion of "anatomical complementarity" say anything about actual body parts.[38] Instead, almost all of these passages speak negatively of how the passive partner in male-male sex is degraded, and either forced or deceived into abandoning his "natural" manliness and acting like a woman instead. Jewish writers are particularly derisive of those passive partners in male-male sex who exhibit feminine appearance or behavior. In other words, what these early Jewish texts have in mind is not anatomical complementarity but the violation of socially normed gender roles, in which the male was expected to be active, rational, shorthaired, and in control, and the woman was expected to be passive, emotional, longhaired, and subservient. These texts hardly support an interpretation of nature as referring to

---

36. Philo, *Decalogue* 1:142 (italics added).

37. Hence Gagnon is certainly wrong when he declares, "Passions, which are not material and hence not visible to sight, are excluded from consideration as indications of God's intentions manifest in nature" (Gagnon, *The Bible and Homosexual Practice,* pp. 257-58). Paul refers explicitly to lust and passion throughout this passage, in the closest possible connection with what is "unnatural" (Rom. 1:24, 26, 27).

38. See Gagnon, *The Bible and Homosexual Practice,* pp. 169-76.

"the anatomical fittedness of the male penis and the female vagina." Indeed, they say absolutely nothing about the relationship of penis to vagina at all.

There are a number of ancient texts that speak of the *kinaidoi*, male cult prostitutes of the ancient cult of Cybele, or Magna Mater, that may address the issue of anatomical differences between men and women. Some worshipers would castrate themselves and devote themselves to sacral prostitution.[39] Philo speaks derisively of these as an extreme manifestation of this feminization process.[40] But this concern with anatomy is only one element in a much larger concern of Philo in this passage: the blurring of gender roles defined in terms of dress, behavior, and authority/control. It is this latter problem, rather than the violation of an "anatomical norm," that shapes Philo's discourse as a whole.

In other words, even though Gagnon wishes to interpret nature in Romans 1 as referring to "anatomical complementarity," the texts that he cites to support this claim fail to do so. They speak instead either of procreation or of the violation of gender roles more broadly. Nowhere does Gagnon cite a single ancient text that speaks specifically of the fittedness of penis and vagina. This is a striking and ominous silence, particularly in Gagnon's argument, where "anatomical complementarity" comprises the very heart and essence of his entire case against homosexual practice. It appears that the notion of "anatomical gender complementarity" is really a modern concept rather than a category that actually shaped ethical thought about sex in the ancient world. To the extent that ancient references to "nature" in sexual ethics envisioned anatomy and biology, they clearly had procreation in mind.[41] Beyond this, however, references to na-

---

39. See Nissinen, *Homoeroticism in the Biblical World*, pp. 57-88; see also Jeramy Townsley, "Paul, the Goddess Religions, and Queers: Romans 1:23-28," *Journal of Biblical Literature*, forthcoming, which provides extensive documentation of the place of the *kinaidoi* in ancient Greek and Roman culture.

40. Philo, *Special Laws* 3:42.

41. Another ancient text, not cited by Gagnon, that links the anatomy of sex organs with procreation specifically, is found in Cicero's *De Finibus*: "Again, it is held by the Stoics to be important to understand that nature creates in parents an affection for their children; and parental affection is the germ of that social community of the human race to which we afterwards attain. This cannot but be clear in the first place from the conformation of the body and its members, which by themselves are enough to show that nature's scheme included the procreation of children" (III:62). Here, if anywhere, differences of sex organs are mentioned; but this difference is only noted in the service of the broader vision we have already noted: the critical link between nature and procreation, as well as the "naturalness" of social rela-

ture in ancient sexual ethics bring us back to the first two categories of this chapter: one's individual nature and nature defined as established social order (including gender roles).

Summarizing the Nature Debate in Romans 1:26-27: Three Streams

With this broad survey of the debate about nature in place, we can now step back and synthesize what Paul may have meant when he spoke of sexual behavior that was "unnatural" in Romans 1:26-27. I believe that the most obvious place to begin is with nature as procreative capacity and intent. Clearly, the natural link between sex and procreation is more fully documented in the ancient sources than any other understanding of the relationship between nature and sex. Many texts from the ancient world regard men having sex with other men as unnatural because such sexual expression does not move toward the manifest purpose of sex seen throughout the natural world — the propagation of the species. As we have seen, the writings of Philo, Josephus, and other Jewish writers contain multiple passages supporting this line of interpretation, as do many other ancient authors. Moreover, as we have also noted earlier, for the first 300 years of the church's life, Romans 1:26 (referring to women who "exchanged natural intercourse for unnatural") was understood to refer, not to lesbian sexual activity, but to nonprocreative forms of *heterosexual* intercourse. This also suggests that the early church saw the common theme between the sexual misconduct of women in Romans 1:26 and that of men in verse 27 to center on the *nonprocreative* character of both forms of sexual misconduct (rather than the alleged commonality of same-sex eroticism). In short, any sexual activity of women that was not directed toward procreation was "unnatural" in the ancient world; same-sex eroticism between men was "unnatural" for the same reason; the neglect of the "natural" procreative purpose of sex made all such behavior "unnatural."

---

tionships and affection. What is notably absent in this passage from Cicero, on the other hand, is any sense in which genital complementarity might lead to affection or bonding between husband and wife. Such a conclusion is not at all warranted here; gender differences are envisioned solely in the service of procreation. This calls into question Gagnon's attempt to broaden genital complementarity beyond anatomy to other categories, such as "sexual stimulation" and "relational expectations" (see Via and Gagnon, *Homosexuality and the Bible*, p. 65). This is simply not the way people in the ancient world thought about the anatomical differences between men and women.

Hence, because the link between procreation and nature occupies a central place in the way people in the ancient world thought about sex, Paul used that common point of reference in condemning the sexual excesses in Romans 1:26-27. However, it is unlikely that Paul's readers would have thought *only* of procreation when he characterized the sexual behavior in those verses as "unnatural." Particularly when Paul also speaks of such behavior as "degrading," Paul's readers would likely have recalled the assumption, widely attested throughout the ancient world, that it was not only unnatural but also inherently shameful and degrading for a man to be reduced to the status of a female by playing the passive role in sexual intercourse. Such a violation of socially established hierarchies was understood to be shocking and dangerous. Indeed, Paul's reference to the "due penalty" that males received for their error (Rom. 1:27) underscores the social anxiety and instability that such behavior engendered in the ancient world. Such flagrant disruption of social norms could not go unpunished. Male-male sex in particular was "unnatural" because it degraded the passive partner into acting like a woman, confusing and distorting "natural" — that is, socially embedded — gender roles. For the active partner to inflict such shame on the passive partner was equally culpable.

Finally, Paul's readers would also have assumed that the behavior described in Romans 1:26-27 was "unnatural" because it violated the true personal and individual *natures* of the persons involved. Here again we should note the preponderance of the language of lust and desire in this text. As we have seen in earlier discussion, Jews and Christians in the ancient world generally thought that same-sex eroticism was driven by an unnatural lust that was not content with the natural and procreative purposes of sex but was selfishly driven to increasingly exotic forms of stimulation. The characterization of such sexual behavior as both lustful and unnatural depicts two sides of the same coin. Because the participants are driven by insatiable desires, they violate their own deepest and truest nature, which should normally be content with the "natural" purpose of heterosexual procreation for sexual expression.

This brief summary underscores how important it is to avoid a pitfall common to much scholarship in the contemporary debate over the interpretation of this text, a pitfall that involves focusing exclusively on one of the three streams of interpretation we have explored, while ignoring or downplaying the others. "Nature" in the ancient world included one's individual or personal nature, but extended beyond that. It included conventional social expectations regarding gender roles, but extended beyond that as well. And it also included a sense of the biological significance of procreation as well. Indeed, the Stoic understanding of "nature," understood as the implicit norm for all life, envisioned a convergence and harmony between the personal and individual, the communal, and the biological worlds. We will not understand what Paul meant when he spoke of these sexual behaviors as "unnatural" unless we see these behaviors as violating this deep convergence and resonance in multiple ways. Paul envisions the sexual misbehavior he describes in Romans 1:26-27 as a violation of one's individual nature or identity, as a violation of deeply established social norms regarding gender, and as a violation of the "biological imperative" to bear children. All of this is conveyed in his characterization of these behaviors as "unnatural."

What contemporary Christians must realize, however, is that this "natural" convergence of the personal, the communal, and the biological worlds does not take place for us today in the same way that it took place in the ancient world, quite apart from the question of same-sex relationships. The advent of reliable contraception has altered the way we think about the relationship between sex and procreation, dramatically increasing the significance of sex as intimate bonding in addition to — and in some cases displacing — the procreative meaning and purpose of sex. The modern world no longer understands "natural" gender roles in the way they were understood in the ancient world. For most Western Christians today, women are not naturally passive, subservient, and subject to the passions. Most Western Christians do not regard it as degrading for a male employee to have a female boss. Moreover, recent discoveries about sexual orientation have changed the way we think about the sexual "nature" of individuals. Psychologists now recognize a persistent, nonpathological pattern of same-sex sexual orientation as a natural phenomenon, resulting from a complex interaction between genetics, in-utero hormonal influences, and social context.[42]

In other words, the grand "natural" synthesis championed by the Stoics and assumed throughout much of the ancient world is much more problematic for Western Christians today. Our understanding of personal natures, of natural social and gender roles, and even of the natural procreative purpose of sex has grown and changed in many ways. We cannot simply adopt this ancient vision of nature without significant qualifica-

42. See Wilson and Rahman, *Born Gay;* see also Simon LeVay, *Gay, Straight, and the Reason Why: The Science of Sexual Orientation* (Oxford: Oxford University Press, 2011).

tions and adaptations. These include not only considerations of same-sex intimacy, but also considerations about contraception, the meaning of heterosexual intimacy, the "natural" casting of gender roles, and the proper boundaries of "natural" desire.

This does not mean that contemporary Christians reject the will of God as it is revealed in creation. But it does mean that our understanding of exactly how the will of God is revealed in the natural order is subject to change, deepening, and growth over time. Indeed, the desire to understand how God's will is embedded in the created order should in fact lead us to investigate the natural world more carefully, with a view to discovering the intentions and purposes of God that may be reflected in the shape and structure of the created order. Thus, even though the ancient "natural" synthesis requires substantial adaptation before it can be embraced by contemporary Christians, the call to live in accordance with nature still embodies an important vision worthy of our consideration. When people in the ancient world thought about nature, they thought comprehensively about a synthetic vision encompassing the personal, the social, and the natural world. Even if contemporary Christians may think differently about what is natural, they still can learn from the ancients and can reach toward an analogous contemporary synthesis. Far too much contemporary popular thinking fractures the realms of the personal, social, and physical world into separate spheres that are disconnected from each other. However, we still need and long for a vision that unites these spheres, a vision where individuals live in harmony with themselves and with each other in a healthy society that reconciles intimacy and public life, rich and poor, women and men, friend and stranger, old and young, and where that society lives in harmony with its natural environment. In other words, the specific ways in which we interpret what is natural may change over time, but the need for a comprehensive and embodied vision of what is natural remains as urgent as it ever was — and as elusive today as it was in the world Paul talks about in Romans 1.

Indeed, it is precisely the elusiveness of this vision of an ordered, "natural" world that makes Romans 1 the beginning, rather than the end, of Paul's discourse. Paul speaks of nature here in order to chronicle our alienation from it and to evoke our longing for that coherence of the personal, social, and physical that so persistently eludes our grasp. But seeing nature through this lens only raises a deeper and more important question: What is the relationship between "nature" as Paul speaks of it in Romans 1 and the redemption in Christ that is narrated in the following chapters of Romans?

Nature and Redeemed Life in Christ

One does not need to probe too deeply before encountering tensions between the comprehensive Stoic concept of nature (which almost all scholars think is evoked in Romans 1) and the will and purpose of God revealed in Paul's gospel of Christ. The Stoics attempted to ground their understanding of nature — and the moral vision implicit in that understanding of nature — in what seemed obvious and self-evident in the natural world. Troels Engberg-Pedersen summarizes this vision: "[S]ince the Stoics were philosophers, their favoured procedure was to show that 'rightly understood' the *ordinary* perception of good and bad could be seen to point in the direction of their own view."[43] Appeals to nature entailed appeals to the most common forms of experience and observation that would seem self-evident to all rational people of good will. Yet Paul's characterization of his gospel as "foolishness" to Gentiles (1 Cor. 1:23) suggests that redemption in Christ stands in some tension with "the ordinary perception of good and bad."[44] For Paul, Christian life entailed a powerful and important movement from the old creation to the new creation. This movement creates for Paul some profound discontinuities, for example, in the role of the law, particularly for Gentile believers. For Paul, even though "nature" may accurately describe where we have come from, it does not necessarily and comprehensively describe where we as Christians are going.

Therefore, Paul can speak in Romans 2:27 of those who are "by nature" uncircumcised, but who nonetheless keep God's law, demonstrating a "circumcision of the heart" (Rom. 2:27) despite the absence of "natural" circumcision. Similarly, in Romans 11:24, God acts "contrary to nature" by grafting the (Gentile) wild olive branches into what is "by nature" a cultivated (Jewish) olive tree. But perhaps the most striking text that speaks of how redemption moves beyond the framework of "nature" is Galatians 3:28: "There is no longer Jew or Greek, there is no longer slave or free, there is no longer male and female; for all of you are one in Christ Jesus." In this context, the "natural" distinction (cf. Rom 2:27) of circumcised and uncircumcised no longer has any meaning in Christ. Likewise, the "natural" division of humanity into male and female for the purpose of procre-

43. Engberg-Pedersen, *Paul and the Stoics*, p. 79 (italics in original).
44. See the more extended discussion of this issue in J. Louis Martyn, "De-Apocalpyticizing Paul: An Essay Focused on *Paul and the Stoics* by Troels Engberg-Pedersen," *Journal for the Study of the New Testament* 86 (2002): 77.

ation loses its ultimate significance in Christ. Even the distinction between slave and free, while rejected as unnatural by some Stoic writers, is regarded as entirely natural by others. Indeed, Aristotle considered the slave/ master polarity one of the fundamental bases on which all of society is built. The opening of his political treatise includes these words:

> Now that it is clear what are the components of the state, we have first of all to discuss household management; for every state is composed of households . . . . The investigation of everything should begin with the smallest parts, and the primary and smallest parts of the household are master and slave, husband and wife, father and children; we ought therefore to examine the proper constitution and character of each of these relationships, I mean that of mastership, that of marriage . . . and thirdly the progenitive relationship.[45]

Clearly, for Aristotle at least, the relationship of masters to slaves was just as basic and essential to the "natural" ordering of society as that of husband and wife or parents and children. But all this "natural" ordering of the world is radically transformed by Paul's gospel, where "there is neither slave nor free," and where "neither circumcision nor uncircumcision is anything, but a new creation is everything" (Gal. 6:15).

In this sense, Paul's approach to "nature," when viewed against the backdrop of his theological perspective in its totality, stands in marked contrast to the approach we find in Jewish writers like Philo, Josephus, and Pseudo-Phocylides. In these Jewish writers, "nature" becomes synonymous with "the will of God revealed in the creation accounts and the rest of the law." However, for Paul, the death of Christ forced a radical rereading of the law itself and its significance in the redeemed life; and the resurrection of Christ opened up a vision of a new creation in which the "second Adam" fulfilled the intent of the original creation, but moved far beyond it as well, drawing humanity into participation in the Trinitarian divine communion. The death and resurrection of Christ is hardly the "natural" means of redemption for the world that would make sense to all rational people of good will. Rather, it entails a kind of "foolishness," by which Paul declares that Christians have died to "the world" — the entire system of relationships and assumptions that shapes ordinary human life (Col. 2:20, Gal. 6:14). In other words, as far as Paul is concerned, the violations of "nature" that he narrates in Romans 1 expose the irresolvable and destructive tensions and ruptures

---

45. Aristotle, *Politics* 1.1253b.

that have destroyed the capacity of humans to live in harmony with themselves, with others, and with the natural world. But contrary to Stoic teaching, Paul did not believe that nature had the capacity to teach us how to fix this problem with any effectiveness at all. The way forward is not found by a return to a pristine, original nature — or even by more focused attempts to keep the whole law — but rather by following the crucified Messiah, who is ushering in a new creation, empowered by the Spirit of God.

Hence we arrive at an important eschatological tension running throughout Paul's theology. Christian life takes place in this world, which was created by God and distorted through the Fall. It is this world — in both its beauty and brokenness — where the incarnation took place, where the gospel is proclaimed, where the Spirit is at work. This is the natural world that God came to redeem, not to destroy or replace. Therefore, redemption does not displace or escape nature; rather, it fulfills nature. But that fulfillment does not take place apart from dramatic transformation. The book of Revelation speaks of a "new heaven and a new earth," but the word for "new" *(kainos)* connotes not "novel" or "unprecedented," but "fresh, improved, and renewed." Revelation 21:1 goes on to declare that, in this new heaven and new earth, "there was no longer any sea." In ancient thought, the sea connoted the threat of randomness and dissolution that always marked the bounds of the habitable creation. In the creation narrative God separated the waters below from the waters above, to make space for life to flourish (Gen. 1:6). When Jesus calmed the sea and walked on it, he demonstrated his power over the forces of chaos that threaten to undo the stable created order (Matt. 8:24ff.; 14:25ff.; Mark 4:39ff.; 6:48ff.; John 6:19ff.). But in the new heaven and the new earth, the sea is no more: the divine life knows no boundaries, but extends its life-giving power everywhere, leaving no threat remaining to God's good order and purpose for all of life. Hence we cannot simply read God's final purposes for the creation from the original, natural order. Instead, we must look to the vision of the future disclosed in the gospel of Christ.

This is the "not yet" of Christian existence, the hope that "the creation itself will be set free from its bondage to decay, and will obtain the freedom of the glory of the children of God" (Rom. 8:21). But this hope is not yet entirely present in our current experience. Paul speaks of how the creation is "groaning in labor pains until now," and how humans, having received the "first fruits" of the Spirit, groan along with it (Rom. 8:22-23). The natural world points beyond itself, hinting at a redemption for which it can only groan — without any clear articulation.

Natural Law, the New Creation, and Committed Gay Unions

This is the place where Christians must locate the presence and function of "natural law" — the attempt to frame moral life in harmony with the natural world. The created order is not abandoned or dismissed, but no longer is it necessarily considered normative, apart from its transformation by the gospel of Christ. In the new creation that is opened up by the reconciling power of the Spirit, the traditional bonds of marriage are deepened and marked by the gospel (Eph. 5:21-33). Yet there are also those who have made themselves eunuchs for the sake of the kingdom of God (Matt. 19:12) — a vocation inconceivable if "nature" is the norm for all of life. The divine choice of Phoebe as minster/deacon (Rom. 16:1) or Junia, who is "prominent among the apostles" (Rom. 16:7), suggests that "natural" gender roles are already being displaced in the emerging new creation, where there is "no longer male and female." Already in the New Testament, the "new creation" does not merely restore the old natural order but transforms it.

Might committed gay unions find a place in such a transformed creation, part of a harmonious nature renewed and transformed by the Spirit of God? If nature is simply determined by anatomy, then this can never happen; but if nature is simply determined by anatomy, neither could places be found that are created in the New Testament for the leadership of Phoebe and Junia, or by the inclusion of the Ethiopian eunuch. The New Testament clearly sets out to reenvision what is "natural" in light of the gospel of Christ, and in so doing it calls into question many things that the ancient world regarded as self-evidently natural. That pattern is one we must continue to pursue in ongoing and fresh ways. But what does this reenvisioning look like? We have noted the importance of a continued call to live in accordance with nature as the convergence of individual disposition, social order, and the physical world. If committed gay unions are to find a place in a nature renewed by the Spirit of God, we should expect to find a similar convergence of a sanctified individual disposition, social order, and physical environment.

But why should we expect to find committed gay and lesbian unions in such a renewed "nature" in the first place? Here we confront a central problem that this book has been probing from a variety of different angles: the fact that the New Testament does not envision the kind of committed, mutual, lifelong, loving, moderated gay and lesbian unions that are emerging today. The New Testament also does not envision the elimination of the institution of slavery, or birth control, or women as leaders in society. These are never imagined as part of the natural order in the ancient world, and they were not part of the experience of the early church either. As this chapter has made clear, there are gaps between our own understanding of nature and those understandings we see in the ancient world. We cannot simply replicate the ancient understanding of nature in our own context today. But we can and must seek to continue the pattern already begun in the New Testament itself: imagining a renewed convergence of the personal, the social, and the physical world in our context, under the redeeming influence of the Spirit of God.

Such a renewed and sanctified natural order must be shaped by the contours of the divine purposes for sexuality that we have been exploring throughout this book. We have seen the way in which sex and one-flesh bonding go hand in hand, how sex is directly related to the overcoming of our aloneness in relationships that persist over a lifetime. Can we imagine a world in which the divine pronouncement at the beginning of creation, "It is not good for the man to be alone" (Gen. 2:18), might find a range of deeply satisfying resolutions, from heterosexual marriage, to celibate communities, to gay and lesbian committed unions?[46] Can we imagine both those with heterosexual and same-sex sexual orientation finding the deep kind of intimate, one-flesh communion that satisfies the longings of the heart and the body, builds stable households in society, and draws all persons more deeply into the experience of interpersonal grace that echoes and leads into the divine communion itself? Can we imagine these diverse households all contributing toward a fruitful and just society where children are conceived, sometimes adopted, and nurtured, where the hungry are fed, where the poor and the sick are cared for, and where creativity and productivity are unleashed in the natural energy and vitality of communal life? Such exercises in imagination reach toward the same synthesis we saw in the ancient Stoic vision — the harmony of one's individual "nature," the "natural" ordering of society, and the wider natural world. But such a vision is only imaginable in light of the power of the Holy Spirit, who continues to draw human life, both individually and collectively, into communion with the divine life.

But it is one thing to imagine such a vision; it is another to say that

---

46. See Eugene F. Rogers, *Sexuality and the Christian Body: Their Way into the Triune God* (Oxford: Blackwell, 1999), which develops this threefold vision in a remarkable engagement with the Orthodox tradition.

such a vision can have normative authority for Christians, that gay and lesbian committed unions might actually find affirmation and support within the life of a church that seeks to be faithful to the gospel. Yet there are at least two ways in which Christians might argue for the embrace of such a vision. For some Christians, this vision is imaginable as a form of "accommodation" in a broken world. They may not be able to see same-sex sexual orientation as itself expressive of the divine will (just as the castration of the Ethiopian eunuch can scarcely be said to reflect the will and purpose of God). Yet in a broken world, where life does not follow the perfect "natural" plan, God's redemptive purpose can embrace eunuchs and barren women — as well as gay and lesbian people — and draw them into a wider and deeper divine purpose moving toward the new creation in Christit.[47] In a sinful and broken world, the incarnation declares that God meets us where we are, and then begins the work of transformation, not by magically changing us or our circumstances, but by pervading our lives in surprising ways, in the midst of our brokenness or our lack of conformity with common assumptions or expectations of society.

Other Christians may be more ready to acknowledge that, throughout the natural order, same-sex attraction is a naturally recurring "minority" experience. These Christians may celebrate the way in which, by the providence of God, such "queer" folk can naturally deconstruct the pervasive tendencies of majority voices to become oppressive and exclusionary. In this vision, the inclusion of committed gay and lesbian unions represents, not an accommodation to a sexually broken world, but rather an offbeat redemptive purpose in the new creation. That purpose can destabilize the assumed exclusivity of the heterosexual majority, challenging all of God's people to discover more deeply the richness of interpersonal communion, beyond socially constructed roles and responsibilities shaped by a heterosexual majority that is too often oblivious to the ways it can oppress minority voices.

In either case, what emerges is a vision of a redeemed and transformed "natural" order, where the convergence of individual natures, the larger social order, and the natural world ushers in a deeper harmony and provides a transforming vision that can shape and guide individual choices toward a future in which the creation moves toward its culmination in Christ. In that final culmination, neither gay nor straight people will marry or be

---

47. Something like this is the position of Lewis B. Smedes, "Like the Wideness of the Sea," *Perspectives* 14, no. 5 (1999).

given in marriage (Matt. 22:30; Mark 12:25; Luke 20:34-35). Instead, all our experiences of intimacy, fruitfulness, and communion in this life will be seen as only hints and foretastes of a deeper intimacy, fruitfulness, and communion that our present experiences of faithfulness, love, and intimacy in this life can only suggest and prefigure, as the old creation gives way to the new.

This vision affirms the deep intent of what Paul says in Romans 1. Sex must not be driven by self-serving lust and passion. The intimacy of sexual expression must be a place where people can be most authentically their true selves. Sex must not degrade or shame its participants. The procreative purpose of sex remains an important — though not all-defining — aspect of sexual existence for most men and women. But even where procreation is not a possible goal to pursue, whether the couples be gay, lesbian, or heterosexual, sex must still serve deeper purposes than mere self-gratification or a will to power. Instead, it must move toward establishing enduring social relationships that can contribute to the well-being of society as a whole. The sexual brokenness Paul describes in Romans 1 graphically illustrates the failure to fulfill all these "natural" purposes of sex. It thus provides a compelling image, within the context of the ancient world, of human life gone wrong, out of touch with itself, the wider society, and the natural world. But the advent of new life in Christ invites us to imagine a way forward, from our present state, toward the new creation, where the personal, the social, and the physical realms live in perfect harmony amidst rich diversity. To reach this world, we need to read and live into the rest of Romans, with its remarkable message of radical grace, freedom from law, transformation in Christ, and hope of a new creation.

Summing Up

- Central to the debates about the applicability of Romans 1:24-27 to contemporary committed gay and lesbian relationships is Paul's claim that the sexual misbehavior he describes in these verses is "unnatural," or "contrary to nature." We must understand the moral logic underlying this claim in order to discern how to apply these verses to contemporary life.
- The Greek word that Paul uses for "nature" here *(phusis)* does not occur in the Septuagint, the early translation of the Hebrew Bible into Greek. Rather, it arises in Jewish discourse after 200 BCE, when Jewish

writers make use of it as a Stoic category in order to interpret Jewish ethics to Gentiles.

- In the ancient world there were three dimensions to the understanding of *nature,* and we find each of these reflected in Paul's use of the word:
    - Nature was understood as one's individual nature or disposition. Paul's language in Romans 1 thus reflects the ancient notion that same-sex eroticism was driven by an insatiable thirst for the exotic by those who were not content with "natural" desires for the same sex. The ancient world had no notion of sexual orientation.
    - Nature was also understood as what contributed to the good order of society as a whole. In this sense, it looks very much like social convention, and many ancient understandings of what is natural, particularly those concerning gender roles, seem quaint at best to us today.
    - Nature was also understood in the ancient world in relationship to biological processes, particularly procreation. Paul's references to sexual misbehavior in Romans 1:24-27 as "unnatural" spring in part from their nonprocreative character. Yet there is no evidence that people in the ancient world linked natural gender roles more specifically to the complementary sexual organs of male and female, apart from a general concern with the "naturalness" of procreation.
- While we as modern persons should still seek a convergence of the personal, social, and physical worlds, just as the ancients did under the category of *nature,* we must recognize, even apart from the question of same-sex relationships, that this convergence will look different to us than it looked in the ancient world.
- The biblical vision of a *new* creation invites us to imagine what living into a deeper vision of "nature" as the convergence of individual disposition, social order, and the physical world might look like, under the guidance and power of the Spirit of God. This might also entail the cultivation of a vision for how consecrated and committed gay and lesbian relationships might fit into such a new order.

PART IV

Conclusions

12

Conclusions

W eaving through the various threads of this book is the concept of "moral logic." At one level, this concept of moral logic is simple and uncontroversial: When interpreting scriptural commands or prohibitions, we must ask not only *what* is commanded or prohibited but *why.* The reason for asking why emerges when we attempt to apply the commands and prohibitions of Scripture in new and diverse contexts. It is only when we know *why* Scripture prohibits the charging of interest on loans to fellow Israelites that we can judge whether granting or receiving a home mortgage between Christians today is right or wrong (see Exod. 22:25; Lev. 25:36-37; Deut. 23:19-20; Ps. 15:5; Ezek. 18:8ff.). We need to understand *why* Paul says that nature teaches that it is disgraceful for a man to wear long hair (1 Cor. 11:14) if we are to make appropriate moral judgments about length of hair among men today, or even if we are to make sense of other biblical passages where some men were commanded *not* to cut their hair (Num. 6; Judg. 13:2-5; 1 Sam. 1:11).

Discerning the "moral logic" underpinning a command or prohibition involves uncovering the deeper values and commitments that give rise to the command or prohibition in the first place. Often, these underlying assumptions are stated explicitly. For example, the prohibition of murder in Genesis 9:6 bases the command not to shed the blood of another explicitly on the fact that "in his own image God made humankind." At other points, however, discerning the underlying moral logic requires a broader exegetical exploration of the whole witness of Scripture, along with other ancient texts. Only in this way can the underlying rationale for any specific command or prohibition be interpreted with clarity and confidence. For

example, chapter 4 of this book described an emerging "trajectory" regarding women in leadership that emerges from the canon as a whole,
which helps to frame a wide diversity of perspectives on this issue in various biblical texts.

When we turn to those passages of Scripture that seem to prohibit or
denigrate same-sex erotic relationships, however, Christians disagree
about *why* these texts say what they do. Traditionalists believe that these
prohibitions and negative portrayals are rooted in a fundamental vision of
divinely intended gender complementarity, which is discerned in the differences in bodies and personalities between males and females. In this
view, the "one-flesh" union spoken of in Genesis 2:24 can thus be constituted only by the joining of male and female, who bring to this union their
complementary bodies and personalities.

By contrast, I have argued that the language of "one flesh" refers not to
complementarity but to kinship. The relationship of kinship is not based
on complementarity, but on similarity and mutual obligation. Kin are
those who have something essential in common with each other, and who
accept the obligation to help and support each other in distinctive ways.
Moreover, nowhere in Scripture is the notion of anatomical or biological
complementarity of male and female explicitly portrayed or discussed.
The absence of confirming texts calls into question whether this vision of
gender complementarity truly underlies the antipathy Scripture shows toward the same-sex erotic relationships it addresses.

So if gender complementarity is not the basic moral logic underlying
Genesis 2:24, as well as those texts that denigrate same-sex erotic relationships, what is the underlying moral logic? The more detailed discussion of
Romans 1 in the previous section of this book clearly shows the moral logic
that shapes Paul's rejection of the same-sex erotic activity he discusses, using his own vocabulary as the reference point. He characterizes such behavior as lustful, as impure, as shameful, and as a distortion of that convergence of individual disposition, social convention, and biological order
understood in the ancient world as "nature."

Traditionalists do not contest the claim that Paul portrays same-sex
erotic relationships in Romans 1 as lustful, impure, shameful, and unnatural. What they also claim, however, is that at the root of the lust, shame,
and impurity of such behavior is a core problem: its "unnaturalness," conceived as the violation of divinely intended gender complementarity. This,
they argue, is what is assumed or taken for granted by Paul when he writes,
even if he explicitly only uses the more general and (as we have seen in

chapter 11) somewhat ambiguous category of "contrary to nature." It is this "unnaturalness," they argue, that makes these desires inappropriate (and therefore lustful), that makes these behaviors a violation of proper boundaries (and therefore impure) and results in a failure to live out one's true identity (and therefore shameful).

Taking a very different perspective, I have argued that the same-sex eroticism Paul derides in Romans 1 reflects an expression of excessive and self-centered desire — and is thus *lustful*. For Paul, lust is determined not so much by the object of desire but by the excess of desire. When Paul describes this behavior as *impurity*, he is speaking not so much about the violation of boundaries but about an inward problem — a heart that seeks its own benefit and power. When Paul says that this behavior is *shameful*, he focuses attention on the violation of male honor specifically, as well as gender roles more generally. Finally, when Paul speaks of this behavior as *unnatural*, he focuses attention not on the violation of gender complementarity but on the ways in which this behavior violates assumptions taken for granted throughout the culture of that day regarding what is natural for men and women as individuals, as members of society, and as part of the physical world. For Paul, all of these dispositions are expressive of a fundamentally disordered state arising from humanity's proclivity to idolatry and its failure to worship the one true God. I argue that, at the same time, we cannot assume that all committed same-sex relationships are *necessarily* prone to the errors and problems that Paul narrates in Romans 1. There is thus room to evaluate these relationships using broader biblical understandings of sexuality and intimate faithfulness, quite apart from a doctrinal commitment to "gender complementarity."

Note that both sides of this debate agree on important issues. Both sides of the debate, at least as it has been presented in this book, agree that the behavior that Paul speaks of in Romans 1 is rightly rejected and identified as an expression of sinfulness and idolatry, even if we disagree about the reasons Paul has for rejecting the behavior. For traditionalists, Paul rejects the behavior because it violates divinely intended gender complementarity inherent in the creation narrative. I contend, however, that the same-sex eroticism Paul envisions is either an expression of the monstrous ego of the Roman imperial house, or an expression of prostitution, child abuse, or promiscuity, an absence of mutuality, a neglect of the obligation to procreate, or a failure of persons to express with their bodies what they say with the rest of their lives. Such persons "receive back the due penalty for their error," in self-evident forms of judgment, showing the obvious consequences of their misbehavior (Rom. 1:27). In either case, both sides of the debate can agree that Paul is correct in what he says here. In other words, both sides accept the authority of the text in what it is directly teaching. This is an important point that should not be passed over lightly. Neither side of the debate denies the authority and truthfulness of Scripture. The point of difference centers on the underlying moral logic that shapes the text, and thus its applicability to contemporary life.

Consequently, the two sides disagree on how Paul's discussion (and the rest of the biblical witness) speaks to our contemporary experience, particularly the experience of gay and lesbian couples in committed relationships. Traditionalists locate the center of the problem with same-sex erotic relationships in their violation of the gender complementarity that was intended at creation. For them, such relationships can *never* be regarded as appropriate, regardless of whether same-sex committed relationships may reflect disciplined desire, whether they arise from a self-giving and loving heart, whether there is a desire to honor the partner, whether commitments are deep and abiding, or whether there is evidence of an intention to live out a form of life that is in harmony with one's self, with others, and with the natural world. Even if such relationships appear to lead to a flourishing life rather than to the self-evident forms of judgment that Paul alludes to somewhat cryptically in Romans 1:27, they are unacceptable to the traditionalists. None of these admirable qualities are sufficient to overcome the core problem: these relationships violate divinely intended gender complementarity.

By contrast, I have argued that gender complementarity is never directly taught in Scripture in such generic terms. To the extent that language that might suggest gender complementarity appears at all in Scripture, it is a way of speaking about one of several more specific things:

- the hierarchy of the genders (in which case we also see a movement in Scripture away from such hierarchical understandings);
- other culturally defined role differences between men and women (which change quite radically from one culture to another — even within Scripture itself);
- or else as an expression of the procreative purpose of sexuality (which, I have argued, is an important, though not essential, meaning of sexual relations).

Over against this entire line of interpretation focusing on gender complementarity, I have argued that at the heart of the Bible's understanding of the meaning of sexual relationships lies the one-flesh kinship bond. This bond is formed when the desire for self-gratification *(eros)* comes to recognize that one's own gratification is only possible in the context of loving self-giving to the other *(agapē)*. Hence, longing turns to loving, as intimacy unfolds into long-term kinship bonds of service, commitment, and mutual care. Therefore, a fundamental rejection of promiscuity lies at the heart of the Bible's vision for sex, and it also undergirds Paul's rejection of the lewd behavior he describes in Romans 1:24-27. In other words, one can locate Paul's entire discussion in quite a different world of discourse, identifying quite different underlying values and assumptions that shape his rhetoric.

How is one to navigate such an impasse? At one level, the challenge is an exegetical one. Which vision of the heart and significance of the "one-flesh" bond can be more fully documented in the biblical witness and related ancient sources? I argue that the exegetical evidence tilts strongly toward "one flesh" as a loving kinship bond, rather than as an expression of gender complementarity.

But the debate is not only an exegetical one. Elements of personal experience factor largely into this discussion as well, but often remain implicit and hidden. I would suggest that most heterosexual persons who have fallen in love, married, and lived for any period of time with someone of the opposite sex know deep in their hearts something of the mystery that stands at the heart of such a relationship. That mystery is characterized by a deep and profound interaction of similarity and difference — in other words, *complementarity.* Many men and women think differently, solve problems differently, tend to experience the world differently. Those differences enrich many heterosexual marriages in countless ways, both great and small. It is enormously tempting simply to assume that this is what the Bible has in mind when it speaks of the "one-flesh" union in Genesis 2:24. It is also tempting, in this light, to wonder whether same-sex intimate relationships must necessarily lack something that many heterosexual marriages find of enormous beauty and value.

But two important cautionary points must be raised here. The first has to do with changes that have taken place over the centuries in the institution of marriage itself. It is undoubtedly true that many modern marriages experience and value intimacy and complementarity much more highly than was true in the ancient world. Stephanie Coontz's history of marriage has shown that modern notions of love and intimacy in marriage arose for the first time in the nineteenth century.[1] Prior to that, marriage was driven centrally by economic concerns, a desire for social advancement, and the need for social alliances. If some marriages also found deep love, complementarity, and intimacy, that was a welcome bonus, but it was not of the essence of the relationship. Therefore, we must be cautious about reading our experience back into the biblical texts, as wonderful and as valuable as our experience may be. This is not to diminish the significance of the experience of complementarity in intimate relationships; it is simply to note that this kind of experience was probably not broadly shared by the original writers and readers of the biblical text. We should not assume that these categories or experiences are assumed or implicit in the text. The biblical writers were far more pragmatic about marriage than we are. (Moreover, the escalating divorce rate in most modern cultures suggests that modern expectations of intimacy and complementarity may not always be easy to fulfill.)

A second qualifier on the contemporary experience of complementarity is even more important. We cannot clearly distinguish, even in modern experiences of intimate complementarity, between those patterns of similarity and difference that are inherent to gender (understood biologically) and those patterns that are simply a function of the *otherness* of one's life partner. Indeed, many heterosexual marriages take on very different role divisions and patterns, depending on the partners' strengths and dispositions. In one marriage, for example, the husband cleans the house, and the wife keeps the books; in another, the wife sets the social agenda, but the husband is the better listener. Role differentiation abounds, but it doesn't always line up along stereotypically gendered lines, and it often has little to do with the biological differences between men and women. I believe that this is why so many discussions about "gender complementarity" in Scripture stay at such a general and nonspecific level. In modern society, we have intense experiences of complementarity, and these are clearly related to our individual gendered identities. Yet it is hard to press further and to characterize these in ways that might be more universally applicable. Our bodily desires tell us that our partner's gender matters, and the patterns of similarities and differences with our partner shape the relationship in profound ways. However, we cannot specify in more detail exactly those pat-

1. See Coontz, *Marriage, a History: From Obedience to Intimacy, or How Love Conquered Marriage* (New York: Viking, 2005).

terns of similarities and differences that apply normatively, not only to us as individuals, but to everyone. Indeed, when we look at a wide range of patterns, structures, and styles of marriage across different times and cultures, such universal commonalities seem very elusive.

This raises a profound and important question. Perhaps what heterosexuals are experiencing in marriage is not essentially a complementarity of gender understood biologically, but simply a form of *otherness* that usually takes shape along gendered lines, even if those gendered lines may shift significantly from one context to the next. Indeed, my own limited conversations with gay and lesbian couples who have lived with each other over extended periods of time leads me to believe that intimacy and complementarity, desire and otherness, play very significant roles in gay and lesbian committed relationships as well as in heterosexual ones. Otherness is an unavoidable aspect of our humanness, and as our relationships move toward deeper intimacy, the profound mingling of similarity and difference becomes more, not less, pronounced. Surely, our closest nonsexual friendships with others of the same sex share the same deep characteristics: points of deep commonality along with points of otherness and difference that enrich and enliven the friendship. In other words, one need not relinquish the deep value of complementarity — nor its gendered manifestations — in offering greater approval to gay and lesbian committed relationships. Instead, one may simply recognize that this mingling of similarity and difference, fueled by desire and longing, may take different but equally meaningful forms in gay and lesbian relationships, alongside its wonderful heterosexual expressions. One need not relinquish complementarity; one must only loosen its essential link to a hard-wired understanding of gender in order to account for a wide range of experience of longing, love, and intimacy amidst difference — shaped in long-term bonds of love and faithfulness.

In short, I argue that the Bible neither assumes nor teaches a normative understanding of gender complementarity. The Bible regards procreative complementarity as an important — though not essential — feature of one-flesh unions; and it assumes in some passages a hierarchical relationship between the genders. But the larger trajectory of Scripture as a whole moves away from this assumption. The Bible also looks at gender issues through the ancient lens of an honor-shame culture; but again, Scripture does not absolutize that honor-shame framework. Indeed, there are many passages in the Bible that deconstruct or reframe ancient assumptions regarding honor and shame. My conclusion — that the Bible does not teach a normative gender complementarity — should thus not be regarded as surprising. Furthermore, there is nothing of such a notion whatsoever in the creedal tradition of the church: we find nothing of gender complementarity in the Apostles' Creed, the Nicene Creed, or any other of the ancient ecumenical creeds. We also find no mention of gender complementarity in the great confessional documents of the Reformation: the Augsburg Confession, the Westminster Confession of Faith,[2] the Second Helvetic Confession, or the Belgic Confession. Nor do we find gender complementarity taught in any of the great catechisms of the Reformation. While different gender roles have been taken for granted throughout the life of the church, the formulation of specific understandings of normative gender complementarity has never emerged in the church's creeds or confessions. Such a doctrine is not taught in Scripture, considered in its entirety, and has never been part of normative Christian teaching.

To the extent that the Bible views same-sex erotic relationships, then, it does so through lenses other than a normative understanding of biological gender complementarity. As the previous chapters have demonstrated, when we broadly peruse early Jewish and Christian literature (and particularly Paul's letter to the Romans), we see four forms of moral logic that form the central framework for objections against same-sex erotic relationships in the ancient world:

- First, Paul viewed these relationships as an expression of excessive lust that is not content with heterosexual relationships but is driven to increasingly exotic forms of stimulation, leading to the loss of purity of heart. The notion that someone might not be significantly attracted to persons of the opposite sex — but to persons of the same sex — is never even considered by early Jewish or Christian writers.

---

2. The Westminster Confession of Faith defines marriage as "between one man and one woman" (chapter XXIV), but the concern is clearly focused on the rejection of polygamy and incest and on restrictions regarding divorce. No mention is made of gender roles, or of the biological differences between the sexes, or of anything that might be construed directly as a doctrine of gender complementarity. Hence, while we can safely say that the Westminster Confession of Faith assumes a heterosexual understanding of marriage, we cannot say with any confidence that this assumption is based on a normative understanding of gender complementarity. The most natural and contextual reading of the reference to "one man and one woman" is that the text is constructed so as to explicitly rule out both polygyny (more than one wife) and polyandry (more than one husband). Cf. similar discussions in the Second Helvetic Confession (chapter XXIX).

- Second, he viewed these relationships as shameful, particularly because they treated a man as a woman, inherently degrading the passive partner, and more generally because they violated understood gender roles in the conventions of the ancient world.
- Third, because same-sex relationships are nonprocreative, Paul regarded these relationships as selfish and socially irresponsible, neglecting the obligation of procreation.
- Finally, Paul regarded these relationships as "unnatural" because they violated ancient society's understanding of the natural order, the commonly accepted synthesis of understanding one's individual disposition, larger social values, and the surrounding physical world.

To be sure, the church should continue to stand against those sinful dispositions that motivate the Bible's concerns in sexual ethics, including its discussion in Romans 1. This includes, first, a rejection of promiscuity of all kinds and a deep valuing of committed love that cultivates and flourishes in lifelong relationships. Such love disciplines and moderates our natural desires, which all too readily become merely self-serving. The church should continue to stand against lust. The church should also continue to reject all sexual relationships that are marked by domination, control, lack of consent, and lack of mutuality, including especially relationships marked by pederasty. The church should thus continue to insist that all sexual relationships be mutual and consensual — that they must honor both persons involved. Finally, the church should stand against the modern assumption that sexual relationships are merely "private" matters between consenting adults and that wider concerns about social order and the larger social and environmental context are irrelevant to sexual ethics. Instead, the church should urge the cultivation of a robust vision of sexual ethics that leads to a flourishing of life for all, marked by the convergence of individual disposition, social order, and harmony with the world around us.

But I have also argued that there are significant reasons why Christians today should reconsider whether the strictures against the same-sex relationships known in the ancient world should also apply to contemporary committed and intimate same-sex relationships. To explore this thesis more closely, we need to turn again to rest of the "seven passages," those few biblical texts that are commonly understood to refer explicitly to same-sex erotic relationships. We need to summarize what these passages say, why they say it, and how their concerns reflect or diverge from the experience of gay and lesbian Christians in committed relationships today.

Reviewing the Rest of the "Seven Passages"

Sodom and Gomorrah and the Levite's Concubine

The first two passages are "texts of terror" that share a similar shape and focus. Both the story of Sodom and Gomorrah in Genesis 19 and the story of the Levite's concubine in Judges 19 show the same pattern. A foreigner spends the night in the house of a local host. The men of the town surround the house, and they demand that the visitor be brought out; their intention is to rape him. In both cases, the owner of the home offers a woman from the house to the locals as a substitute victim. The Bible narration presents both stories as evidence of extreme degradation and corruption. Both stories regard a man being raped by other men as an expression of violence and extreme degradation; both assume that the rape of female members of the household would be preferable to the rape of the male visitors, which underscores the deep violation of male honor that is assumed in both stories to be attached to the rape of a male by another male.

All Christians today will agree that sexual violence is a profound violation of human dignity. All Christians can also agree, I believe, that these stories reflect a limited moral perspective: that is, they assume that the rape of a female is less offensive than the rape of a male. Christians may also agree that these two stories can help illuminate the antipathy shown elsewhere in the Bible to sexual relations between men, given the fact that these two stories associate this behavior with humiliation, violence, and inhospitality toward strangers — expressed in its most extreme form. But precisely because of this extremity, Christians should also recognize that these stories are of no more value in assessing lifelong, loving, committed same-sex relationships than stories of heterosexual rape can be used to morally evaluate loving heterosexual relationships. The failure to distinguish between consensual, committed, and loving sexual relationships and violent, coercive relationships represents a serious case of moral myopia. I do not wish to provide moral justification for all consensual sexual relationships; but I do wish to state clearly that *all* nonconsensual, violent, or coercive sexual relationships are always morally wrong, because they are inherently incapable of deepening the relational kinship bonds intended by God to be established and nurtured by sexual relations. To attempt to derive further moral guidance from these stories is to fail to recognize the focus of their moral concern. As numerous commentators have noted, the canonical treatment of these stories elsewhere in the Bible does not focus on the offense of male-male sex, but rather on violence and inhospitality. In one case (Jude 7), Sodom and Gomorrah also serve as an example of "unnatural lust" because of the desire of the residents for the angelic visitors, though the language used in Jude cannot be understood to focus on same-sex eroticism. In short, while the stories of Sodom and Gomorrah and the Levite's concubine graphically portray the horror of rape, they simply do not speak to committed same-sex intimate relationships.

The Levitical Prohibitions of "Lying with a Male as with a Woman" (Lev. 18:22; 20:13)

As I noted in chapter 9, which deals with purity and impurity, there are broad forms of moral logic that shape many of the purity laws in general terms, including these texts from Leviticus. The purity laws attempt, in general, to replicate the order of the original creation, where there was "a place for everything, and everything was in its place." They tend toward preserving what was perceived as the order of creation, and avoiding inappropriate mixtures. These concerns covered food to be eaten, clothes to be worn, and many other things, including the boundaries of appropriate sexual relationships. In this context, I also focused in chapter 9 on the generative processes whereby life comes into the world. Purity laws seek to keep these processes carefully regulated. Emissions of blood and semen were regarded as especially problematic. One can see how this concern for a man "lying with a man as with a woman" would raise concerns in the context of both of these broad forms of moral logic.

However, chapter 9 also explores the larger canonical movement in which these general concerns about purity need to be viewed. There I argue that we see an overall canonical movement regarding purity laws —

- away from defining purity *externally* toward defining purity in terms of the motives and dispositions of the *heart and will;*
- away from *defensiveness* and separateness toward *confidence* and engagement;
- away from a *backward* look toward the old creation, and shifting to a *forward* look toward the new creation.

This larger canonical context is important in evaluating these passages, and it certainly challenges any attempt to apply these texts to contemporary life without qualification. But it will also be helpful to discern some further nuances in these passages that address same-sex relationships in particular. We need to explore the more immediate context of these passages in order to discern the underlying forms of moral logic that shape them in a more specific way, beyond the general characteristics of purity laws already explored in chapter 9.

The first thing to note is that the immediate contexts of both of these prohibitions against "lying with a male as with a woman" are closely linked to two other problems: injunctions against the practices of idolatry and the urgency of avoiding the practices of surrounding nations. Immediately before Leviticus 18:22 ("You shall not lie with a male as with a woman; it is an abomination"), Leviticus 18:21 declares: "You shall not give any of your offspring to sacrifice them to Molech, and so profane the name of your God: I am the LORD." Immediately following this command against "lying with a male as with a woman," we see another summary injunction: "Do not defile yourselves in any of these ways, for by all these practices the nations I am casting out before you have defiled themselves." We see the same pattern in Leviticus 20, with injunctions against idolatrous practice in verses 2-7; we also find a call to practices distinct from the surrounding nations in verses 22-23. Similarly, the characterization of male-male sex as an "abomination" in both of these passages (Hebrew *toēvah*) makes use of a strong word of abhorrence that is closely linked to idolatrous practices in at least thirty-eight other passages in Scripture (Deut. 7:25-36; 12:31; 13:14; 17:4; 18:9, 12; 20:18; 23:18; 27:15; 32:16; 1 Kings 14:24; 2 Kings 16:3; 21:2, 11; 23:13; 28:3; 33:2; 34:33; 36:8, 14; Ezra 9:1, 11, 13; Jer. 2:7; 7:10; 16:18; 32:35; 44:4; Ezek. 6:9; 7:20; 8:9; 14:6; 16:2; 16:36, 47; 18:12; 44:7; Mal. 2:11).

There is evidence linking same-sex eroticism, particularly among males, to cultic prostitution and other idolatrous practices in the ancient world generally; there is no literary evidence for consensual male-male sexual relations in the land of Israel and surrounding regions specifically, apart from that cultic context.[3] This linkage with temple or cultic prostitution also helps to explain the death penalty for male-male sex in Leviticus 20:13: it would make no sense to apply such a penalty in the context of gang rape portrayed in the stories of Sodom and Gomorrah or of the Levite's

---

3. Martti Nissinen, *Homoeroticism in the Biblical World: A Historical Perspective* (Minneapolis: Fortress, 1998). Of course, ancient Greece and the eastern Mediterranean have a different history, with different patterns, but it is unlikely that the book of Leviticus has these in mind.

concubine. In those cases of rape, the death penalty for the victim would be monstrous. So we can say with reasonable confidence that the activity envisioned in the Levitical prohibitions is assumed to be consensual, and that it is probably envisioned to take place in cultic contexts, with clear linkages to idolatry and other religious practices foreign to the nation of Israel. As such, the prohibition of these practices is part of Israel's call to be both separate from other nations and holy to the Lord.

Yet many traditionalists, while perhaps acknowledging some significance to these cultic connections, insist that the moral logic underlying this prohibition is not exhausted merely by its cultic connections. Instead, they insist that the wording of the prohibition itself points to a different form of moral logic that shapes — at an even deeper level — the Levitical prohibitions. By speaking of "lying with a male as with a woman," these passages focus attention on the failure to act out one's proper gender role in sexual relationships. Thus, traditionalists argue, the concern is not merely with the avoidance of idolatry and cultic prostitution (if that is a concern at all). Rather, there is a deeper concern: to conduct oneself sexually in light of the purposes God has for one's sexual identity revealed in creation — in keeping with one's gender. They argue that this concern focusing on gender is not culturally specific, but rather rooted in biological gender. Indeed, many traditionalists have argued that Paul's use of the Greek word *arsenokoitēs* in reference to same-sex behavior in passages such as 1 Corinthians 6:9-10 is rooted in the language of Leviticus 18:22 and 20:13, thus confirming the cross-cultural relevance of the Levitical prohibitions for Christian ethics in a way that focuses specifically on the violation of biologically shaped gender roles.[4]

This attempt to link Paul's Greek vocabulary directly to the Levitical texts, however, is speculative and lacks external confirming evidence. But there is also a deeper reason to be suspicious of this reading, which assumes that the moral logic of the Levitical prohibitions is based on upholding biological gender distinctions: that is, there is no parallel injunction against same-sex relations between women in Leviticus. Of course, one might note that female-female sexual relations are rarely discussed in the ancient world generally, and there is no evidence linking such sexual

---

4. Robert A. J. Gagnon, *The Bible and Homosexual Practice: Texts and Hermeneutics* (Nashville: Abingdon, 2001), p. 327; Stanley J. Grenz, *Welcoming But Not Affirming: An Evangelical Response to Homosexuality* (Louisville: Westminster John Knox, 1998), p. 58; Marion L. Soards, *Scripture and Homosexuality: Biblical Authority and the Church Today* (Louisville: Westminster John Knox, 1995), p. 19.

behavior directly to idolatrous or cultic practices. So the absence of any prohibition of female-female sex in Leviticus makes sense from the perspective of a moral logic that focuses primarily on opposition to cultic practices. However, if the concern is not with cultic practices but with the violation of gender, why are women not mentioned? This is particularly noteworthy in light of the explicit prohibition of sex with animals — both for women and for men — in these same chapters of Leviticus (18:23; 20:15-16). There is even scanter evidence of bestiality in the ancient world than there is of same-sex erotic relationships; yet the rarity of the case does not prevent the author of Leviticus from forbidding both male and female sex with animals. Why, then, is there no analogous prohibition of a "woman lying with a female as with a man"? If violations of biological gender roles constituted the primary moral logic underlying the prohibition, one would expect the corresponding injunction against female same-sex eroticism as well. But it is absent.

The absence of any concern about female-female sex in Leviticus suggests that it is not gender as an abstract or biological concept that these prohibitions have in mind; instead, to the extent that these passages are concerned with gender at all (beyond a concern with pagan cultic practices), they have a more specific focus that we can also see in the stories of Sodom and Gomorrah and the Levite's concubine — that is, the preservation of male *honor*. From the perspective of Leviticus, to "lie with a male as with a woman" is to reduce a male to the status of a female, which inherently degrades him and fails to honor his divinely given status as a male. For a male to willingly accept such degradation makes him equally culpable in the Leviticus author's mind. Sex between females is not mentioned simply because there is no such degradation operative in these cases. This suggests that, in addition to a concern with cultic practices, the Levitical prohibitions should be read in light of assumptions regarding honor and shame that were shared throughout the ancient world. Male-male sex is thus linked with the behavior of alien nations, with idolatry and cultic prostitution, and with the degradation of distinctively male honor. It may also be the case that, since the ancient world assumed that men held the "seed" for future generations, that male-male sex was rejected because of its nonprocreative character, and that female-female sex was left out because there was no "seed" involved. When all these considerations are taken together, Leviticus concludes that "lying with a male as with a woman" is an "abomination" to both God and Israelite sensibilities, and its presence could not be tolerated within Israel.

But how should one respond to gay and lesbian couples who want to commit themselves to each other in lifelong, socially sanctioned relationships, as faithful Christians who seek to honor each other? In such a context, Leviticus's concerns about idolatry, violations of male honor, and the like seem distinctly out of place. We can appreciate the way the ancient writer is seeking to preserve the integrity of Israelite life in Leviticus without assuming that the same concerns are relevant to life today. This is particularly true in light of the larger canonical movement evident in the Bible's treatment of purity laws in the New Testament (outlined in chapter 9 above). In short, the religious, purity, procreative, and honor-shame contexts that form the underlying moral logic of the Levitical prohibitions, understandable and coherent as they may be in their own context, simply do not apply to contemporary committed Christian gay and lesbian relationships.[5]

Finally, it is also worth noting that this analysis applies quite apart from the more general problem that Christians no longer regard much of the Levitical law as applying to the church today. The overall agenda established by the book of Leviticus concerning purity was radically transformed by the gospel of Christ. It is simply inadequate, from a Christian perspective, to attempt to build an ethic based on the prohibitions of Leviticus alone. This is important material to reflect on, but it cannot stand at the center of a responsible Christian moral position on committed gay or lesbian relationships.

References to Same-Sex Erotic Behavior in the New Testament Vice Lists (1 Corinthians 6:9 and 1 Timothy 1:10)

When we turn to the New Testament, we find two references to male same-sex eroticism; these are found in longer catalogs of misbehavior known as "vice lists." The most important thing to realize about these texts is that the reference is found in multiple words, not just one. Neither list refers to same-sex erotic behavior with a single word — such as the English word "homosexual." Instead, the lists use multiple words to reflect widely ac-

---

5. Robert Gagnon has also argued that the Levitical prohibitions of male same-sex eroticism should be seen as analogous to the forbidding of incest in these texts, and thus as having universal, cross-cultural relevance (Dan Otto Via and Robert A. J. Gagnon, *Homosexuality and the Bible: Two Views* [Minneapolis: Fortress, 2003], pp. 48ff.). For a refutation of these arguments, see chapter 9 above.

cepted roles that were part of male same-sex erotic behavior in the ancient world. For example, 1 Corinthians 6:9 uses two words: *malakoi* (literally meaning "soft," or "effeminate" ones), and *arsenokoitai* (literally "man-bedders"). The latter term is particularly problematic because there is no attested usage of this word preceding the New Testament documents — that is, in extrabiblical literature — that might provide additional information about its range of meaning. But the most important thing to recognize is that there are two words, not just one. Most scholars recognize that the presence of these two words reflects widespread assumptions throughout the ancient world about male-male homosexual activity: almost all the documents discussing male same-sex eroticism assume a distinction between active older men (commonly referred to in Greek as *erastai*) and passive younger males (commonly referred to as *erōmenoi*) — in other words, the practice of pederasty. The *malakoi* ("softies") are the younger, passive *erōmenoi*, and the *arsenokoitai* ("man-bedders") are the older, active *erastai*.[6]

The vice list in 1 Timothy 1:10 includes three interrelated terms in reference to male-male erotic activity: *pornoi* (translated by the NRSV as "fornicators," but can also mean "male prostitutes"), *arsenokoitai* ("man-bedders," the same term that appears in 1 Cor. 6:9), and *andropodistai* ("slave-dealers," or "kidnappers"). Many scholars believe that the three terms belong together in this list: that is, we see kidnappers or slave dealers *(andropodistai)* acting as "pimps" for their captured and castrated boys (the *pornoi*, or male prostitutes), servicing the *arsenokoitai*, the men who make use of these boy prostitutes. Scholars have noted that the Roman Empire tried on several occasions to pass laws banning this practice — but with minimal success.[7]

The assumption of the practice of pederasty, or male prostitution, in

6. The definitive scholarly discussion of these issues is found in Robin Scroggs, *The New Testament and Homosexuality: Contextual Background for Contemporary Debate* (Philadelphia: Fortress, 1983). Other scholars dispute this analysis, however, claiming that we cannot know in detail what either of these words means. Nonetheless, I am convinced that the pairing of words in 1 Cor. 6:9-10 reflects common pederastic assumptions about male-male sex in the ancient world. For a more detailed exploration of these problems, see Nissinen, *Homoeroticism in the Biblical World*, pp. 113-18; see also Dale Martin, *Sex and the Single Savior: Gender and Sexuality in Biblical Interpretation* (Louisville: Westminster John Knox, 2006), pp. 37-50.

7. See, for example, Johnson, *A Time to Embrace: Same-Gender Relationships in Religion, Law, and Politics* (Grand Rapids: Eerdmans, 2006), p. 133.

both of these lists complicates their applicability to contemporary experience. The NIV translation, for example, unhelpfully blurs this cultural gap by rendering the Greek word *arsenokoitai,* which in its original context refers to the active partners in pederastic relationships, as "homosexuals." In so doing, the NIV shifts the meaning of the word to the notion of sexual orientation, which is completely lacking in the ancient world among Jews and Christians. But when we take the original social context of these vice lists seriously, we again recognize a gap between what these vice lists are rejecting and what is happening in committed same-sex relationships today. In the ancient world, these pederastic relationships were transitory rather than permanent and committed; they were driven by the desires of the older partner rather than being mutual and shared; and they were often characterized by abuse, slavery, and prostitution. One can readily agree that all sexual relationships that have these characteristics are rightly rejected by Christians, and one can still question whether committed gay and lesbian relationships should be painted with the same brush of rejection.

This becomes particularly important when one recognizes the rhetorical function of vice lists in the ancient world generally — and in the New Testament in particular. Vice lists are not the place where fine moral distinctions are on display. Rather, they single out stereotypically abhorrent behavior that is widely regarded in the community with condemnation, ridicule, or rejection. Hence they are of limited use in the morally more nuanced conversation taking place in the church today about long-term committed same-sex relationships.

The Application of the "Seven Passages" to Committed Same-Sex Relationships Today

This overview of the entire range of explicit biblical texts addressing same-sex eroticism suggests that the forms of moral logic that undergird this wider range of texts are similar to the forms of moral logic that we saw in the more in-depth analysis of Romans 1:24-27 in the previous chapters of this book. In the stories of Sodom and Gomorrah and of the Levite's concubine we have seen concerns about the violence of rape and a deep concern about preserving male honor, even at the expense of subjecting women to rape in the place of males. In Leviticus, in addition to broader purity concerns, we have seen concerns with avoiding cultic behavior, maintaining Israel's distinctness as a nation, preserving the integrity of procreation, and preserving male honor. In the vice lists we have seen concerns with pederasty, prostitution, abuse, sexual slavery, and lust. But in none of these passages have we seen a primary or central concern with upholding anatomical or biological gender complementarity.

Some of these concerns clearly transcend their particular cultural setting and continue to serve as forms of moral logic that should shape Christian moral frameworks today. This is particularly true with concerns about rape and other forms of sexual violence and coercion, concerns about pederasty, sexual slavery, and other forms of nonmutual, short-term sexual behaviors, as well as those concerns that focus on excessive lust and prostitution. Even today, any forms of same-sex eroticism that exhibit these characteristics should be rejected by Christians, just as behavior in heterosexual relationships that exhibits these characteristics should be rejected. In this sense, these texts continue to have a normative impact on Christian moral reflection.

However, there are other aspects of the moral logic undergirding these texts that are more culture-specific, and they require a cross-cultural perspective when we attempt to apply them in contemporary contexts. The dynamics of honor and shame vary dramatically from one culture to another, and those forms of sexual behavior that are regarded as inherently degrading may also shift dramatically from one culture to another. The call to honor each other persists in all cultures, but its particular behavioral manifestations may vary from one culture to another.

Similarly, we have seen how understandings of gender, including masculine and feminine identity, shift dramatically from one culture to another. In Paul's day, it was assumed that "nature" itself taught that it was degrading for a man to wear long hair (1 Cor. 11:14). Assumptions about masculine and feminine identities — and the roles and behaviors appropriate to those identities — have undergone massive shifts, and the vast majority of Western Christians recognize these variations as different cultural forms rather than as deviations from a divine norm. Attempts to establish universal norms regarding gender identity have never been part of the core of Christian teaching, insofar as that core has been identified by the great creeds and confessions of the church.

Finally, we have seen how assumptions regarding the centrality of procreation in sexual relations exercise a powerful role in many of these passages. At the same time, the modern development of contraception has underscored what we see elsewhere in Scripture: a central way of thinking about sexuality that is based not on procreation but on the one-flesh kinship bond established by sexual relations. This unitive meaning of marriage and sexuality represents the essential center and heart of biblical teaching on the meaning of marriage and sexuality.

To the extent that some of these more culturally variable forms of moral logic inform the Bible's disposition toward same-sex intimacy in those passages where it is discussed, a cross-cultural analysis is required. Not everything that the biblical writers assume or take for granted is to be considered normative for Christians today, particularly when these assumptions are based on culturally variable norms that Scripture itself engages in a variety of ways. For example, the church of the nineteenth century had to reread the biblical texts on slavery in a more deep and penetrating way. Even the biblical writers, particularly in the New Testament, had simply assumed, without question, that the institution of slavery existed and would continue to exist. So much of the advice offered by the New Testament had to do with "humanizing" the master-slave relationship. But during the nineteenth century the church began to discern deeper and more pervasive principles from the biblical witness, which called into question whether the institution of slavery itself should be supported by Christians. In light of the fresh experience of the church in the nineteenth century, Christians grew in their ability to discern deeper and more abiding forms of moral logic that shape the biblical narrative at its deepest levels.

Might committed same-sex relationships present a similar kind of challenge to the church today? This study, along with the reflection of many other Christians, raises an important question: Should the moral logic that informs the condemnation of same-sex erotic activity in the "seven passages" apply categorically to all committed same-sex relationships today? The evidence suggests that there are no forms of moral logic underpinning these passages that clearly and unequivocally forbid all contemporary forms of committed same-sex intimate relationships. This is particularly clear when these contemporary relationships are not lustful or dishonoring to one's partner, are marked positively by moderated and disciplined desire, and when intimacy in these relationships contributes to the establishment of lifelong bonds of kinship, care, and mutual concern. Such same-sex intimate relationships were never considered by the biblical writers, which leaves us with the need to discern more clearly how the church should respond to these relationships today.

Recognizing this gap between the biblical discussions of same-sex eroticism and the experience of committed gay and lesbian couples today is vitally important. If the core moral logic underpinning the biblical witness is a concern for anatomical or biological gender complementarity, as traditionalists argue, then there can be no gap. Since biology has not changed, the same moral logic applies today. But if there are various forms of moral logic at work, some of them culturally specific and rooted in the ancient world, then the exploration of this gap between the ancient and modern worlds is necessary and urgent. To recognize this gap is not to say that the Bible has nothing to say to contemporary life, but to note that one must discern more particularly the reasons undergirding scriptural commands and prohibitions — and the cross-cultural relevance of those reasons.

Obviously, much more could be said — indeed, much more needs to be said — on the question of the church's approach to committed same-sex relationships today. Different churches struggle with a variety of more detailed questions about the legal definitions of marriage and the church's role in marriage vis-à-vis the state, about ordination and the recognition of gay and lesbian persons as Christian leaders, and about how to balance grace and law in dealing with gay and lesbian persons. This book has not directly addressed these more detailed contemporary questions. Moreover, this book has said nothing about some of the more specific and unique issues arising in the lives of bisexual and transgendered persons today.

My focus in this book has been more specifically on the interpretation of Scripture in relationship to these questions. I am convinced that the church needs to move away from an interpretation of Scripture that assumes that the Bible teaches a normative form of biological or anatomical gender complementarity. In its place I have offered a more complex moral vision, one that looks at sexuality through the central category of the exclusive one-flesh kinship bond and sees the core meaning of sexuality expressed in

- a delight in the other;
- a deep desire for gratification and union;
- the attendant call to honor and serve the other in committed bonds of loving mutuality;
- and a fruitful vision of committed love that overflows in many ways — in procreation, adoption, service to the community, and hospitality to others.

This central meaning of our sexuality is hedged and bounded by warnings against excessive and self-centered desire and against behaviors that shame or degrade the other. This vision of a redeemed sexuality offers glimpses of a still deeper dance of sameness and otherness in the new creation, where "they neither marry nor are given in marriage." That final vision is not the negation of our deepest experiences of intimacy and communion; rather, it is their culmination and fulfillment — in ways we cannot yet fully imagine.

I believe that the church is only beginning to glimpse the ways in which those outside the heterosexual mainstream might participate in the complex journey toward that final destiny. Much of what we have assumed in the past regarding scriptural teaching on same-sex relationships will need to be reconsidered. There are many questions along the way on that journey. But if this book is helpful in providing a framework for biblical interpretation that guides the church on that journey, I will be most deeply gratified.

Summing Up

- One must read biblical commands and prohibitions in terms of their underlying forms of moral logic. The moral logic underpinning the negative portrayal of same-sex eroticism in Scripture does not directly address committed, loving, consecrated same-sex relationships today.
- Although Scripture does not teach a normative form of gender complementarity, the experience of *complementarity* itself may be helpful and important in both heterosexual and same-sex relationships, even if complementarity is not construed along hard-wired gender lines.
- The stories of Sodom and Gomorrah (Gen. 19) and the Levite's concubine (Judg. 19) focus on the horror of rape and the ancient abhorrence of the violation of male honor in rape. As such, they help to explain Scripture's negative stance toward the types of same-sex eroticism the Bible addresses, but they do not directly address the case of committed and loving same-sex relationships.
- The prohibitions in Leviticus against "lying with a male as with a woman" (18:22; 20:13) make sense in an ancient context, where there were concerns about purity, pagan cults, the distinctiveness of Israel as a nation, violations of male honor, and anxieties concerning procreative processes. However, these prohibitions do not speak directly to committed and consecrated same-sex relationships. Nor are they

based on a form of moral logic grounded in biology-based gender complementarity.

- The references to same-sex eroticism found in two New Testament vice lists (1 Cor. 6:9 and 1 Tim. 1:10) focus attention on the ancient practice of pederasty — the use of boy prostitutes in male-male sex. As such, they also do not address committed and mutual same-sex relationships today.

- There are many more questions to be explored, but this book has attempted to focus on core issues involving the interpretation of Scripture, as the church continues to wrestle with a multitude of questions that arise outside the heterosexual mainstream.

Bibliography of Works Cited

Alison, James. *Faith Beyond Resentment: Fragments Catholic and Gay*. New York: Crossroad, 2001.

Althaus, Paul. *The Theology of Martin Luther*. Philadelphia: Fortress, 1966.

Aquinas, Thomas. *Aquinas Scripture Series*. Translated by Matthew L. Lamb. Albany, NY: Magi Books, 1966.

Aristotle. *The Politics*. Translated by Harris Rackham, Loeb Classical Library. London/New York: W. Heinemann/G. Putnam, 1932.

Augustine. *Concerning the City of God against the Pagans*. Penguin Classics. London/New York: Penguin Books, 2003.

Banister, Jamie A. "Ὁμοίως and the Use of Parallelism in Romans 1:26-27." *Journal of Biblical Literature* 128, no. 3 (2009): 569-90.

Barth, Karl, Geoffrey Bromiley, Thomas F. Torrance, Frank McCombie, and Princeton Theological Seminary. *Church Dogmatics*. Study edition. London/New York: T & T Clark, 2009.

Beker, Johan Christiaan. *Heirs of Paul: Paul's Legacy in the New Testament and in the Church Today*. Minneapolis: Fortress, 1991.

———. *Paul the Apostle: The Triumph of God in Life and Thought*. Philadelphia: Fortress, 1980.

Blanchard, Kathryn D. "The Gift of Contraception: Calvin, Barth, and a Lost Protestant Conversation." *Journal of the Society of Christian Ethics* 27, no. 1 (2007): 225-49.

Blankenhorn, David, Don S. Browning, and Mary Stewart Van Leeuwen. *Does Christianity Teach Male Headship? The Equal-Regard Marriage and Its Critics*. Religion, Marriage, and Family. Grand Rapids: Eerdmans, 2004.

Boswell, John. *Christianity, Social Tolerance, and Homosexuality: Gay People in Western Europe from the Beginning of the Christian Era to the Fourteenth Century*. Chicago: University of Chicago Press, 1980.

————. *Same-Sex Unions in Premodern Europe*. New York: Villard Books, 1994.

Brooten, Bernadette J. *Love between Women: Early Christian Responses to Female Homoeroticism*. The Chicago Series on Sexuality, History, and Society. Chicago: University of Chicago Press, 1996.

Bruner, Frederick Dale. *Matthew: A Commentary*. Revised and expanded edition. Grand Rapids: Eerdmans, 2004.

Cahill, Lisa Sowle. *Sex, Gender, and Christian Ethics*. New Studies in Christian Ethics. Cambridge, UK: Cambridge University Press, 1996.

Calvin, John. *Commentaries on the Four Last Books of Moses: Arranged in the Form of a Harmony*. Translated by Charles William Bingham. Vol. 3, Calvin's Commentaries. Grand Rapids: Eerdmans, 1950.

————. *The Epistles of Paul the Apostle to the Galatians, Ephesians, Philippians and Colossians*. Translated by T. H. L. Parker. Edited by David W. Torrance and Thomas F. Torrance. Grand Rapids: Eerdmans, 1965.

Campbell, Douglas Atchison. *The Deliverance of God: An Apocalyptic Rereading of Justification in Paul*. Grand Rapids: Eerdmans, 2009.

Christian Reformed Church. *Ecumenical Creeds and Reformed Confessions*. Grand Rapids: CRC Publications, 1987.

Chrysostom, Dio. *Dio Chrysostom*. Translated by J. W. Cohoon and H. Lamar Crosby. The Loeb Classical Library. London/New York: W. Heinemann/Putnam, 1932.

Cook, James I., and Reformed Church in America, Commission on Theology. *The Church Speaks: Papers of the Commission on Theology, Reformed Church in America, 1959-1984*, Historical Series of the Reformed Church in America, No. 15. Grand Rapids: Eerdmans, 1985.

Coontz, Stephanie. *Marriage, a History: From Obedience to Intimacy, or How Love Conquered Marriage*. New York: Viking, 2005.

Countryman, Louis William. *Dirt, Greed, and Sex: Sexual Ethics in the New Testament and Their Implications for Today*. Revised edition. Minneapolis: Fortress, 2007.

Curran, Charles E., and Richard A. McCormick. *Dialogue about Catholic Sexual Teaching*. Readings in Moral Theology, No. 8. New York: Paulist, 1993.

Curran, Charles E., and Julie Hanlon Rubio. *Marriage*. Readings in Moral Theology. New York: Paulist, 2009.

Davies, Margaret. "New Testament Ethics and Ours: Homosexuality and Sexuality in Romans 1:26-27." *Biblical Interpretation* 3 (1995).

Deming, Will. *Paul on Marriage and Celibacy: The Hellenistic Background of 1 Corinthians 7*. Second edition. Grand Rapids: Eerdmans, 2004.

De Young, Kevin. *Freedom and Boundaries: A Pastoral Primer on the Role of Women in the Church*. Enumclaw, WA: Pleasant Word, 2006.

Douglas, Mary. *Purity and Danger: An Analysis of Concepts of Pollution and Taboo*. London: Routledge & Kegan Paul, 1966.

Elliott, Neil. *The Arrogance of Nations: Reading Romans in the Shadow of Empire*. Paul in Critical Contexts. Minneapolis: Fortress, 2008.

————. *Liberating Paul: The Justice of God and the Politics of the Apostle*. The Bible and Liberation. Maryknoll, NY: Orbis Books, 1994.

Ellis, J. Edward. *Paul and Ancient Views of Sexual Desire: Paul's Sexual Ethics in 1 Thessalonians 4, 1 Corinthians 7 and Romans 1*. Library of New Testament Studies, 354. London/New York: T & T Clark, 2007.

Engberg-Pedersen, Troels. *Paul and the Stoics*. Louisville: Westminster John Knox, 2000.

Farley, Margaret A. *Just Love: A Framework for Christian Sexual Ethics*. New York: Continuum, 2006.

Fee, Gordon D. *The First Epistle to the Corinthians*. The New International Commentary on the New Testament. Grand Rapids: Eerdmans, 1987.

Fowler, James W. *Faithful Change: The Personal and Public Challenges of Postmodern Life*. Nashville: Abingdon, 1996.

Fredrickson, David E. "Natural and Unnatural Use in Romans 1:24-27." In *Homosexuality, Science, and the "Plain Sense" of Scripture*, edited by David Balch, pp. 197-222. Grand Rapids: Eerdmans, 2000.

Gagnon, Robert A. J. *The Bible and Homosexual Practice: Texts and Hermeneutics*. Nashville: Abingdon, 2001.

Grenz, Stanley J. *Welcoming But Not Affirming: An Evangelical Response to Homosexuality*. Louisville: Westminster John Knox, 1998.

Grimsrud, Ted, and Mark Nation. *Reasoning Together: A Conversation on Homosexuality*. Scottdale, PA: Herald Press, 2008.

Grudem, Wayne A. *Evangelical Feminism: A New Path to Liberalism?* Wheaton, IL: Crossway Books, 2006.

————. *The Gift of Prophecy in the New Testament and Today*. Revised edition. Wheaton, IL: Crossway Books, 2000.

Hays, Richard. "Relations Natural and Unnatural: A Response to J. Boswell's Exegesis of Rom. 1." *Journal of Religious Ethics* 14, no. 1 (1986): 184-215.

————. *The Moral Vision of the New Testament: Community, Cross, New Creation; A Contemporary Introduction to New Testament Ethics*. San Francisco: HarperSanFrancisco, 1996.

Hefling, Charles C. *Our Selves, Our Souls, and Bodies: Sexuality and the Household of God*. Cambridge, MA: Cowley Publications, 1996.

Heim, D., M. L. Stackhouse, L. T. Johnson, and D. M. McCarthy. "Homosexuality, Marriage and the Church: A Conversation." *Christian Century*, July 1-8, 1998, pp. 644-50.

Jewett, Paul King, and Marguerite Shuster. *Who We Are: Our Dignity as Human; A Neo-Evangelical Theology*. Grand Rapids: Eerdmans, 1996.

Jewett, Robert, Roy David Kotansky, and Eldon Jay Epp. *Romans: A Commentary*. Hermeneia — A Critical and Historical Commentary on the Bible. Minneapolis: Fortress, 2007.

John Paul VI. *Humanae Vitae*. (1968): http://www.vatican.va/holy_father/paul_vi/ encyclicals/documents/hf_p-vi_enc_25071968_humanae-vitae_en.html.

Johnson, William Stacy. "Empire and Order: The Gospel and Same-Gender Relationships." *Biblical Theology Bulletin* 37, no. 4 (2007): 161-73.

————. *A Time to Embrace: Same-Gender Relationships in Religion, Law, and Politics*. Grand Rapids: Eerdmans, 2006.

LeVay, Simon. *Gay, Straight, and the Reason Why: The Science of Sexual Orientation*. Oxford/New York: Oxford University Press, 2011.

Lincoln, Andrew T. *Ephesians*. Word Biblical Commentary. Dallas: Word Books, 1990.

Loader, William R. G. *Sexuality and the Jesus Tradition*. Grand Rapids: Eerdmans, 2005.

Malina, Bruce J. *The New Testament World: Insights from Cultural Anthropology*. Revised edition. Louisville: Westminster John Knox Press, 1993.

Martin, Dale B. *Sex and the Single Savior: Gender and Sexuality in Biblical Interpretation*. Louisville: Westminster John Knox, 2006.

Martyn, J. Louis. "De-Apocalpyticizing Paul: An Essay Focused on *Paul and the Stoics* by Troels Engberg-Pedersen." *Journal for the Study of the New Testament* 86 (2002): 61-102.

Mauser, Ulrich. "Creation, Sexuality, and Homosexuality in the New Testament." In *Homosexuality and Christian Community*, edited by Choon-Leong Seow, pp. 39-49. Louisville: Westminster John Knox, 1996.

Meilaender, Gilbert. *The Way That Leads There: Augustinian Reflections on the Christian Life*. Grand Rapids: Eerdmans, 2006.

Metzger, Bruce Manning. *A Textual Commentary on the Greek New Testament: A Companion Volume to the United Bible Societies' Greek New Testament*. Fourth revised edition. London/New York: United Bible Societies, 1994.

Milgrom, Jacob. *Leviticus: A Book of Ritual and Ethics*. Continental Commentaries. Minneapolis: Fortress, 2004.

Miller, James. "The Practices of Romans 1:26: Homosexual or Heterosexual?" *Novum Testamentum* 37 (1995): 1-11.

Myers, David G., and Letha Scanzoni. *What God Has Joined Together: A Christian Case for Gay Marriage*. San Francisco: HarperSanFrancisco, 2005.

Nissinen, Martti. *Homoeroticism in the Biblical World: A Historical Perspective*. Minneapolis: Fortress, 1998.

Penn, Michael Philip. *Kissing Christians: Ritual and Community in the Late Ancient Church*. Divinations. Philadelphia: University of Pennsylvania Press, 2005.

Philo. *Philo*. Translated by F. H. Colson. Nine volumes. Vol. VI, Loeb Classical Library. Cambridge/London: Cambridge University Press/Heinemann, 1935.

Pierce, Ronald W., Rebecca Merrill Groothuis, and Gordon D. Fee. *Discovering Biblical Equality: Complementarity without Hierarchy*. Second edition. Downers Grove, IL: InterVarsity, 2005.

Piper, John, and Wayne A. Grudem. *Recovering Biblical Manhood and Womanhood: A Response to Evangelical Feminism.* Wheaton, IL: Crossway Books, 1991.

Plato. *The Collected Dialogues of Plato, Including the Letters.* Edited by Edith Hamilton and Huntington Cairns. Bollingen Series, 71. New York: Pantheon Books, 1961.

Poirier, John C. "Purity Beyond the Temple in the Second Temple Era." *Journal of Biblical Literature* 122, no. 2 (2003): 247-65.

Pokorný, Petr. *Colossians: A Commentary.* Peabody, MA: Hendrickson, 1991.

Rogers, Eugene F. *Sexuality and the Christian Body: Their Way into the Triune God.* Oxford: Blackwell, 1999.

Rogers, Jack. *Jesus, the Bible, and Homosexuality: Explode the Myths, Heal the Church.* Revised and expanded edition. Louisville: Westminster John Knox, 2009.

Satlow, M. L. "'Wasted Seed,' the History of a Rabbinic Idea." *Hebrew Union College Annual* 65 (1994): 137-75.

Schmidt, Thomas E. *Straight and Narrow? Compassion and Clarity in the Homosexuality Debate.* Downers Grove, IL: InterVarsity, 1995.

Scroggs, Robin. *The New Testament and Homosexuality: Contextual Background for Contemporary Debate.* Philadelphia: Fortress, 1983.

Siker, Jeffrey S. *Homosexuality in the Church: Both Sides of the Debate.* Louisville: Westminster John Knox, 1994.

Smedes, Lewis B. "Like the Wideness of the Sea." *Perspectives* 14, no. 5 (1999): 8-12.

———. *Sex for Christians: The Limits and Liberties of Sexual Living.* Revised edition. Grand Rapids: Eerdmans, 1994.

Smith, Mark D. "Ancient Bisexuality and the Interpretation of Romans 1:26-27." *Journal of the American Academy of Religion* 64, no. 2 (1996): 223-56.

Soards, Marion L. *Scripture and Homosexuality: Biblical Authority and the Church Today.* Louisville: Westminster John Knox, 1995.

Stott, John R. W. *Same-Sex Partnerships? A Christian Perspective.* Grand Rapids: F. H. Revell, 1998.

Suetonius. *Suetonius.* Translated by J. C. Rolfe. The Loeb Classical Library. London/New York: Heinemann/Harvard University Press, 1920.

Suicide Prevention Resource Center. "Suicide Risk and Prevention for Lesbian, Gay, Bisexual and Transgender Youth." Newton, MA: Education Development Center, Inc., 2008.

Swartley, Willard M. *Slavery, Sabbath, War, and Women: Case Issues in Biblical Interpretation.* The Conrad Grebel Lectures, 1982. Scottdale, PA: Herald Press, 1983.

Thiselton, Anthony C. *The First Epistle to the Corinthians: A Commentary on the Greek Text.* New International Greek Testament Commentary. Grand Rapids: Eerdmans, 2000.

Thrall, Margaret E., Trevor J. Burke, and J. K. Elliott, eds. *Paul and the Corinthians:*

Studies on a Community in Conflict; Essays in Honour of Margaret Thrall. Supplements to Novum Testamentum. Leiden/Boston: Brill, 2003.

Vaaler, Margaret L., Christopher G. Ellison, and Daniel A. Powers. "Religious Influences on the Risk of Marital Dissolution." *Journal of Marriage and Family* 71 (November 2009): 917-34.

Via, Dan Otto, and Robert A. J. Gagnon. *Homosexuality and the Bible: Two Views.* Minneapolis: Fortress, 2003.

Von Rad, Gerhard. *Genesis: A Commentary.* Revised edition. The Old Testament Library. Philadelphia: Westminster, 1972.

Webb, William J. *Slaves, Women and Homosexuals: Exploring the Hermeneutics of Cultural Analysis.* Downers Grove, IL: InterVarsity, 2001.

Wenham, Gordon J. *Genesis.* Two volumes. Word Biblical Commentary. Waco, TX: Word Books, 1987.

Wilson, Glenn D., and Qazi Rahman. *Born Gay: The Psychobiology of Sex Orientation.* London/Chester Springs, PA: Peter Owen, 2005.

Witte, John. *From Sacrament to Contract: Marriage, Religion, and Law in the Western Tradition.* The Family, Religion, and Culture. Louisville: Westminster John Knox, 1997.

Witte, John, and Eliza Ellison. *Covenant Marriage in Comparative Perspective.* Grand Rapids: Eerdmans, 2005.

Wright, David F. "Homosexuality: The Relevance of the Bible." *Evangelical Quarterly* 61 (1989).

Yarhouse, Mark A., and Stanton L. Jones. *Homosexuality: The Use of Scientific Research in the Church's Moral Debate.* Downers Grove, IL: InterVarsity, 2000.

Index of Names and Subjects

287

Index of Scripture References